Everyman, I will go with thee,
and be thy guide

Matthew Arnold

SELECTED POEMS
AND PROSE

Edited by
MIRIAM ALLOTT

University of London

EVERYMAN
J. M. DENT · LONDON
CHARLES E. TUTTLE
VERMONT

First published in Everyman's Library 1978
Reprinted 1985
Reissued 1991
New edition 1993

Printed in Great Britain by
The Guernsey Press Co. Ltd
Guernsey, Channel Islands

J. M. Dent
Orion Publishing Group
Orion House, 5 Upper St Martin's Lane
London WC2H 9EA
and
Charles E. Tuttle Co.
28 South Main Street, Rutland, Vermont
05701, USA

British Library Cataloguing-in-Publication Data
is available upon request.

ISBN 0 460 87392 X

CONTENTS

Note on the Author and Editor   vii
Chronology of Arnold's Life and Times   viii
Introduction   xix
Note on the Text   liii

POEMS
Shakespeare   3
In Harmony with Nature   3
In Utrumque Paratus   4
The Sick King in Bokhara   5
Resignation : To Fausta   12
The Forsaken Merman   19
To a Friend   23
Quiet Work   24
Meeting   24
Isolation. To Marguerite   25
To Marguerite – Continued   26
A Farewell   27
Stanzas in Memory of the Author of 'Obermann'   30
Self-dependence   35
Empedocles on Etna   36
From Tristram and Iseult   68
Memorial Verses   74
Dover Beach   76
The Youth of Nature   78
A Summer Night   81
The Buried Life   84
Stanzas from the Grande Chartreuse   87

From Sohrab and Rustum (coda)   92
The Scholar-Gipsy   94
Requiescat   101
From Haworth Churchyard   102
Thyrsis   105
Growing Old   111

PROSE

Preface to First Edition of *Poems* (1853)   115
From Preface to Second Edition of *Poems* (1854)   128
From On the Modern Element in Literature   129
From On Translating Homer : Last Words   138
From Democracy   149
From Maurice de Guérin   154
From Heinrich Heine   156
From Spinoza and the Bible   161
From Joubert   164
From Pagan and Religious Medieval Sentiment   169
From The Literary Influence of Academies   172
From The Function of Criticism at the Present Time 174
From On the Study of Celtic Literature   187
From Friendship's Garland   193
From Culture and Anarchy   197
From God and the Bible   211
From Wordsworth   216
The Study of Poetry   225

Notes   251
Suggestions for Further Reading   289
Acknowledgements   295

NOTE ON THE AUTHOR AND EDITOR

MATTHEW ARNOLD was born in Laleham-on-Thames on 24 December 1822 and died suddenly of heart failure in Liverpool on 15 April 1888. An outline of his life appears on pp. ix–xii below.

MIRIAM ALLOTT has held professorships at London and at Liverpool, where she succeeded her husband Kenneth Allott as A. C. Bradley Professor of Modern Literature. She has written on nineteenth-century poetry and fiction, is editor of the complete poems of Keats for Longman, and also editor of the revised edition of the complete poems of Arnold, first published by Kenneth Allott in 1969. She is currently working on an edition of Arnold's poems for OUP, a critical biography of Arthur Hugh Clough, and the Faber Book of Poets on Poetry.

Year	Age	Life
1822		Born (24 December) at Laleham-on-Thames as the eldest son of the Reverend Thomas Arnold and Mary Arnold (née Penrose)
1828	6	The family move to Rugby on Dr Arnold's appointment as Headmaster of Rugby School
1831	9	Arnold is tutored by his uncle, the Reverend John Buckland, at Laleham (January to December) and makes his first visit to the Lake District (August)
1833	11	Southey's cousin, Herbert Hill, engaged by Dr Arnold as tutor for his sons (May)
1834	12	Fox How, near Ambleside, completed (July) and from now on becomes the holiday home of the Arnolds in the Lakes. Wordsworth is a neighbour and frequent visitor
1836	14	Arnold's first attempts at writing verse, including 'The First Sight of Italy' (March) and 'Lines written on the seashore at Eaglehurst' (July). With his brother Tom enters Winchester College (his father's old school) as a Commoner
1837	15	Arnold wins a school verse-speaking prize with a speech from Byron's *Marino Faliero* and makes his first visit to France (August); leaves Winchester and enters the Fifth Form at Rugby
1838	16	First number of the manuscript *Fox How Magazine* (January); brought out twice yearly by Arnold with Tom's help until January 1842. He wins the Fifth Form prize for Latin verse and removes to the Sixth Form under his father
1840	18	Arnold wins school prize for English essay and English verse (June) and his prize poem, 'Alaric at Rome', printed at Rugby; gains open scholarship to Balliol College, Oxford
1841	19	Arnold shares school prizes for Latin essay and Latin verse (June); his father appointed Regius Professor of Modern History at Oxford (October). He goes into residence at Oxford, when his close friendship with Arthur Hugh Clough begins. He deeply admires Newman's preaching at St Mary's but is not drawn into the Oxford Movement

CHRONOLOGY OF HIS TIMES

Year	Artistic Events	Historical Events
1832	Tennyson, *Poems*	
1833	Carlyle, *Sartor Resartus*	John Keble preaches his 'National Apostasy' sermon; beginning of the Oxford Movement
1837	Carlyle, *The French Revolution* and *Lectures on German Literature*	
1838	Dr Arnold, *Early History of Rome* (concluded 1843)	
1839	Carlyle, *Chartism*	Walter Pater born
1841	Newman, 'Tract 90'; Carlyle, *Heroes, Hero -Worship and the Heroic in History*; Emerson, *Essays: First Series* (second series 1844)	

Year	Age	Life
1842	20	Arnold *proximo accessit* for Hertford Latin Scholarship (March). Sudden death of his father of heart disease (12 June)
1842-5	20-23	Arnold reads and is influenced by Carlyle, Emerson, George Sand, Goethe and Spinoza. Member of the 'Decade' undergraduate society
1843	21	Arnold's Newdigate prize-poem *Cromwell* printed
1844	22	Arnold obtains B.A. Second Class in 'Greats' (November)
1845	23	Arnold appointed temporary assistant master at Rugby (February–April) and elected Fellow of Oriel College, Oxford (March)
1846	24	Arnold visits France; meets George Sand at Nohant (July) and sees Rachel act in Paris (December), where he stays until February 1847. Probably begins his close reading of Senancour and Sainte-Beuve at this time
1847	25	Arnold becomes Private Secretary to Lord Landsdowne, Lord President of the Council and Whig elder statesman (April). Tom Arnold emigrates to New Zealand in search of 'Liberty, Equality and Fraternity' (November)
1848	26	Arnold's brother William Delafield leaves Oxford for India as ensign in the Bengal Army of the East India Company (February). Arnold himself visits Switzerland and meets 'Marguerite'at Thun (September)
1849	27	Arnold publishes his first volume, *The Strayed Reveller, and Other Poems* (February). He visits Switzerland and meets 'Marguerite' for the second and last time (September)
1850	28	Arnold publishes 'Memorial Verses' in *Fraser's Magazine*. His favourite sister Jane marries W. E. Foster (August), but his own engagement to Frances Lucy Wightman is delayed because of his need to find a settled source of livelihood. Meets Charlotte Brontë at Fox How
1851	29	Arnold appointed Inspector of Schools (15 April), marries Lucy, daughter of Sir William Wightman, Justice of the Queen's Bench, at Hampton (10 June) and goes on a delayed honeymoon journey in France, Italy and Switzerland, during which he visits the Grande Chartreuse (September to October). Begins work as a school-inspector (11 October), and from now on is committed to a heavy programme of work and constant travelling as an inspector and, for some years, marshal to his father-in-law on circuit

Year	Artistic Events	Historical Events
1842	Dr Arnold, *Study of Modern History*	
1843	Wordsworth Poet Laureate; Carlyle, *Past and Present*	
1844	A. P. Stanley, *Life and Correspondence of Thomas Arnold*	
1845	Carlyle, *Cromwell*	
1848	Cough writes 'The Bothie of Toperna-Fuosich' (November), after having resigned his fellowship at Oriel College because of scruples about religious subscription	
1850	Tennyson made Poet Laureate and publishes *In Memoriam*; Wordsworth, *The Prelude*; Carlyle, *Latter-Day Pamphlets*; Emerson, *Representative Men*	Death of Wordsworth (23 April)

Year	Age	Life
1852	30	Arnold publishes *Empedocles on Etna, and Other Poems* (October)
1853	31	Arnold publishes *Poems, A New Edition*, a selection of his poems, excluding 'Empedocles on Etna' and including among new poems 'Sohrab and Rustum' and 'The Scholar-Gipsy'
1854	32	Arnold publishes *Poems, Second Series*, a further selection from his two earlier volumes, with 'Balder Dead' as the single important new poem
1855	33	'Stanzas from the Grande Chartreuse' and 'Haworth Churchyard' published in *Fraser's Magazine* (April, May)
1857	35	Arnold elected Professor of Poetry at Oxford (May) and delivers his Inaugural lecture, 'On the Modern Element in Literature' (14 November); creates a precedent by lecturing in English; re-elected at the end of his first term of five years; publishes *Merope* (December)
1858	36	Arnold settles in London at 2, Chester Square (February: '... it will be something to unpack one's portmanteau for the first time since I was married, now nearly seven years ago'). Takes a walking holiday in Switzerland with Theodore Wolrond (August to September)
1859	37	Arnold visits France, Holland and Switzerland as Foreign Assistant Commissioner to the Newcastle Commission on Elementary Education (March to August); his brother William dies at Gibraltar (April); his *England and the Italian Question* published (August)
1861	39	Arnold publishes *On Translating Homer* (January) and *The Popular Education of France*, with the introductory essay 'Democracy' (November)
1862	40	Arnold risks official hostility by publishing in *Fraser's Magazine* 'The Twice Revised Code', attacking Robert Lowe's 'Payment by Results' as a method of distributing government grants for education (March); also publishes *On Translating Homer: Last Words*
1864	42	Arnold publishes *A French Eton*. From now on most of his work appears in periodicals before being published in book form
1865	43	Arnold publishes *Essays in Criticism: First Series* (February); visits France, Italy, Germany, Switzerland as Foreign Assistant Commissioner to the Taunton Commission (Schools Inquiry)

Year	Artistic Events	Historical Events

1856   Carlyle, *Collected Works*
        Emerson, *English Tracts*

1858   Carlyle, *Frederick the Great*
        Goethe, *Poems and Ballads*,
        translated by Aytonn and
        Martin; Clough, *Amours de
        Voyage*

1860   *Cornhill Magazine* started, with
        Thackeray as editor (until 1862)
1861   Palgrave, *Golden Treasury*   Clough dies in Florence
        (revised 1896)

1862   Clough, *Collected Works* with
        memoir by Palgrave

Year	Age	Life
1866	44	Arnold applies unsuccessfully for the Librarianship of the House of Commons (April). Publishes *On the Study of Celtic Literature* (July), *New Poems* (restoring *Empedocles on Etna* on Browning's request). From now on writes little verse, and is increasingly known for his controversial social and religious writings
1868	46	Arnold loses two of his sons, his infant son Basil (January) and his eldest son Thomas, aged 16 and a Harrow schoolboy (November). Moves to Byron House, Harrow (March)
1869	47	Arnold publishes *Culture and Anarchy*, his major work of social criticism (January), the first collected edition of his *Poems* (two volumes, June); his essay on 'Obermann' in the *Academy* (October), and, after the death of Sainte-Beuve, his commemorative essay also in the *Academy* (November). Applies unsuccessfully for appointment as one of the three commissioners under the Endowed Schools Act
1870	48	Arnold publishes *St Paul and Protestantism* (May), receives the Honorary Degree of DCL at Oxford (June) and is promoted to Senior Inspector of Schools
1871	49	Arnold publishes *Friendship's Garland*, his 'half serious, half playful' letters on English life and culture (February) and visits France and Switzerland with his wife and his son Richard (August)
1872	50	Arnold loses a third son, William Trevenen, aged 18 (February)
1873	51	Arnold publishes *Literature and Dogma*, his most important work on religion (February), takes a holiday leave from school inspection with his wife in Italy (February to May) and moves to Pains Hill Cottage, Cobham, Surrey. His mother dies at Fox How (November)
1875	53	Arnold publishes *God and the Bible*, reviewing objections to *Literature and Dogma* (November)
1876	54	Arnold reprints 'The New Sirens' in *Macmillan's Magazine* (December)
1877	55	Arnold declines re-nomination for the Professorship of Poetry at Oxford (February) and nomination for the Lord Rectorship of St Andrew's University (November). He publishes *Last Essays on Church and Religion* (April to May) and 'George Sand' in *The Fortnightly Review* (June)

Year	Artistic Events	Historical Events
1867	Carlyle, *Shooting Niagara* (*Macmillan Magazine*); Pater, *Essay on Winckelmann* (*Westminster Review*)	
1869	Clough, *Poems and Prose Remains*, with *Selections from his Letters*, ed. by his wife	
1873	Pater, *Studies in the Renaissance*	
1876	Thomas Arnold's edition of *Beowulf*	George Sand dies (June)
1877	W. H. Mallock portrays Arnold as 'Mr Luke' in his *The New Republic* (April, May)	

Year	Age	Life
1878	56	*Selected Poems of Matthew Arnold* (Golden Treasury Series) published (June)
1879	57	Arnold publishes *Mixed Essays* (c. March) and his selected *Poems of Wordsworth* (August)
1880	58	Arnold attends the reception in London given in honour of Cardinal Newman by the Duke of Norfolk 'because I wanted to have spoken once in my life to Newman' (12 May). He contributes three essays to T. H. Ward's *The English Poets*: Introduction (later called 'On the Study of Poetry'), 'Thomas Gray' and 'John Keats'. Holiday in Switzerland and Italy (September)
1881	59	Arnold publishes his selected *Poetry of Byron* (June)
1882	60	Arnold publishes 'Westminster Abbey', his elegy on Stanley, in the *Nineteenth Century* (March) and *Irish Essays*
1883 1879	61	Arnold accepts Civil List Pension of £50 a year 'in public recognition of service to the poetry and literature of England' (August). Begins his lecture tour in the USA (October to March 1884)
1884	62	Arnold becomes Chief Inspector of Schools
1885	63	Arnold publishes *Discourses in America* (June) and his three-volume collected edition of poems (Library Edition: c. August). He again declines re-nomination for the Professorship of Poetry in spite of a memorial from Oxford heads of colleges and another from four hundred under graduates (October: 'Everyone is very kind as one grows old...'). Visits Germany for the Royal Commission (November to December)
1886	64	Arnold abroad again in France, Switzerland and Germany for the Royal Commission in Education (February - March). He retires from Inspectorship of Schools (30 April) and makes his second visit to USA (May to August)
1888	66	Arnold dies suddenly of heart failure at Liverpool while awaiting the arrival of his married daughter from America (15 April). His *Essays in Criticism, Second Series* published posthumously (November)

Year	Artistic Events	Historical Events
1880		Arnold's brother-in-law, W. E. Forster, appointed Chief Secretary for Ireland by Gladstone (resigned 1882, shortly before the Phoenix Park murders)
1885	Pater, *Marius the Epicurean*	
1887	Carlyle, *Early Letters* and *Correspondence with Goethe*, ed. Norton	

INTRODUCTION

'To see the object as in itself it really is': the unity in diversity of
Arnold's poetry and prose.

I

Matthew Arnold is among the most attractive of the Eminent
Victorians. The play of intelligence felt everywhere in his work,
the intimate reflection in both his poetry and his prose of move-
ments of thought and feeling which were central in his time and
have affected our own, and the personal temper which allowed
him to be serious without stuffiness and entertaining without
being frivolous, make for our sympathetic response and are
fortunately much better understood now than they were earlier in
this century, thanks to the devoted labours of Arnoldian editors
and critics during the past twenty-five years or so. On 5 May 1857,
when he and his wife were awaiting news of the polling at the
Convention for the Oxford Chair of Poetry, the message came,
'Nothing certain is known, but it is rumoured that you are ahead.'
The rumour was correct and, in the words of a recent author, the
message 'has its engaging import for us and for Arnold's future.'[1]

Arnold's election to the Professorship of Poetry at Oxford in
1857, when he was thirty-five, marked what turned out to be the
closing stages of his career as a poet and the opening of his career
as a writer of prose. The change of direction ensured that by the
end of his life – he died in 1888 in his sixty-sixth year – he would
be widely known in England and abroad, not so much perhaps as
the elegiac poet of loss and separation but certainly as one of the
liveliest and most discerning commentators on the England of his
day. He took a modest pleasure in being 'ahead' in the controver-
sies fostered by his lively polemics at the expense of the
narrowness of mind, heart and spirit which he saw as a universal
threat to the welfare of his country, recording in his affectionate

letters to members of his family the responses, friendly or acrimonious, which he had managed to arouse in his countrymen. Those who found their faculties quickened by his play of mind came from varied walks of life. We can trace the effects of his vivacity in the testimony of the teacher in a Welsh school, whom he met in his capacity as Schools Inspector (this was the gruelling job by which he earned his living from the time of his marriage to Lucy Wightman in 1851 until his retirement in 1886) and with whom he shared an admiration for 'Mark Rutherford', urging him on no account to miss any work by this author;[2] in the interest expressed by prominent political, literary and ecclesiastical figures of the day; and in the august commendations of Royalty. His mother, then for twenty-seven years bereft of her eminent husband, Dr Arnold of Rugby,[3] must have been amused and gratified to learn in June 1869 that her son's recently published *Culture and Anarchy* – in which he first sets out a full explanation of his celebrated description of the three English social classes as Barbarians, Philistines and Populace – was being eagerly read by Princess Alice, who 'is quite fascinated . . . uses all its phrases, and knows long bits by heart. The Crown Princess is now reading the book'.[4]

By the summer of 1869 he had long been in the forefront of controversy, at first in the relatively specialized areas covered, for example, by the preface to *Poems* (1853) and *On Translating Homer* (1861), but more prominently and popularly since the period in 1866 to 1867 when the pages of the *Pall Mall Gazette* were enlivened by the first seven of his 'Arminius letters', the enjoyably provocative precursors to the articles on 'Culture and its Enemies' for the *Cornhill Magazine* gathered in his book, and themselves, with five later letters, to be reprinted in turn as *Friendship's Garland* (1871). Moreover the publication of *Culture and Anarchy* in January was followed in the June by the first collected, two-volume edition of his *Poems*. This was a good moment, then, to take soundings of what he had accomplished as a poet and as a critic, that is in the wide sense which his individual practice had attached to this term. It is well known that 'disinterested' contemplation of 'the object as in itself it really is', the 'Indian virtue' as he calls it in his celebrated 1864 essay on 'The Function of Criticism at the Present Time',[5] is one of the cluster of rallying watchwords – 'sweetness and light', 'high seriousness', 'Hebraism and Hellenism', 'adequacy', '*architectonicè*', literature as 'a criticism of life' are among the others – which crystallized his thinking and have now more or less passed into the language (Disraeli pleased him by praising his 'great achievement in launching phrases'). He could recognize with amusement lapses in his own 'disinterestedness': when a member of his family demurred at his disapproval of Ruskin for being dogmatic, since he was no less so himself, he replied that the difference was that Ruskin was 'dogmatic and *wrong*'.[6] All the same, the informal remarks which he made about his work in various letters written during 1869 attest his power of looking at the object with his 'Indian virtue' and also the advantages of doing so. What he says reads like a prophecy. The unity and value of his work spring from its representativeness in

> this iron time
> Of doubts, disputes, distractions, fears...[7]

and the quality guarantees that in some future day its being 'ahead' would amount to more than a rumour:

> My poems represent, on the whole, the main movement of mind of the last quarter of a century, and thus they will probably have their day as people become conscious to themselves of what that movement of mind is, and interested in the literary productions which reflect it. It might be fairly urged that I have less practical sentiment than Tennyson, and less intellectual vigour and abundance than Browning; yet, because I have perhaps more of a fusion of the two than either of them, and have more regularly applied that fusion to the main line of modern development, I am likely enough to have my turn, as they have had theirs...[8]

It is a matter of record that in a well known survey of recent Victorian research the pages devoted to Arnold outnumber those devoted to Tennyson and Browning, whose 'turn' lasted far into this century, surviving the long period, even now not altogether at an end, when 'the Victorians' were looked upon in the sour light of post-Strachey disenchantment with incomprehension and distaste.[9] 'You will see', Arnold added a few days later in a letter referring to *Culture and Anarchy*, 'that it will have a considerable effect in the end, and the chapters on Hebraism and Hellenism are in the main, I am convinced, so true that they will form a kind of centre for English thought and speculation on the matters treated in them'.[10]

It is the centrality of his work, then, that Arnold rightly stresses and for the modern reader the quality is reinforced by the interplay between the two sides of his career and by the pressures – some of them reflecting Dr Arnold's still formidably surviving presence in his son's life – which saw to it that a robust and animating master of prose and 'imaginative reason'[11] should take over from the youthful, melancholy poet who made himself heard in the 1840s and early 1850s. For H. F. Lowry, who as early as 1932 furnished us with his indispensable edition of Arnold's letters to his friend and fellow poet, Arthur Hugh Clough,

> The real truth is that his efforts in the two fields are *inseparable*, and the reader who knows only one body of his work can hardly know even that. Voices reverberate back and forth between the verse and the essays; the questions raised in the one are answered in the other...[12]

And the tone of the one, we might add, is responded to by the tone of the other. The differences are partly owed to the normal processes of change from youth to age, but Arnold's individual temper, in which gaiety and seriousness were intermingled from the beginning, precludes any simple divorce between his younger and his older self. In his early Oxford days – he went up to Balliol in 1841, took a Second in 'Greats' in 1844 and was elected Fellow of Oriel in 1845 – he was remembered as debonair and dandyish, with a passion for things French. George Sand, whom he visited at Nohant in 1846 in his 'days of *Lélia*', saw him as ' *un Milton, jeune et voyageant*'.[13] 'Matt is full of Parisianism', wrote his friend Clough, 'he enters the room with a song of Béranger's on his lips ... his carriage shows him in fancy parading the Rue de Rivoli ... his hair is guiltless of English scissors ... in ... 8 days ... he has been to chapel *once*'.[14] No wonder Charlotte Brontë when she met him in 1850 felt that 'the shade of Dr Arnold seemed to frown on his young representative'. But she also saw 'a real modesty ... under his assumed conceit', together with 'intellectual aspiration, as well as high educational acquirements'.[15] Had she seen further into his self-protective pose she might have detected that there was more of his father in his moral make-up than he knew and might have made out the 'hidden ground/Of thought and of austerity within ... ' – the passage is from his own 'Austerity of Poetry' (1867) – which gives its sad reflective flavour to all his poetry and made his first volume, *The Strayed Reveller and other Poems* (1849), so surprising to his sister because of 'the knowledge of life and conflict ... *strangely like experience*' which she found in it.[16]

The difference in the later Arnold is that the gaiety and high spirits are now placed at the service of that missionary conscience which hastened the decline of his poetic talent and so has tempted many modern readers to accept as true Auden's pronouncement that he 'thrust his gift in prison till it died'.

It is certainly the case that the decline of his poetic creativity went *pari passu* with his increasing dedication to public concerns. There was also the matter of changes in his personal life: his farewell to youthful passion and to the French girl who inspired it, which we know about only through the troubled 'Marguerite' poems of 1848–9; his settling down some three years later to a contented marriage with Judge Wightman's daughter; and his dutiful acceptance of a taxing means of livelihood in the Education Office, which he supplemented by acting as marshal to his father-in-law. He continued to write poetry until the 1860s and, if we set aside verses written for pleasure in childhood and in schooldays at Winchester and Rugby, we can say that he produced most of his poetry between 1843 and 1867, writing few poems of any importance after that year. But the fact remains that his best poetry belongs to the ten years from 1843–52, the year in which he 'settled down', though not in any restful sense. His work carried him on long tiring journeys by rail to different parts of the country and, in order to prepare literary work of his own, including, after 1857, his Oxford lectures, he would rise in the early dawn. We have his spare, bitten-off, testimony to the difficulty of writing poetry in the few moments left free in a life filled with one-night stands in dismal lodgings, the interminable marking of examination papers and a heavy programme of observing lessons.[17] When we add the difficulty he experienced in composing ('you may often hear my sinews cracking under the effort to unite matter', he once told Clough),[18] it is hardly surprising to find that after his first two volumes, *The Strayed Reveller, and other Poems* and *Empedocles on Etna, and Other Poems* of 1849 and 1852, his collections should be largely new editions of earlier work, with varying omissions and a diminishing number of new pieces. These are, memorably, 'The Scholar-Gipsy' and 'Sohrab and Rustum' in *Poems* (1853), from which he dropped 'Empedocles on Etna'; 'Balder Dead', the 'blameless excursion into Scandinavian mythology' intended as a companion piece to 'Sohrab and Rustum' in *Poems. Second Series* (1855); *Merope*, a frigid quasi-Greek tragedy published in 1858; and 'Thyrsis', his celebrated elegy for Clough, which, together with 'Obermann Once More', appeared in his last collection, *Poems* (1867), where he at last reprinted his major poem,'Empedocles on Etna'. 'Obermann Once More', the sequel to his 1852 poem, 'Stanzas in Memory of the Author of "Obermann" ', and 'Thyrsis' have been fairly described as 'Parthian shots':

> Arnold was looking back over his shoulder at the past. 'Thyrsis', with its nostalgic echoes of 'The Scholar Gipsy', recalls his Oxford years, 'the *freest* and most delightful part, perhaps, of my life', as Arnold once described them; 'Obermann Once More' revives the memory of Senancour and of visits to Switzerland in 1848 and 1849 [where he met Marguerite] when the poet in Arnold was still keeping the moralist at arm's length.[19]

The 'moralist' made his first significant public appearance in the preface to *Poems* (1853), which explains that 'Empedocles on Etna' had been dropped because it was too 'morbid'. He is very much on the scene too in Arnold's letter to Clough written during the November when the volume was published.

> I am glad you like the Gipsy-Scholar – but what does it *do* for you? Homer *animates* – Shakespeare *animates* – in its poor way I think 'Sohrab and Rustum' *animates* – the Gipsy-Scholar at its best awakens a pleasing melancholy. But this is not what we want.
>
> The complaining millions of men
> Darken in labour and pain –
>
> what they want is something to *animate* and *ennoble* them ... I believe a feeling of this kind is the basis of my nature – and of my poetics.[20]

But it was not the basis of his poetic talent:

> It is obvious that a vein of melancholy resisted and explored rather than simply indulged is a main component of Arnold's poetic nature, and that when he mastered the discontent of 'the mobile, straining, passionate poetic temperament' in the interests of 'morality and character' (though the mastery was never to be complete) the poetry slowed to a trickle and then disappeared.

So one of his warmest modern admirers has written of him, finding in the late lyric, 'The Progress of Poesy', with its imagery of the bright stream struck from the rock in youth, whose 'sacred drops' vanish with the years until 'the old man ... feebly rakes among the stones', an emblematic account of individual poetic development which carries autobiographical weight as well as its wider application to the fate of the Romantic poet.[21]

If the process hastened the transmogrification of the poet into the critic it also made for a discontinuity in the work which the poet produced. For the same critic this is

> analogous to the line of a geological fault in a landscape, although the scenery, so to speak, has a family likeness on both sides of the broken and tilted streak. The discontinuity is glaring between 'Empedocles on Etna', the culmination of Arnold's earlier poetic development and his most ambitious poem, and *Merope*, the most open application of the doctrines of the 1853 preface.[22]

From the period of his would-be 'animating' narrative poem, 'Sohrab and Rustum', the story of a youthful son slain by a robust, upright father which nevertheless seems to gather personal significance and win a degree of vitality from this,[23] Arnold increasingly tries for perfection of form instead of exploring the individual feeling which informs his most haunting cadences and, like the sound of the sea in his own 'Dover Beach', 'brings the eternal note of sadness in'. 'People do not understand', he wrote when discussing the mixed reception accorded to *Merope*, 'what a temptation there is if you cannot bear anything *not very good* to transfer your operation to a region where form is everything. Perfection of a kind may be attained or approached without knocking yourself to pieces'.[24] Even in his fresher creative days he was a long way from approaching Browning's energetic verbal resourcefulness or Tennyson's unfailingly fine and delicate metrical ear, though he possessed impressive metrical gifts of his own. As he said of his admired Sainte-Beuve (in whom once again the critic took over from the poet), there was always 'some want of flame, of breadth, of passion'. Henry James, in an attaching phrase, found 'a certain abuse of meagreness for distinction's sake'. But the poems which the moralist in him least approved display his poetic voice at its most authentic. If he laments in them hope and joy irrecoverably impaired by a prevailing melancholy, he also defines with honesty and precision the sources of the pain and, as in 'Resignation', the poem written to encourage a sister recently made unhappy by a broken love affair but addressed as much to himself as to her, he repeats, like a refrain, the necessity

of escaping from self-absorption by schooling the spirit to a quiet
vision of things entire.

> The poet, to whose mighty heart
> Heaven doth a quicker pulse impart,
> Subdues that energy to scan,
> Not his own course, but that of man.

> [...] tears
> Are in his eyes, and in his ears
> The murmur of a thousand years.
> Before him he sees life unroll,
> A placid and continuous whole –
> That general life, which does not cease,
> Whose secret is not joy, but peace. [...]

> Be passionate hopes not ill resigned
> For quiet, and a fearless mind [...]

It is his tracing of distress to its sources in the movements of a
modern sensibility which finally confirms the unity in diversity of
this poet-critic and strengthens his appeal for us today. The 1853
preface opens with regret for the passing of 'the calm, the cheer-
fulness, the disinterested objectivity' which he associates with the
high period of Greek antiquity before the days of Empedocles:

> The dialogue of the mind with itself has commenced; modern
> problems have presented themselves; we hear already the
> doubts, we witness the discouragement, of Hamlet and of
> Faust.[25]

To Clough in 1852 he wrote, '[...] woe was upon me if I analysed
not my situation [...] Werter, René and suchlike, none of them
analyse the modern situation in its true *blankness* and *barrenness*
and *unpoetrylessness*.'[26] In his prose he takes arms against this sea
of troubles, urging the need for an 'adequate' literature, a liberal
education, a state government representing the nation's 'best self',
an unsuperstitious reverence for 'the power not ourselves which
makes for righteousness' (he came no nearer than this to the
orthodox God of his father's faith), an acceptance of poetry as a
magister vitae which would do the work of religion by lighting up
morality and so help to mitigate the harshness of Hebraism with
the grace and flexibility of his Hellenic ideal. Thus equipped we
might come to 'see life steadily and see it whole', with the
Sophoclean composure praised in his early sonnet 'To a Friend'.

Such are the central ideas, spun from the feelings which first made him into a poet, which he gradually wove into a single web as he moved on through the years from his inaugural Oxford lecture 'On the Modern Element in Literature', with its plea for balance and 'adequacy', to the continuously developing but still interrelated themes of his lectures on Homer; his first series of *Essays in Criticism* (1865), where the loving emphasis on European writers and European culture ministers to English parochialism; his reports on English and French education, with unstinted praise for the superior intellectual attainments of the latter; his trouncing of middle class Philistinism in *Culture and Anarchy* and *Friendship's Garland*; his plea for an imaginative response to the Bible in *Literature and Dogma* (1883), which turned out to be his best selling book; his glance at transatlantic *moeurs* in *Discourses in America*(1885), published after his six-month lecture tour in 1883–4, and in his two 'Notes' on America also of the 1880s; and the fine, late, critical pieces, including those on Wordsworth and 'The Study of Poetry', which were eventually collected, and published just after his death, as the second series of *Essays in Criticism* (1888).

II

Making itself universally felt in these works of criticism is Arnold's desire to minister to an ailing public, 'to pull out a few more stops', as he put it, 'in that powerful but at present somewhat narrow organ, the modern Englishman'. As a critic he diagnoses with increasing alertness to their social and cultural causes the ills which press on his consciousness in a more undifferentiated way in his poems, whether he calls them 'lyrical', 'elegiac', 'dramatic' or 'narrative' (these are the labels which he tried to fix on them, restlessly chopping and changing the classifications from one edition to another).[27] Images of sickness and fever gather as he contemplates his contemporary waste land, its people debilitated by

> this strange disease of modern life,
> With its sick hurry, its divided arms,
> Its heads o'ertax'd, its palsied hearts [...]

from which he urges his Scholar Gipsy to 'Fly hence [...] Still fly, plunge deeper in the bowering wood!'[28] The title of his early

narrative poem, 'The Sick King in Bokhara', signals the presence
in the poem of a spiritual as well as a physical malaise.[29] There is
'something that infects the world', the poet sadly tells Fausta in
'Resignation'.[30] For the bardic narrator in the third part of
'Tristram and Iseult' it is not the normal personal sorrows of life
but 'the gradual furnace of the world' which shrivels feeling and

> [...] kills in us the bloom, the youth, the spring –
> Which leaves the fierce necessity to feel
> But takes away the power [...][31]

– 'bloom', with its dual associations of youth and transience, is,
like 'calm', one of Arnold's favourite words. In his 'Stanzas from
the Grande Chartreuse' (1852), which voice, says T. S. Eliot, 'a
moment of historic doubt recorded by its most representative
mind',[32] we trace the source of the infection in the unmistakable
tones of the 'lost generation' of the later 1840s, that post Chartist,
post Oxford Movement period, when the old simple certainties
were no longer either simple or certain and the seismic shocks
caused by the religious, political and social upheavals of the
'hungry 'Forties', which saw the Year of Revolutions abroad and
the last flare-up of Chartism at home, made permanent casualties
of the sensitive and reflective. As he contemplates this Carthusian
retreat, home of the 'last of the people who believe', the poet
grieves for his plight,

> Wandering between two worlds, one dead,
>   The other powerless to be born ...

echoing, less analytically but with individual urgency, others who
had already recognized such uncertainties; Carlyle, for instance,
who knew in the 1830s that 'the Old has passed away but, alas,
the New appears not in its stead', and John Stuart Mill, another
who had seen in the early 1830s that 'Mankind have outgrown old
institutions and old doctrines, and have not yet acquired new ones'.[33]

Arnold's fullest and most consciously deliberated poetic treat-
ment of 'modern feeling' and 'modern thought' is found of course
in 'Empedocles on Etna', which he dismissed in 1853, with no
regard for its poetic merit, because it seemed to him to reflect the
ills without attempting to treat them. Any moderately attentive
reading of this important work at once reveals the imaginative
consistency with which it focuses its author's most characteristic
attitudes and reworks the literary and philosophical influences to

which he was drawn by certain answering qualities in them, especially the instilling of a particular kind of composure. We recognize the urgency of this need in his poetry's recurring images of calm – a wide and tranquil sea, a quiet landscape or seascape silvered by the moon, the shining of the steadfast stars (the many echoes of Keats's 'Bright Star!' sonnet are no accident)[34] – which reply to his images of fever and illness and make their appealing pictorial contribution to the individual flavour of his poetic world. The writers most affecting him – chiefly the Stoic philosophers, Lucretius, Spinoza, Senancour – share much of his melancholy. (Carlyle, with his authoritarian gusto, was something of an exception and, in spite of the early debt to his thinking which is reflected in Empedocles's long discourse on 'modern thought' in Act I, Arnold had already described him to Clough with typical verve as a 'moral desperado'.[35]) But they also possess the 'gravity and severity' which he distinguishes in Etienne Pivert de Senancour, whom he celebrates in his two 'Obermann' poems and whose representative 'modern feeling' shapes Empedocles' meditations in Act II.[36] Epictetus and Marcus Aurelius reappear as 'the great masters of morals' in his *Essays in Criticism* of 1865, joining Goethe, Sainte-Beuve, Spinoza and Heine, and other admired lucid, reflective intelligences, some of these – like Joubert and Maurice de Guérin – barely known in England until Arnold wrote about them. But they are brought now under the scrutiny of the author of the 1853 preface. Man 'can be borne over the thousand impediments of the narrow way, only by the tide of a joyful and bounding emotion' he says, and in spite of the power of Epictetus, the 'charm' suffusing and softening the austerity of Marcus Aurelius, it is impossible to rise from reading either without a sense of constraint and melancholy, 'without feeling that the burden laid upon man is well-nigh greater than he can bear'.[37] It is not from these, then, that succour will come for the 'heads o'ertax'd' and the 'palsied hearts' of his beleagured age.

And yet partly through their help, partly through the operations of a temperament naturally flexible and subtle, the feelings of restlessness, dissatisfaction and uncertainty for which Arnold early sought relief in his 'presiders' – his first study of Stoicism belongs to the period in 1846–7 when he was reading Epictetus and Senancour – generate in his poetry, together with its plangent images of tranquillity, certain lyrical movements of phrase and line which suggest an easing of the spirit and make for a calmative effect of the kind he sought in his reading. The pressure of this personal feeling, generating an equally urgent need to bring the feeling under command, seems to have quickened his considerable metrical skill to give to his early poetry qualities of suppleness and variety which disappeared once he tried to suppress his melancholy and submit himself to the formal disciplines discovered in poems on the other side of his 'geological fault'. In 'Empedocles on Etna', the climax of his achievement on its hither side, the variations, as I have said elsewhere, 'signal and help to define the complex feelings which shape the poem'.[38] In each of the two Acts, Empedocles's long despondent meditations are framed by the joyful songs of Callicles, who represents a young, undisenchanted self. The lyrical utterances, affected by Arnold's familiarity with Pindar, Hesiod and Ovid, are sometimes cast into rhyming three- or four-stressed lines but also fall into the irregularly stressed unrhymed chant which is Arnold's individual melodic achievement, first found in 'The Strayed Reveller' and used with perhaps his finest success in 'The Forsaken Merman', the much admired poem – it is part elegy, part narrative, part dramatic monologue – which had also appeared in the 1849 volume. Empedocles's meditations are themselves differentiated metrically, in keeping with their respective concerns with the 'thought' and 'feeling' already described. The skilled handling of the hexameters in Act I is sustained throughout their seventy-one stanzas and the blank verse in Act II flows more easily than that of 'Sohrab and Rustum' or *Merope*, preserving a more graceful allegiance to the speaker's tones of voice than Arnold permitted himself in either the latter or in 'Balder Dead', both of which represent later attempts at 'dramatic' representation. So the poem's thematic and emotional movement between contrarieties is enacted metrically as well as in the imagery and diction. It carries us from the measured expression of Empedocles's commentary on Nature's indifference to man,

> Nature, with equal mind,
> Sees all her sons at play;
> Sees man control the wind,
> The wind sweep man away,
> Allows the proudly-riding and the foundering bark,

to Callicles's freely moving delight in the 'leaping stream' which, with its 'eternal showers of spray', freshens the surrounding air

and the plants lining its wet banks; from Empedocles's complex
dissection of his want of single vision,

> Hither and thither spins
> The wind-borne mirroring soul,
> A thousand glimpses wins,
> And never sees a whole [...]

which engenders feelings of isolation and loneliness,

> [...] with men thou canst not live,
> Their thoughts, their ways, their wishes, are not thine;
> And being lonely thou art miserable,
> For something has impaired thy spirit's strength
> And dried its self-sufficing fount of joy [...]

to the simple balance of Callicles's acceptance of the whole,

> The day in his hotness
> The strife with the palm
> The night in her silence,
> The stars in their calm.[39]

These lines form part of the coda following Empedocles's leap
into the crater and their final point of rest in that favourite word
– since 'calm' always suggests a tranquillity longed for, rarely
found, and if found feared to exact a high price in the power to
feel – hints at the different kind of acceptance advocated by the
older poet's brand of stoicism. 'Make us not fly to dreams, but
moderate desire', he pleads.[40] For the truth is that Arnold could
never be a Callicles. This image of youthful freshness and freedom
haunts his poetry from as early as 'The Strayed Reveller' to as late
as *Merope*, where the figure makes a fleeting appearance in
Aepytus, who is conceived as a man of action but nevertheless,

> [...] in the glens
> Of Lycaeus afar
> A gladsome hunter of deer
> Basks in his morning of youth [...]

and, in lines which have little to do with Arnold's Sophoclean
sources,

> [...] with a light uncareworn spirit, turns
> Quick from distressful thought and floats in joy [...][41]

The seductiveness of the figure is in proportion to its remoteness
from the poet who once wrote to Clough, 'I am past thirty and

already three parts iced over' and, as another letter tells us, grieved for his 'lost spring of life' in 'The Scholar-Gipsy', a poem which he classified as an elegy and where the scholar gipsy is, after all, 'a Callicles miraculously preserved from turning into an Empedocles'.[42] The passing of youth and with it the shrivelling of that sense of what Hopkins called 'the freshness deep down things', is always the main source of the elegiac note in Arnold's poems. It is wholly in keeping with his poetic temper that so many of his memorable poems should have been designed as elegies. The best known include 'Thyrsis', his poem for Clough, where – as in 'The Scholar-Gipsy'– the strong Keatsian resonance is associated with the theme of transience and the movement away from and back to actuality which characterize Keats's major 1819 odes;[43] the mysterious little poem, 'Requiescat', 'Haworth Churchyard', written after Charlotte Brontë's death in 1855 as a celebration of all the Brontës but especially Emily,

> [...] whose soul
> Knew no fellow for might,
> Passion, vehemence, grief,
> Daring, since Byron died [...]

and 'The Youth of Nature' and 'Memorial Verses', the 'pindarics' written for Wordsworth after his death in 1850. It seems oddly fitting that of the few verses Arnold managed to write in the 1880s the most charming and touching were inspired by the deaths of household pets, a canary ('Poor Mathias') and two dogs, one of them his beloved dachshund, for whom he wrote the last poem of his own life, 'Kaiser Dead'.[44]

But it is when he engages directly with passionate experience – for example in his love poems, especially the 'Switzerland' series inspired by 'Marguerite', or his narrative poem 'Tristram and Iseult', which recalls youthful passion and sets it beside a sorrowful austere present – that the 'something that infects the world' is felt with particular poignancy. In the best of his shorter poems this obsessive theme simultaneously stimulates and disciplines his poetic imagination. 'The Forsaken Merman', inspired by a legendary tale about loss and separation and linked emotionally with the Marguerite poems, is saved from an unbalancing subjectivity by the ordering of the narrative sequence to preserve an unobtrusive interplay between the poet's various voices – the narrator's, the protagonist's, that of the personal self – and between the bright past and the sadness of the present and future. The flexible metrical movement records the ebb and flow of the lament, which opens with a 'lyrical cry', since the forsaken merman and his children are still 'wild with pain', and closes with sorrowful resignation to inevitable loss, the final vision of the moonlit shore summoning a characteristically individual image of longed-for calm. The struggle between the head and the heart, which lies at the centre of Arnold's romanticism as it lies at the centre of the imaginative literature produced by his most creative and representative contemporaries, finds emblematic expression in the separation of the land from the sea, the decorous 'white-walled' town with its 'grey church' from the magical undersea world. The pulse of the same sorrow beats in the Marguerite poems, where love heightens rather than lessens loneliness and the 'different fate' separating the lovers offers no hope of reconciling contraries outside the poetic statements which themselves still 'strive to unite matter'. 'To Marguerite – Continued', beginning 'Yes, in the sea of life enisled [...], attempts to bring together in a single act of perception the isolation of human beings, the alien world they inhabit, and the subjection of both man and nature to the same ineluctable laws. The islands 'dotted' in unbounded seas, and visited from time to time by benign spring air which renews belief that 'they were once parts of a single continent', parallel rather than symbolize isolated human beings quickened by the experience of romantic love into a momentary hope that separation is not an eternal condition of existence. But the hope is 'as soon as kindled cooled'. The burden of the 'Switzerland' sequence is the impossibility of communion.

> Far, far from each other
>   Our spirits have grown;
> And what heart knows another?
>   Ah! who knows his own?

'Happier men', perhaps,

> Have *dream'd* two human hearts might blend
> In one, and were through faith released
> From isolation without end
> Prolonged; nor knew, although not less
> Alone than thou, their loneliness.

But for himself the longing is 'like despair' and there is no reply to the arbitrary force which ordains that, for this temperament with its 'sad lucidity of soul', there is no other truth than that 'we mortal millions' shall remain isolated like the islands dotted in the sea.

> A God, a God their severance ruled!
> And bade betwixt their shores to be
> The unplumbed, salt, estranging sea.[45]

The sea of life is an image Arnold uses several times in other poems to suggest lonely voyages over long distances – 'we stem across the sea of life by night', he writes in 'Human Life'. Elsewhere, as in 'The Forsaken Merman' and in this haunting line from the second poem on 'Isolation' addressed to 'Marguerite', the sea is a sundering force and reveals something of his profoundly un-Wordsworthian attitude to Nature. 'Ah love, let us be true to one another', he pleads in the famous lyric 'Dover Beach', a poem not written for 'Marguerite' but on his honeymoon with Lucy,

> [...] for the world, which seems
> To lie before us like a land of dreams,
> So various, so beautiful, so new,
> Hath really neither joy, nor love, nor light,
> Nor certitude, nor peace, nor help for pain [...]

It is not only in 'Resignation', then, that he replies to Wordsworth, suggesting that Nature does not lead us, as we are assured in 'Tintern Abbey', from 'joy to joy' but remains indifferent to man while suffering under the same pitiless laws.[46] 'The Youth of Nature', which mourns the passing of the poet who

> [...] was a priest to us all
> Of the wonder and bloom of the world [...]

conveys inescapably that Arnold also laments both his own lost youthful freedom and the vanished youth of 'this iron time', which requires more than Wordsworth's 'healing power' to remedy the plight of those who 'darken in labour and pain' or hear with consternation the 'melancholy long withdrawing roar' of the ebbing sea of faith. His ambivalent feelings are more explicit in his first poem for Senancour, written before Wordsworth's death:

> [...] of the spirits who have reigned
> In this our troubled day,
> I know but two, who have attained,
> Save thee, to see their way.

These are Goethe, a pre-eminent figure among his 'presiders', dead since 1832, and Wordsworth:

> But Wordsworth's eyes avert their ken
> From half of human fate [...][47]

He 'plunged himself in the inward life, he voluntarily cut himself off from the modern spirit', Arnold adds in the course of his essay on Heine. But here he also calls him the 'gravest' of the Romantic poets. And in his introduction to his selections from Wordsworth's poetry, which were designed to arouse admiration and respect in an audience for whom Wordsworth was perhaps an unfamiliar or an unattractive figure, he praises him confidently as England's major poet after Shakespeare and Milton.[48]

III

Yeats said that a man makes from the quarrel with himself poetry and from the quarrel with others rhetoric. It would be hard to find a better way of summing up this movement from troubled debate with himself to rousing argument directed to others which distinguishes Arnold the poet from Arnold the critic of literature and society. But the 'rhetoric' here, we need to add, is governed by principles possessing a family resemblance to those which told the poet that he must 'animate' and 'rejoice' the reader, suppress morbid introspection, and avoid the exhaustion which attends poetic creation when 'you descend into yourself and produce the best of your thought and feeling naturally'. 'It is very animating', he wrote in 1863, when he was beginning to skim before the wind in his public role, 'to think that one has at last a chance of *getting at* the English public. Such a public as it is and such a work as one wants to do with it!' But this 'work' exacted its own disciplines. 'Partly through nature, partly time and study', he had thoroughly learnt

> the precious truth that everything turns upon one's exercising
> the powers of *persuasion*, of *charm*; that without this all fury, en-
> ergy, reasoning power, acquirement, are thrown away and only
> render their owner more miserable. Even in one's ridicule one
> must preserve a sweetness and good-humour.[49]

His 'fury' at this stage was extending itself beyond the short-comings of particular individuals to the intransigencies of an entire class. In his lectures 'On Translating Homer' he had

pounded away at Francis Newman because he was an example of
the misdirected energy which – for want of 'a public force of correct
literary opinion' – led 'men of ability and learning' to add to

> the chaos of false tendencies, wasted efforts, impotent conclu-
> sions, works which ought never to have been undertaken.[50]

His own 'energy, reasoning, acquirement' were now directed to
that whole section of middle-class society which he had already
tried to arouse by his arguments for state education in
'Democracy' (1861) and by his appeal in 'The Function of Criti-
cism at the Present Time' (1864) for the openness of mind, the
breadth of knowledge and the self-awareness which he felt were
urgently needed in what he described as the 'epoch of expansion'
which was now following hard upon the previous century's 'epoch
of concentration'.[51] But 'the endeavour in all branches of knowl-
edge – theology, philosophy, history, art, science – to see the object
as in itself it really is' was apparently, so far, too strenuous or too
incomprehensible a proposition to stir the English public to
action. Hence the need for a still more energetically seductive
strategy and the right kind of moral trim to support it.

> [...] si vis me flere, dolendum est
> Primum ipsi tibi [...]

and by the same token to win others to 'sweetness and light' one
must take to honeysuckle and beeswax oneself, all the more since,
the public being what it was, candour was likely to break in. 'I often
wished that I too had a little sweetness and light', wrote Leslie
Stephen, 'that I might be able to say such nasty things of my
enemies'.[52]

It should perhaps be urged at this stage that Arnold's prose
writings fill eleven volumes in R. W. Super's magnificent chron-
ological compilation, *The Complete Works of Matthew Arnold*
(1960 –1977). It is obviously impossible to attempt here anything
remotely approaching a comprehensive account, but certain gen-
eralizations may perhaps be permitted, bearing in mind that
several close studies of Arnold's prose exist which trace the
development of his ideas and the accompanying shades of differ-
ence in his style and manner with a scrupulous attention to 'the
object' which would have won his approval.[53] One generalization
perhaps worth risking has to do with the consonancy between
Arnold's concerns and the literary form he found to express them.

In that age of vociferous public debate, Arnold's prose, so far from being a monologue in masquerade as one critic has found, sustains like his poems his habit of dialogue and self-debate, now increasingly recognised as his principal mode of discourse.[54] It is hardly surprising that Arnold should have been as alert to the existence of the individual's different 'selves' as he shows himself to be in the poem 'The Buried Self' and in the lines written in the late 1860s which he mentioned in a letter to his mother with the comment, 'I think them good':

> Of what we *say* we feel – below the stream,
> As light, of what we *think* we feel – there flows
> With noiseless current strong, obscure and deep,
> The central stream of what we feel indeed.[55]

The stylistic peculiarities referred to are associated with his public polemical self and become increasingly noticeable once he extends his attention beyond his 'literary' essays and begins to write regularly for periodicals. The disciplines governing his 'quarrel with others' dictated an arrangement naturally different from the imaginative order governing the 'quarrel with himself', when he would 'knock himself to pieces' in the 'effort to unite matter'. Even the articles gathered in the first series of *Essays in Criticism*, almost all of which were originally designed as lectures, suggest a mind accustomed to ordering a winning 'spoken' argument but with little leisure in which to select and refine. 'Maurice de Guérin' is unusually shapely because Arnold took loving pains over this first attempt at critical appreciation of an individual creative sensibility; so is his lively Preface, written for the second edition and revealing the play of his irony at its most sardonically effective. On the other hand, his essays on Spinoza and on 'Pagan and Medieval Religious Sentiment' were both severely cut before appearing in the collection, while the publication of 'On the Modern Element in Literature' was delayed for many years because of its digressiveness. His public concerns in the 1860s fostered his liking for an expansive freewheeling discursiveness and a cheerful running before the sidewinds of local impulse, especially when he hit upon the latest lucubrations of Mr Bottles or Mr Roebuck or any of the emblems of Philistinism encountered in his running battles with the hosts of Midian. He is not, then, a polished essayist in the chiselled manner of Bacon or the unbuttoned manner of Lamb, whose casual air is the result of a particularly uncasual control of a chosen idiom. Nor did he possess a highly developed gift for abstract thinking. It is not their close reasoning which makes *Culture and Anarchy* and many of his writings on religion seem pretty indigestible when they are read as wholes, even taking into account their numerous local vivacities. They retain, rather, many distracting signs of their origin as contributions to the running debate with his adversaries (most of them now unfamiliar to the ordinary reader) which Arnold had conducted in the periodicals and indeed continued to conduct in these new pages. His discourse moves circularly around the handful of themes which occupied him from the beginning to the end of his critical career, expanding freshly upon them with each new revolution as his engagements with Mr Bottles and his recent practical experiences decide. These, it must be said, almost always brought into sharper focus for him the sorry failings of the country for which he felt so deeply; how deeply can be measured by the enormous pains he took during more than thirty years to contribute in some measure to the 'intellectual deliverance' which he insists upon as a crying need in 'The Modern Element in Literature'.

This essay belongs to the first stage of his critical career when his Oxford lectures drew him to 'literary' subjects, though his concern with a social, imaginative and intellectual 'deliverance' informed everything he chose to say and made itself felt again in his selection of material for the first series of *Essays in Criticism*. Of the nine essays he collected here, six are devoted to figures who through their individual fineness of sensibility and intelligence capture his sympathy and admiration. This personal warmth quickens the clarity and delicacy of his discriminating assessments of talents as diverse as those of Maurice de Guérin and his sister Eugénie, Heinrich Heine, Spinoza and Marcus Aurelius. His underlying concern with excellence in these discussions is given an explicit public application in the remaining three essays. The need for 'a high correct standard in intellectual matters', a quickened consciousness of 'our shortcomings and excess', of our 'vulgarity', of our 'provincialism', is his burden in 'The Literary Influence of Academies', the necessity in the present age for the balance of head and heart is the point towards which his entire discussion of Theocritus and St Francis moves in 'Pagan and Medieval Religious Sentiment'; and 'The Function of Criticism at the Present Time', placed at the beginning of the volume and one of his most important essays, is, in effect, his manifesto. The 'sense of a creative activity belongs only to genuine creation; in literature we must never forget that'. But in some ages, and this 'age of expansion' is one, criticism must take the centre of the stage. 'To have the sense of creative activity is the great happiness and the great proof of being alive', he declares in the closing paragraphs which recapitulate his central argument,

> and it is not denied to criticism to have it; but then criticism must be sincere, simple, flexible, ardent, ever widening its knowledge. Then it may have [...] a joyful sense of creative activity; a sense which a man of insight and conscience will prefer to what he might derive from a poor, starved, fragmentary, inadequate creation. And at some epochs no other creation is possible [...]

Three stages in his later critical career show him exerting with renewed energy his passionate efforts on behalf of vitality and truth in public life. The first opened in 1859 when he was appointed Foreign Assistant Commissioner to the Newcastle Commission on elementary education, an assignment which – to his delight – took him abroad to France, Switzerland and Holland, where he was to investigate their systems of education and write a report. He took great pains over this and published it in 1861 as *The Popular Education of France*, a study displaying impressive practical and moral acumen which should be required reading today, when Arnold would have found many of his worries about the future of English education dismally justified. He commends the French system which has 'undertaken to put the means of education within its people's reach' and contrasts the English habit of fostering, at one end of the scale, its great and admirable public schools and, at the other, an unequal system of elementary education. The French system

> altogether diverges from ours, which has by no means undertaken to put the means of education within the people's reach, but only to make the best and richest elementary schools better and richer [...] Where everything is left to be done by voluntary effort, schools where most needed are not established at all. Where everything, again, is left to be done by the State, there is wasteful extravagance and local apathy. Where everything, finally, is left to be done by the parish, there is niggardly pinching [...] The French plan [...] tempers the parsimony of the parish with the more liberal views of the central power; and between the parish contributor and the state contributor it places a third contributor of less narrow spirit than the first, of more economical spirit than the second, – the Department or County [...][56]

He provided a rudder for his whole discussion in his important opening essay, 'Democracy', which defends the State in a time when the aristocracy has lost its virtue, the middle class is ill-educated and the working class not educated at all. But there is still a 'best self' in the country from which those who govern are drawn. This looks ahead to *Culture and Anarchy*, but by then his 'fury' at the betrayal of its 'best self' in each class had sharpened his satirical tone. The crudities of the aristocracy make them Barbarians, the materialism and pusillanimousness of the middle classes make them Philistines (the term long ago fastened on when he was first reading Heine), and the working class is the Populace, whose recently revealed capacity for frightening acts of violence had become a general source of anxiety in this time of the Second Reform Act and the Hyde Park Riots. But even so 'aliens' exist in each class on whom hope may rest. These now are to represent the nation's 'best selves' in government and by their flexibility and intelligence guard against 'anarchy', the depredations of '*laissez-faire*', the Hebraic narrowness of Dissent and all the ills that mid-Victorian flesh is heir to.

Arnold's second period of renewed critical activity in these later years opened shortly after the publication of *Culture and Anarchy* when he turned his attention to religion, beginning in 1870 with *St Paul and Protestantism* and going on to *Literature and Dogma* (1873) and *God and the Bible* (1875). This interest is commonly held to coincide with the increasing 'Christianizing' of his thought, but as early as his essay on 'Marcus Aurelius' he had contrasted the austerities of that otherwise *sympathique* Roman Emperor and the 'coldness' of Epictetus with the 'exquisite' powers of Thomas à Kempis's *Imitation of Christ*, which was 'second only' to the New Testament in its power to 'light up morality' by the 'sweetness' and 'warmth' of its message.[57] This feeling was almost certainly deepened by the personal griefs which visited him in the years between 1868 and 1873, when he lost in succession his three young sons, two in 1868 (his infant son Basil and Thomas, a sixteen-year-old Harrow schoolboy), the third in 1872 (William Trevenen, aged eighteen) and, in the next year, his long-widowed mother. But everywhere in these books his major interest is to develop and drive home the ideas set going in 1862 when he had made sport of Bishop Colenso's aridly 'liberal' interpretation of the Bible in an article which gave him the starting-point for 'Spinoza and the Bible'. Superstition is not to be routed by simple mathematics:

[...] as to the account in the Book of Exodus of the Israelites dwelling in tents – '*Allowing 10 persons for each tent (and a Zulu hut in Natal contains on average only 3 ½), how many tents would 2,000,000 persons require?* The parenthesis in that problem is hardly worthy of such a master of arithmetical statement as Dr Colenso; but with or without the parenthesis, the problem, when answered, disposes of the Book of Exodus. [...] Take Numbers, and the total of first-borns there given, as compared with the number of male adults: '*If, of 900,000 males, 22,273 are first-borns, how many boys must there be in each family?*' That disposes of Numbers. For Deuteronomy, take the number of lambs slain at the Sanctuary, as compared with the space for slaying them: '*In an area of 1,692 square yards, how many lambs per minute can 150,000 persons kill in two hours?*' Certainly not 1,250, the number required; and the Book of Deuteronomy, therefore, shares the fate of its predecessors. *Omnes eodem cogimur.*[58]

Arnold's response is governed by an ethical not a metaphysical passion. Like his fellow 'agnostic angels' – Basil Willey's term for the age's devout sceptics who abandoned Christian dogma while retaining the Christian ethos and holding to belief in unalterable moral law (George Eliot is very close to Arnold in this) – he grounded his defence of religion in its value for man's harmonious development as a creature with a need 'for intellect and knowledge, desire for beauty, instinct for society, and for pleasurable and graceful forms of society' as well as for material advantages and the support of 'high seriousness'. Perhaps one may be forgiven for quoting here this brief epitome of his position:

To Arnold metaphysical reasoning was simply methodical self-bewilderment, but he had as strongly as George Eliot the conviction that the moral law exists and speaks unequivocally in experience. On the one side, then, religion was ceremonial practices, which he supported *because* they were absurd – much as Bagehot defended the decorative elements in the English constitution as 'social cement'; on the other side, religion was morality, which religious feeling could 'light up' and transform into a driving-force. The rest was 'over-belief' (*Aberglaube*) [...] Miracles did not occur, theology was a pseudo-science, and literary tact discerned that theologians had done enormous violence to the loose figurative language of the Bible – language never meant to be precise, but 'thrown out' at objects of consciousness 'not fully grasped' [...] Arnold was quite sure that the traditional idea of

God arose from a failure to distinguish the scientific and poetic uses of language.

He believed that he was 'defending religion by surrendering its untenable outposts', but, this argument goes on,

we are more likely to feel that he was attempting – in an adaptation of Hartley Coleridge's phrase about Wordsworth – to smuggle Spinoza into the pulpit in a curate's ragged surplice.[59]

As it turned out, *God and the Bible*, his reply two years later to objections raised by the enormously successful *Literature and Dogma*, was much less popular with the general public. But for the modern reader the book has something of the same effect as *On Translating Homer. Last Words*, Arnold's reply to criticisms of his first series of Homer lectures. The challenge, reviving his polemical *élan*, encourages him to rehearse and clarify his central themes, so that the third of his major religious discussions can serve us nowadays as an introduction to the ideas first developed in its two studiously pondered predecessors.

It might be said of the stage of his career which follows this that Arnold 'returned' to literary criticism since he now committed himself to a series of major literary assignments, many of which have held their place as centre-pieces of nineteenth-century criticism and have proved to be as influential as anything he wrote. He contributed selections from Gray and Keats to T. H. Ward's *The English Poets* (1880), writing introductions for each and agreeing to add a General Introduction. This became his important and frequently misunderstood essay, 'The Study of Poetry'. He compiled his own selections from Wordsworth in 1879 and from Byron in 1881, the introductions for these once again turning out to be among the finest examples of his critical talent. Between 1877 and 1887 he wrote in addition articles for various periodicals on Milton, Shelley, Amiel and Sainte-Beuve, to whose influence he had paid constant tribute throughout his critical career. He also published two pieces which are among the few commentaries we have from him on novelists. His essay on Tolstoy (whom he admired far beyond Flaubert because of his wholesome avoidance of the 'Goddess Lubricity') virtually introduced this writer to the English reading public for the first time. The tribute to George Sand was written shortly after her death in 1876 and contains a moving account of his first and only visit to her in his long ago 'days of *Lélia*'. His assessment of her gift carries equally strong personal overtones. 'The hour of revolt, of agony', which belongs to the period of her early novels (*Valentine, Lélia, Jacques, Mauprat* are all of the 1830s), 'passed away for George Sand as it passed away for Goethe, as it passes away for their readers likewise. It passes away and does not return ... we shall read the books no more ...' And yet 'the immense vibration of George Sand's voice upon the ear of Europe will not soon die away' because she had more than this to express:

> [...] in the evolution of these three elements, – the passion of agony and revolt, the consolation from nature and from beauty, the ideas of social renewal – in the evolution of these is [...] George Sand's life and power [...][60]

This pronouncement alone, with its reiterated emphasis on 'aspiration towards a purged and renewed human society' is enough to remind us that we cannot justly speak of a 'return', nor yet of a new development, in this final decade of Arnold's life. We find him, shortly after completing work on Wordsworth, writing with his customary political verve on 'The Future of Liberalism', armed *cap à pie* as 'a Liberal of the future' against both the Tories and his fellow Liberals, their complacencies refreshed by their recent victory in the General Election. 'They reproach me, sometimes', he says,

> with having drawn the picture of the Radical and Dissenting Bottles, but left the Tory Bottles unportrayed. Yet he exists, they urge, and is very baneful; and his ignoble Toryism it is, the shoddy Toryism of the City and of the Stock Exchange, and not, as pompous leading articles say, the intelligence and sober judgment of the educated classes and of mercantile sagacity, which carried the elections in the City of London and in the metropolitan counties for the Conservatives [...][61]

But Liberalism has done nothing as yet for inequality. 'Our present state' is still as bad as he has always described it, with 'an upper class materialized, a middle class vulgarized, a lower class brutalized'. Moreover England carries her infection into Ireland, where inequality produces yet 'more pressing and evident troubles' and whose dark political situation and dire educational plight had occupied him to such an extent since his essay in 1878 on 'Irish Catholicism and British Liberalism' that he called his next collection *Irish Essays*. 'His principle, in all Irish matters', Robert Super reminds us, 'is that a national, a racial, a religious minority must decide for itself what it wants; it cannot be told what is good for it by a dominant but alien majority, it need not even convince that majority that what it wants is in the long run best and most reasonable'.[62]

If there is a 'development' in these years, then, there is one in no sense other than that his best work shows him writing with the freshness, ease and fullness of mind which we should expect from a lifetime devoted to the practice and encouragement of the utmost possible flexibility, variety and openness to experience. Here lies the abiding principle which makes 'criticism' and 'culture' synonymous terms in Arnold's vocabulary. Criticism requires qualities of tact and delicacy which are ultimately matters of morality and character as well as intellect and sensibility:

> The critic of poetry should have the finest tact, the nicest moder-
> ation, the most free, flexible, and elastic spirit imaginable; he
> should be indeed the 'ondoyant et divers', the *undulating and di-*
> *verse* being of Montaigne ... [63]

His emphasis on this 'best self' – for this is what is involved here as in all his statements about the criticism of literature and society – is perhaps responsible for what we may see in our disenchanted day as the limitations of his liberal idealism, his over-optimistic belief that we will be made better people by reading 'the best that has been thought and said' and the curious myopia which prevented him acknowledging either the richness of some of the literature of his day (in the novel, for example) or, in his 1853 preface, how dark was the vision attending the 'excellent actions' in the great Greek tragic dramatists who are supposed to 'animate' and 'rejoice' us. But his refusal to separate the man who suffers from the poet who creates is also the main source of the remarkable strength and assurance of his criticism. Most of his literary themes – 'natural magic', '*architectonicé*', literature as 'a criticism of life', the 'interpretative power' of poetry – arise from his grasp of the ruling qualities of a writer's temperament and the conditions which shape the experience recreated in his work: his nationality, his age, the setting of his day-to-day life. 'Natural magic' is associated with the Celtic imaginative temperament, Spinoza's strength as a philosopher with his nobility of character, Maurice de Guérin's delicate perception with his gentle melancholy. *Architectonicé*, 'high seriousness', 'the grand style' are the effects of morality and character too, since they depend on disciplining oneself to 'know enough' – as the Romantic poets did not – and so triumph over the world's 'multitudinousness', 'see life steadily and see it whole' and speak with the authority, breadth and wisdom which can give literature the magisterial power to which Arnold summons it in 'The Study of Poetry'. His 'touchstones' in this essay do not guide us to this power because of any strength or beauty they may possess on their own; this would be totally contrary to his assertion that the whole matters more than the parts, however vivid local imagery and style may be. 'I hate all over-preponderance of single elements', he had said at the start of his critical career, when he found that Keats and Shelley were 'on a false track' when

> they set themselves to reproduce the exuberance of expression [...] the richness of images [...] of the Elizabethan poets [...] critics still think that the object of poetry is to reproduce exquisite bits and images [...][64]

Our 'touchstones' should recall to us the 'excellence', the 'high seriousness', the 'profound application of ideas to life', characterizing their context in the *Iliad*, or *Hamlet*, or the *Divina Commedia* or *Paradise Lost*. The idea of 'wholeness' penetrates this entire nineteenth-century 'Defence of Poetry' and carries with it a kind of pre-Yeatsian desire for unity of being. So it is that the critic cannot bring his various faculties fully into play, cannot be '*ondoyant et divers*', if he permits the 'historical' and the 'personal' estimate to distort his vision and prevent him seeing the object 'as it is'. So, even more, with the creative writer, for whom the critic, however important his function, remains a servant, providing in certain periods of a country's history the current of fresh ideas and the necessary intellectual climate in which imaginative literature can flourish.[65] The concern helps to explain incidental judgments which have troubled readers over the years, for example that Chaucer in a final view lacks 'high seriousness', that Dryden and Pope are 'not masters of our poetry' but are respectively the 'founder' and the 'high priest' of 'our age of prose and reason, our excellent and indispensable eighteenth century'. There is in them a lack of 'high seriousness', of a powerful 'poetic' application of ideas to life, a want of 'largeness, freedom, insight, benignity'.[66] Arnold may well be accused of want of insight into the virtues of Augustan poetry and the imaginative range which gave us *Troylus and Cryseyde* as well as *The Canterbury Tales*. But these estimates make a certain sense in the context of his critical thinking. His gnomic phrase, 'imaginative reason', which he defines as the 'element by which the modern spirit, if it would live aright, has chiefly to live',[67] epitomizes his lifelong Romantic struggle to reconcile 'head' and 'heart' and we may discern in its light a movement of thought which led him to see a predominancy of the former in the eighteenth century and of the latter in Chaucer. If the art of criticism lies in the capacity to make distinctions, to see the object as itself and not another thing, this order of discrimination is perfectly justifiable. Whatever the critical rights and wrongs here, it was certainly his belief in their imbalance which made him disapprove of his own early poems and try for greater breadth and composure, even if the heart still struggled to make itself felt through the more austere disciplines of his later poetry.

'The Study of Poetry' is designed, we should remember, to encourage people to buy a new anthology by quickening their sense of what poetry might mean to them as a moral and imaginative force. A similar purpose directs the essays about individual writers represented in Arnold's own selections, especially perhaps those on Wordsworth, Byron and Keats, in whom in spite of recognized weaknesses Arnold finds a promise so immense that he places him, after all, 'with Shakespeare'. His gifts for drawing on his feeling for character and depicting the interplay of 'the man' and 'the moment' are forcefully in evidence in his essay on Byron, a writer who can be slovenly and careless, guilty of 'trailing relatives [...] crying grammatical solecism [...] inextricable anacolouthon' and, what is more, is often lacking in Leopardi's weight and gravity. But this is not all:

> There is the Byron who posed, there is the Byron with his affectations and silliness, the Byron whose weakness Lady Blessington [...] so admirably seized: 'His great defect is flippancy and a total want of self-possession.' But when this theatrical and easily criticized personage betook himself to poetry, and when he had fairly warmed to his work, then he became another man [...] at last came forth into light that true and puissant personality, with its direct strokes, its ever-welling force, its satire, its energy, and its agony [...]

It may be true, as Goethe said, that 'the moment he reflects he is a child', but his heart is in the right place. He warred throughout his life against a British Philistinism 'far more deep and dark than it is now'. He 'shattered himself to pieces' to no avail against the cant which revolted him 'in the great middle part of the English nation' and 'the cant of his own class' which 'revolted him still more'. But 'this passionate and dauntless soldier of a forlorn hope [...] waged against [...] the old impossible world [...] a fiery battle; waged it till he fell', and did so with 'splendid and imperishable excellence of sincerity and strength'.[68]

There is a passionate ring in this which reminds us that Arnold was never fully equipped to act finally on Carlyle's advice to 'close thy Byron; open thy Goethe'.[69] It conveys something of the romantic feeling invading his moral commitment to keep 'breast to breast with reality', the ambition which he expressed in one of his early letters to Clough, which are rivalled only by those of Keats and Hopkins as the utterances of a vivacious individual poetic sensibility. Keats's letters (as I have said in another context) are indispensable reading for anyone concerned with poetry, the poetic temperament and the poetic process.[70] So are Arnold's, for they afford us an intimate insight into the mental and emotional hinterland of his journey from poetry to criticism. When we read them alongside his public writings we perceive still more clearly the complexities of a temperament recently described as 'an individual mixture of eighteenth-century rationality, Romantic idealism, Victorian scepticism, and, if we like the overworn word, modern existentialism'; sharing with so many of his contemporaries the loss of traditional Christian faith, 'in his troubled search for light and direction he found help in such heterogeneous guides as George Sand, Senancour, Goethe, Spinoza, Carlyle (whose influence survived repudiation), Emerson, the ancient classics and Stoics, the *Bhagavad-Gita*, the Bible and Thomas à Kempis'.[71] We come 'breast to breast' with some of the more intimate aspects of this struggle with his *daemon* in his letters to Clough. In exploring his situation he strikes off, with the confident freedom of one friend to another, some of his finest early flashes of insight. They herald his public skills, anticipating the quality which he speaks of many years later in his Byron essay:

> Surely the critic who does most for his author is the critic who gains readers for his author himself, not for any lucubrations on his author; – gains more readers for him, and enables those readers to read him with more admiration ...[72]

It would be pleasant to think that these introductory remarks, and the selections which follow, might go some way towards serving Arnold as he served the writers who aroused his own sense of acceptance, relief, admiration and delight, and in doing so helped to quicken our own.

NOTES

1. Fraser Neiman, 'A Reader's Guide to Arnold', *Allott* 12.
2. See J. W. Gulland's unpublished letter of 24 June 1913, cited in Irvin Stock, *William Hale White (Mark Rutherford)* (1956), 3n. The teacher was William Jones, later MP and Welsh Whip. Hale White's *The Autobiography of Mark Rutherford* was published 1881 and his translation of Spinoza's *Ethic* in 1883.
3. The Reverend Thomas Arnold died suddenly of heart disease in 1842, fourteen years after being appointed Headmaster of Rugby School.
4. *Letters* ii. 11. See also *Letters* ii. 131 for the Bishop who 'told me that my poems were the centre of his mental life, and that he had read many of them hundreds of times'.
5. See p. 189 below.
6. *Letters* i. 200.
7. See 'Memorial Verses' ll. 43 – 4, p. 87 below.
8. *Letters* ii. 9.
9. Lytton Strachey's *Eminent Victorians* (1918), including biographies of Cardinal Manning, Florence Nightingale, Dr Arnold and General Gordon, was followed in 1921 by his *Life of Queen Victoria*. He describes his method as avoiding 'scrupulous narration', attacking 'his subject in unexpected places', and sending 'a sudden revealing searchlight into obscure recesses'. The method had a salutary effect on unthinking reverence, but also encouraged some equally unthinking reactions. The survey referred to is *Victorian Prose: A Guide to Research*, ed. D. J. DeLaura (1973); the chapter on Arnold refers to work on his poetry as well as his prose.
10. *Letters* ii. 11.
11. Arnold calls Dryden and Pope masters of 'our excellent and indispensable age of prose and reason'. See 'On the Study of Poetry' pp. 256–8 below, and for 'imaginative reason' p. 186 below.
12. *Letters to Clough*, 36.
13. 'George Sand speaks somewhere of her "days of *Corinne*", Days of *Valentine*, many of us may in like manner say, – days of *Valentine*, days of *Lélia*, days never to return' (Arnold's 1877 essay on George Sand, *CPW* viii. 220). Patricia Thompson uses the phrase as the title for her lively chapter on Arnold and George Sand, *George Sand and*

the Victorians (1977), 90 –120. Arnold learnt of the impression he had made many years later; see his letter of June 1876, 'I [...] heard from Morley yesterday that G. Sand had said to Renan that when she saw me years ago, "*Je lui faisait l'effet d'un Milton jeune et voyage-ant*", Renan told him this. Her death has been much in my mind; she was the greatest spirit in our European world from the time that Goethe departed. With all her faults and Frenchism she was this. I must write a few pages about her', *Letters* ii. 131; see also 'The New Sirens', *Poems* 33 –5.

14.　*Letters to Clough*, 25.

15.　Letter to James Taylor, 15 Jan. 1851, *The Brontës: Their Lives, Friendships and Correspondence* (ed. Wise and Symons, 1932), iii. 199.

16.　Quoted in Mrs Humphry Ward's, *A Writer's Recollections* (1918), 44.

17.　'Here is my programme for this afternoon: Avalanches – The Steam Engine – The Thames – India Rubber – Bricks – The Battle of Poictiers – Subtraction – The Reindeer – The Gunpowder Plot – The Jordan. Alluring is it not? Twenty minutes each, and the days of one's life are only threescore years and ten', letter to Lady de Rothschild, *Letters* i. 242. See also his letter after completing 'Sohrab and Rustum', 'it is pain and grief composing with such interruptions as I have', *Letters to Clough*, 136.

18.　*Letters to Clough*, 65.

19.　*Matthew Arnold. Poems*, ed. Kenneth Allott (Everyman 1965) vi.

20.　*Letters to Clough*, 146. The lines quoted are from 'The Youth of Nature,' ll. 51–2 (p. 91 below).

21.　Allott, 74.

22.　Ibid., 75.

23.　'[...] it is almost impossible not to find [...] at least a shadowy personal significance. The strong son is slain by the mightier father; and in the end Sohrab draws his father's spear from his own side to let out his life [...] We watch Arnold in his later youth and we must wonder if he is not, in a psychical sense, doing the same thing', Trilling 134 –5.

24.　*Letters*, i. 62.

25.　See p. 129 below.

26.　*Letters to Clough*, 126.

27.　On his taxonomic problems see K. and M. Allott, 'Arnold the Poet: (ii) Narrative and Dramatic Poems', Allott 70 –3.

28.　'The Scholar-Gipsy' ll. 203–7 (pp. 113–14 below).

29.　See K. and M. Allott, op. cit., 84–7.

30.　See the close of 'Resignation' (ll. 277–8, p. 20 below) where 'action's dizzying eddy' expresses feelings akin to 'the sick fatigue' and 'the sick hurry' of 'The Scholar-Gipsy' (ll. 164, 204) and to 'Eddying at large in blind uncertainty' in 'The Buried Life', l. 43 (pp. 112, 113, 98 below).

31. 'Tristram and Iseult' III. ll. 122–24 (pp. 82–3 below).

32. In his *A choice of Kipling's Verse* (1941) 17.

33. 'Stanzas from the Grande Chartreuse' ll. 85– 6 (p. 102 below); Carlyle's 'Characteristics' (1831), *Traill* xxviii. 29–30, 32; Mill's 'The Spirit of the Age' (1831), rpt. *Essays on Literature and Society* ed. J. B. Schneewind (1965) 30.

34. Arnold wrote out this sonnet in the gift copy to his sister of the 1852 Moxon edition of Keats's *Poems*, from which the sonnet is omitted. Expressions of his mingled admiration for and reserves about Keats's talent appear here and there in his writings from 1848 (date of Monckton Milnes's edition of Keats's *Life, Letters and Literary Remains*) until his late essay for T. H. Ward. See above, pp. xxxviii–ix and below, pp. 169–70, 203–5 and *Letters to Clough* 96–7, 100–1, 124.

35. 'My dearest Clough these are damned times – everything is against one – the height to which knowledge is come, the spread of luxury, our physical enervation, the absence of great *natures*, the unavoidable contact with millions of small ones, newspapers, cities, light profligate friends, moral desperadoes like Carlyle, our own selves, and the sickening consciousness of our difficulties: but for God's sake let us neither be fanatics nor yet chaff blown by the wind', *Letters to Clough* 111.

36. See below, p. 64. For Arnold's note on Senancour's qualities attached to his second 'Obermann' poem see *Poems* 129.

37. 'Marcus Aurelius', *CPW* iii. 134.

38. *Allott* 78.

39. Quotations from 'Empedocles on Etna' I. ii. 257– 61, I. ii. 46–50, I. ii. 82–5, II. i. 18–22, II. i. 465–8 (pp. 55, 48–9, 50, 64, 78 below).

40. I. ii. 386 (p. 60 below).

41. *Merope* 518–20, 614–16; *Poems* 412, 415.

42. See *Poems* 332.

43. For the influence of Keats's odes on the versification and poetic texture of these poems see further pp. 107, 282–3, 284–5 below.

44. *Poems* 547, 557, 562. On Arnold's 'pindarics' see *Poems* 244–5.

45. Quotations from 'Isolation. To Marguerite', ll. 37–42; 'Resignation' l. 198; 'To Marguerite – Continued' ll. 22– 4 (pp. 28, 18, 29 below); 'Parting' ll. 71– 4 (*Poems* 120).

46. See 'Human Life' l. 27 (*Poems* 140); 'Dover Beach' ll. 23–5, 29–34; 'The Youth of Nature' ll. 51– 4; headn. to 'Resignation' (pp. 89, 91, 12 below).

47. 'Stanzas in Memory of the Author of "Obermann" ', ll. 45–8, 53– 4 (p. 34 below). Arnold's letter of 25 Sept. 1854 describes Wordsworth and Goethe as 'the two moderns (very different) I most care for' *Letters*

i. 241. For detailed discussions of Arnold's response to these 'moderns' see 'Arnold and Wordsworth' in Leon A. Gottfried's *Matthew Arnold and the Romantics* (1963) and James Simpson, 'Arnold and Goethe', *Allott* 286 –318.

48. See 'Heinrich Heine', 'Wordsworth', pp. 170, 231 below.

49. *Letters* i. 201.

50. *On Translating Homer: Last Words, CPW* i. 172.

51. See pp. 196–7 below. This conception of history is intimately connected with Arnold's emphasis on the importance of understanding the spirit of the time, the *Zeit-geist*: cp. his first Arminius letter p. 207 below and Peter Keating, 'by the close of [the 1860s] the whole argument of "Democracy" [p. 164 below] was to be contained in Arminius's defiant scream, "Get Geist" ', *Matthew Arnold: Selected Prose* (Penguin English Library 1970) 17.

52. In his *Studies of a Biographer* II. (1898). On 'Sweetness and Light' see *Culture and Anarchy*, p. 212 below.

53. For example the various studies by David J. DeLaura, Robert Super, Basil Willey and Warren Anderson in *Allott*; and by Peter Keating in the same volume and in *Matthew Arnold: Selected Prose*. See further Bibliography below.

54. For a recent account of such 'dialogue' in Arnold's poems and prose see Miriam Allott, 'Voices Across the Echoing Straits. Dialogue, Translation and Irony in Arnold and Clough', *Tensions and Translations. The Mediating Imagination* (Faber and Faber, 1990), 47–64. The reference to Arnold's 'monologue' appears in Peter Keating, op. cit. 18.

55. *Letters* ii. 28; *Poems* 543.

56. Chapter XIII 'The Popular Education of France and England Compared–Legislation', *CPW* ii. 145.

57. 'Marcus Aurelius', *CPW* iii. 133–5.

58. 'The Bishop and the Philosopher', *CPW* iii. 48.

59. K. Allott, *Matthew Arnold*, in Writers and Their Work (1955), repr. British Writers and Their Works (1963), 62–3.

60. *CPW* viii. 220.

61. *CPW* ix. 138–9.

62. *CPW* viii. 465.

63. *On Translating Homer, CPW* i. 174.

64. *Letters to Clough* 124.

65. 'The Function of Criticism at the Present Time' pp. 191–2 below.

66. 'The Study of Poetry' pp. 255, 258 below.

67. 'Pagan and Medieval Religious Sentiment', p. 186 below.

68. 'Byron', *CPW* ix. 223, 233 – 4, 236.

69. *Sartor Resartus* (1838), Traill i. 153.

70. *John Keats*, Writers and their Work (1976) 49.

71. Douglas Bush, *Matthew Arnold* xv–xvi (1971).

72. 'Byron', loc. cit., 235.

NOTE ON THE TEXT

Wherever possible the text of the poems and the prose has been set up from earlier editions in Everyman's Library: notably *Matthew Arnold. Poems* (first reprinted in Everyman's Library 1906; revised and enlarged 1944; new edition with introduction by Kenneth Allott, 1965); and Matthew Arnold's *Essays in Criticism, First and Second Series* (1964) which carries a note on the text by the same editor, explaining that *Essays in Criticism, Second Series*, with the Preface to the second edition (1869) of *Essays in Criticism, First Series*, now both out of copyright, have replaced certain of the contents included in *Essays, Literary and Critical*, first added to the Library in 1906: namely, *On Translating Homer* (1861) and *Last Words on Translating Homer* (1862); and Francis Newman's *Homeric Translation in Theory and Practice* (1861). When it has been found necessary to go beyond *Essays in Criticism, First and Second Series*, the choice of readings has been guided by texts reproduced in R. H. Super's *The Complete Prose Works of Matthew Arnold*.

The representation of both sides of Matthew Arnold's creative talent in a single volume is still a relatively rare undertaking, and the more we know about his work the easier it is to see why this is so. His prose writings occupy eleven volumes in R. H. Super's *The Complete Prose Works of Matthew Arnold*, completed in 1977, and the documentation in this edition and in Kenneth Allott's *The Poems of Matthew Arnold*, published in 1965 and shortly to be reprinted, leaves us with no excuse to doubt the extraordinary range and diversity of his interests. It is obvious, then, that anyone compiling a selection of the kind proposed here is faced with acute editorial problems and is unlikely to be really satisfied with the manner in which they have been met. But at least it can be said that the present choice has been guided by a consistent effort to observe, as honourably as possible in the available space, the unity in variety of a creative intelligence which always tried to examine and understand its own laws of development ('I will write historically as I can write naturally in no other way', Arnold told Clough in 1853); and which found increasingly at its service from the 1850s onwards, when the poet began to cede to the critic of literature and society, the dual qualities of sensitive insight into and toughly reasonable command of the perplexing troubles of the age which had helped to shape it.

This accounts for the emphasis throughout this volume on the interplay between Arnold's poetic achievement and his critical responsiveness, which has its own light to shed on the brevity of his poetic life and also on the personal pressures which first brought that life into being. It also accounts for various departures from editorial custom, especially the exclusion of certain much anthologized pieces in the interests of others more in keeping with a concern for representativeness and centrality. 'Sohrab and Rustum', for example, yields – apart from its famous coda – to 'Empedocles on Etna', which is Arnold's, and perhaps also the age's, major long poem, and is here printed in full. The same concern, reinforced by Arnold's discursive mannerisms as a polemical essayist (these are discussed in the introductory essay), explains the printing of extracts from the prose – some short, some very substantial – to illustrate characteristic turns of his thought and style over the years. Thus *Culture and Anarchy* is not represented by the two or three complete chapters which have so often been reprinted from it, but by key passages which link themselves with passages from other works chosen to represent Arnold's lively *sorties* in his running battle with the hosts of Midian.

All the same a multitude of regrets haunts an editor obliged by want of space to omit so much. I should have liked to represent, among many other pieces, the preface to *Essays in Criticism, First Series* and much more of *Friendship's Garland* (including 'My Countrymen'), as examples of Arnold's liveliest satirical style; the excellent essays on Emerson and 'A French Critic on Milton', which reiterate with fresh lucidity some of his fundamental critical principles; 'Falkland', a memorable late essay, which reveals the abiding presence in the critic of the creative writer who had deeply desired to give poetic expression to noble and 'excellent' human actions; and, as an instance of one aspect of his daily observation which is hardly known, the still very topical 'A Comment on Christmas'. But space has been found for what seems to be, at least in the present editor's view, the absolute *sine qua non* for any introductory study of Arnold's prose. The task of choosing among the poems has seemed less taxing because the quantity is so much less overwhelming, though, as happens with almost any selection, readers will probably regret the absence of some of their favourite pieces. I think it is fair to say that the poems which do appear represent the most characteristic expression of Arnold's poetic voice in the brief fruitful decade from 1847–57 and illustrate its intermittent renewals in the years which followed. One hardly needs to add in conclusion that serious students of Arnold will find it essential to supplement whatever may be gleaned from any selection of his work by proper reference to the definitive editions of the poetry and prose referred to at the beginning of this preface.

POEMS

Shakespeare

Dated 1 Aug. 1844 in A.'s fair copy; one of eleven sonnets pub. *1849*. The octet is Italian, with the 'Wordsworthian' variant of a third rhyme ll. 6–7; in the sestet a Shakespearian quatrain followed by a couplet.

Others abide our question. Thou art free.
We ask and ask – Thou smilest and art still,
Out-topping knowledge. For the loftiest hill,
Who to the stars uncrowns his majesty,

Planting his steadfast footsteps in the sea,
Making the heaven of heavens his dwelling-place,
Spares but the cloudy border of his base
To the foiled searching of mortality;

And thou, who didst the stars and sunbeams know,
Self-school'd, self-scann'd, self-honour'd, self-secure,   10
Didst tread on earth unguessed at. – Better so!

All pains the immortal spirit must endure,
All weakness which impairs, all griefs which bow,
Find their sole speech in that victorious brow.

In Harmony with Nature

TO A PREACHER

Probably composed 1844–7; pub. *1849* as 'To an Independent Preacher, who preached that we should be "In Harmony with Nature."' Repr. later edns. with present title. See A. in *Literature and Dogma* (1873) on 'pitfalls ... in that word *Nature* ... Do you mean that we are to give full swing to our inclinations ... the constitution of things turns out to be somehow or other against it ... the free development ... of our *apparent* self, has to undergo a profound modification from the law of our higher *real* self, the law of righteousness' (*CPW* vi. 389, 391–2).

'In harmony with Nature?' Restless fool,
Who with such heat dost preach what were to thee,
When true, the last impossibility –
To be like Nature strong, like Nature cool!

Know, man hath all which Nature hath, but more,
And in that *more* lie all his hopes of good.

Nature is cruel, man is sick of blood;
Nature is stubborn, man would fain adore;

Nature is fickle, man hath need of rest;
Nature forgives no debt, and fears no grave;   10
Man would be mild, and with safe conscience blest.

Man must begin, know this, where Nature ends;
Nature and man can never be fast friends.
Fool, if thou canst not pass her, rest her slave!

In Utrumque Paratus

Probably written 1846 when A. was reading Plotinus; pub. *1849.* 'The alternatives of
the title are the world of emanation (man has descended) or as eternal matter achieving
consciousness in man (man has ascended)' (*Poems* 54).

If, in the silent mind of One all-pure,
        At first imagined lay
The sacred world; and by procession sure
From those still deeps, in form and colour drest,
Seasons alternating, and night and day,
The long-mused thought to north, south, east, and west,
        Took then its all-seen way;

O waking on a world which thus-wise springs!
        Whether it needs thee count
Betwixt thy waking and the birth of things   10
Ages or hours – O waking on life's stream!
By lonely pureness to the all-pure fount
(Only by this thou canst) the colour'd dream
        Of life remount!

Thin, thin the pleasant human noises grow,
        And faint the city gleams;
Rare the lone pastoral huts – marvel not thou!
The solemn peaks but to the stars are known,
But to the stars, and the cold lunar beams;
Alone the sun arises, and alone   20
        Spring the great streams.

But, if the wild unfather'd mass no birth

In divine seats hath known;
In the blank echoing solitude if Earth,
Rocking her obscure body to and fro,
Ceases not from all time to heave and groan,
Unfruitful oft, and at her happiest throe
    Forms, what she forms, alone;

O seeming sole to awake, thy sun-bathed head
    Piercing the solemn cloud   30
Round thy still dreaming brother-world outspread!
O man, whom Earth, thy long-vext mother, bare
Not without joy – so radiant, so endow'd
(Such happy issue crown'd her painful care) –
    Be not too proud!

Oh when most self-exalted most alone,
    Chief dreamer, own thy dream!
Thy brother-world stirs at thy feet unknown,
Who hath a monarch's hath no brother's part;
Yet doth thine inmost soul with yearning teem.   40
– Oh, what a spasm shakes the dreamer's heart!
    '*I, too, but seem.*'

The Sick King in Bokhara

Probably written 1847–8; pub. *1849*. Source is Alexander Burnes's *Travels into Bokhara* ... (1834), also used for 'The Strayed Reveller' (1849) and *Sohrab and Rustum* (p. 92 below), especially the story (i. 307–9), illustrating with topographical and pictorial detail, 'the rigour of the Mohammedan law' in the case of a mullah 'who ... violated the law, proceeded to the palace, and demanded justice according to the Koran'. On the parallel with Raskolnikov seeking punishment to expiate his guilt see *Trilling* (104–6) and, on A.'s interest in the story for its emphasis on the sanctioning of moral law by the individual conscience, *Poems* 76.

HUSSEIN:
O most just Vizier, send away
The cloth-merchants, and let them be,
Them and their dues, this day! the King
Is ill at ease, and calls for thee.

THE VIZIER:
O merchants, tarry yet a day

Here in Bokhara! but at noon,
To-morrow, come, and ye shall pay
Each fortieth web of cloth to me,
As the law is, and go your way.
O Hussein, lead me to the King!   10
Thou teller of sweet tales, thine own,
Ferdousi's, and the others', lead!
How is it with my lord?

HUSSEIN:
                                        Alone,
Ever since prayer-time, he doth wait,
O Vizier! without lying down,
In the great window of the gate,
Looking into the Registàn,
Where through the sellers' booths the slaves
Are this way bringing the dead man. –
O Vizier, here is the King's door!   20

THE KING:
O Vizier, I may bury him?

THE VIZIER:
O King, thou know'st, I have been sick
These many days, and heard no thing
(For Allah shut my ears and mind),
Not even what thou dost, O King!
Wherefore, that I may counsel thee,
Let Hussein, if thou wilt, make haste
To speak in order what hath chanced.

THE KING:
O Vizier, be it as thou say'st!

HUSSEIN:
Three days since, at the time of prayer   30
A certain Moollah, with his robe
All rent, and dust upon his hair,
Watch'd my lord's coming forth, and push'd
The golden mace-bearers aside,
And fell at the King's feet, and cried:
'Justice, O King, and on myself!
On this great sinner, who did break

The law, and by the law must die!
Vengeance, O King!'

                    But the King spake:
'What fool is this, that hurts our ears   40
With folly? or what drunken slave?
My guards, what, prick him with your spears!
Prick me the fellow from the path!'
As the King said, so it was done,
And to the mosque my lord pass'd on.

But on the morrow, when the King
Went forth again, the holy book
Carried before him, as is right,
And through the square his way he took;
My man comes running, fleck'd with blood   50
From yesterday, and falling down
Cries out most earnestly: 'O King,
My lord, O King, do right, I pray!

'How canst thou, ere thou hear, discern
If I speak folly? but a king,
Whether a thing be great or small,
Like Allah, hears and judges all.

'Wherefore hear thou! Thou know'st, how fierce
In these last days the sun hath burn'd;
That the green water in the tanks   60
Is to a putrid puddle turn'd;
And the canal, which from the stream
Of Samarcand is brought this way,
Wastes, and runs thinner every day.

'Now I at nightfall had gone forth
Alone, and in a darksome place
Under some mulberry-trees I found
A little pool; and in short space,
With all the water that was there
I fill'd my pitcher, and stole home   70
Unseen; and having drink to spare,
I hid the can behind the door,
And went up on the roof to sleep.

'But in the night, which was with wind

And burning dust, again I creep
Down, having fever, for a drink.

'Now meanwhile had my brethren found
The water-pitcher, where it stood
Behind the door upon the ground,
And call'd my mother; and they all,   80
As they were thirsty, and the night
Most sultry, drain'd the pitcher there;
That they sate with it, in my sight,
Their lips still wet, when I came down.

'Now mark! I, being fever'd, sick
(Most unblest also), at that sight
Brake forth, and cursed them – dost thou hear? –
One was my mother—Now, do right!'

But my lord mused a space, and said:
'Send him away, Sirs, and make on!   90
It is some madman!' the King said.
As the King bade, so was it done.

The morrow, at the self-same hour,
In the King's path, behold, the man,
Not kneeling, sternly fix'd! he stood
Right opposite, and thus began,
Frowning grim down: 'Thou wicked King,
Most deaf where thou shouldst most give ear!

What, must I howl in the next world,
Because thou wilt not listen here?   100

'What, wilt thou pray, and get thee grace,
And all grace shall to me be grudged?
Nay but, I swear, from this thy path
I will not stir till I be judged!'

Then they who stood about the King
Drew close together and conferr'd;
Till that the King stood forth and said:
'Before the priests thou shalt be heard.'

But when the Ulemas were met,
And the thing heard, they doubted not;   110
But sentenced him, as the law is,
To die by stoning on the spot.

Now the King charged us secretly:
'Stoned must he be, the law stands so.
Yet, if he seek to fly, give way;
Hinder him not, but let him go.'

So saying, the King took a stone,
And cast it softly; – but the man,
With a great joy upon his face,
Kneel'd down, and cried not, neither ran.   120

So they, whose lot it was, cast stones,
That they flew thick and bruised him sore.
But he praised Allah with loud voice,
And remain'd kneeling as before.

My lord had cover'd up his face;
But when one told him, 'He is dead,'
Turning him quickly to go in,
'Bring thou to me his corpse,' he said.

And truly, while I speak, O King,
I hear the bearers on the stair;   130
Wilt thou they straightway bring him in?
– Ho! enter ye who tarry there!

THE VIZIER:
O King, in this I praise thee not!
Now must I call thy grief not wise.
Is he thy friend, or of thy blood,
To find such favour in thine eyes?

Nay, were he thine own mother's son,
Still, thou art king, and the law stands.
It were not meet the balance swerved,
The sword were broken in thy hands.   140

But being nothing, as he is,
Why for no cause make sad thy face? –
Lo, I am old! three kings, ere thee,
Have I seen reigning in this place.

But who, through all this length of time,
Could bear the burden of his years,
If he for strangers pain'd his heart
Not less than those who merit tears?

Fathers we *must* have, wife and child,
And grievous is the grief for these;   150
This pain alone, which *must* be borne,
Makes the head white, and bows the knees.

But other loads than this his own
One man is not well made to bear.
Besides, to each are his own friends,
To mourn with him, and show him care.

Look, this is but one single place,
Though it be great; all the earth round,
If a man bear to have it so,
Things which might vex him shall be found.   160

Upon the Russian frontier, where
The watchers of two armies stand
Near one another, many a man,
Seeking a prey unto his hand,

Hath snatch'd a little fair-hair'd slave;
They snatch also, towards Mervè,
The Shiah dogs, who pasture sheep,
And up from thence to Orgunjè.

And these all, labouring for a lord,
Eat not the fruit of their own hands;   170
Which is the heaviest of all plagues,
To the man's mind, who understands.

The kaffirs also (whom God curse!)
Vex one another, night and day;
There are the lepers, and all sick;
There are the poor, who faint alway.

All these have sorrow, and keep still,
Whilst other men make cheer, and sing.
Wilt thou have pity on all these?
No, nor on this dead dog, O King!   180

THE KING:
O Vizier, thou art old, I young!
Clear in these things I cannot see.
My head is burning, and a heat
Is in my skin which angers me.

But hear ye this, ye sons of men!
They that bear rule, and are obey'd,
Unto a rule more strong than theirs
Are in their turn obedient made.

In vain therefore, with wistful eyes
Gazing up hither, the poor man,   190
Who loiters by the high-heap'd booths,
Below there, in the Registàn,

Says: 'Happy he, who lodges there!
With silken raiment, store of rice,
And for this drought, all kinds of fruits,
Grape-syrup, squares of colour'd ice,

'With cherries serv'd in drifts of snow.'
In vain hath a king power to build
Houses, arcades, enamell'd mosques;
And to make orchard-closes, fill'd   200

With curious fruit-trees brought from far
With cisterns for the winter-rain,
And, in the desert, spacious inns
In divers places – if that pain

Is not more lighten'd, which he feels,
If his will be not satisfied;
And that it be not, from all time
The law is planted, to abide.

Thou wast a sinner, thou poor man!
Thou wast athirst; and didst not see,   210
That, though we take what we desire,
We must not snatch it eagerly.

And I have meat and drink at will,
And rooms of treasures, not a few.
But I am sick, nor heed I these;
And what I would, I cannot do.

Even the great honour which I have,
When I am dead, will soon grow still;
So have I neither joy, nor fame.
But what I can do, that I will.   220

I have a fretted brick-work tomb

Upon a hill on the right hand,
Hard by a close of apricots,
Upon the road of Samarcand;

Thither, O Vizier, will I bear
This man my pity could not save,
And, plucking up the marble flags,
There lay his body in my grave.

Bring water, nard, and linen rolls!
Wash off all blood, set smooth each limb!   230
Then say: 'He was not wholly vile,
Because a king shall bury him.'

Resignation

TO FAUSTA

Probably begun c. July 1843 (date of the poem's second walk) and worked upon under
the influences of A.'s reading 1845–8, notably Goethe's *Wilhelm Meister*, the Stoics,
Spinoza and *Obermann* (see p. 30 below); pub. *1849*. 'Fausta' is Jane Arnold, A.'s
elder sister (see *n.* to sub-title). The poem recalls Wordsworth's 'Tintern Abbey' in
addressing to a sister reflections on revisiting a place after a long interval, but here
Nature does not 'lead/From joy to joy' ('Tintern Abbey' 124–5) but 'Seems to bear
rather than rejoice' (l.270 below).

To die be given us, or attain!
Fierce work it were, to do again.
So pilgrims, bound for Mecca, pray'd
At burning noon; so warriors said,
Scarf'd with the cross, who watch'd the miles
Of dust which wreathed their struggling files
Down Lydian mountains; so, when snows
Round Alpine summits, eddying, rose,
The Goth, bound Rome-wards; so the Hun,
Crouch'd on his saddle, while the sun   10
Went lurid down o'er flooded plains
Through which the groaning Danube strains
To the drear Euxine; – so pray all,
Whom labours, self-ordain'd, enthrall;
Because they to themselves propose
On this side the all-common close

A goal which, gain'd, may give repose.
So pray they; and to stand again
Where they stood once, to them were pain;
Pain to thread back and to renew   20
Past straits, and currents long steer'd through.

But milder natures, and more free –
Whom an unblamed serenity
Hath freed from passions, and the state
Of struggle these necessitate;
Whom schooling of the stubborn mind
Hath made, or birth hath found, resign'd –
These mourn not, that their goings pay
Obedience to the passing day.
These claim not every laughing Hour   30
For handmaid to their striding power;
Each in her turn, with torch uprear'd,
To await their march; and when appear'd,
Through the cold gloom, with measured race,
To usher for a destined space
(Her own sweet errands all forgone)
The too imperious traveller on.
These, Fausta, ask not this; nor thou,
Time's chafing prisoner, ask it now!

    We left, just ten years since, you say,   40
That wayside inn we left to-day.
Our jovial host, as forth we fare,
Shouts greeting from his easy chair.
High on a bank our leader stands,
Reviews and ranks his motley bands,
Makes clear our goal to every eye –
The valley's western boundary.
A gate swings to! our tide hath flow'd
Already from the silent road.
The valley-pastures, one by one,   50
Are threaded, quiet in the sun,
And now beyond the rude stone bridge
Slopes gracious up the western ridge.
Its woody border, and the last
Of its dark upland farms is past –
Cool farms, with open-lying stores,

Under their burnish'd sycamores;
All past! and through the trees we glide,
Emerging on the green hill-side.
There climbing hangs, a far-seen sign,   60
Our wavering, many-colour'd line;
There winds, upstreaming slowly still
Over the summit of the hill.
And now, in front, behold outspread
Those upper regions we must tread!
Mild hollows, and clear heathy swells,
The cheerful silence of the fells.
Some two hours' march with serious air,
Through the deep noontide heats we fare;
The red-grouse, springing at our sound,   70
Skims, now and then, the shining ground;
No life, save his and ours, intrudes
Upon these breathless solitudes.
O joy! again the farms appear.
Cool shade is there, and rustic cheer;
There springs the brook will guide us down,
Bright comrade, to the noisy town.
Lingering, we follow down; we gain
The town, the highway, and the plain.
And many a mile of dusty way,   80
Parch'd and road-worn, we made that day;
But, Fausta, I remember well,
That as the balmy darkness fell
We bathed our hands with speechless glee,
That night, in the wide-glimmering sea.
Once more we tread this self-same road,
Fausta, which ten years since we trod;
Alone we tread it, you and I,
Ghosts of that boisterous company.
Here, where the brook shines, near its head,   90
In its clear, shallow, turf-fringed bed;
Here, whence the eye first sees, far down,
Capp'd with faint smoke, the noisy town;
Here sit we, and again unroll,
Though slowly, the familiar whole.
The solemn wastes of healthy hill
Sleep in the July sunshine still;

The self-same shadows now, as then,
Play through this grassy upland glen;
The loose dark stones on the green way   100
Lie strewn, it seems, where then they lay;
On this mild bank above the stream,
(You crush them!) the blue gentians gleam.
Still this wild brook, the rushes cool,
The sailing foam, the shining pool!
These are not changed; and we, you say,
Are scarce more changed, in truth, than they.

The gipsies, whom we met below,
They, too, have long roam'd to and fro;
They ramble, leaving, where they pass,   110
Their fragments on the cumber'd grass.
And often to some kindly place
Chance guides the migratory race,
Where, though long wanderings intervene,
They recognise a former scene.
The dingy tents are pitch'd; the fires
Give to the wind their wavering spires;
In dark knots crouch round the wild flame
Their children, as when first they came;
They see their shackled beasts again   120
Move, browsing, up the gray-wall'd lane.
Signs are not wanting, which might raise
The ghost in them of former days –
Signs are not wanting, if they would;
Suggestions to disquietude.
For them, for all, time's busy touch,
While it mends little, troubles much.
Their joints grow stiffer – but the year
Runs his old round of dubious cheer;
Chilly they grow – yet winds in March,   130
Still, sharp as ever, freeze and parch;
They must live still – and yet, God knows,
Crowded and keen the country grows;
It seems as if, in their decay,
The law grew stronger every day.
So might they reason, so compare,
Fausta, times past with times that are.

But no! – they rubb'd through yesterday
In their hereditary way,
And they will rub through, if they can,   140
To-morrow on the self-same plan,
Till death arrive to supersede,
For them, vicissitude and need.

The poet, to whose mighty heart
Heaven doth a quicker pulse impart,
Subdues that energy to scan
Not his own course, but that of man.
Though he move mountains, though his day
Be pass'd on the proud heights of sway,
Though he hath loosed a thousand chains,   150
Though he hath borne immortal pains,
Action and suffering though he know –
He hath not lived, if he lives so.
He sees, in some great-historied land,
A ruler of the people stand,
Sees his strong thought in fiery flood
Roll through the heaving multitude
Exults – yet for no moment's space
Envies the all-regarded place.
Beautiful eyes meet his – and he   160
Bears to admire uncravingly;
They pass – he, mingled with the crowd,
Is in their far-off triumphs proud.
From some high station he looks down,
At sunset, on a populous town;
Surveys each happy group, which fleets,
Toil ended, through the shining streets,
Each with some errand of its own –
And does not say: *I am alone.*
He sees the gentle stir of birth   170
When morning purifies the earth;
He leans upon a gate and sees
The pastures, and the quiet trees.
Low, woody hill, with gracious bound,
Folds the still valley almost round;
The cuckoo, loud on some high lawn,
Is answer'd from the depth of dawn;

In the hedge straggling to the stream,
Pale, dew-drench'd, half-shut roses gleam;
But, where the farther side slopes down,   180
He sees the drowsy new-waked clown
In his white quaint-embroider'd frock
Make, whistling, tow'rd his mist-wreathed flock –
Slowly, behind his heavy tread,
The wet, flower'd grass heaves up its head.
Lean'd on his gate, he gazes – tears
Are in his eyes, and in his ears
The murmur of a thousand years.
Before him he sees life unroll,
A placid and continuous whole –   190
That general life, which does not cease,
Whose secret is not joy, but peace;
That life, whose dumb wish is not miss'd
If birth proceeds, if things subsist;
The life of plants, and stones, and rain,
The life he craves – if not in vain
Fate gave, what chance shall not control,
His sad lucidity of soul.

You listen – but that wandering smile,
Fausta, betrays you cold the while!   200
Your eyes pursue the bells of foam
Wash'd eddying, from this bank, their home.
Those gipsies, so your thoughts I scan,
Are less, the poet more, than man.
They feel not, though they move and see;
Deeper the poet feels; but he
Breathes, when he will, immortal air,
Where Orpheus and where Homer are.
In the day's life, whose iron round
Hems us all in, he is not bound;   210
He leaves his kind, o'erleaps their pen,
And flees the common life of men.
He escapes thence, but we abide –
Not deep the poet sees, but wide.

The world in which we live and move
Outlasts aversion, outlasts love,
Outlasts each effort, interest, hope,

Remorse, grief, joy; – and were the scope
Of these affections wider made,
Man still would see, and see dismay'd,   220
Beyond his passion's widest range,
Far regions of eternal change.
Nay, and since death, which wipes out man,
Finds him with many an unsolved plan,
With much unknown, and much untried,
Wonder not dead, and thirst not dried,
Still gazing on the ever full
Eternal mundane spectacle –
This world in which we draw our breath,
In some sense, Fausta, outlasts death.   230
Blame thou not, therefore, him who dares
Judge vain beforehand human cares;
Whose natural insight can discern
What through experience others learn;
Who needs not love and power, to know
Love transient, power an unreal show;
Who treads at ease life's uncheer'd ways –
Him blame not, Fausta, rather praise!
Rather thyself for some aim pray
Nobler than this, to fill the day;   240
Rather that heart, which burns in thee,
Ask, not to amuse, but to set free;
Be passionate hopes not ill resign'd
For quiet, and a fearless mind.
And though fate grudge to thee and me
The poet's rapt security,
Yet they, believe me, who await
No gifts from chance, have conquer'd fate.
They, winning room to see and hear,
And to men's business not too near,   250
Through clouds of individual strife
Draw homeward to the general life.
Like leaves by suns not yet uncurl'd;
To the wise, foolish; to the world,
Weak; – yet not weak, I might reply,
Not foolish, Fausta, in His eye,
To whom each moment in its race,
Crowd as we will its neutral space,

Is but a quiet watershed
Whence, equally, the seas of life and death are fed.   260

Enough, we live! – and if a life,
With large results so little rife,
Though bearable, seem hardly worth
This pomp of words, this pain of birth;
Yet, Fausta, the mute turf we tread,
The solemn hills around us spread,
This stream which falls incessantly,
The strange-scrawl'd rocks, the lonely sky,
If I might lend their life a voice,
Seem to bear rather than rejoice.   270
And even could the intemperate prayer
Man iterates, while these forbear,
For movement, for an ampler sphere,
Pierce Fate's impenetrable ear;
Not milder is the general lot
Because our spirits have forgot,
In action's dizzying eddy whirl'd,
The something that infects the world.

The Forsaken Merman

Probably written between 1848 and Jan. 1849; pub. *1849*. The name Margaret and
the themes of loss and separation may indicate a link with the 'Switzerland' poems (pp.
24–30 below) and hence a date of composition after c. Sept. 1848. A. may have known
Hans Andersen's account of the ballad about Agnes and the Merman in *The story of
my Life* (Mary Howitt's transl. 1849) but the poem follows George Borrow's fuller
version in his review of J.M. Thiele's *Danske Folkesagn*, *Universal Review* ii. 563–4
(1825). The poem was widely popular with A.'s friends and the reviewers of *1849*: on
the form and style see Introduction (pp. above).

Come, dear children, let us away;
Down and away below!
Now my brothers call from the bay,
Now the great winds shoreward blow,
Now the salt tides seaward flow;
Now the wild white horses play,
Champ and chafe and toss in the spray.
Children dear, let us away!

This way, this way!

Call her once before you go –   10
Call once yet!
In a voice that she will know:
'Margaret! Margaret!'
Children's voices should be dear
(Call once more) to a mother's ear;
Children's voices, wild with pain –
Surely she will come again!
Call her once and come away;
This way, this way!
'Mother dear, we cannot stay!   20
The wild white horses foam and fret.'
Margaret! Margaret!

Come, dear children, come away down;
Call no more!
One last look at the white wall'd town,
And the little grey church on the windy shore;
Then come down!
She will not come though you call all day;
Come away, come away!

Children dear, was it yesterday   30
We heard the sweet bells over the bay?
In the caverns where we lay,
Through the surf and through the swell,
The far-off sound of a silver bell?
Sand-strewn caverns, cool and deep,
Where the winds are all asleep;
Where the spent lights quiver and gleam,
Where the salt weed sways in the stream,
Where the sea-beasts, ranged all round,
Feed in the ooze of their pasture-ground;   40
Where the sea-snakes coil and twine,
Dry their mail and bask in the brine;
Where great whales come sailing by,
Sail and sail, with unshut eye,
Round the world for ever and aye?
When did music come this way?
Children dear, was it yesterday?

Children dear, was it yesterday
(Call yet once) that she went away?
Once she sate with you and me, 50
On the red gold throne in the heart of the sea,
And the youngest sate on her knee.
She comb'd its bright hair, and she tended it well,
When down swung the sound of a far-off bell.
She sigh'd, she look'd up through the clear green sea;
She said: 'I must go, for my kinsfolk pray
In the little grey church on the shore to-day.
'Twill be Easter-time in the world – ah me!
And I lose my poor soul, Merman! here with thee.
I said: 'Go up, dear heart, through the waves; 60
Say thy prayer, and come back to the kind sea-caves.
She smiled, she went up through the surf in the bay.
Children dear, was it yesterday?

Children dear, were we long alone?
'The sea grows stormy, the little ones moan;
Long prayers,' I said, 'in the world they say;
Come!' I said; and we rose through the surf in the bay
We went up the beach, by the sandy down
Where the sea-stocks bloom, to the white-wall'd town
Through the narrow paved streets, where all was still, 70
To the little grey church on the windy hill.
From the church came a murmur of folk at their prayers
But we stood without in the cold blowing airs.
We climb'd on the graves, on the stones worn with rains
And we gazed up the aisle through the small leaded panes
She sate by the pillar; we saw her clear:
'Margaret, hist! come quick, we are here!
Dear heart,' I said, 'we are long alone;
The sea grows stormy, the little ones moan.'
But, ah, she gave me never a look, 80
For her eyes were seal'd to the holy book!
Loud prays the priest; shut stands the door.
Come away, children, call no more!
Come away, come down, call no more!

Down, down, down!
Down to the depths of the sea!
She sits at her wheel in the humming town,

Singing most joyfully.
Hark what she sings: 'O joy, O joy,
For the humming street, and the child with its toy!   90
For the priest, and the bell, and the holy well;
For the wheel where I spun,
And the blessed light of the sun!'
And so she sings her fill,
Singing most joyfully,
Till the spindle drops from her hand,
And the whizzing wheel stands still.
She steals to the window, and looks at the sand,
And over the sand at the sea;
And her eyes are set in a stare;   100
And anon there breaks a sigh,
And anon there drops a tear,
From a sorrow-clouded eye,
And a heart sorrow-laden,
A long, long sigh;
For the cold strange eyes of a little Mermaiden
And the gleam of her golden hair.

　　Come away, away children;
Come children, come down!
The hoarse wind blows coldly;   110
Lights shine in the town
She will start from her slumber
When gusts shake the door;
She will hear the winds howling,
Will hear the waves roar.
We shall see, while above us
The waves roar and whirl,
A ceiling of amber,
A pavement of pearl.
Singing: 'Here came a mortal,   120
But faithless was she!
And alone dwell for ever
The kings of the sea.'

But, children, at midnight,
When soft the winds blow,
When clear falls the moonlight,
When spring-tides are low;

When sweet airs come seaward
From heaths starr'd with broom,
And high rocks throw mildly   130
On the blanch'd sands a gloom;
Up the still, glistening beaches,
Up the creeks we will hie,
Over banks of bright seaweed
The ebb-tide leaves dry.
We will gaze, from the sand-hills,
At the white, sleeping town;
At the church on the hill-side –
And then come back down.
Singing: 'There dwells a loved one,   140
But cruel is she!
She left lonely for ever
The kings of the sea.'

To a Friend

Probably written Aug. 1848 when A. was reading Epictetus (ll. 5–9*n*. below); pub.
1849. The 'friend' is almost certainly Clough.

Who prop, thou ask'st, in these bad days, my mind?
He much, the old man, who, clearest-souled of men,
Saw The Wide Prospect, and the Asian Fen,
And Tmolus hill, and Smyrna bay, though blind.

Much he, whose friendship I not long since won,
That halting slave, who in Nicopolis
Taught Arrian, when Vespasian's brutal son
Cleared Rome of what most shamed him. But be his

My special thanks, whose even-balanced soul,
From first youth tested up to extreme old age,   10
Business could not make dull, nor passion wild;

Who saw life steadily, and saw it whole;
The mellow glory of the Attic stage,
Singer of sweet Colonus, and its child.

Quiet Work

Probably written 1848; pub. *1849*, as the introductory poem ('... banished from its pre-eminence' in *1869*: see A. to F.T. Palgrave 1869, G.W. Russell, *Matthew Arnold* (Second edn. 1904) 43). With Nature's 'one lesson' cp. 'Self-Dependence', p. 35 below.

One lesson, Nature, let me learn of thee,
One lesson which in every wind is blown,
One lesson of two duties kept at one
Though the loud world proclaim their enmity –

Of toil unsever'd from tranquillity!
Of labour, that in lasting fruit outgrows
Far noisier schemes, accomplish'd in repose,
Too great for haste, too high for rivalry!

Yes, while on earth a thousand discords ring,
Man's fitful uproar mingling with his toil,   10
Still do thy sleepless ministers move on,
Their glorious tasks in silence perfecting;
Still working, blaming still our vain turmoil,
Labourers that shall not fail, when man is gone.

Switzerland

MEETING

This and the three following poems probably written or begun c. Sept. 1849 and – except 'Isolation. To Marguerite' (*1857*) – pub. *1852*. They form part of the 'Switzerland' sequence (first so titled *1853*) expressing A.'s feelings for 'Marguerite', a French girl seemingly met at Thun Sept. 1848 and Sept. 1849, of whom nothing is known beyond the descriptions in the poems and A.'s fleeting allusions in two letters to Clough: the first speaks of lingering in Thun 'for the sake of a pair of blue eyes' (Sept. 1848); the second, written a year later (23 Sept. 1849), quotes an early version of 'Parting' after referring to A.'s being in Switzerland in 'a curious and not altogether comfortable state' and planning to take his 'aching head' to the mountains for a few days (*CL* 91. 110–11). The other poems in the series, besides 'Parting' (*1852*), are 'Absence' (*1852*) and 'On the Terrace at Berne', recording A.'s Swiss visit of 1859 (pub. *1867*, added to 'Switzerland' *1869*).

Again I see my bliss at hand,
The town, the lake are here;
My Marguerite smiles upon the strand,

Unalter'd with the year.

I know that graceful figure fair,
That cheek of languid hue;
I know that soft, enkerchief'd hair,
And those sweet eyes of blue.

Again I spring to make my choice;
Again in tones of ire   10
I hear a God's tremendous voice:
'Be counsell'd, and retire.'

Ye guiding Powers who join and part,
What would ye have with me?
Ah, warn some more ambitious heart,
And let the peaceful be!

ISOLATION. TO MARGUERITE

See headnote. to 'Meeting', above. 'To Marguerite' *1857*; present title *1869*.

We were apart; yet, day by day,
I bade my heart more constant be.
I bade it keep the world away,
And grow a home for only thee;
Nor fear'd but thy love likewise grew,
Like mine, each day, more tried, more true.

The fault was grave! I might have known,
What far too soon, alas! I learn'd –
The heart can bind itself alone,
And faith may oft be unreturn'd.   10
Self-sway'd our feelings ebb and swell –
Thou lov'st no more; – Farewell! Farewell!

Farewell! – and thou, thou lonely heart,
Which never yet without remorse
Even for a moment didst depart
From thy remote and spheréd course
To haunt the place where passions reign –
Back to thy solitude again!

Back! with the conscious thrill of shame
Which Luna felt, that summer-night,   20
Flash through her pure immortal frame,
When she forsook the starry height
To hang over Endymion's sleep
Upon the pine-grown Latmian steep.

Yet she, chaste queen, had never proved
How vain a thing is mortal love,
Wandering in Heaven, far removed.
But thou hast long had place to prove
This truth – to prove, and make thine own:
'Thou hast been, shalt be, art, alone.'   30

Or, if not quite alone, yet they
Which touch thee are unmating things –
Ocean and clouds and night and day;
Lorn autumns and triumphant springs;
And life, and others' joy and pain,
And love, if love, of happier men.

Of happier men – for they, at least,
Have *dream'd* two human hearts might blend
In one, and were through faith released
From isolation without end   40
Prolong'd; nor knew, although not less
Alone than thou, their loneliness.

TO MARGUERITE – CONTINUED

See headnote. to 'Meeting', p. 24 above. A. uses the stanza form of the preceding poem, 'Isolation. To Marguerite', to continue reflections about the separateness of lovers and his own separation from Marguerite in particular. Other uses of the sea isolating human beings from each other, some of them probably influential, recorded in K. Tillotson, 'Yes: in the sea of life', *RES* n.s. (1952) 346–64. K.A., *Poems* 122, notes 'the estranging sea' is additionally the English Channel 'soon to flow between [A.] and Marguerite'.

Yes! in the sea of life enisled,
With echoing straits between us thrown,
Dotting the shoreless watery wild,
We mortal millions live *alone*.

The islands feel the enclasping flow,
And then their endless bounds they know.

But when the moon their hollows lights,
And they are swept by balms of spring,
And in their glens, on starry nights,
The nightingales divinely sing; 10
And lovely notes, from shore to shore,
Across the sounds and channels pour –

Oh! then a longing like despair
Is to their farthest caverns sent;
For surely once, they feel, we were
Parts of a single continent!
Now round us spreads the watery plain –
Oh might our marges meet again!

Who order'd, that their longing's fire
Should be, as soon as kindled, cool'd? 20
Who renders vain their deep desire? –
A God, a God their severance ruled!
And bade betwixt their shores to be
The unplumb'd, salt, estranging sea.

A Farewell

See headnote to 'Meeting', p. 24 above.

My horse's feet beside the lake,
Where sweet the unbroken moonbeams lay,
Sent echoes through the night to wake
Each glistening strand, each heath-fringed bay.

The poplar avenue was passed,
And the roofed bridge that spans the stream;
Up the steep street I hurried fast,
Led by thy taper's starlike beam.

I came! I saw thee rise! – the blood
Poured flushing to thy languid cheek. 10
Locked in each other's arms we stood,
In tears, with hearts too full to speak.

Days flew; ah, soon I could discern
A trouble in thine altered air!
Thy hand lay languidly in mine,
Thy cheek was grave, thy speech grew rare.

I blame thee not! – this heart, I know,
To be long loved was never framed;
For something in its depths doth glow
Too strange, too restless, too untamed.   20

And women – things that live and move
Mined by the fever of the soul –
They seek to find in those they love
Stern strength, and promise of control.

They ask not kindness, gentle ways –
These they themselves have tried and known;
They ask a soul which never sways
With the blind gusts that shake their own.

I too have felt the load I bore
In a too strong emotion's sway;   30
I too have wished, no woman more,
This starting, feverish heart away.

I too have longed for trenchant force,
And will like a dividing spear;
Have praised the keen, unscrupulous course,
Which knows no doubt, which feels no fear.

But in the world I learnt, what there
Thou too wilt surely one day prove,
That will, that energy, though rare,
Are yet far, far less rare than love.   40

Go, then! – till time and fate impress
This truth on thee, be mine no more!
They will! – for thou, I feel, not less
Than I, wast destined to this lore.

We school our manners, act our parts –
But He, who sees us through and through
Knows that the bent of both our hearts
Was to be gentle, tranquil, true.

And though we wear out life, alas!

Distracted as a homeless wind,   50
In beating where we must not pass,
In seeking what we shall not find;

Yet we shall one day gain, life past,
Clear prospect o'er our being's whole;
Shall see ourselves, and learn at last
Our true affinities of soul.

We shall not then deny a course
To every thought the mass ignore;
We shall not then call hardness force,
Nor lightness wisdom any more.   60

Then, in the eternal Father's smile,
Our soothed, encouraged souls will dare
To seem as free from pride and guile,
As good, as generous, as they are.

Then we shall know our friends! – though much
Will have been lost – the help in strife,
The thousand sweet, still joys of such
As hand in hand face earthly life –

Though these be lost, there will be yet
A sympathy august and pure;   70
Ennobled by a vast regret,
And by contrition sealed thrice sure.

And we, whose ways were unlike here,
May then more neighbouring courses ply;
May to each other be brought near,
And greet across infinity.

How sweet, unreached by earthly jars,
My sister! to maintain with thee
The hush among the shining stars,
The calm upon the moonlit sea!   80

How sweet to feel, on the boon air,
All our unquiet pulses cease!
To feel that nothing can impair
The gentleness, the thirst for peace –

The gentleness too rudely hurled
On this wild earth of hate and fear;

The thirst for peace a raving world
Would never let us satiate here.

Stanzas in Memory of the
Author of 'Obermann'

NOVEMBER, 1849

Written Sept.–Nov. 1849; pub. *1852. Obermann*, epistolary novel of romantic
introspection by Etienne Pivert de Senancour (1770–1846), was widely influential in
the French Romantic movement, affecting among others George Sand's *Lélia* (1833),
Sainte-Beuve's *Volupté and Balzac's Le Lys dans la Vallée* (1836). A. celebrated
Senancour again in 'Obermann Once More' (1867), his essay, *Obermann* (*The
Academy*, 9 Oct. 1869) and his *n*. in *1869* (quoted in full *Poems* 129–30) on 'the
profound inwardness, the austere sincerity, of Senancour's principal work, *Obermann*, the
delicate feeling for nature which it exhibits and the melancholy eloquence of many
passages of it'. Sainte-Beuve included a translation of A.'s poem in his *Chateaubriand et
son groupe littéraire* (1860): brief passages from their correspondence are cited in the Notes.

In front the awful Alpine track
Crawls up its rocky stair;
The autumn storm-winds drive the rack,
Close o'er it, in the air.

Behind are the abandon'd baths
Mute in their meadows lone;
The leaves are on the valley-paths.
The mists are on the Rhone –

The white mists rolling like a sea!
I hear the torrents roar.   10
– Yes, Obermann, all speaks of thee;
I feel thee near once more!

I turn thy leaves! I feel their breath
Once more upon me roll;
That air of languor, cold, and death,
Which brooded o'er thy soul.

Fly hence, poor wretch, whoe'er thou art,
Condemn'd to cast about,
All shipwreck in thy own weak heart,
For comfort from without!   20

A fever in these pages burns
Beneath the calm they feign;
A wounded human spirit turns,
Here, on its bed of pain.

Yes, though the virgin mountain-air
Fresh through these pages blows;
Though to these leaves the glaciers spare
The soul of their white snows;

Though here a mountain-murmur swells
Of many a dark-bough'd pine;   30
Though, as you read, you hear the bells
Of the high-pasturing kine –

Yet, through the hum of torrent lone,
And brooding mountain-bee,
There sobs I know not what ground-tone
Of human agony.

Is it for this, because the sound
Is fraught too deep with pain,
That, Obermann! the world around
So little loves thy strain?   40

Some secrets may the poet tell,
For the world loves new ways;
To tell too deep ones is not well –
It knows not what he says.

Yet, of the spirits who have reign'd
In this our troubled day,
I know but two, who have attain'd,
Save thee, to see their way.

By England's lakes, in grey old age,
His quiet home one keeps;   50
And one, the strong much-toiling sage,
In German Weimar sleeps.

But Wordsworth's eyes avert their ken
From half of human fate;
And Goethe's course few sons of men
May think to emulate.

For he pursued a lonely road,

His eyes on Nature's plan;
Neither made man too much a God,
Nor God too much a man.   60

Strong was he, with a spirit free
From mists, and sane, and clear;
Clearer, how much! than ours – yet we
Have a worse course to steer.

For though his manhood bore the blast
Of a tremendous time,
Yet in a tranquil world was pass'd
His tenderer youthful prime.

But we, brought forth and rear'd in hours
Of change, alarm, surprise –   70
What shelter to grow ripe is ours?
What leisure to grow wise?

Like children bathing on the shore,
Buried a wave beneath,
The second wave succeeds, before
We have had time to breathe.

Too fast we live, too much are tried,
Too harass'd, to attain
Wordsworth's sweet calm, or Goethe's wide
And luminous view to gain.   80

And then we turn, thou sadder sage,
To thee! we feel thy spell!
– The hopeless tangle of our age,
Thou too hast scann'd it well!

Immoveable thou sittest, still
As death, composed to bear!
Thy head is clear, thy feeling chill,
And icy thy despair.

Yes, as the son of Thetis said,
I hear thee saying now: 90
Greater by far than thou art dead;
Strive not! die also thou!

Ah! two desires toss about
The poet's feverish blood.

One drives him to the world without,
And one to solitude.

The glow, he cries, *the thrill of life*,
Where, where do these abound? –
Not in the world, not in the strife
Of men, shall they be found.   100

He who hath watch'd, not shared, the strife,
Knows how the day hath gone.
He only lives with the world's life,
Who hath renounced his own.

To thee we come, then! Clouds are roll'd
Where thou, O seer! art set;
Thy realm of thought is drear and cold –
The world is colder yet!

And thou hast pleasures, too, to share
With those who come to thee –   110
Balms floating on thy mountain-air,
And healing sights to see.

How often, where the slopes are green
On Jaman, hast thou sate
By some high chalet-door, and seen
The summer-day grow late;

And darkness steal o'er the wet grass
With the pale crocus starr'd,
And reach that glimmering sheet of glass
Beneath the piny sward,   120

Lake Leman's waters, far below!
And watch'd the rosy light
Fade from the distant peaks of snow;
And on the air of night

Heard accents of the eternal tongue
Through the pine branches play –
Listen'd, and felt thyself grow young!
Listen'd and wept – Away!

Away the dreams that but deceive
And thou, sad guide, adieu!   130
I go, fate drives me; but I leave

Half of my life with you.

We, in some unknown Power's employ,
Move on a rigorous line;
Can neither, when we will, enjoy,
Nor, when we will, resign.

I in the world must live; but thou,
Thou melancholy shade!
Wilt not, if thou canst see me now,
Condemn me, nor upbraid.   140

For thou art gone away from earth,
And place with those dost claim,
The Children of the Second Birth,
Whom the world could not tame;

And with that small, transfigured band,
Whom many a different way
Conducted to their common land,
Thou learn'st to think as they.

Christian and pagan, king and slave,
Soldier and anchorite,   150
Distinctions we esteem so grave,
Are nothing in their sight.

They do not ask, who pined unseen,
Who was on action hurl'd,
Whose one bond is, that all have been
Unspotted by the world.

There without anger thou wilt see
Him who obeys thy spell
No more, so he but rest, like thee,
Unsoil'd! – and so, farewell.   160

Farewell! – Whether thou now liest near
That much-loved inland sea,
The ripples of whose blue waves cheer
Vevey and Meillerie:

And in that gracious region bland,
Where with clear-rustling wave
The scented pines of Switzerland
Stand dark round thy green grave,

Between the dusty vineyard-walls
Issuing on that green place   170
The early peasant still recalls
The pensive stranger's face,

And stoops to clear thy moss-grown date
Ere he plods on again; –
Or whether, by maligner fate,
Among the swarms of men,

Where between granite terraces
The blue Seine rolls her wave,
The Capital of Pleasure sees
The hardly-heard-of grave; –   180

Farewell! Under the sky we part,
In the stern Alpine dell.
O unstrung will! O broken heart!
A last, a last farewell!

Self-dependence

Written probably late 1849, or early 1850; pub. *1852*. The sea-journey and the
emotional tone suggest a link with the Marguerite poems, pp. 24–30 above. Basil
Willey notes of the poem, 'as concise a summary of Stoic teaching as we could hope to
find' (*The English Moralists* 1965) 67.

Weary of myself, and sick of asking
What I am, and what I ought to be,
At this vessel's prow I stand, which bears me
Forwards, forwards, o'er the starlit sea.

And a look of passionate desire
O'er the sea and to the stars I send:
'Ye who from my childhood up have calmed me,
Calm me, ah, compose me to the end!

'Ah, once more,' I cried, 'ye stars, ye waters,
On my heart your mighty charm renew;   10
Still, still let me, as I gaze upon you,
Feel my soul becoming vast like you!'

From the intense, clear, star-sown vault of heaven,
Over the lit sea's unquiet way,
In the rustling night-air came the answer:
'Wouldst thou *be* as these are? *Live* as they.

'Unaffrighted by the silence round them,
Undistracted by the sights they see,
These demand not that the things without them
Yield them love, amusement, sympathy.   20

'And with joy the stars perform their shining,
And the sea its long moon-silvered roll;
For self-poised they live, nor pine with noting
All the fever of some differing soul.

'Bounded by themselves, and unregardful
In what state God's other works may be,
In their own tasks all their powers pouring,
These attain the mighty life you see.'

O air-born voice! long since, severely clear,
A cry like thine in mine own heart I hear: 30
'Resolve to be thyself; and know that he,
Who finds himself, loses his misery!'

Empedocles on Etna

A DRAMATIC POEM

Written during 1849–52; pub. *1852*, suppressed *1853*, repr. (at Browning's request) *1867*. Seemingly evolved from A.'s projected but unwritten tragedy on Lucretius (evidence includes his letter of March 1849 on 'a tragedy I have long had in mind' and his list of poems to be composed 1849; see also I. ii. 397–410*n*.). J.C. Shairp informed Clough 30 June 1849, 'A. was working at an "Empedocles" – which seemed to be not much about the man who leaps into the crater – but his name and outward circumstances are used for the drapery of his own thoughts' (*AHC* I. 270). For A.'s notes on S. Karsten's *Philosophorum Graecorum Veterum ...* ii (1838) see *Commentary* ll. 289–90 and for his analysis in *Yale MS* of Empedocles's character and motive, *Poems* 148. The latter is in keeping with A.'s description of modern feeling in Lucretius, in 'On the Modern Element in Literature', and in the 1853 Preface (pp. 151–2, 129 below): W.E. Houghton discusses I. ii. on 'modern thought', II. i. on 'modern feeling' in *Vict. Stud.* i. 311–36 (1958). Principal sources for A.'s ideas include Empedocles, Lucretius, Epictetus, M. Aurelius, Carlyle's *Sartor Resartus*, and *Obermann*; for the songs of Callicles – the character, though not the name, is A.'s own invention – Pindar, Hesiod and Ovid; and for the dramatic form and treatment of the action, Byron's

Manfred (see K. Allott, *N&Q* n.s. ix. 300–3 (1962) and 'A background for "Empedocles on Etna"', *Essays and Studies by Members of the English Association*, n.s. *xxi (1968). On A.'s reasons for suppressing the poem in 1853 see Preface, p. 115 below.

PERSONS

EMPEDOCLES

PAUSANIAS, *a Physician*

CALLICLES, *a young Harp-player*

The Scene of the Poem is on Mount Etna; at first in the forest region, afterwards on the summit of the mountain

ACT I: SCENE I

Morning. A Pass in the forest region of Etna

CALLICLES
(Alone, resting on a rock by the path)
The mules, I think, will not be here this hour;
They feel the cool wet turf under their feet
By the stream-side, after the dusty lanes
In which they have toiled all night from Catana,
And scarcely will they budge a yard. O Pan,
How gracious is the mountain at this hour!
A thousand times have I been here alone,
Or with the revellers from the mountain-towns,
But never on so fair a morn; the sun
Is shining on the brilliant mountain-crests,   10
And on the highest pines; but farther down,
Here in the valley, is in shade; the sward
Is dark, and on the stream the mist still hangs;
One sees one's footprints crush'd in the wet grass,
One's breath curls in the air; and on these pines
That climb from the stream's edge, the long grey tufts,
Which the goats love, are jewell'd thick with dew.
Here will I stay till the slow litter comes.
I have my harp too – that is well. Apollo!
What mortal could be sick or sorry here?   20
I know not in what mind Empedocles,
Whose mules I follow'd, may be coming up,
But if, as most men say, he is half mad
With exile, and with brooding on his wrongs,

Pausanias, his sage friend, who mounts with him,
Could scarce have lighted on a lovelier cure.
The mules must be below, far down. I hear
Their tinkling bells, mix'd with the song of birds,
Rise faintly to me – now it stops! Who's here?
Pausanias! and on foot? alone?

PAUSANIAS

                    And thou, then?   30
I left thee supping with Peisianax,
With thy head full of wine, and thy hair crown'd,
Touching thy harp as the whim came on thee,
And praised and spoil'd by master and by guests
Almost as much as the new dancing-girl.
Why hast thou follow'd us?

CALLICLES

                     The night was hot,
And the feast past its prime; so we slipp'd out,
Some of us, to the portico to breathe –
Peisianax, thou know'st, drinks late; and then,
As I was lifting my soil'd garland off,   40
I saw the mules and litter in the court,
And in the litter sate Empedocles;
Thou, too, wast with him. Straightway I sped home:
I saddled my white mule, and all night long
Through the cool lovely country follow'd you,
Pass'd you a little since as morning dawn'd,
And have this hour sate by the torrent here,
Till the slow mules should climb in sight again.
And now?

PAUSANIAS

           And now, back to the town with speed!
Crouch in the wood first, till the mules have pass'd;   50
They do but halt, they will be here anon.
Thou must be viewless to Empedocles;
Save mine, he must not meet a human eye.
One of his moods is on him that thou know'st;
I think, thou wouldst not vex him.

CALLICLES

                     No – and yet

I would fain stay, and help thee tend him. Once
He knew me well, and would oft notice me;
And still, I know not how, he draws me to him,
And I could watch him with his proud sad face,
His flowing locks and gold-encircled brow   60
And kingly gait, for ever; such a spell
In his severe looks, such a majesty
As drew of old the people after him,
In Agrigentum and Olympia,
When his star reign'd, before his banishment,
Is potent still on me in his decline.
But oh! Pausanias, he is changed of late;
There is a settled trouble in his air
Admits no momentary brightening now,
And when he comes among his friends at feasts,   70
'Tis as an orphan among prosperous boys.
Thou know'st of old he loved this harp of mine,
When first he sojourn'd with Peisianax;
He is now always moody, and I fear him;
But I would serve him, soothe him, if I could,
Dared one but try.

PAUSANIAS
                    Thou wast a kind child ever!
He loves thee, but he must not see thee now.
Thou hast indeed a rare touch on thy harp,
He loves that in thee, too;—there was a time
(But that is pass'd), he would have paid thy strain   80
With music to have drawn the stars from heaven.
He hath his harp and laurel with him still,
But he has laid the use of music by,
And all which might relax his settled gloom.
Yet thou may'st try thy playing, if thou wilt –
But thou must keep unseen; follow us on,
But at a distance! in these solitudes,
In this clear mountain-air, a voice will rise,
Though from afar, distinctly; it may soothe him.
Play when we halt, and, when the evening comes   90
And I must leave him (for his pleasure is
To be left musing these soft nights alone
In the high unfrequented mountain-spots),

Then watch him, for he ranges swift and far,
Sometimes to Etna's top, and to the cone;
But hide thee in the rocks a great way down,
And try thy noblest strains, my Callicles,
With the sweet night to help thy harmony!
Thou wilt earn my thanks sure, and perhaps his.

CALLICLES
More than a day and night, Pausanias,   100
Of this fair summer-weather, on these hills,
Would I bestow to help Empedocles.
That needs no thanks; one is far better here
Than in the broiling city in these heats.
But tell me, how hast thou persuaded him
In this his present fierce, man-hating mood,
To bring thee out with him alone on Etna?

PAUSANIAS
Thou hast heard all men speaking of Pantheia,
The woman who at Agrigentum lay
Thirty long days in a cold trance of death,   110
And whom Empedocles call'd back to life.
Thou art too young to note it, but his power
Swells with the swelling evil of this time,
And holds men mute to see where it will rise.
He could stay swift diseases in old days,
Chain madmen by the music of his lyre,
Cleanse to sweet airs the breath of poisonous streams,
And in the mountain-chinks inter the winds.
This he could do of old; but now, since all
Clouds and grows daily worse in Sicily,   120
Since broils tear us in twain, since this new swarm
Of sophists has got empire in our schools
Where he was paramount, since he is banish'd
And lives a lonely man in triple gloom –
He grasps the very reins of life and death.
I ask'd him of Pantheia yesterday,
When we were gathered with Peisianax,
And he made answer, I should come at night
On Etna here, and be alone with him,
And he would tell me, as his old, tried friend,   130
Who still was faithful, what might profit me;

That is, the secret of this miracle.

CALLICLES
Bah! Thou a doctor! Thou art superstitious.
Simple Pausanias, 'twas no miracle!
Pantheia, for I know her kinsmen well,
Was subject to these trances from a girl.
Empedocles would say so, did he deign;
But he still lets the people, whom he scorns,
Gape and cry *wizard* at him, if they list.
But thou, thou art no company for him!   140
Thou art as cross, as sour'd as himself!
Thou hast some wrong from thine own citizens,
And then thy friend is banish'd, and on that,
Straightway thou fallest to arraign the times,
As if the sky was impious not to fall.
The sophists are no enemies of his;
I hear, Gorgias, their chief, speaks nobly of him,
As of his gifted master, and once friend.
He is too scornful, too high-wrought, too bitter.
'Tis not the times, 'tis not the sophists vex him;   150
There is some root of suffering in himself,
Some secret and unfollowed vein of woe,
Which makes the time look black and sad to him.
Pester him not in this his sombre mood
With questionings about an idle tale,
But lead him through the lovely mountain-paths,
And keep his mind from preying on itself,
And talk to him of things at hand and common,
Not miracles! thou art a learned man,
But credulous of fables as a girl.   160

PAUSANIAS
And thou, a boy whose tongue outruns his knowledge,
And on whose lightness blame is thrown away.
Enough of this! I see the litter wind
Up by the torrent-side, under the pines.
I must rejoin Empedocles. Do thou
Crouch in the brushwood till the mules have passed;
Then play thy kind part well. Farewell till night!

SCENE II

Noon. A Glen on the highest skirts of the woody region of Etna.
EMPEDOCLES – PAUSANIAS

PAUSANIAS
The noon is hot. When we have cross'd the stream,
We shall have left the woody tract, and come
Upon the open shoulder of the hill.
See how the giant spires of yellow bloom
Of the sun-loving gentian, in the heat,
Are shining on those naked slopes like flame!
Let us rest here; and now, Empedocles,
Pantheia's history!

                         [*A harp-note below is heard.*

EMPEDOCLES
              Hark! what sound was that
Rose from below? If it were possible,
And we were not so far from human haunt,   10
I should have said that some one touch'd a harp.
Hark! there again!

PAUSANIAS
             'Tis the boy Callicles,
The sweetest harp-player in Catana.
He is for ever coming on these hills,
In summer, to all country-festivals,
With a gay revelling band; he breaks from them
Sometimes, and wanders far among the glens.
But heed him not, he will not mount to us;
I spoke with him this morning. Once more, therefore,
Instruct me of Pantheia's story, Master,   20
As I have pray'd thee.

EMPEDOCLES
             That? and to what end?

PAUSANIAS
It is enough that all men speak of it.
But I will also say, that when the Gods
Visit us as they do with sign and plague,
To know those spells of thine which stay their hand

Were to live free from terror.

EMPEDOCLES

Spells? Mistrust them!
Mind is the spell which governs earth and heaven.
Man has a mind with which to plan his safety;
Know that, and help thyself!

PAUSANIAS

But thine own words?
'The wit and counsel of man was never clear,   30
Troubles confound the little wit he has.'
Mind is a light which the Gods mock us with,
To lead those false who trust it.

[The harp sounds again.

EMPEDOCLES

Hist! once more!
Listen, Pausanias! – Ay, 'tis Callicles;
I know these notes among a thousand. Hark!

CALLICLES
(*Sings unseen, from below*)
The track winds down to the clear stream,
To cross the sparkling shallows; there
The cattle love to gather, on their way
To the high mountain-pastures, and to stay,
Till the rough cow-herds drive them past,   40
Knee-deep in the cool ford; for 'tis the last
Of all the woody, high, well-water'd dells
On Etna; and the beam
Of noon is broken there by chestnut-boughs
Down its steep verdant sides; the air
Is freshen'd by the leaping stream, which throws
Eternal showers of spray on the moss'd roots
Of trees, and veins of turf, and long dark shoots
Of ivy-plants, and fragrant hanging bells
Of hyacinths, and on late anemonies,   50
That muffle its wet banks; but glade,
And stream, and sward, and chestnut-trees,
End here; Etna beyond, in the broad glare
Of the hot noon, without a shade,
Slope behind slope, up to the peak, lies bare;

The peak, round which the white clouds play.

   In such a glen, on such a day,
   On Pelion, on the grassy ground,
   Chiron, the aged Centaur lay,
   The young Achilles standing by.   60
   The Centaur taught him to explore
   The mountains; where the glens are dry
   And the tired Centaurs come to rest,
   And where the soaking springs abound
   And the straight ashes grow for spears,
   And where the hill-goats come to feed,
   And the sea-eagles build their nest.
   He showed him Phthia far away,
   And said: O boy, I taught this lore
   To Peleus, in long distant years!   70
   He told him of the Gods, the stars,
   The tides; and then of mortal wars,
   And of the life which heroes lead
   Before they reach the Elysian place
   And rest in the immortal mead;
   And all the wisdom of his race.

The music below ceases, and EMPEDOCLES *speaks, accompanying
   himself in a solemn manner on his harp.*

   The out-spread world to span
   A cord the Gods first slung,
   And then the soul of man
   There, like a mirror, hung,   80
And bade the winds through space impel the gusty toy.

   Hither and thither spins
   The wind-borne, mirroring soul,
   A thousand glimpses wins,
   And never sees a whole;
Looks once, and drives elsewhere, and leaves its last employ.

   The Gods laugh in their sleeve
   To watch man doubt and fear,
   Who knows not what to believe
   Since he sees nothing clear,   90
And dares stamp nothing false where he finds nothing sure.

Is this, Pausanias, so?
And can our souls not strive,
But with the winds must go,
And hurry where they drive?
Is fate indeed so strong, man's strength indeed so poor?

I will not judge. That man,
Howbeit, I judge as lost,
Whose mind allows a plan,
Which would degrade it most;   100
And he treats doubt the best who tries to see least ill.

Be not, then, fear's blind slave!
Thou art my friend; to thee,
All knowledge that I have,
All skill I wield, are free.
Ask not the latest news of the last miracle,

Ask not what days and nights
In trance Pantheia lay,
But ask how thou such sights
May'st see without dismay;   110
Ask what most helps when known, thou son of Anchitus!

What? hate, and awe, and shame
Fill thee to see our time;
Thou feelest thy soul's frame
Shaken and out of chime?
What? life and chance go hard with thee too, as with us;

Thy citizens, 'tis said,
Envy thee and oppress,
Thy goodness no men aid,
All strive to make it less;   120
Tyranny, pride, and lust, fill Sicily's abodes;

Heaven is with earth at strife,
Signs make thy soul afraid,
The dead return to life,
Rivers are dried, winds stay'd;
Scarce can one think in calm, so threatening are the Gods;

And we feel, day and night,
The burden of ourselves –

Well, then, the wiser wight
In his own bosom delves,   130
And asks what ails him so, and gets what cure he can.

The sophist sneers: Fool, take
Thy pleasure, right or wrong.
The pious wail: Forsake
A world these sophists throng.
Be neither saint nor sophist-led, but be a man!

These hundred doctors try
To preach thee to their school.
We have the truth! they cry;
And yet their oracle,   140
Trumpet it as they will, is but the same as thine.

Once read thy own breast right,
And thou hast done with fears;
Man gets no other light,
Search he a thousand years.
Sink in thyself! there ask what ails thee, at that shrine!

What makes thee struggle and rave?
Why are men ill at ease? –
'Tis that the lot they have
Fails their own will to please;   150
For man would make no murmuring, were his will obey'd.

And why is it, that still
Man with his lot thus fights? –
'Tis that he makes this *will*
The measure of his *rights*,
And believes Nature outraged if his will's gainsaid.

Couldst thou, Pausanias, learn
How deep a fault is this;
Couldst thou but once discern
Thou hast no *right* to bliss,   160
No title from the Gods to welfare and repose;

Then thou wouldst look less mazed
Whene'er of bliss debarr'd,
Nor think the Gods were crazed
When thy own lot went hard.

But we are all the same – the fools of our own woes!

       For, from the first faint morn
       Of life, the thirst for bliss
       Deep in man's heart is born;
       And, sceptic as he is,   170
He fails not to judge clear if this be quench'd or no.

       Nor is the thirst to blame.
       Man errs not that he deems
       His welfare his true aim,
       He errs because he dreams
The world does but exist that welfare to bestow.

       We mortals are no kings
       For each of whom to sway
       A new-made world up-springs,
       Meant merely for his play;   180
No, we are strangers here; the world is from of old.

       In vain our pent wills fret,
       And would the world subdue.
       Limits we did not set
       Condition all we do;
Born into life we are, and life must be our mould.

       Born into life! – man grows
       Forth from his parents' stem,
       And blends their bloods, as those
       Of theirs are blent in them;   190
So each new man strikes root into a far fore-time.

       Born into life! – we bring
       A bias with us here,
       And, when here, each new thing
       Affects us we come near;
To tunes we did not call our being must keep chime.

       Born into life! – in vain,
       Opinions, those or these,
       Unaltered to retain
       The obstinate mind decrees;   200
Experience, like a sea, soaks all-effacing in.

       Born into life! – who lists

May what is false hold dear,
And for himself make mists
Through which to see less clear;
The world is what it is, for all our dust and din.

Born into life! – 'tis we,
And not the world, are new;
Our cry for bliss, our plea,
Others have urged it too –   210
Our wants have all been felt, our errors made before.

No eye could be too sound
To observe a world so vast,
No patience too profound
To sort what's here amass'd;
How man may here best live no care too great to explore.

But we – as some rude guest
Would change, where'er he roam,
The manners there profess'd
To those he brings from home –   220
We mark not the world's course, but would have *it* take *ours*.

The world's course proves the terms
On which man wins content;
Reason the proof confirms –
We spurn it, and invent
A false course for the world, and for ourselves, false powers.

Riches we wish to get,
Yet remain spendthrifts still;
We would have health, and yet
Still use our bodies ill;   230
Bafflers of our own prayers, from youth to life's last scenes.

We would have inward peace,
Yet will not look within;
We would have misery cease,
Yet will not cease from sin;
We want all pleasant ends, but will use no harsh means;

We do not what we ought,
What we ought not, we do,
And lean upon the thought

That chance will bring us through; 240
But our own acts, for good or ill, are mightier powers.

    Yet, even when man forsakes
    All sin – is just, is pure,
    Abandons all which makes
    His welfare insecure, –
Other existences there are, that clash with ours.

    Like us, the lightning-fires
    Love to have scope and play;
    The stream, like us, desires
    An unimpeded way; 250
Like us, the Libyan wind delights to roam at large.

    Streams will not curb their pride
    The just man not to entomb,
    Nor lightnings go aside
    To give his virtues room;
Nor is that wind less rough which blows a good man's barge.

    Nature, with equal mind,
    Sees all her sons at play;
    Sees man control the wind,
    The wind sweep man away; 260
Allows the proudly-riding and the foundering bark.

    And, lastly, though of ours
    No weakness spoil our lot,
    Though the non-human powers
    Of Nature harm us not,
The ill deeds of other men make often *our* life dark.

    What were the wise man's plan?—
    Through this sharp, toil-set life,
    To work as best he can,
    And win what's won by strife.— 270
But we an easier way to cheat our pains have found.

    Scratch'd by a fall, with moans
    As children of weak age
    Lend life to the dumb stones
    Whereon to vent their rage,
And bend their little fists, and rate the senseless ground,

So, loth to suffer mute,
We, peopling the void air,
Make Gods to whom to impute
The ills we ought to bear;   280
With God and Fate to rail at, suffering easily.

Yet grant – as sense long miss'd
Things that are now perceived,
And much may still exist
Which is not yet believed –
Grant that the world were full of Gods we cannot see;

All things the world which fill
Of but one stuff are spun,
That we who rail are still,
With what we rail at, one;   290
One with the o'erlabour'd Power that through the
   breadth and length

Of earth, and air, and sea,
In men, and plants, and stones,
Hath toil perpetually,
And travails, pants, and moans;
Fain would do all things well, but sometimes fails in strength.

And patiently exact
This universal God
Alike to any act
Proceeds at any nod,   300
And quietly declaims the cursings of himself.

This is not what man hates,
Yet he can curse but this.
Harsh Gods and hostile Fates
Are dreams! this only *is* –
Is everywhere; sustains the wise, the foolish elf.

Nor only, in the intent
To attach blame elsewhere,
Do we at will invent
Stern Powers who make their care   310
To embitter human life, malignant Deities;

But, next, we would reverse

The scheme ourselves have spun,
And what we made to curse
We now would lean upon,
And feign kind Gods who perfect what man vainly tries.

Look, the world tempts our eye,
And we would know it all!
We map the starry sky,
We mine this earthen ball,   320
We measure the sea-tides, we number the sea-sands;

We scrutinise the dates
Of long-past human things,
The bounds of effaced states,
The lines of deceased kings;
We search out dead men's words, and works of dead men's hands;

We shut our eyes, and muse
How our own minds are made.
What springs of thought they use,
How righten'd, how betray'd –   330
And spend our wit to name what most employ unnamed.

But still, as we proceed
The mass swells more and more
Of volumes yet to read,
Of secrets yet to explore.
Our hair grows grey, our eyes are dimm'd, our heat is tamed;

We rest our faculties,
And thus address the Gods:
'True science if there is,
It stays in your abodes!   340
Man's measures cannot mete the immeasurable All.

'You only can take in
The world's immense design.
Our desperate search was sin,
Which henceforth we resign,
Sure only that your mind sees all things which befal.'

Fools! That in man's brief term
He cannot all things view,
Affords no ground to affirm

That there are Gods who do;   350
Nor does being weary prove that he has where to rest.

    Again. — Our youthful blood
    Claims rapture as its right;
    The world, a rolling flood
    Of newness and delight,
Draws in the enamoured gazer to its shining breast;

    Pleasure, to our hot grasp,
    Gives flowers, after flowers;
    With passionate warmth we clasp
    Hand after hand in ours;   360
Nor do we soon perceive how fast our youth is spent.

    At once our eyes grow clear!
    We see, in blank dismay,
    Year posting after year,
    Sense after sense decay;
Our shivering heart is mined by secret discontent;

    Yet still, in spite of truth,
    In spite of hopes entomb'd,
    That longing of our youth
    Burns ever unconsumed,   370
Still hungrier for delight as delights grow more rare.

    We pause; we hush our heart,
    And thus address the Gods:
    'The world hath failed to impart
    The joy our youth forebodes,
Fail'd to fill up the void which in our breasts we bear.

    'Changeful till now, we still
    Look'd on to something new;
    Let us, with changeless will,
    Henceforth look on to you,   380
To find with you the joy we in vain here require!'

    Fools! That so often here
    Happiness mock'd our prayer,
    I think might make us fear
    A like event elsewhere;
Make us, not fly to dreams, but moderate desire.

And yet, for those who know
Themselves, who wisely take
Their way through life, and bow
To what they cannot break,   390
Why should I say that life need yield but *moderate* bliss?

Shall we, with temper spoil'd,
Health sapp'd by living ill,
And judgment all embroil'd
By sadness and self-will,
Shall *we* judge what for man is not true bliss or is?

Is it so small a thing
To have enjoy'd the sun,
To have lived light in the spring,
To have loved, to have thought, to have done;   400
To have advanced true friends, and beat down baffling foes –

That we must feign a bliss
Of doubtful future date,
And, while we dream on this,
Lose all our present state,
And relegate to worlds yet distant our repose?

Not much, I know, you prize
What pleasures may be had,
Who look on life with eyes
Estranged, like mine, and sad: 410
And yet the village-churl feels the truth more than you,

Who's loth to leave this life
Which to him little yields –
His hard-task'd sunburnt wife,
His often-labour'd fields,
The boors with whom he talk'd, the country-spots he knew.

But thou, because thou hear'st
Men scoff at Heaven and Fate,
Because the Gods thou fear'st
Fail to make blest thy state,   420
Tremblest, and wilt not dare to trust the joys there are!

I say: Fear not! Life still
Leaves human effort scope.

But, since life teems with ill,
Nurse no extravagant hope;
Because thou must not dream, thou need'st not then despair!

*A long pause. At the end of it the notes of a harp below are again
heard, and* CALLICLES *sings:*
Far, far from here,
The Adriatic breaks in a warm bay
Among the green Illyrian hills; and there
The sunshine in the happy glens is fair,   430
And by the sea, and in the brakes,
The grass is cool, the sea-side air
Buoyant and fresh, the mountain flowers
More virginal and sweet than ours.
And there, they say, two bright and aged snakes,
Who once were Cadmus and Harmonia,
Bask in the glens or on the warm sea-shore,
In breathless quiet, after all their ills;
Nor do they see their country, nor the place
Where the Sphinx lived among the frowning hills,   440
Nor the unhappy palace of their race,
Nor Thebes, nor the Ismenus, any more.
     There those two live, far in the Illyrian brakes!
They had stay'd long enough to see,
In Thebes, the billow of calamity
Over their own dear children rolled,
Curse upon curse, pang upon pang,
For years, they sitting helpless in their home,
A grey old man and woman; yet of old
The Gods had to their marriage come,   450
And at the banquet all the Muses sang.

Therefore they did not end their days
In sight of blood; but were rapt, far away,
To where the west-wind plays,
And murmurs of the Adriatic come
To those untrodden mountain-lawns; and there
Placed safely in changed forms, the pair
Wholly forget their first sad life, and home,
And all that Theban woe, and stray
For ever through the glens, placid and dumb.   460

EMPEDOCLES
That was my harp-player again! – where is he?
Down by the stream?

PAUSANIAS
                    Yes, Master, in the wood.

EMPEDOCLES
He ever loved the Theban story well!
But the day wears. Go now, Pausanias,
For I must be alone. Leave me one mule;
Take down with thee the rest to Catana.
And for young Callicles, thank him from me;
Tell him, I never failed to love his lyre –
But he must follow me no more to-night.

PAUSANIAS
Thou wilt return to-morrow to the city?   470

EMPEDOCLES
Either to-morrow or some other day,
In the sure revolutions of the world,
Good friend, I shall revisit Catana.
I have seen many cities in my time,
Till mine eyes ache with the long spectacle,
And I shall doubtless see them all again;
Thou know'st me for a wanderer from of old.
Meanwhile, stay me not now. Farewell, Pausanias!
                    He departs on his way up the mountain.

PAUSANIAS *(alone)*
I dare not urge him further – he must go;
But he is strangely wrought! – I will speed back   480
And bring Peisianax to him from the city;
His counsel could once soothe him. But, Apollo!
How his brow lighten'd as the music rose!
Callicles must wait here, and play to him;
I saw him through the chestnuts far below,
Just since, down at the stream. – 'Ho! Callicles!'
                    He descends, calling.

ACT II
Evening. The Summit of Etna.

EMPEDOCLES
                                        Alone! –
On this charr'd, blacken'd, melancholy waste,
Crown'd by the awful peak, Etna's great mouth,
Round which the sullen vapour rolls – alone!
Pausanias is far hence, and that is well,
For I must henceforth speak no more with man
He hath his lesson too, and that debt's paid;
And the good, learned, friendly, quiet man
May bravelier front his life, and in himself
Find henceforth energy and heart. But I –   10
The weary man, the banished citizen,
Whose banishment is not his greatest ill,
Whose weariness no energy can reach,
And for whose hurt courage is not the cure –
What should I do with life and living more?

   No, thou art come too late, Empedocles!
And the world hath the day, and must break thee,
Not thou the world. With men thou canst not live,
Their thoughts, their ways, their wishes, are not thine;
And being lonely thou art miserable,   20
For something has impair'd thy spirit's strength,
And dried its self-sufficing fount of joy.

Thou canst not live with men nor with thyself –
O sage! O sage! Take then the one way left;
And turn thee to the elements, thy friends,
Thy well-tried friends, thy willing ministers,
And say: Ye helpers, hear Empedocles,
Who asks this final service at your hands!
Before the sophist-brood hath overlaid
The last spark of man's consciousness with words –   30
Ere quite the being of man, ere quite the world
Be disarrayed of their divinity –
Before the soul lose all her solemn joys,
And awe be dead, and hope impossible,
And the soul's deep eternal night come on –
Receive me, hide me, quench me, take me home!

*He advances to the edge of the crater. Smoke and fire break
forth with a loud noise, and* CALLICLES *is heard below singing:*

The lyre's voice is lovely everywhere;
In the court of Gods, in the city of men,
And in the lonely rock-strewn mountain-glen,
In the still mountain air.   40

Only to Typho it sounds hatefully;
To Typho only, the rebel o'erthrown,
Through whose heart Etna drives her roots of stone
To imbed them in the sea.

Wherefore dost thou groan so loud?
Wherefore do thy nostrils flash,
Through the dark night, suddenly,
Typho, such red jets of flame?—
Is thy tortured heart still proud?
Is thy fire-scathed arm still rash?   50
Still alert thy stone-crush'd frame?
Doth thy fierce soul still deplore
Thine ancient rout by the Cilician hills,

And that curst treachery on the Mount of Gore?
Do thy bloodshot eyes still weep
The fight which crown'd thine ills,
Thy last mischance on this Sicilian deep?
Hast thou sworn, in thy sad lair,
Where erst the strong sea-currents suck'd thee down,
Never to cease to writhe, and try to rest,   60
Letting the sea-stream wander through thy hair?
That thy groans, like thunder prest,
Begin to roll, and almost drown
The sweet notes whose lulling spell
Gods and the race of mortals love so well,
When through thy caves thou hearest music swell?

But an awful pleasure bland
Spreading o'er the Thunderer's face,
When the sound climbs near his seat,
The Olympian council sees;   70
As he lets his lax right hand,
Which the lightnings doth embrace,
Sink upon his mighty knees.

And the eagle, at the beck
Of the appeasing, gracious harmony,
Droops all his sheeny, brown, deep-feather'd neck,
Nestling nearer to Jove's feet;
While o'er his sovran eye
The curtains of the blue films slowly meet.
And the white Olympus-peaks   80
Rosily brighten, and the soothed Gods smile
At one another from their golden chairs,
And no one round the charméd circle speaks.
Only the loved Hebe bears
The cup about, whose draughts beguile
Pain and care, with a dark store
Of fresh-pull'd violets wreathed and nodding o'er;
And her flush'd feet glow on the marble floor.

EMPEDOCLES
He fables, yet speaks truth!
The brave, impetuous heart yields everywhere   90
To the subtle, contriving head;
Great qualities are trodden down,
And littleness united
Is become invincible.

These rumblings are not Typho's groans, I know!
These angry smoke-bursts
Are not the passionate breath
Of the mountain-crush'd, tortured, intractable Titan king –
But over all the world
What suffering is there not seen   100
Of plainness oppressed by cunning,
As the well-counsell'd Zeus oppressed
That self-helping son of earth!
What anguish of greatness,
Rail'd and hunted from the world,
Because its simplicity rebukes
This envious, miserable age!

I am weary of it.
– Lie there, ye ensigns
Of my unloved preëminence   110
In an age like this!

Among a people of children,
Who throng'd me in their cities,
Who worshipp'd me in their houses,
And ask'd, not wisdom,
But drugs to charm with,
But spells to mutter –
All the fool's-armoury of magic!—Lie there,
My golden circlet,
My purple robe!   120

CALLICLES *(from below)*
As the sky-brightening south-wind clears the day,
And makes the mass'd clouds roll,
The music of the lyre blows away
The clouds which wrap the soul.
Oh! that Fate had let me see
That triumph of the sweet persuasive lyre,
That famous, final victory,
When jealous Pan with Marsyas did conspire;

When, from far Parnassus' side,
Young Apollo, all the pride   130
Of the Phrygian flutes to tame,
To the Phrygian highlands came;
Where the long green reed-beds sway
In the rippled waters grey
Of that solitary lake
Where Mæander's springs are born;
Whence the ridged pine-wooded roots
Of Messogis westward break,
Mounting westward, high and higher.
There was held the famous strife;   140
There the Phrygian brought his flutes,
And Apollo brought his lyre;
And, when now the westering sun
Touch'd the hills, the strife was done,
And the attentive Muses said:
'Marsyas, thou art vanquishéd!'
Then Apollo's minister
Hang'd upon a branching fir
Marsyas, that unhappy Faun,
And began to whet his knife.   150

But the Mænads, who were there,
Left their friend, and with robes flowing
In the wind, and loose dark hair
O'er their polished bosoms blowing,
Each her ribbon'd tambourine
Flinging on the mountain-sod,
With a lovely frighten'd mien
Came about the youthful God.
But he turned his beauteous face
Haughtily another way,   160
From the grassy sun-warm'd place
Where in proud repose he lay,
With one arm over his head,
Watching how the whetting sped.

    But aloof, on the lake-strand,
Did the young Olympus stand,
Weeping at his master's end;
For the Faun had been his friend.
For he taught him how to sing,
And he taught him flute-playing.   170
Many a morning had they gone
To the glimmering mountain-lakes,
And had torn up by the roots
The tall crested water-reeds
With long plumes and soft brown seeds,
And had carved them into flutes,
Sitting on a tabled stone
Where the shoreward ripple breaks.
And he taught him how to please
The red-snooded Phrygian girls,   180
Whom the summer evening sees
Flashing in the dance's whirls
Underneath the starlit trees
In the mountain-villages.
Therefore now Olympus stands,
At his master's piteous cries
Pressing fast with both his hands
His white garment to his eyes,
Not to see Apollo's scorn;—
Ah, poor Faun, poor Faun! ah, poor Faun!   190

EMPEDOCLES
And lie thou there,
My laurel bough!
Scornful Apollo's ensign, lie thou there!
Though thou hast been my shade in the world's heat –
Though I have loved thee, lived in honouring thee –
Yet lie thou there,
My laurel bough!

I am weary of thee.
I am weary of the solitude
Where he who bears thee must abide –   200
Of the rocks of Parnassus,
Of the gorge of Delphi,
Of the moonlit peaks, and the caves.
Thou guardest them, Apollo!
Over the grave of the slain Pytho,
Though young, intolerably severe!
Thou keepest aloof the profane,
But the solitude oppresses thy votary!
The jars of men reach him not in thy valley –
But can life reach him?   210
Thou fencest him from the multitude –
Who will fence him from himself?
He hears nothing but the cry of the torrents,
And the beating of his own heart.
The air is thin, the veins swell,
The temples tighten and throb there –
Air! air!

Take thy bough, set me free from my solitude;
I have been enough alone!

Where shall thy votary fly then? back to men?—   220
But they will gladly welcome him once more,
And help him to unbend his too tense thought,
And rid him of the presence of himself,
And keep their friendly chatter at his ear,
And haunt him, till the absence from himself,
That other torment, grow unbearable;
And he will fly to solitude again,
And he will find its air too keen for him,

And so change back; and many thousand times
Be miserably bandied to and fro   230
Like a sea-wave, betwixt the world and thee,
Thou young, implacable God! and only death
Can cut his oscillations short, and so
Bring him to poise. There is no other way.

And yet what days were those, Parmenides!
When we were young, when we could number friends
In all the Italian cities like ourselves,
When with elated hearts we join'd your train,
Ye Sun-born Virgins! on the road of truth.
Then we could still enjoy, then neither thought   240
Nor outward things were closed and dead to us;
But we received the shock of mighty thoughts
On simple minds with a pure natural joy;
And if the sacred load oppress'd our brain,
We had the power to feel the pressure eased,
The brow unbound, the thoughts flow free again,
In the delightful commerce of the world.
We had not lost our balance then, nor grown
Thought's slaves, and dead to every natural joy.
The smallest thing could give us pleasure then –   250
The sports of the country-people,
A flute-note from the woods,
Sunset over the sea;
Seed-time and harvest,
The reapers in the corn,
The vinedresser in his vineyard,
The village-girl at her wheel.

Fullness of life and power of feeling, ye
Are for the happy, for the souls at ease,
Who dwell on a firm basis of content!   260
But he, who has outlived his prosperous days –
But he, whose youth fell on a different world
From that on which his exiled age is thrown –
Whose mind was fed on other food, was train'd
By other rules than are in vogue to-day –
Whose habit of thought is fix'd, who will not change,
But, in a world he loves not, must subsist
In ceaseless opposition, be the guard

Of his own breast, fetter'd to what he guards,
That the world win no mastery over him –   270
Who has no friend, no fellow left, not one;
Who has no minute's breathing space allow'd
To nurse his dwindling faculty of joy –
Joy and the outward world must die to him,
As they are dead to me.

A long pause, during which EMPEDOCLES *remains motionless, plunged in thought. The night deepens. He moves forward and gazes round him, and proceeds:*

And you, ye stars,
Who slowly begin to marshal,
As of old, in the fields of heaven,
Your distant, melancholy lines!
Have you, too, survived yourselves?   280
Are you, too, what I fear to become?
You, too, once lived;
You, too, moved joyfully
Among august companions,
In an older world, peopled by Gods,
In a mightier order,
The radiant, rejoicing, intelligent Sons of Heaven.
But now, ye kindle
Your lonely, cold-shining lights,
Unwilling lingerers   290
In the heavenly wilderness,
For a younger, ignoble world;
And renew, by necessity,
Night after night your courses,
In echoing, unnear'd silence,
Above a race you know not –
Uncaring and undelighted,
Without friend and without home;
Weary like us, though not
Weary with our weariness.   300

No, no, ye stars! there is no death with you,
No languor, no decay! languor and death,
They are with me, not you! ye are alive –
Ye, and the pure dark ether where ye ride

Brilliant above me! And thou, fiery world,
That sapp'st the vitals of this terrible mount
Upon whose charr'd and quaking crust I stand –
Thou, too, brimmest with life! – the sea of cloud,
That heaves its white and billowy vapours up
To moat this isle of ashes from the world,   310
Lives; and that other fainter sea, far down,
O'er whose lit floor a road of moonbeams leads
To Etna's Liparëan sister-fires
And the long dusky line of Italy –
That mild and luminous floor of waters lives,
With held-in joy swelling its heart; I only,
Whose spring of hope is dried, whose spirit has fail'd,
I have not, like these, in solitude
Maintain'd courage and force, and in myself
Nursed an immortal vigour – I alone   320
Am dead to life and joy, therefore I read
In all things my own deadness.

                              A long silence. He continues:

Oh, that I could glow like this mountain!
Oh, that my heart bounded with the swell of the sea!
Oh, that my soul were full of light as the stars!
Oh, that it brooded over the world like the air!
But no, this heart will glow no more; thou art
A living man no more, Empedocles!
Nothing but a devouring flame of thought –
But a naked, eternally restless mind!   330

                                        After a pause:

To the elements it came from
Everything will return –
Our bodies to earth,
Our blood to water,
Heat to fire,
Breath to air,
They were well born, they will be well entomb'd –
But mind? ...

And we might gladly share the fruitful stir
Down in our mother earth's miraculous womb;   340
Well would it be

With what roll'd of us in the stormy main;
We might have joy, blent with the all-bathing air,
Or with the nimble, radiant life of fire.

But mind, but thought –
If these have been the master part of us –
Where will *they* find their parent element?
What will receive *them*, who will call *them* home?
But we shall still be in them, and they in us,
And we shall be the strangers of the world,   350
And they will be our lords, as they are now;
And keep us prisoners of our consciousness,
And never let us clasp and feel the All
But through their forms, and modes, and stifling veils.
And we shall be unsatisfied as now;
And we shall feel the agony of thirst,
The ineffable longing for the life of life
Baffled for ever; and still thought and mind
Will hurry us with them on their homeless march,
Over the unallied unopening earth,   360
Over the unrecognising sea; while air
Will blow us fiercely back to sea and earth,
And fire repel us from its living waves.
And then we shall unwillingly return
Back to this meadow of calamity,
This uncongenial place, this human life;
And in our individual human state
Go through the sad probation all again,
To see if we will poise our life at last,
To see if we will now at last be true   370
To our own only true, deep-buried selves,
Being one with which we are one with the whole world;
Or whether we will once more fall away
Into some bondage of the flesh or mind,
Some slough of sense, or some fantastic maze
Forged by the imperious lonely thinking-power.
And each succeeding age in which we are born
Will have more peril for us than the last;
Will goad our senses with a sharper spur,
Will fret our minds to an intenser play,   380
Will make ourselves harder to be discern'd.
And we shall struggle awhile, gasp and rebel –

And we shall fly for refuge to past times,
Their soul of unworn youth, their breath of greatness;
And the reality will pluck us back,
Knead us in its hot hand, and change our nature.
And we shall feel our powers of effort flag,
And rally them for one last fight – and fail;
And we shall sink in the impossible strife,
And be astray for ever.

                Slave of sense   390
I have in no wise been; but slave of thought? ...
And who can say: I have been always free,
Lived ever in the light of my own soul? –
I cannot; I have lived in wrath and gloom,
Fierce, disputatious, ever at war with man,
Far from my own soul, far from warmth and light.
But I have not grown easy in these bonds –
But I have not denied what bonds these were.
Yea, I take myself to witness,
That I have loved no darkness,   400
Sophisticated no truth,
Nursed no delusion,
Allowed no fear!

  And therefore, O ye elements! I know –
Ye know it too – it hath been granted me
Not to die wholly, not to be all enslaved.
I feel it in this hour. The numbing cloud
Mounts off my soul; I feel it, I breathe free.

        Is it but for a moment?
        – Ah, boil up, ye vapours!   410
        Leap and roar, thou sea of fire!
        My soul glows to meet you.
        Ere it flag, ere the mists
        Of despondency and gloom
        Rush over it again,
        Receive me, save me!

                        [He plunges into the crater.

CALLICLES
(*from below*)
Through the black, rushing smoke-bursts,

Thick breaks the red flame;
All Etna heaves fiercely
Her forest-clothed frame.

420

Not here, O Apollo!
Are haunts meet for thee.
But, where Helicon breaks down
In cliff to the sea,

Where the moon-silver'd inlets
Send far their light voice
Up the still vale of Thisbe,
O speed, and rejoice!

On the sward at the cliff-top
Lie strewn the white flocks,
On the cliff-side the pigeons
Roost deep in the rocks.

430

In the moonlight the shepherds,
Soft lulled by the rills,
Lie wrapt in their blankets
Asleep on the hills.

– What forms are these coming
So white through the gloom?
What garments out-glistening
The gold-flower'd broom?

440

What sweet-breathing presence
Out-perfumes the thyme?
What voices enrapture
The night's balmy prime?

'Tis Apollo comes leading
His choir, the Nine.
– The leader is fairest,
But all are divine.

They are lost in the hollows!
They stream up again!
What seeks on this mountain
The glorified train?—

450

They bathe on this mountain,
In the spring by their road;

Then on to Olympus,
Their endless abode.

– Whose praise do they mention?
Of what is it told?—
What will be for ever;
What was from old.   460

First hymn they the Father
Of all things; and then,
The rest of immortals,
The action of men.

The day in his hotness,
The strife with the palm;
The night in her silence,
The stars in their calm.

From Tristram and Iseult

The whole poem, the first treatment in England of this legend, probably conceived and planned in Switzerland Sept. 1849, begun shortly after A.'s return to England, and further worked on before Oct. 1852; pub. *1852*. A. 'read the story ... in Thun [p. 24 above] in an article ... on the romance literature: I have never met with it before and it fastened on me' (letter of 5 Nov. 1852, *TLS* 19 May 1932); 'that the whole story developed a shadowy personal significance for A. (with Marguerite and Frances Lucy Wightman as the "two Iseults who did sway/Each his hour of Tristram's day" [l. 68–9]) can hardly be doubted' (*Poems* 196). Besides La Villemarqué's article (*Revue de Paris*, 3rd Series xxiv. 266–82, 1841), A. drew on Malory, Southey's edn. (1817) of the Life of King Arthur, and Dunlop's *History of Fiction* (1845 edn.). Part I, Tristram, shows T. mortally sick and recalling his passion for the first Iseult, while in the care of his wife, the gentle second Iseult. Part II, Iseult of Ireland, brings her to his bedside and records their Liebestod. Part III, Iseult of Brittany, shows the surviving Iseult, 'dying in a mask of youth', caring for her children and telling them stories, here that of Merlin and Vivian (drawn from Southey) 'of which I am especially fond' (A.'s Nov. 1852 letter) and which is significantly another tale of enchantment and loss. Some variant readings from the *Yale MS.* are recorded *Poems* 216–24.

III
Iseult of Brittany

A year had flown, and o'er the sea away,
In Cornwall, Tristram and Queen Iseult lay;
In King Marc's chapel, in Tyntagel old –
There in a ship they bore those lovers cold.

The young surviving Iseult, one bright day,
Had wander'd forth. Her children were at play
In a green circular hollow in the heath
Which borders the sea-shore – a country path
Creeps over it from the till'd fields behind.
The hollow's grassy banks are soft-inclined,   10
And to one standing on them, far and near
The lone unbroken view spreads bright and clear
Over the waste. This cirque of open ground
Is light and green; the heather, which all round
Creeps thickly, grows not here; but the pale grass
Is strewn with rocks, and many a shiver'd mass
Of vein'd white-gleaming quartz, and here and there
Dotted with holly-trees and juniper.
In the smooth centre of the opening stood
Three hollies side by side, and made a screen,   20
Warm with the winter-sun, of burnish'd green
With scarlet berries gemm'd, the fell-fare's food.
Under the glittering hollies Iseult stands,
Watching her children play; their little hands
Are busy gathering spars of quartz, and streams
Of staghorn for their hats; anon, with screams
Of mad delight they drop their spoils, and bound
Among the holly-clumps and broken ground,
Racing full speed, and startling in their rush
The fell-fares and the speckled missel-thrush   30
Out of their glossy coverts; – but when now
Their cheeks were flush'd, and over each hot brow,
Under the feather'd hats of the sweet pair,
In blinding masses shower'd the golden hair –
Then Iseult call'd them to her, and the three
Cluster'd under the holly-screen, and she
Told them an old-world Breton history.

   Warm in their mantles wrapt the three stood there,
Under the hollies, in the clear still air –
Mantles with those rich furs deep glistering   40
Which Venice ships do from swart Egypt bring.
Long they stay'd still – then, pacing at their ease,
Moved up and down under the glossy trees.
But still, as they pursued their warm dry road,

From Iseult's lips the unbroken story flow'd,
And still the children listen'd, their blue eyes
Fix'd on their mother's face in wide surprise;
Nor did their looks stray once to the sea-side,
Nor to the brown heaths round them, bright and wide,
Nor to the snow, which, though 't was all away   50
From the open heath, still by the hedgerows lay,
Nor to the shining sea-fowl, that with screams
Bore up from where the bright Atlantic gleams,
Swooping to landward; nor to where, quite clear,
The fell-fares settled on the thickets near.
And they would still have listen'd, till dark night
Came keen and chill down on the heather bright;
But, when the red glow on the sea grew cold,
And the grey turrets of the castle old
Look'd sternly through the frosty evening-air,   60
Then Iseult took by the hand those children fair,
And brought her tale to an end, and found the path,
And led them home over the darkening heath.

And is she happy? Does she see unmoved
The days in which she might have lived and loved
Slip without bringing bliss slowly away,
One after one, to-morrow like to-day?
Joy has not found her yet, nor ever will –
Is it this thought which makes her mien so still,
Her features so fatigued, her eyes, though sweet,   70
So sunk, so rarely lifted save to meet
Her children's? She moves slow; her voice alone
Hath yet an infantine and silver tone,
But even that comes languidly; in truth,
She seems one dying in a mask of youth.
And now she will go home, and softly lay
Her laughing children in their beds, and play
Awhile with them before they sleep; and then
She'll light her silver lamp, which fishermen
Dragging their nets through the rough waves, afar,   80
Along this iron coast, know like a star,
And take her broidery-frame, and there she'll sit
Hour after hour, her gold curls sweeping it;
Lifting her soft-bent head only to mind

Her children, or to listen to the wind.
And when the clock peals midnight, she will move
Her work away, and let her fingers rove
Across the shaggy brows of Tristram's hound
Who lies, guarding her feet, along the ground;
Or else she will fall musing, her blue eyes   90
Fixt, her slight hands clasp'd on her lap; then rise,
And at her prie-dieu kneel, until she have told
Her rosary-beads of ebony tipp'd with gold,
Then to her soft sleep – and to-morrow'll be
To-day's exact repeated effigy.

Yes, it is lonely for her in her hall.
The children, and the grey-hair'd seneschal,
Her women, and Sir Tristram's aged hound,
Are there the sole companions to be found.
But these she loves; and noisier life than this   100
She would find ill to bear, weak as she is.
She has her children, too, and night and day
Is with them; and the wide heaths where they play,
The hollies, and the cliff, and the sea-shore,
The sand, the sea-birds, and the distant sails,
These are to her dear as to them; the tales
With which this day the children she beguiled
She gleaned from Breton grandames, when a child,
In every hut along this sea-coast wild.
She herself loves them still, and, when they are told,   110
Can forget all to hear them, as of old.

Dear saints, it is not sorrow, as I hear,
Not suffering, which shuts up eye and ear
To all that has delighted them before,
And lets us be what we were once no more.
No, we may suffer deeply, yet retain
Power to be moved and soothed, for all our pain,
By what of old pleased us, and will again.
No, 'tis the gradual furnace of the world,
In whose hot air our spirits are upcurl'd   120
Until they crumble, or else grow like steel –
Which kills in us the bloom, the youth, the spring –
Which leaves the fierce necessity to feel,
But takes away the power – this can avail,

By drying up our joy in everything,
To make our former pleasures all seem stale.
This, or some tyrannous single thought, some fit
Of passion, which subdues our souls to it,
Till for its sake alone we live and move –
Call it ambition, or remorse, or love –   130
This too can change us wholly, and make seem
All which we did before, shadow and dream.

  And yet, I swear, it angers me to see
How this fool passion gulls men potently;
Being, in truth, but a diseased unrest,
And an unnatural overheat at best.
How they are full of languor and distress
Not having it; which when they do possess,
They straightway are burnt up with fume and care,
And spend their lives in posting here and there   140
Where this plague drives them; and have little ease,
Are furious with themselves, and hard to please.
Like that bold Cæsar, the famed Roman wight,
Who wept at reading of a Grecian knight
Who made a name at younger years than he;
Or that renown'd mirror of chivalry,
Prince Alexander, Philip's peerless son,
Who carried the great war from Macedon
Into the Soudan's realm, and thundered on
To die at thirty-five in Babylon.   150

What tale did Iseult to the children say,
Under the hollies, that bright winter's day?

She told them of the fairy-haunted land
Away the other side of Brittany,
Beyond the heaths, edged by the lonely sea;
Of the deep forest-glades of Broce-liande,
Through whose green boughs the golden sunshine creeps,
Where Merlin by the enchanted thorn-tree sleeps.
For here he came with the fay Vivian,
One April, when the warm days first began.   160
He was on foot, and that false fay, his friend,
On her white palfrey; here he met his end,
In these lone sylvan glades, that April-day.

This tale of Merlin and the lovely fay
Was the one Iseult chose, and she brought clear
Before the children's fancy him and her.

Blowing between the stems, the forest-air
Had loosen'd the brown locks of Vivian's hair,
Which play'd on her flush'd cheek, and her blue eyes
Sparked with mocking glee and exercise.   170
Her palfrey's flanks were mired and bathed in sweat,
For they had travell'd far and not stopp'd yet.
A brier in that tangled wilderness
Had scored her white right hand, which she allows
To rest ungloved on her green riding-dress;
The other warded off the drooping boughs.
But still she chatted on, with her blue eyes
Fix'd full on Merlin's face, her stately prize.
Her 'haviour had the morning's fresh clear grace,
The spirit of the woods was in her face.   180
She look'd so witching fair, that learned wight
Forgot his craft, and his best wits took flight;
And he grew fond, and eager to obey
His mistress, use her empire as she may.

They came to where the brushwood ceased, and day
Peer'd 'twixt the stems; and the ground broke away,
In a sloped sward down to a brawling brook;
And up as high as where they stood to look
On the brook's farther side was clear, but then
The underwood and trees began again.   190
This open glen was studded thick with thorns
Then white with blossom; and you saw the horns,
Through last year's fern, of the shy fallow-deer
Who come at noon down to the water here.
You saw the bright-eyed squirrels dart along
Under the thorns on the green sward; and strong
The blackbird whistled from the dingles near,
And the weird chipping of the woodpecker
Rang lonelily and sharp; the sky was fair,
And a fresh breath of spring stirr'd everywhere.   200
Merlin and Vivian stopp'd on the slope's brow,
To gaze on the light sea of leaf and bough
Which glistering plays all round them, lone and mild,

As if to itself the quiet forest smiled.
Upon the brow-top grew a thorn, and here
The grass was dry and moss'd, and you saw clear
Across the hollow; white anemonies
Starr'd the cool turf, and clumps of primroses
Ran out from the dark underwood behind.
No fairer resting-place a man could find.   210
'Here let us halt,' said Merlin then; and she
Nodded, and tied her palfrey to a tree.

They sate them down together, and a sleep
Fell upon Merlin, more like death, so deep.
Her finger on her lips, then Vivian rose,
And from her brown-lock'd head the wimple throws,
And takes it in her hand, and waves it over
The blossom'd thorn-tree and her sleeping lover.
Nine times she waved the fluttering wimple round,
And made a little plot of magic ground.   220
And in that daised circle, as men say,
Is Merlin prisoner till the judgment-day;
But she herself whither she will can rove –
For she was passing weary of his love.

Memorial Verses

Written c. 27 April 1850, date of Wordsworth's burial at Grasmere, at the request of Wordsworth's son-in-law Edward Quillinan; pub. *Fraser's Magazine* June 1850; repr. 1852.

APRIL, 1850

Goethe in Weimar sleeps, and Greece,
Long since, saw Byron's struggle cease.
But one such death remain'd to come;
The last poetic voice is dumb –
We stand to-day by Wordsworth's tomb.

When Byron's eyes were shut in death,
We bow'd our head and held our breath.
He taught us little; but our soul
Had *felt* him like the thunder's roll.

With shivering heart the strife we saw 10
Of passion with eternal law;
And yet with reverential awe
We watch'd the fount of fiery life
Which served for that Titanic strife.

When Goethe's death was told, we said:
Sunk, then, is Europe's sagest head.
Physician of the iron age,
Goethe has done his pilgrimage.
He took the suffering human race,
He read each wound, each weakness clear; 20
And stuck his finger on the place,
And said: *Thou ailest here, and here!*
He look'd on Europe's dying hour
Of fitful dream and feverish power;
His eye plunged down the weltering strife,
The turmoil of expiring life –
He said: *The end is everywhere,*
Art still has truth, take refuge there!
And he was happy, if to know
Causes of things, and far below 30
His feet to see the lurid flow
Of terror, and insane distress,
And headlong fate, be happiness.

And Wordsworth! – Ah, pale ghosts, rejoice!
For never has such soothing voice
Been to your shadowy world convey'd,
Since erst, at morn, some wandering shade
Heard the clear song of Orpheus come
Through Hades, and the mournful gloom.
Wordsworth has gone from us – and ye, 40
Ah, may ye feel his voice as we!
He too upon a wintry clime
Had fallen – on this iron time
Of doubts, disputes, distractions, fears.
He found us when the age had bound
Our souls in its benumbing round;
He spoke, and loosed our heart in tears.
He laid us as we lay at birth
On the cool flowery lap of earth,

Smiles broke from us and we had ease;   50
The hills were round us, and the breeze
Went o'er the sun-lit fields again;
Our foreheads felt the wind and rain.
Our youth return'd; for there was shed
On spirits that had long been dead,
Spirits dried up and closely furl'd,
The freshness of the early world.

Ah, since dark days still bring to light
Man's prudence and man's fiery might,
Time may restore us in his course   60
Goethe's sage mind and Byron's force;
But where will Europe's latter hour
Again find Wordsworth's healing power?

Others will teach us how to dare,
And against fear our breast to steel;
Others will strengthen us to bear –
But who, ah! who, will make us feel?
The cloud of mortal destiny,
Others will front it fearlessly –
But who, like him, will put it by?   70

Keep fresh the grass upon his grave
O Rotha, with thy living wave!
Sing him thy best! for few or none
Hears thy voice right, now he is gone.

Dover Beach

Probably written late June 1851; pub. *1867*. Arguments for the dating of 'A.'s most
famous lyric' are summarized *Poems* 239 and supported by S.O.A. Ullmann, 'Dating
through Calligraphy: The example of "Dover Beach",' *Studies in Bibliography* (1973)
xxvi. 19–36. Evidence includes A.'s pencilled autograph of ll. 1–28 on the back of
notes about Empedocles from Karsten (headnote., p. 36 above) and his visit of Dover
with his wife after their marriage 10 June 1851.

The sea is calm to-night.
The tide is full, the moon lies fair
Upon the straits; – on the French coast the light

Gleams and is gone; the cliffs of England stand,
Glimmering and vast, out in the tranquil bay.
Come to the window, sweet is the night-air!
Only, from the long line of spray
Where the sea meets the moon-blanch'd land,
Listen! You hear the grating roar
Of pebbles which the waves draw back, and fling,   10
At their return, up the high strand,
Begin, and cease, and then again begin,
With tremulous cadence slow, and bring
The eternal note of sadness in.
Sophocles long ago
Heard it on the Aegaean, and it brought
Into his mind the turbid ebb and flow
Of human misery; we
Find also in the sound a thought,
Hearing it by this distant northern sea.   20

The Sea of Faith
Was once, too, at the full, and round earth's shore
Lay like the folds of a bright girdle furl'd.
But now I only hear
Its melancholy, long, withdrawing roar,
Retreating, to the breath
Of the night-wind, down the vast edges drear
And naked shingles of the world.

Ah, love, let us be true
To one another! for the world, which seems   30
To lie before us like a land of dreams,
So various, so beautiful, so new,
Hath really neither joy, nor love, nor light,
Nor certitude, nor peace, nor help for pain;
And we are here as on a darkling plain
Swept with confused alarms of struggle and flight,
Where ignorant armies clash by night.

The Youth of Nature

Written between June 1850 (1.63) – Jan. 1852; pub. *1852*. See A.'s entry in his unpub. diary 4 Jan 1852, '... walked alone along Rydal and Grasmere during afternoon service – finished Wordsworth's pindaric' – A.'s term for his unrhymed lyric consisting of verse paragraphs possessing an irregular number of chiefly three-stressed lines. (Used again for 'The Youth of Man' which also celebrates Nature 'in a way that may indicate a recent reading of *The Prelude* (1850)', *Poems* 245.)

Raised are the dripping oars,
Silent the boat! the lake,
Lovely and soft as a dream,
Swims in the sheen of the moon.
The mountains stand at its head
Clear in the pure June-night,
But the valleys are flooded with haze.
Rydal and Fairfield are there;
In the shadow Wordsworth lies dead.
So it is, so it will be for aye.   10
Nature is fresh as of old,
Is lovely; a mortal is dead.

The spots which recall him survive,
For he lent a new life to these hills.
The Pillar still broods o'er the fields
Which border Ennerdale Lake,
And Egremont sleeps by the sea.
The gleam of The Evening Star
Twinkles on Grasmere no more,
But ruin'd and solemn and grey   20
The sheepfold of Michael survives;
And, far to the south, the heath
Still blows in the Quantock coombs,
By the favourite waters of Ruth.
These survive! – yet not without pain,
Pain and dejection to-night,
Can I feel that their poet is gone.

He grew old in an age he condemn'd.
He look'd on the rushing decay
Of the times which had shelter'd his youth;   30
Felt the dissolving throes

Of a social order he loved;
Outlived his brethren, his peers;
And, like the Theban seer,
Died in his enemies' day.

Cold bubbled the spring of Tilphusa,
Copais lay bright in the moon,
Helicon glass'd in the lake
Its firs, and afar rose the peaks
Of Parnassus, snowily clear;   40
Thebes was behind him in flames,
And the clang of arms in his ear,
When his awe-struck captors led
The Theban seer to the spring.
Tiresias drank and died.
Nor did reviving Thebes
See such a prophet again.

Well may we mourn, when the head
Of a sacred poet lies low
In an age which can rear them no more!   50
The complaining millions of men
Darken in labour and pain;
But he was a priest to us all
Of the wonder and bloom of the world,
Which we saw with his eyes, and were glad.
He is dead, and the fruit-bearing day
Of his race is past on the earth;
And darkness returns to our eyes.

For, oh! is it you, is it you,
Moonlight, and shadow, and lake,   60
And mountains, that fill us with joy,
Or the poet who sings you so well?
Is it you, O beauty, O grace,
O charm, O romance, that we feel,
Or the voice which reveals what you are?
Are ye, like daylight and sun,
Shared and rejoiced in by all?
Or are ye immersed in the mass
Of matter, and hard to extract,
Or sunk at the core of the world   70
Too deep for the most to discern?

Like stars in the deep of the sky,
Which arise on the glass of the sage,
But are lost when their watcher is gone.

'They are here' – I heard, as men heard
In Mysian Ida the voice
Of the Mighty Mother, or Crete,
The murmur of Nature reply –
'Loveliness, magic and grace,
They are here! they are set in the world,   80
They abide; and the finest of souls
Hath not been thrill'd by them all,
Nor the dullest been dead to them quite.
The poet who sings them may die,
But they are immortal and live,
For they are the life of the world.
Will ye not learn it, and know,
When ye mourn that a poet is dead,
That the singer was less than his themes,
Life, and emotion, and I?   90

'More than the singer are these.
Weak is the tremor of pain
That thrills in his mournfullest chord
To that which once ran through his soul.
Cold the elation of joy
In his gladdest, airiest song,
To that which of old in his youth
Fill'd him and made him divine.
Hardly his voice at its best
Gives us a sense of the awe,   100
The vastness, the grandeur, the gloom
Of the unlit gulph of himself.

'Ye know not yourselves; and your bards –
The clearest, the best, who have read
Most in themselves – have beheld
Less than they left unreveal'd.
Ye express not yourselves; – can you make
With marble, with colour, with word,
What charm'd you in others re-live?
Can thy pencil, O artist! restore   110
The figure, the bloom of thy love,

As she was in her morning of spring?
Canst thou paint the ineffable smile
Of her eyes as they rested on thine?
Can the image of life have the glow,
The motion of life itself?

'Yourselves and your fellows ye know not; and me,
The mateless, the one, will ye know?
Will ye scan me, and read me, and tell
Of the thoughts that ferment in my breast,   120
My longing, my sadness, my joy?
Will ye claim for your great ones the gift
To have render'd the gleam of my skies,
To have echoed the moan of my seas,
Utter'd the voice of my hills?'
When your great ones depart, will ye say:
All things have suffer'd a loss,
Nature is hid in their grave?

'Race after race, man after man,
Have thought that my secret was theirs,   130
Have dream'd that I lived but for them,
That they were my glory and joy.
– They are dust, they are changed, they are gone!
I remain.'

A Summer Night

Probably written 1849–52; pub. *1852*. The circumstances are unknown
but may be connected with A.'s courtship of Frances Wightman rather
than with memories of Marguerite and Thun.

In the deserted, moon-blanched street,
How lonely rings the echo of my feet!
Those windows, which I gaze at, frown,
Silent and white, unopening down,
Repellent as the world; but see,
A break between the housetops shows
The moon! and, lost behind her, fading dim
Into the dewy dark obscurity

Down at the far horizon's rim,
Doth a whole tract of heaven disclose!   10

And to my mind the thought
Is on a sudden brought
Of a past night, and a far different scene.
Headlands stood out into the moonlit deep
As clearly as at noon;
The spring-tide's brimming flow
Heaved dazzlingly between;
Houses, with long white sweep,
Girdled the glistening bay;
Behind, through the soft air,   20
The blue haze-cradled mountains spread away.
That night was far more fair –
But the same restless pacings to and fro,
And the same vainly throbbing heart was there,
And the same bright, calm moon.

And the calm moonlight seems to say:
Hast thou then still the old unquiet breast,
Which neither deadens into rest,
Nor ever feels the fiery glow
That whirls the spirit from itself away,   30
But fluctuates to and fro,
Never by passion quite possessed
And never quite benumbed by the world's sway?

And I, I know not if to pray
Still to be what I am, or yield and be
Like all the other men I see.
For most men in a brazen prison live,
Where, in the sun's hot eye,
With heads bent o'er their toil, they languidly
Their lives to some unmeaning taskwork give,   40
Dreaming of nought beyond their prison-wall.
And as, year after year,
Fresh products of their barren labour fall
From their tired hands, and rest
Never yet comes more near,
Gloom settles slowly down over their breast;
And while they try to stem

The waves of mournful thought by which they are pressed,
Death in their prison reaches them,
Unfreed, having seen nothing, still unblest.   50

And the rest, a few,
Escape their prison and depart
On the wide ocean of life anew.
There the freed prisoner, where'er his heart
Listeth, will sail;
Nor doth he know how there prevail,
Despotic on that sea,
Trade-winds which cross it from eternity.
Awhile he holds some false way, undebarred
By thwarting signs, and braves   60
The freshening wind and blackening waves.
And then the tempest strikes him; and between
The lightning-bursts is seen
Only a driving wreck,
And the pale master on his spar-strewn deck
With anguished face and flying hair
Grasping the rudder hard,
Still bent to make some port he knows not where,
Still standing for some false, impossible shore.
And sterner comes the roar   70
Of sea and wind, and through the deepening gloom
Fainter and fainter wreck and helmsman loom,
And he too disappears, and comes no more.

Is there no life, but these alone?
Madman or slave, must man be one?

Plainness and clearness without shadow of stain!
Clearness divine!
Ye heavens, whose pure dark regions have no sign
Of languor, though so calm, and, though so great,
And yet untroubled and unpassionate;   80
Who, though so noble, share in the world's toil,
And, though so tasked, keep free from dust and soil!
I will not say that your mild deeps retain
A tinge, it may be, of their silent pain
Who have longed deeply once, and longed in vain –
But I will rather say that you remain

A world above a man's head, to let him see
How boundless might his soul's horizons be,
How vast, yet of what clear transparency!
How it were good to abide there, and breathe free;   90
How fair a lot to fill
Is left to each man still!

The Buried Life

Probably written between 1850–52; pub. 1852. According to *Commentary* (195) the opening is linked in feeling and theme with the Marguerite poems and the second half with 'Dover Beach' (p. 76 above), but the temper of ll. 1–25 seems closer to 'Faded Leaves' than 'Switzerland'.

Light flows our war of mocking words, and yet,
Behold, with tears mine eyes are wet!
I feel a nameless sadness o'er me roll.
Yes, yes, we know that we can jest,
We know, we know that we can smile!
But there's a something in this breast,
To which thy light words bring no rest,
And thy gay smiles no anodyne.
Give me thy hand, and hush awhile,
And turn those limpid eyes on mine,   10
And let me read there, love! thy inmost soul.

Alas! is even love too weak
To unlock the heart, and let it speak?
Are even lovers powerless to reveal
To one another what indeed they feel?
I knew the mass of men conceal'd
Their thoughts, for fear that if revealed
They would by other men be met
With blank indifference, or with blame reproved;
I knew they lived and moved   20
Trick'd in disguises, alien to the rest
Of men, and alien to themselves – and yet
The same heart beats in every human breast!

But we, my love! – doth a like spell benumb
Our hearts, our voices? must we too be dumb?

Ah! well for us, if even we,
Even for a moment, can get free
Our heart, and have our lips unchain'd;
For that which seals them hath been deep-ordain'd!

Fate, which foresaw   30
How frivolous a baby man would be –
By what distractions he would be possess'd,
How he would pour himself in every strife,
And well-nigh change his own identity –
That it might keep from his capricious play
His genuine self, and force him to obey
Even in his own despite his being's law,
Bade through the deep recesses of our breast
The unregarded river of our life
Pursue with indiscernible flow its way;   40
And that we should not see
The buried stream, and seem to be
Eddying at large in blind uncertainty,
Though driving on with it eternally.

But often, in the world's most crowded streets,
But often, in the din of strife,
There rises an unspeakable desire
After the knowledge of our buried life;
A thirst to spend our fire and restless force
In tracking out our true, original course;   50
A longing to inquire
Into the mystery of this heart which beats
So wild, so deep in us – to know
Whence our lives come and where they go.
And many a man in his own breast then delves,
But deep enough, alas! none ever mines.
And we have been on many thousand lines,
And we have shown, on each, spirit and power;
But hardly have we, for one little hour,
Been on our own line, have we been ourselves   60
Hardly had skill to utter one of all
The nameless feelings that course through our breast,
But they course on for ever unexpress'd.
And long we try in vain to speak and act
Our hidden self, and what we say and do

Is eloquent, is well – but 'tis not true!
And then we will no more be rack'd
With inward striving, and demand
Of all the thousand nothings of the hour
Their stupefying power;   70
Ah yes, and they benumb us at our call!
Yet still, from time to time, vague and forlorn,
From the soul's subterranean depth upborne
As from an infinitely distant land,
Come airs, and floating echoes, and convey
A melancholy into all our day.
Only – but this is rare –
When a beloved hand is laid in ours,
When, jaded with the rush and glare
Of the interminable hours,   80
Our eyes can in another's eyes read clear,
When our world-deafen'd ear
Is by the tones of a loved voice caress'd –
A bolt is shot back somewhere in our breast,
And a lost pulse of feeling stirs again.
The eye sinks inward, and the heart lies plain,
And what we mean, we say, and what we would, we know.
A man becomes aware of his life's flow,
And hears its winding murmur; and he sees
The meadows where it glides, the sun, the breeze.   90

And there arrives a lull in the hot race
Wherein he doth for ever chase
That flying and elusive shadow, rest.
An air of coolness plays upon his face,
And an unwonted calm pervades his breast.
And then he thinks he knows
The hills where his life rose,
And the sea where it goes.

Stanzas from the Grande Chartreuse

Written between 7 Sept. 1851 and March 1855, pub. *Fraser's Magazine* April 1855, repr. *1867*. A. visited the Grande Chartreuse with his wife on their honeymoon Sunday 7 Sept. 1851. With the stanza form cp. 'Isolation. To Marguerite', p. 25 above. For the influence of Carlyle, and for T.S. Eliot on the poem voicing a moment of historic doubt 'recorded by its most representative mind', see Introduction p. xxviii above.

Through Alpine meadows soft-suffused
With rain, where thick the crocus blows,
Past the dark forges long disused,
The mule-track from Saint Laurent goes.
The bridge is cross'd, and slow we ride,
Through forest, up the mountain-side.

The autumnal evening darkens round,
The wind is up, and drives the rain;
While, hark! far down, with strangled sound
Doth the Dead Guier's stream complain,   10
Where that wet smoke, among the woods,
Over his boiling cauldron broods.

Swift rush the spectral vapours white
Past limestone scars with ragged pines,
Showing – then blotting from our sight! –
Halt – through the cloud-drift something shines!
High in the valley, wet and drear,
The huts of Courrerie appear.

Strike leftward! cries our guide; and higher
Mounts up the stony forest-way.   20
At last the encircling trees retire;
Look! through the showery twilight grey
What pointed roofs are these advance? –
A palace of the Kings of France?

Approach, for what we seek is here!
Alight, and sparely sup, and wait
For rest in this outbuilding near;
Then cross the sward and reach that gate.
Knock; pass the wicket! Thou art come
To the Carthusians' world-famed home.   30

The silent courts, where night and day
Into their stone-carved basins cold

The splashing icy fountains play –
The humid corridors behold!
Where, ghostlike in the deepening night,
Cowl'd forms brush by in gleaming white.

The chapel, where no organ's peal
Invests the stern and naked prayer –
With penitential cries they kneel
And wrestle; rising then, with bare   40
And white uplifted faces stand,
Passing the Host from hand to hand;

Each takes, and then his visage wan
Is buried in his cowl once more.
The cells! – the suffering Son of Man
Upon the wall – the knee-worn floor –
And where they sleep, that wooden bed,
Which shall their coffin be, when dead!

The library, where tract and tome
Not to feed priestly pride are there,   50
To hymn the conquering march of Rome,
Nor yet to amuse, as ours are!
They paint of souls the inner strife,
Their drops of blood, their death in life.

The garden, overgrown – yet mild,
See, fragrant herbs are flowering there!
Strong children of the Alpine wild
Whose culture is the brethren's care;
Of human tasks their only one,
And cheerful works beneath the sun.   60

Those halls, too, destined to contain
Each its own pilgrim-host of old,
From England, Germany, or Spain –
All are before me! I behold
The House, the Brotherhood austere!
–And what am I, that I am here?

For rigorous teachers seized my youth,
And purged its faith, and trimm'd its fire,
Show'd me the high, white star of Truth,
There bade me gaze, and there aspire.   70

Even now their whispers pierce the gloom:
What dost thou in this living tomb?

Forgive me, masters of the mind!
At whose behest I long ago
So much unlearnt, so much resign'd –
I come not here to be your foe!
I seek these anchorites, not in ruth,
To curse and to deny your truth;

Not as their friend, or child, I speak!
But as, on some far northern strand,   80
Thinking of his own Gods, a Greek
In pity and mournful awe might stand
Before some fallen Runic stone –
For both were faiths, and both are gone.

Wandering between two worlds, one dead,
The other powerless to be born,
With nowhere yet to rest my head,
Like these, on earth I wait forlorn.
Their faith, my tears, the world deride –
I come to shed them at their side.   90

Oh, hide me in your gloom profound,
Ye solemn seats of holy pain!
Take me, cowl'd forms, and fence me round,
Till I possess my soul again;
Till free my thoughts before me roll,
Not chafed by hourly false control!

For the world cries your faith is now
But a dead time's exploded dream;
My melancholy, sciolists say,
Is a pass'd mode, an outworn theme –   100
As if the world had ever had
A faith, or sciolists been sad!

Ah, if it *be* pass'd, take away,
At least, the restlessness, the pain;
Be man henceforth no more a prey
To these out-dated stings again!
The nobleness of grief is gone –
Ah, leave us not the fret alone!

But – if you cannot give us ease –
Last of the race of them who grieve   110
Here leave us to die out with these
Last of the people who believe!
Silent, while years engrave the brow;
Silent – the best are silent now.

Achilles ponders in his tent,
The kings of modern thought are dumb;
Silent they are, though not content,
And wait to see the future come.
They have the grief men had of yore,
But they contend and cry no more.   120

Our fathers water'd with their tears
This sea of time whereon we sail,
Their voices were in all men's ears
Who pass'd within their puissant hail.
Still the same ocean round us raves,
But we stand mute, and watch the waves.

For what avail'd it, all the noise
And outcry of the former men? –
Say, have their sons achieved more joys,
Say, is life lighter now than then?   130
The sufferers died, they left their pain –
The pangs which tortured them remain.

What helps it now, that Byron bore,
With haughty scorn which mock'd the smart,
Through Europe to the Aetolian shore
The pageant of his bleeding heart?
That thousands counted every groan,
And Europe made his woe her own?

What boots it, Shelley! that the breeze
Carried thy lovely wail away,   140
Musical through Italian trees
Which fringe thy soft blue Spezzian bay?
Inheritors of thy distress
Have restless hearts one throb the less?

Or are we easier, to have read,
O Obermann! the sad, stern page,

Which tells us how thou hidd'st thy head
From the fierce tempest of thine age
In the lone brakes of Fontainebleau,
Or chalets near the Alpine snow?   150

Ye slumber in your silent grave! –
The world, which for an idle day
Grace to your mood of sadness gave,
Long since hath flung her weeds away.
The eternal trifler breaks your spell;
But we – we learnt your lore too well!

Years hence, perhaps, may dawn an age,
More fortunate, alas! than we,
Which without hardness will be sage,
And gay without frivolity.   160
Sons of the world, oh, speed those years;
But, while we wait, allow our tears!

Allow them! We admire with awe
The exulting thunder of your race;
You give the universe your law,
You triumph over time and space!
Your pride of life, your tireless powers,
We laud them, but they are not ours.

We are like children rear'd in shade
Beneath some old-world abbey wall,   170
Forgotten in a forest-glade,
And secret from the eyes of all.
Deep, deep the greenwood round them waves,
Their abbey, and its close of graves!

But, where the road runs near the stream,
Oft through the trees they catch a glance
Of passing troops in the sun's beam –
Pennon, and plume, and flashing lance!
Forth to the world these soldiers fare,
To life, to cities, and to war!   180

And through the wood, another way,
Faint bugle-notes from far are borne,
Where hunters gather, staghounds bay,
Round some fair forest-lodge at morn.

Gay dames are there, in sylvan green;
Laughter and cries – those notes between!

The banners flashing through the trees
Make their blood dance and chain their eyes
That bugle-music on the breeze
Arrests them with a charm'd surprise.   190
Banner by turns and bugle woo:
Ye shy recluses, follow too!

O children, what do ye reply? –
'Action and pleasure, will ye roam
Through these secluded dells to cry
And call us? – but too late ye come!
Too late for us your call ye blow,
Whose bent was taken long ago.

'Long since we pace this shadow'd nave;
We watch those yellow tapers shine,   200
Emblems of hope over the grave,
In the high altar's depth divine;
The organ carries to our ear
Its accents of another sphere.

'Fenced early in this cloistral round
Of reverie, of shade, of prayer,
How should we grow in other ground?
How can we flower in foreign air?
– Pass, banners, pass, and bugles, cease;
And leave our desert to its peace!'   210

From Sohrab and Rustum

Composed Dec. 1852–1 May 1853; copied out by Aug. and pub. Nov. 1853. The whole poem is written in keeping with A.'s principles in the 1853 preface (p. 115 below), especially in its consciously elevating subject-matter (story from Sir J. Malcolm's *History of Persia* (1815), and its careful attention to form and structure. On completing it, A. thought it 'by far the best thing I have done' (L i. 130) and in Nov. 1853 wrote, 'Homer *animates* – Shakespeare *animates* – in its poor way Sohrab and Rustum *animates* – the Gipsy Scholar [p. 93 below] at best awakens a pleasing melancholy. But this is not what we want' (*CL* 146); but he had confessed, after copying it out Aug. 1853, 'I like it less' (*CL* 139). Its critical reception was mixed,

notably over the extensive and frequent use of epic similes; today it is generally felt
that such success as it has depends on the pressure of subjective feeling which it was
A.'s purpose to subdue: '... at least a shadowy personal significance. The strong son is
slain by the mightier father; and in the end, Sohrab draws his father's spear from his
own side to let out his life ... We watch A. in his later youth and we must wonder if he is
not, in a psychical sense, doing the same thing' (Trilling 134–5). See further
Introduction p. xxv above.
The coda, on the River Oxus, given below, is one of A.'s most famous passages. Source
is Burnes's *Travels* ii. 186–7 (see 'The Sick King ...', p. 5 above) and for one
interpretative commentary see Maud Bodkin, *Archetypal Patterns in Poetry* 1934, 66
(1934), ending,
'... the poet or his reader, dreaming on the river that breaks at last into the free ocean,
sees in this image his own life and death ... in accordance with a deep organic need for
release from conflict and tension'.

...

But the majestic river floated on,
Out of the mist and hum of that low land,
Into the frosty starlight, and there moved,
Rejoicing, through the hush'd Chorasmian waste,
Under the solitary moon; – he flow'd
Right for the polar star, past Orgunjè,
Brimming, and bright, and large; then sands begin
To hem his watery march, and dam his streams,
And split his currents; that for many a league
The shorn and parcell'd Oxus strains along   10
Through beds of sand and matted rushy isles –
Oxus, forgetting the bright speed he had
In his high mountain-cradle in Pamere,
A foil'd circuitous wanderer – till at last
The long'd-for dash of waves is heard, and wide
His luminous home of waters opens, bright
And tranquil, from whose floor the new-bathed stars
Emerge, and shine upon the Aral Sea.

The Scholar-Gipsy

Written 1852–3; pub. *1853*. Story from Joseph Glanvil, *The Vanity of Dogmatising* (1661), bought by A. 1844. For A.'s and Clough's interest in the 'scholar-gipsy' while at Oxford see 'Thyrsis' ll. 28–30, p. 103 below, and for the dating, A.'s summary of the story and mixed feelings about the poem, together with various critical commentaries, *Poems* 331–3; see also Introduction p. xxiv above. The stanzaic structure is affected by Keats's 'Ode to a Nightingale' and the presenting of contrasted ways of life by Gray's 'Elegy written in a Country Church-yard'.

Go, for they call you, shepherd, from the hill;
  Go, shepherd, and untie the wattled cotes!
   No longer leave thy wistful flock unfed,
  Nor let thy bawling fellows rack their throats,
   Nor the cropp'd herbage shoot another head.
   But when the fields are still,
  And the tired men and dogs all gone to rest,
   And only the white sheep are sometimes seen
   Cross and recross the strips of moon-blanch'd green,
Come, shepherd, and again begin the quest!   10

Here, where the reaper was at work of late –
  In this high field's dark corner, where he leaves
   His coat, his basket, and his earthen cruse,
  And in the sun all morning binds the sheaves,
   Then here, at noon, comes back his stores to use –
   Here will I sit and wait,
  While to my ear from uplands far away
   The bleating of the folded flocks is borne,
   With distant cries of reapers in the corn –
All the live murmur of a summer's day.   20

Screen'd is this nook o'er the high, half-reap'd field,
  And here till sun-down, shepherd! will I be.
   Through the thick corn the scarlet poppies peep,
  And round green roots and yellowing stalks I see
   Pale pink convolvulus in tendrils creep;
   And air-swept lindens yield
  Their scent, and rustle down their perfumed showers
   Of bloom on the bent grass where I am laid,
   And bower me from the August sun with shade;
And the eye travels down to Oxford's towers.   30

And near me on the grass lies Glanvil's book –
   Come, let me read the oft-read tale again!
     The story of the Oxford scholar poor,
  Of pregnant parts and quick inventive brain,
     Who, tired of knocking at preferment's door,
       One summer-morn forsook
  His friends, and went to learn the gipsy-lore,
  And roam'd the world with that wild brotherhood,
    And came, as most men deem'd, to little good,
But came to Oxford and his friends no more.   40

But once, years after, in the country-lanes,
   Two scholars, whom at college erst he knew,
     Met him, and of his way of life enquired;
  Whereat he answer'd, that the gipsy-crew,
     His mates, had arts to rule as they desired
       The workings of men's brains,
  And they can bind them to what thoughts they will.
    'And I,' he said, 'the secret of their art,
    When fully learn'd, will to the world impart;
But it needs heaven-sent moments for this skill.'   50

This said, he left them, and return'd no more. –
   But rumours hung about the country-side,
     That the lost Scholar long was seen to stray,
  Seen by rare glimpses, pensive and tongue-tied,
     In hat of antique shape, and cloak of grey,
       The same the gipsies wore.
  Shepherds had met him on the Hurst in spring;
    At some lone alehouse in the Berkshire moors,
    On the warm ingle-bench, the smock-frock'd boors
Had found him seated at their entering,   60

But, 'mid their drink and clatter, he would fly.
   And I myself seem half to know thy looks,
     And put the shepherds, wanderer! on thy trace;
  And boys who in lone wheatfields scare the rooks
     I ask if thou hast pass'd their quiet place;
       Or in my boat I lie
  Moor'd to the cool bank in the summer-heats,
    'Mid wide grass meadows which the sunshine fills,
    And watch the warm, green-muffled Cumner hills,

And wonder if thou haunt'st their shy retreats.   70

For most, I know, thou lov'st retired ground!
   Thee at the ferry Oxford riders blithe,
      Returning home on summer-nights, have met
   Crossing the stripling Thames at Bab-lock-hithe,
      Trailing in the cool stream thy fingers wet,
         As the punt's rope chops round;
   And leaning backward in a pensive dream,
      And fostering in thy lap a heap of flowers
      Pluck'd in shy fields and distant Wychwood bowers,
   And thine eyes resting on the moonlit stream.   80

And then they land, and thou are seen no more! –
   Maidens, who from the distant hamlets come
      To dance around the Fyfield elm in May,
   Oft through the darkening fields have seen thee roam,
      Or cross a stile into the public way.
         Oft thou hast given them store
Of flowers – the frail-leaf'd, white anemony,
   Dark bluebells drench'd with dews of summer eves,
   And purple orchises with spotted leaves –
But none hath words she can report of thee.   90

And, above Godstow Bridge, when hay-time's here
   In June, and many a scythe in sunshine flames,
      Men who through those wide fields of breezy grass
   Where black-wing'd swallows haunt the glittering Thames,
      To bathe in the abandon'd lasher pass,
         Have often pass'd thee near
Sitting upon the river bank o'ergrown;
   Mark'd thine outlandish garb, thy figure spare,
   Thy dark vague eyes, and soft abstracted air –
But, when they came from bathing, thou wast gone!   100

At some lone homestead in the Cumner hills,
   Where at her open door the housewife darns,
      Thou hast been seen, or hanging on a gate
To watch the threshers in the mossy barns.
      Children, who early range these slopes and late
         For cresses from the rills,
Have known thee eyeing, all an April-day,
   The springing pastures and the feeding kine;

And mark'd thee, when the stars come out and shine,
    Through the long dewy grass move slow away.   110

In autumn, on the skirts of Bagley Wood –
    Where most the gipsies by the turf-edged way
        Pitch their smoked tents, and every bush you see
    With scarlet patches tagg'd and shreds of grey,
            Above the forest-ground called Thessaly –
                The blackbird, picking food,
        Sees thee, nor stops his meal, nor fears at all;
            So often has he known thee past him stray,
            Rapt, twirling in thy hand a wither'd spray,
    And waiting for the spark from heaven to fall.   120

And once, in winter, on the causeway chill
    Where home through flooded fields foot-travellers go,
        Have I not pass'd thee on the wooden bridge,
    Wrapt in thy cloak and battling with the snow,
            Thy face tow'rd Hinksey and its wintry ridge?
                And thou hast climb'd the hill,
        And gain'd the white brow of the Cumner range;
            Turn'd once to watch, while thick the snowflakes fall,
            The line of festal light in Christ-Church hall –
    Then sought thy straw in some sequester'd grange.   130

But what – I dream! Two hundred years are flown
    Since first thy story ran through Oxford halls,
        And the grave Glanvil did the tale inscribe
    That thou wert wander'd from the studious walls
            To learn strange arts, and join a gipsy-tribe;
                And thou from earth art gone
        Long since, and in some quiet churchyard laid –
            Some country-nook, where o'er thy unknown grave
            Tall grasses and white flowering nettles wave,
    Under a dark, red-fruited yew-tree's shade.   140

– No, no, thou hast not felt the lapse of hours!
    For what wears out the life of mortal men?
        'Tis that from change to change their being rolls;
    'Tis that repeated shocks, again, again,
            Exhaust the energy of strongest souls
                And numb the elastic powers.
        Till having used our nerves with bliss and teen,

And tired upon a thousand schemes our wit,
  To the just-pausing Genius we remit
Our worn-out life, and are – what we have been.   150

Thou hast not lived, why should'st thou perish, so?
  Thou hadst *one* aim, *one* business, *one* desire;
    Else wert thou long since number'd with the dead!
  Else hadst thou spent, like other men, thy fire!
    The generations of thy peers are fled,
      And we ourselves shall go;
  But thou possessest an immortal lot,
    And we imagine thee exempt from age
    And living as thou liv'st on Glanvil's page,
Because thou hadst – what we, alas! have not.   160

For early didst thou leave the world, with powers
  Fresh, undiverted to the world without,
    Firm to their mark, not spent on other things;
  Free from the sick fatigue, the languid doubt,
    Which much to have tried, in much been baffled, brings.
      O life unlike to ours!
  Who fluctuate idly without term or scope,
    Of whom each strives, nor knows for what he strives,
    And each half lives a hundred different lives;
Who wait like thee, but not, like thee, in hope.   170

Thou waitest for the spark from heaven! and we,
  Light half-believers of our casual creeds,
    Who never deeply felt, nor clearly will'd,
  Whose insight never has borne fruit in deeds,
    Whose vague resolves never have been fulfill'd;
      For whom each year we see
  Breeds new beginnings, disappointments new;
    Who hesitate and falter life away,
    And lose to-morrow the ground won to-day –
Ah! do not we, wanderer! await it too?   180

Yes, we await it! – but it still delays,
  And then we suffer! and amongst us one,
    Who most has suffer'd, takes dejectedly
      His seat upon the intellectual throne;
    And all his store of sad experience he
  Lays bare of wretched days;

Tells us his misery's birth and growth and signs,
    And how the dying spark of hope was fed,
      And how the breast was soothed, and how the head,
And all his hourly varied anodynes.   190

This for our wisest! and we others pine,
    And wish the long unhappy dream would end,
      And waive all claim to bliss, and try to bear;
With close-lipp'd patience for our only friend,
      Sad patience, too near neighbour to despair –
        But none has hope like thine!
Thou through the fields and through the woods dost stray,
    Roaming the country-side, a truant boy,
    Nursing thy project in unclouded joy,
And every doubt long blown by time away.   200

O born in days when wits were fresh and clear,
    And life ran gaily as the sparkling Thames;
      Before this strange disease of modern life,
With its sick hurry, its divided aims,
      Its heads o'ertax'd, its palsied hearts, was rife –
        Fly hence, our contact fear!
Still fly, plunge deeper in the bowering wood!
    Averse, as Dido did with gesture stern
    From her false friend's approach in Hades turn,
Wave us away, and keep thy solitude!   210

Still nursing the unconquerable hope,
    Still clutching the inviolable shade,
      With a free, onward impulse brushing through,
By night, the silver'd branches of the glade –
      Far on the forest-skirts, where none pursue,
        On some mild pastoral slope
Emerge, and resting on the moonlit pales
    Freshen thy flowers as in former years
    With dew, or listen with enchanted ears,
From the dark dingles, to the nightingales!   220

But fly our paths, our feverish contact fly!
    For strong the infection of our mental strife,
      Which, though it gives no bliss, yet spoils for rest;
        And we should win thee from thy own fair life,
    Like us distracted, and like us unblest.

Soon, soon thy cheer would die,
Thy hopes grow timorous, and unfix'd thy powers,
    And thy clear aims be cross and shifting made;
    And then thy glad perennial youth would fade,
Fade, and grow old at last, and die like ours.   230

Then fly our greetings, fly our speech and smiles!
    – As some grave Tyrian trader, from the sea,
        Descried at sunrise an emerging prow
    Lifting the cool-hair'd creepers stealthily,
        The fringes of a southward-facing brow
            Among the Aegaean isles;
    And saw the merry Grecian coaster come,
        Freighted with amber grapes, and Chian wine,
        Green, bursting figs, and tunnies steep'd in brine –
    And knew the intruders on his ancient home,   240

The young light-hearted masters of the waves –
    And snatch'd his rudder, and shook out more sail;
        And day and night held on indignantly
    O'er the blue Midland waters with the gale,
        Betwixt the Syrtes and soft Sicily,
            To where the Atlantic raves
    Outside the western straits; and unbent sails
        There, where down cloudy cliffs, through sheets of foam,
        Shy traffickers, the dark Iberians come;
    And on the beach undid his corded bales.   250

Requiescat

Written (?) 1848–53; pub. 1853. The identity of the woman is unknown. Perhaps an exercise in the manner of Wordsworth's 'A Slumber did my spirit seal' (*Poems* 346). The situation of the girl forced to play her part in a busy worldly life she detests is from Victorian stock. See, e.g., Mary Claude's *Twilight Thoughts: Stories for Children and Child-lovers* (1848), 'I have seen a maiden decked in gold and jewels in the lighted hall – her sparkling eye and crimson cheek, her light laughter and her witty words, all but masks to hide the anguish of her heart ... I saw her again in her lovely chamber, pale and drooping, her bright smiles thrown off with her glittering jewels ... I knew she was dying for the love she had not, when I heard her murmured prayer, "My God, release me, for my life is all a lie"' ('An Angel's Tears', *Twilight Thoughts* (1848)). A. wrote a preface for the American edn. (1887) of this book (*CPW* xi. 120–1).

Strew on her roses, roses,
    And never a spray of yew!
In quiet she reposes;
    Ah, would that I did too!

Her mirth the world required;
    She bathed it in smiles of glee.
But her heart was tired, tired,
    And now they let her be.

Her life was turning, turning,
    In mazes of heat and sound.
But for peace her soul was yearning,   10
    And now peace laps her round.

Her cabin'd, ample spirit,
    It flutter'd and fail'd for breath.
To-night it doth inherit
    The vasty hall of death.

From Haworth Churchyard

APRIL 1855

Written in April 1855 shortly after Charlotte Brontë's death (31 March); pub. *Fraser's Magazine*, May 1855; repr. with revisions 1877. The first part (ll. 1–46), omitted here, salutes Harriet Martineau, thought at the time to be mortally ill. A. met Charlotte Brontë and Harriet Martineau at Fox How 21 Dec. 1850 (*L* i. 13). With A.'s 'pindarics' cp. 'The Youth of Nature', p. 77 above.

...
– Turn we next to the dead.
– How shall we honour the young,
The ardent, the gifted? how mourn?
Console we cannot, her ear
Is deaf. Far northward from here,
In a churchyard high 'mid the moors
Of Yorkshire, a little earth
Stops it for ever to praise.

Where, behind Keighley, the road
Up to the heart of the moors   10
Between heath-clad showery hills
Runs, and colliers' carts
Poach the deep ways coming down,
And a rough, grimed race have their homes –
There on its slope is built
The moorland town. But the church
Stands on the crest of the hill,
Lonely and bleak; – at its side
The parsonage-house and the graves.

Strew with laurel the grave   20
Of the early-dying! Alas,
Early she goes on the path
To the silent country, and leaves
Half her laurels unwon,
Dying too soon! – yet green
Laurels she had, and a course
Short, but redoubled by fame.

And not friendless, and not
Only with strangers to meet,

Faces ungreeting and cold, 30
Thou, O mourn'd one, to-day
Enterest the house of the grave!
Those of thy blood, whom thou lov'dst,
Have preceded thee – young,
Loving, a sisterly band;
Some in art, some in gift
Inferior – all in fame.
They, like friends, shall receive
This comer, greet her with joy;
Welcome the sister, the friend; 40
Hear with delight of thy fame!

Round thee they lie – the grass
Blows from their graves to thy own!
She, whose genius, though not
Puissant like thine, was yet
Sweet and graceful; – and she
(How shall I sing her?) whose soul
Knew no fellow for might,
Passion, vehemence, grief,
Daring, since Byron died, 50
That world-famed son of fire – she, who sank
Baffled, unknown, self-consumed;
Whose too bold dying song
Stirr'd, like a clarion-blast, my soul.

Of one, too, I have heard,
A brother – sleeps he here?
Of all that gifted race
Not the least gifted; young,
Unhappy, eloquent – the child
Of many hopes, of many tears. 60
O boy, if here thou sleep'st, sleep well!
On thee too did the Muse
Bright in thy cradle smile;
But some dark shadow came
(I know not what) and interposed.

Sleep, O cluster of friends,
Sleep! – or only when May,
Brought by the west-wind, returns

Back to your native heaths,
And the plover is heard on the moors,   70
Yearly awake to behold
The opening summer, the sky,
The shining moorland – to hear
The drowsy bee, as of old,
Hum o'er the thyme, the grouse
Call from the heather in bloom!
Sleep, or only for this
Break your united repose!

EPILOGUE

So I sang; but the Muse,
Shaking her head, took the harp –   80
Stern interrupted my strain,
Angrily smote on the chords.

April showers
Rush o'er the Yorkshire moors.
Stormy, through driving mist,
Loom the blurr'd hills; the rain
Lashes the newly-made grave.

Unquiet souls!
– In the dark fermentation of earth,
In the never idle workshop of nature,   90
In the eternal movement,
Ye shall find yourselves again!

Thyrsis

A MONODY, *to commemorate the author's friend,*
ARTHUR HUGH CLOUGH, *who died at Florence, 1861*

Projected 1862–3, written 1864–5, completed Jan. 1866; pub. *Macmillan's Magazine*
April 1866; repr. 1860. Thyrsis is the name of the shepherd in Virgil's *Eclogues* vii (cp.
'The Scholar-Gipsy' ll. 1–10, pp. 107–8 above, and A.'s *n.* 1867 'Throughout the
Poem there is reference to another piece, "The Scholar-Gipsy"'); also found in
Theocritus (*Idylls* i), much read by A. 1864–6 (his 'Lament for Bion' strongly
influenced the poem). The heading intentionally echoes that of Milton's 'Lycidas'. For
details of composition and the poem's warm reception at the time see *Poems* 496–8.

How changed is here each spot man makes or fills!
   In the two Hinkseys nothing keeps the same;
      The village street its haunted mansion lacks,
And from the sign is gone Sibylla's name,
      And from the roofs the twisted chimney-stacks –
         Are ye too changed, ye hills?
See, 'tis no foot of unfamiliar men
      To-night from Oxford up your pathway strays!
      Here came I often, often, in old days –
Thyrsis and I; we still had Thyrsis then.   10
Runs it not here, the track by Childsworth Farm,
      Past the high wood, to where the elm-tree crowns
      The hill behind whose ridge the sunset flames?
The signal-elm, that looks on Ilsley Downs,
      The Vale, the three lone weirs, the youthful Thames;
         This winter-eve is warm,
Humid the air! leafless, yet soft as spring,
      The tender purple spray on copse and briers!
      And that sweet city with her dreaming spires,
She needs not June for beauty's heightening,   20

Lovely all times she lies, lovely to-night! –
      Only, methinks, some loss of habit's power
      Befalls me wandering through this upland dim.
Once pass'd I blindfold here, at any hour;
      Now seldom come I, since I came with him.
         That single elm-tree bright
Against the west – I miss it! is it gone?
      We prized it dearly; while it stood, we said,

Our friend, the Gipsy-Scholar, was not dead;
While the tree lived, he in these fields lived on.   30

Too rare, too rare, grow now my visits here,
    But once I knew each field, each flower, each stick;
        And with the country-folk acquaintance made
By barn in threshing-time, by new-built rick.
        Here, too, our shepherd-pipes we first assay'd.
            Ah me! this many a year
My pipe is lost, my shepherd's holiday!
        Needs must I lose them, needs with heavy heart
        Into the world and wave of men depart;
But Thyrsis of his own will went away.   40

It irk'd him to be here, he could not rest.
    He loved each simple joy the country yields,
        He loved his mates; but yet he could not keep,
For that a shadow lour'd on the fields,
        Here with the shepherds and the silly sheep.
            Some life of men unblest
He knew, which made him droop, and fill'd his head.
        He went; his piping took a troubled sound
        Of storms that rage outside our happy ground;
He could not wait their passing, he is dead.   50

So, some tempestuous morn in early June,
    When the year's primal burst of bloom is o'er,
        Before the roses and the longest day –
When garden-walks and all the grassy floor
        With blossoms red and white of fallen May
            And chestnut-flowers are strewn –
So have I heard the cuckoo's parting cry,
        From the wet field, through the vext garden-trees,
        Come with the volleying rain and tossing breeze:
The bloom is gone, and with the bloom go I!   60

Too quick despairer, wherefore wilt thou go?
    Soon will the high Midsummer pomps come on,
        Soon will the musk carnations break and swell,
Soon shall we have gold-dusted snapdragon,
        Sweet-William with his homely cottage-smell,
            And stocks in fragrant blow;
Roses that down the alleys shine afar,

And open, jasmine-muffled lattices,
   And groups under the dreaming garden-trees,
      And the full moon, and the white evening-star.   70

He harkens not! light comer, he is flown!
   What matters it? next year he will return,
      And we shall have him in the sweet spring-days,
   With whitening hedges, and uncrumpling fern,
      And blue-bells trembling by the forest-ways,
         And scent of hay new-mown.
   But Thyrsis never more we swains shall see;
      See him come back, and cut a smoother reed,
      And blow a strain the world at last shall heed –
   For Time, not Corydon, hath conquer'd thee!   80

Alack, for Corydon no rival now! –
   But when Sicilian shepherds lost a mate,
      Some good survivor with his flute would go,
   Piping a ditty sad for Bion's fate;
      And cross the unpermitted ferry's flow,
         And relax Pluto's brow,
   And make leap up with joy the beauteous head
      Of Proserpine, among whose crowned hair
      Are flowers first open'd on Sicilian air,
   And flute his friend, like Orpheus, from the dead.   90

O easy access to the hearer's grace
   When Dorian shepherds sang to Proserpine!
      For she herself had trod Sicilian fields,
   She knew the Dorian water's gush divine,
      She knew each lily white which Enna yields,
         Each rose with blushing face;
   She loved the Dorian pipe, the Dorian strain.
      But ah, of our poor Thames she never heard!
      Her foot the Cumner cowslips never stirr'd;
   And we should tease her with our plaint in vain!   100

Well! wind-dispersed and vain the words will be,
   Yet, Thyrsis, let me give my grief its hour
      In the old haunt, and find our tree-topp'd hill!
   Who, if not I, for questing here hath power?
      I know the wood which hides the daffodil,
         I know the Fyfield tree,

I know what white, what purple fritillaries
 The grassy harvest of the river-fields,
  Above by Ensham, down by Sandford, yields,
And what sedged brooks are Thames's tributaries;   110

I know these slopes; who knows them if not I? –
 But many a dingle on the loved hill-side,
  With thorns once studded, old, white-blossom'd trees,
 Where thick the cowslips grew, and far descried
  High tower'd the spikes of purple orchises,
   Hath since our day put by
 The coronals of that forgotten time;
  Down each green bank hath gone the ploughboy's team,
 And only in the hidden brookside gleam
Primroses, orphans of the flowery prime.   120

Where is the girl, who by the boatman's door,
 Above the locks, above the boating throng,
  Unmoor'd our skiff when through the Wytham flats,
 Red loosestrife and blond meadow-sweet among
  And darting swallows and light water-gnats,
   We track'd the shy Thames shore?
 Where are the mowers, who, as the tiny swell
  Of our boat passing heaved the river-grass,
 Stood with suspended scythe to see us pass? –
They all are gone, and thou art gone as well!   130

Yes, thou art gone! and round me too the night
 In ever-nearing circle weaves her shade.
  I see her veil draw soft across the day,
 I feel her slowly chilling breath invade
  The cheek grown thin, the brown hair sprent with grey;
   I feel her finger light
 Laid pausefully upon life's headlong train; –
  The foot less prompt to meet the morning dew,
 The heart less bounding at emotion new,
And hope, once crush'd, less quick to spring again.   140

And long the way appears, which seem'd so short
 To the less practised eye of sanguine youth;
  And high the mountain-tops, in cloudy air,
 The mountain-tops where is the throne of Truth,
  Tops in life's morning-sun so bright and bare!

Unbreachable the fort
Of the long-batter'd world uplifts its wall;
    And strange and vain the earthly turmoil grows,
    And near and real the charm of thy repose,
And night as welcome as a friend would fall.   150

But hush! the upland hath a sudden loss
    Of quiet! – Look, adown the dusk hill-side,
        A troop of Oxford hunters going home,
    As in old days, jovial and talking, ride!
        From hunting with the Berkshire hounds they come
            Quick! let me fly, and cross
    Into yon farther field! – 'Tis done; and see,
        Back'd by the sunset, which doth glorify
        The orange and pale violet evening-sky,
Bare on its lonely ridge, the Tree! the Tree!   160

I take the omen! Eve lets down her veil,
    The white fog creeps from bush to bush about,
        The west unflushes, the high stars grow bright,
    And in the scatter'd farms the lights come out.
        I cannot reach the signal-tree to-night,
            Yet, happy omen, hail!
    Hear it from thy broad lucent Arno-vale
        (For there thine earth-forgetting eyelids keep
        The morningless and unawakening sleep
Under the flowery oleanders pale),   170

Hear it, O Thyrsis, still our tree is there! –
    Ah, vain! These English fields, this upland dim,
        These brambles pale with mist engarlanded,
    That lone, sky-pointing tree, are not for him;
        To a boon southern country he is fled,
            And now in happier air,
    Wandering with the great Mother's train divine
        (And purer or more subtle soul than thee,
        I trow, the mighty Mother doth not see)
Within a folding of the Apennine,   180

Thou hearest the immortal chants of old! –
    Putting his sickle to the perilous grain
        In the hot cornfield of the Phrygian king,
    For thee the Lityerses-song again

Young Daphnis with his silver voice doth sing;
   Sings his Sicilian fold,
His sheep, his hapless love, his blinded eyes –
   And how a call celestial round him rang,
   And heavenward from the fountain-brink he sprang,
And all the marvel of the golden skies.   190

There thou art gone, and me thou leavest here
   Sole in these fields! yet will I not despair.
      Despair I will not, while I yet descry
   Neath the mild canopy of English air
      That lonely tree against the western sky.
         Still, still these slopes, 'tis clear,
   Our Gipsy-Scholar haunts, outliving thee!
      Fields where soft sheep from cages pull the hay,
      Woods with anemonies in flower till May,
Know him a wanderer still; then why not me?   200

A fugitive and gracious light he seeks,
   Shy to illumine; and I seek it too.
      This does not come with houses or with gold,
   With place, with honour, and a flattering crew;
      'Tis not in the world's market bought and sold –
         But the smooth-slipping weeks
   Drop by, and leave its seeker still untired;
      Out of the heed of mortals he is gone,
      He wends unfollow'd, he must house alone;
Yet on he fares, by his own heart inspired.   210

Thou too, O Thyrsis, on like quest wast bound;
   Thou wanderedst with me for a little hour!
      Men gave thee nothing; but this happy quest,
   If men esteem'd thee feeble, gave thee power,
      If men procured thee trouble, gave thee rest.
         And this rude Cumner ground,
   Its fir-topped Hurst, its farms, its quiet fields,
      Here cam'st thou in thy jocund youthful time,
      Here was thine height of strength, thy golden prime
And still the haunt beloved a virtue yields.   220

What though the music of thy rustic flute
   Kept not for long its happy, country tone;
      Lost it too soon, and learnt a stormy note

Of men contention-tost, of men who groan,
    Which task'd thy pipe too sore, and tired thy throat –
        It fail'd, and thou wast mute!
Yet hadst thou alway visions of our light,
    And long with men of care thou couldst not stay,
    And soon thy foot resumed its wandering way,
Left human haunt, and on alone till night.   230

Too rare, too rare, grow now my visits here!
    'Mid city-noise, not, as with thee of yore,
      Thyrsis! in reach of sheep-bells is my home.
  – Then through the great town's harsh, heart-wearying roar,
    Let in thy voice a whisper often come,
        To chase fatigue and fear:
Why faintest thou? I wander'd till I died.
  Roam on! The light we sought is shining still.
  Dost thou ask proof? Our tree yet crowns the hill,
Our Scholar travels yet the loved hill-side.   240

Growing Old

Probably written between 1864–7; pub. 1867. A.'s unrhymed five-line stanza is his own invention. See Trilling of the 1867 poems, 'They … do not question but reply, do not hint but declare. A note of finality, even of dismissal is here' (*Trilling* 293).

What is it to grow old?
Is it to lose the glory of the form,
The lustre of the eye?
Is it for beauty to forgo her wreath?
– Yes, but not this alone.

Is it to feel our strength –
Not our bloom only, but our strength – decay?
Is it to feel each limb
Grow stiffer, every function less exact,
Each nerve more loosely strung?   10

Yes, this, and more; but not
Ah, 'tis not what in youth we dreamed 'twould be!
'Tis not to have our life
Mellowed and softened as with sunset-glow,
A golden day's decline.

'Tis not to see the world
As from a height, with rapt prophetic eyes,
And heart profoundly stirred;
And weep, and feel the fullness of the past,
The years that are no more.   20

It is to spend long days
And not once feel that we were ever young;
It is to add, immured
In the hot prison of the present, month
To month with weary pain.

It is to suffer this,
And feel but half, and feebly, what we feel.
Deep in our hidden heart
Festers the dull remembrance of a change,
But no emotion – none.   30

It is – last stage of all –
When we are frozen up within, and quite
The phantom of ourselves,
To hear the world applaud the hollow ghost
Which blamed the living man.

PROSE

Preface to First Edition of *Poems* (1853)

A.'s first critical essay, written Aug.–Oct. 1853: 'There is a certain Geist [see Introduction 51*n*, pp. above, pp. 193–7 below] in it ... but it is far less *precise* than I had intended. How difficult it is to write prose ... because of the *articulations of the discourse*: one leaps over those in Poetry – places one thought cheek by jowl with another without introducing them and leaving them – but in prose this will not do' (*CL* 144, Oct. 1853). Less vivacious than A.'s later polemical style but prompted wide debate: see preface to *1854*, p. 128 below. Both prefaces dropped after *1857*; repr. *Irish Essays and Others* (1882).

In two small volumes of Poems, published anonymously, one in 1849, the other in 1852, many of the poems which compose the present volume have already appeared. The rest are now published for the first time.

I have, in the present collection, omitted the poem from which the volume published in 1852 took its title.[1] I have done so, not because the subject of it was a Sicilian Greek born between two and three thousand years ago, although many persons would think this a sufficient reason. Neither have I done so because I had, in my own opinion, failed in the delineation which I intended to effect. I intended to delineate the feelings of one of the last of the Greek religious philosophers, one of the family of Orpheus and Musaeus, having survived his fellows, living on into a time when the habits of Greek thought and feeling had begun fast to change, character to dwindle, the influence of the Sophists to prevail. Into the feelings of a man so situated there entered much that we are accustomed to consider as exclusively modern; how much, the fragments of Empedocles himself which remain to us are sufficient at least to indicate. What those who are familiar only with the great monuments of early Greek genius suppose to be its exclusive characteristics, have disappeared; the calm, the cheerfulness, the disinterested objectivity have disappeared; the dialogue of the mind with itself has commenced; modern problems have presented themselves; we hear already the doubts, we witness the discouragement, of Hamlet and of Faust.

The representation of such a man's feelings must be interesting, if consistently drawn. We all naturally take pleasure, says Aristotle, in any imitation or representation whatever[2] this is the basis of our love of poetry; and we take pleasure in them, he adds, because all knowledge is naturally agreeable to us; not to the philosopher only, but to mankind at large. Every representation, therefore, which is consistently drawn may be supposed to be interesting, inasmuch as it gratifies this natural interest in knowledge of all kinds. What is *not* interesting, is that which does not add to our knowledge of any kind; that which is vaguely conceived and loosely drawn; a representation which is general, indeterminate, and faint, instead of being particular, precise, and firm.

Any accurate representation may therefore be expected to be interesting; but, if the representation be a poetical one, more than this is demanded. It is demanded, not only that it shall interest, but also that it shall inspirit and rejoice the reader; that it should convey a charm, and infuse delight. For the Muses, as Hesiod says,[3] were born that they might be 'a forgetfulness of evils, and a truce from cares:' and it is not enough that the poet should add to the knowledge of men, it is required of him also that he should add to their happiness.[4] 'All art,' says Schiller, 'is dedicated to Joy, and there is no higher and no more serious problem, than how to make men happy. The right art is that alone, which creates the highest enjoyment.'[5]

A poetical work, therefore, is not yet justified when it has been shown to be an accurate, and therefore interesting representation; it has to be shown also that it is a representation from which men can derive enjoyment. In presence of the most tragic circumstances, represented in a work of art, the feeling of enjoyment, as is well known, may still subsist; the representation of the most utter calamity, of the liveliest anguish, is not sufficient to destroy it; the more tragic the situation, the deeper becomes the enjoyment; and the situation is more tragic in proportion as it becomes more terrible.[6]

What then are the situations, from the representation of which, though accurate, no poetical enjoyment can be derived? They are those in which the suffering finds no vent in action; in which a continuous state of mental distress is prolonged, unrelieved by incident, hope, or resistance; in which there is everything to be endured, nothing to be done. In such situations there is inevitably something morbid, in the description of them something monotonous. When they occur in actual life, they are painful, not tragic; the representation of them in poetry is painful also.

To this class of situations, poetically faulty as it appears to me, that of Empedocles, as I have endeavoured to represent him, belongs; and I have therefore excluded the poem from the present collection.

And why, it may be asked, have I entered into this explanation respecting a matter so unimportant as the admission or exclusion of the poem in question? I have done so, because I was anxious to avow that the sole reason for its exclusion was that which has been stated above; and that it has not been excluded in deference to the opinion which many critics of the present day appear to entertain against subjects chosen from distant times and countries: against the choice, in short, of any subjects but modern ones.

'The poet,' it is said,* and by an intelligent critic, 'the poet who would really fix the public attention must leave the exhausted past, and draw his subjects from matters of present import, and *therefore* both of interest and novelty.'

Now this view I believe to be completely false. It is worth examining, inasmuch as it is a fair sample of a class of critical dicta everywhere current at the present day, having a philosophical form and air, but no real basis in fact; and which are calculated to vitiate the judgment of readers of poetry, while they exert, so far as they are adopted, a misleading influence on the practice of those who make it.

What are the eternal objects of poetry, among all nations, and at all times? They are actions; human actions; possessing an inherent interest in themselves, and which are to be communicated in an interesting manner by the art of the poet.[7] Vainly will the latter imagine that he has everything in his own power; that he can make an intrinsically inferior action equally delightful with a more excellent one by his treatment of it. He may indeed compel us to admire his skill, but his work will possess, within itself, an incurable defect.

The poet, then, has in the first place to select an excellent action; and what actions are the most excellent? Those, certainly, which most powerfully appeal to the great primary human affections: to those elementary feelings which subsist permanently in the race, and which are independent of time. These feelings are permanent and the same; that which interests them is permanent and the same also. The modernness or antiquity of an action, therefore, has nothing to do with its fitness for poetical representation; this

---

*In the *Spectator* of April 2, 1853. The words quoted were not used with reference to poems of mine. [The critic was R. S. Rintoul, first editor (1828–58) of *The Spectator*. – Ed.]

depends upon its inherent qualities. To the elementary part of our nature, to our passions, that which is great and passionate is eternally interesting; and interesting solely in proportion to its greatness and to its passion. A great human action of a thousand years ago is more interesting to it than a smaller human action of to-day, even though upon the representation of this last the most consummate skill may have been expended, and though it has the advantage of appealing by its modern language, familiar manners, and contemporary allusions, to all our transient feelings and interests. These, however, have no right to demand of a poetical work that it shall satisfy them; their claims are to be directed elsewhere. Poetical works belong to the domain of our permanent passions; let them interest these, and the voice of all subordinate claims upon them is at once silenced.

Achilles, Prometheus, Clytemnestra, Dido,[8] – what modern poem presents personages as interesting, even to us moderns, as these personages of an 'exhausted past'? We have the domestic epic dealing with the details of modern life which pass daily under our eyes; we have poems representing modern personages in contact with the problems of modern life, moral, intellectual, and social; these works have been produced by poets the most distinguished of their nation and time; yet I fearlessly assert that Hermann and Dorothea, Childe Harold, Jocelyn, the Excursion,[9] leave the reader cold in comparison with the effect produced upon him by the latter books of the Iliad, by the Oresteia, or by the episode of Dido. And why is this? Simply because in the three last-named cases the action is greater, the personages nobler, the situations more intense: and this is the true basis of the interest in a poetical work, and this alone.

It may be urged, however, that past actions may be interesting in themselves, but that they are not to be adopted by the modern poet, because it is impossible for him to have them clearly present to his own mind, and he cannot therefore feel them deeply, nor represent them forcibly. But this is not necessarily the case. The externals of a past action, indeed, he cannot know with the precision of a contemporary; but his business is with its essentials. The outward man of Oedipus or of Macbeth, the houses in which they lived, the ceremonies of their courts, he cannot accurately figure to himself; but neither do they essentially concern him. His business is with their inward man; with their feelings and behaviour in certain tragic situations, which engage their passions as men; these have in them nothing local and casual; they are as accessible to the modern poet as to a contemporary.

The date of an action, then, signifies nothing; the action itself, its selection and construction, this is what is all-important. This the Greeks understood far more clearly than we do. The radical difference between their poetical theory and ours consists, as it appears to me, in this: that, with them, the poetical character of the action in itself, and the conduct of it, was the first consideration; with us, attention is fixed mainly on the value of the separate thoughts and images which occur in the treatment of an action. They regarded the whole; we regard the parts. With them, the action predominated over the expression of it; with us, the expression predominates over the action. Not that they failed in expression, or were inattentive to it; on the contrary, they are the highest models of expression, the unapproached masters of the *grand style*.[10] But their expression is so excellent because it is so admirably kept in its right degree of prominence; because it is so simple and so well subordinated; because it draws its force directly from the pregnancy of the matter which it conveys. For what reason was the Greek tragic poet confined to so limited a range of subjects? Because there are so few actions which unite in themselves, in the highest degree, the conditions of excellence: and it was not thought that on any but an excellent subject could an excellent poem be constructed. A few actions, therefore, eminently adapted for tragedy, maintained almost exclusive possession of the Greek tragic stage. Their significance appeared inexhaustible; they were as permanent problems, perpetually offered to the genius of every fresh poet. This too is the reason of what appears to us moderns a certain baldness of expression in Greek tragedy; of the triviality with which we often reproach the remarks of the chorus, where it takes part in the dialogue: that the action itself, the situation of Orestes, or Merope, or Alcmaeon, was to stand the central point of interest, unforgotten, absorbing, principal; that no accessories were for a moment to distract the spectator's attention from this; that the tone of the parts was to be perpetually kept down, in order not to impair the grandiose effect of the whole. The terrible old mythic story on which the drama was founded stood, before he entered the theatre, traced in its bare outlines upon the spectator's mind; it stood in his memory, as a group of statuary, faintly seen, at the end of a long and dark vista: then came the poet, embodying outlines, developing situations, not a word wasted, not a sentiment capriciously thrown in: stroke upon stroke, the drama proceeded: the light deepened upon the group; more and more it revealed itself to the riveted gaze of the spectator: until at last, when the final words were spoken, it stood before him in broad sunlight, a model of immortal beauty.

This was what a Greek critic demanded; this was what a Greek poet endeavoured to effect. It signified nothing to what time an action belonged. We do not find that the Persae occupied a particularly high rank among the dramas of Aeschylus, because it represented a matter of contemporary interest; this was not what a cultivated Athenian required. He required that the permanent elements of his nature should be moved; and dramas of which the action, though taken from a long-distant mythic time, yet was calculated to accomplish this in a higher degree than that of the Persae, stood higher in his estimation accordingly. The Greeks felt, no doubt with their exquisite sagacity of taste, that an action of present times was too near them, too much mixed up with what was accidental and passing, to form a sufficiently grand, detached, and self-subsistent object for a tragic poem. Such objects belonged to the domain of the comic poet, and of the lighter kinds of poetry. For the more serious kinds, for *pragmatic* poetry, to use an excellent expression of Polybius, they were more difficult and severe in the range of subjects which they permitted. Their theory and practice alike, the admirable treatise of Aristotle, and the unrivalled works of their poets, exclaim with a thousand tongues – 'All depends upon the subject; choose a fitting action, penetrate yourself with the feeling of its situations; this done, everything else will follow.'[11]

But for all kinds of poetry alike there was one point on which they were rigidly exacting; the adaptability of the subject to the kind of poetry selected, and the careful construction of the poem.

How different a way of thinking from this is ours! We can hardly at the present day understand what Menander meant, when he told a man who enquired as to the progress of his comedy that he had finished it, not having yet written a single line, because he had constructed the action of it in his mind. A modern critic would have assured him that the merit of his piece depended on the brilliant things which arose under his pen as he went along. We have poems which seem to exist merely for the sake of single lines and passages; not for the sake of producing any total impression. We have critics who seem to direct their attention merely to detached expressions, to the language about the action, not to the action itself. I verily think that the majority of them do not in their hearts believe that there is such a thing as a total impression to be derived from a poem at all, or to be demanded from a poet; they think the term a common-place of metaphysical criticism. They will permit the poet to select any action he pleases, and to suffer that action to go as it will, provided he gratifies them with occasional bursts of fine writing, and with a shower of isolated thoughts and images. That is, they permit him to leave their poetical sense ungratified, provided that he gratifies their rhetorical sense and their curiosity. Of his neglecting to gratify these, there is little danger. He needs rather to be warned against the danger of attempting to gratify these alone; he needs rather to be perpetually reminded to prefer his action to everything else; so to treat this, as to permit its inherent excellences to develop themselves, without interruption from the intrusion of his personal peculiarities; most fortunate, when he most entirely succeeds in effacing himself, and in enabling a noble action to subsist as it did in nature.

But the modern critic not only permits a false practice; he absolutely prescribes false aims. – 'A true allegory of the state of one's own mind in a representative history,' the poet is told, 'is perhaps the highest thing that one can attempt in the way of poetry.'[12] And accordingly he attempts it. An allegory of the state of one's own mind, the highest problem of an art which imitates actions! No assuredly, it is not, it never can be so: no great poetical work has ever been produced with such an aim. Faust itself, in which something of the kind is attempted, wonderful passages as it contains, and in spite of the unsurpassed beauty of the scenes which relate to Margaret, Faust itself, judged as a whole, and judged strictly as a poetical work, is defective: its illustrious author, the greatest poet of modern times, the greatest critic of all times, would have been the first to acknowledge it; he only defended his work, indeed, by asserting it to be 'something incommensurable.'[13]

The confusion of the present times is great, the multitude of voices counselling different things bewildering, the number of existing works capable of attracting a young writer's attention and of becoming his models, immense. What he wants is a hand to guide him through the confusion, a voice to prescribe to him the aim which he should keep in view, and to explain to him that the value of the literary works which offer themselves to his attention is relative to their power of helping him forward on his road towards this aim. Such a guide the English writer at the present day will nowhere find. Failing this, all that can be looked for, all indeed that can be desired, is, that his attention should be fixed on excellent models; that he may reproduce, at any rate, something of their excellence, by penetrating himself with their works and by catching their spirit, if he cannot be taught to produce what is excellent independently.

Foremost among these models for the English writer stands Shakespeare: a name the greatest perhaps of all poetical names; a name never to be mentioned without reverence. I will venture, however, to express a doubt, whether he influence of his works, excellent and fruitful for the readers of poetry, for the great majority, has been of unmixed advantage to the writers of it. Shakespeare indeed chose excellent subjects; the world could afford no better than Macbeth, or Romeo and Juliet, or Othello; he had no theory respecting the necessity of choosing subjects of present import, or the paramount interest attaching to allegories of the state of one's own mind; like all great poets, he knew well what constituted a poetical action; like them, wherever he found such an action, he took it; like them, too, he found his best in past times. But to these general characteristics of all great poets he added a special one of his own; a gift, namely, of happy, abundant, and ingenious expression, eminent and unrivalled: so eminent as irresistibly to strike the attention first in him, and even to throw into comparative shade his other excellences as a poet. Here has been the mischief. These other excellences were his fundamental excellences *as a poet*; what distinguishes the artist from the mere amateur, says Goethe, is *Architectonicè* in the highest sense; that power of execution, which creates, forms, and constitutes: not the profoundness of single thoughts, not the richness of imagery, not the abundance of illustration.[14] But these attractive accessories of a poetical work being more easily seized than the spirit of the whole, and these accessories being possessed by Shakespeare in an unequalled degree, a young writer having recourse to Shakespeare as his model runs great risk of being vanquished and absorbed by them, and, in consequence, of reproducing, according to the measure of his power, these, and these alone. Of this preponderating quality of Shakespeare's genius, accordingly, almost the whole of modern English poetry has, it appears to me, felt the influence. To the exclusive attention on the part of his imitators to this it is in a great degree owing, that of the majority of modern poetical works the details alone are valuable, the composition worthless. In reading them one is perpetually reminded of that terrible sentence on a modern French poet: *Il dit tout ce qu'il veut, mais malheureusement il n'a rien à dire.*[15]

Let me give an instance of what I mean. I will take it from the works of the very chief among those who seem to have been formed in the school of Shakespeare: of one whose exquisite genius and pathetic death render him for ever interesting. I will take the poem of Isabella, or the Pot of Basil, by Keats. I choose this rather than the Endymion, because the latter work, (which a modern critic has classed with the Fairy Queen!) although undoubtedly there blows through it the breath of genius, is yet as a whole so utterly incoherent, as not strictly to merit the name of a poem at all. The poem of Isabella, then, is a perfect treasure-house of graceful and felicitous words and images: almost in every stanza there occurs one of those vivid and picturesque turns of expression, by which the object is made to flash upon the eye of the mind, and which thrill the reader with a sudden delight. This one short poem contains, perhaps, a greater number of happy single expressions which one could quote than all the extant tragedies of Sophocles. But the action, the story? The action in itself is an excellent one; but so feebly is it conceived by the poet, so loosely constructed, that the effect produced by it, in and for itself, is absolutely null. Let the reader, after he has finished the poem of Keats, turn to the same story in the Decameron: he will then feel how pregnant and interesting the same action has become in the hands of a great artist, who above all things delineates his object; who subordinates expression to that which it is designed to express.[16]

I have said that the imitators of Shakespeare, fixing their attention on his wonderful gift of expression, have directed their imitation to this, neglecting his other excellences. These excellences, the fundamental excellences of poetical art, Shakespeare no doubt possessed them, – possessed many of them in a splendid degree; but it may perhaps be doubted whether even he himself did not sometimes give scope to his faculty of expression to the prejudice of a higher poetical duty. For we must never forget that

Shakespeare is the great poet he is from his skill in discerning and firmly conceiving an excellent action, from his power of intensely feeling a situation, of intimately associating himself with a character; not from his gift of expression, which rather even leads him astray, degenerating sometimes into a fondness for curiosity of expression, into an irritability of fancy, which seems to make it impossible for him to say a thing plainly, even when the press of the action demands the very directest language, or its level character the very simplest. Mr Hallam, than whom it is impossible to find a saner and more judicious critic, has had the courage (for at the present day it needs courage) to remark, how extremely and faultily difficult Shakespeare's language often is.[17] It is so: you may find main scenes in some of his greatest tragedies, King Lear for instance, where the language is so artificial, so curiously tortured, and so difficult, that every speech has to be read two or three times before its meaning can be comprehended. This over-curiousness of expression is indeed but the excessive employment of a wonderful gift, – of the power of saying a thing in a happier way than any other man; nevertheless, it is carried so far that one understands what M. Guizot meant, when he said that Shakespeare appears in his language to have tried all styles except that of simplicity.[18] He had not the severe and scrupulous self-restraint of the ancients, partly no doubt, because he had a far less cultivated and exacting audience. He has indeed a far wider range than they had, a far richer fertility of thought; in this respect he rises above them. In his strong conception of his subject, in the genuine way in which he is penetrated with it, he resembles them, and is unlike the moderns. But in the accurate limitation of it, the conscientious rejection of superfluities, the simple and rigorous development of it from the first line of his work to the last, he falls below them, and comes nearer to the moderns. In his chief works, besides what he has of his own, he has the elementary soundness of the ancients; he has their important action and their large and broad manner; but he has not their purity of method. He is therefore a less safe model; for what he has of his own is personal, and inseparable from his own rich nature; it may be imitated and exaggerated, it cannot be learned or applied as an art. He is above all suggestive; more valuable, therefore, to young writers as men than as artists. But clearness of arrangement, rigour of development, simplicity of style, – these may to a certain extent be learned; and these may, I am convinced, be learned best from the ancients, who, although infinitely less suggestive than Shakespeare, are thus, to the artist, more instructive.

What then, it will be asked, are the ancients to be our sole models? the ancients with their comparatively narrow range of experience, and their widely different circumstances? Not, certainly, that which is narrow in the ancients, nor that in which we can no longer sympathise. An action like the action of the Antigone of Sophocles, which turns upon the conflict between the heroine's duty to her brother's corpse and that to the laws of her country, is no longer one in which it is possible that we should feel a deep interest. I am speaking too, it will be remembered, not of the best sources of intellectual stimulus for the general reader, but of the best models of instruction for the individual writer. This last may certainly learn of the ancients, better than anywhere else, three things which it is vitally important for him to know: the all-importance of the choice of a subject; the necessity of accurate construction; and the subordinate character of expression. He will learn from them how unspeakably superior is the effect of the one moral impression left by a great action treated as a whole, to the effect produced by the most striking single thought or by the happiest image. As he penetrates into the spirit of the great classical works, as he becomes gradually aware of their intense significance, their noble simplicity, and their calm pathos, he will be convinced that it is this effect, unity and profoundness of moral impression, at which the ancient poets aimed; that it is this which constitutes the grandeur of their works, and which makes them immortal. He will direct his own efforts towards producing the same effect. Above all, he will deliver himself from the jargon of modern criticism, and escape the danger of producing poetical works conceived in the spirit of the passing time, and which partake of its transitoriness.

The present age makes great claims upon us; we owe it service, it will not be satisfied without our admiration. I know not how it is, but their commerce with the ancients appears to me to produce, in those who constantly practise it, a steadying and composing effect upon their judgment, not of literary works only, but of men and events in general. They are like persons who have had a very weighty and impressive experience; they are more truly than others under the empire of facts, and more independent of the language current among those with whom they live. They wish neither to applaud nor to revile their age; they wish to know what it is, what it can give them, and whether this is what they want. What they want, they know very well; they want to educe and cultivate what is best and noblest in themselves; they know, too, that this is no easy task – χαλεπόν, as Pittacus said, χαλεπὸν ἐσθλὸν ἔμμεναι[19] – and they ask themselves sincerely whether their age and its literature can assist them in the attempt. If they are endeavouring to practise any art, they remember the plain and simple proceedings of the old artists, who attained their grand results by penetrating themselves with some noble and significant action, not by inflating themselves with a belief in the preeminent importance and greatness of their own times. They do not talk of their mission, nor of interpreting their age, nor of the coming poet; all this, they know, is the mere delirium of vanity; their business is not to praise their age, but to afford to the men who live in it the highest pleasure which they are capable of feeling. If asked to afford this by means of subjects drawn from the age itself, they ask what special fitness the present age has for supplying them. They are told that it is an era of progress, an age commissioned to carry out the great ideas of industrial development and social amelioration. They reply that with all this they can do nothing; that the elements they need for the exercise of their art are greater actions, calculated powerfully and delightfully to affect what is permanent in the human soul; that so far as the present age can supply such actions, they will gladly make use of them; but that an age wanting in moral grandeur can with difficulty supply such, and an age of spiritual discomfort with difficulty be powerfully and delightfully affected by them.

A host of voices will indignantly rejoin that the present age is inferior to the past neither in moral grandeur nor in spiritual health. He who possesses the discipline I speak of will content himself with remembering the judgments passed upon the present age, in this respect, by the men of strongest head and widest culture whom it has produced; by Goethe and by Niebuhr.[20] It will be sufficient for him that he knows the opinions held by these two great men respecting the present age and its literature; and that he feels assured in his own mind that their aims and demands upon life were such as he would wish, at any rate, his own to be; and their judgment as to what is impeding and disabling such as he may safely follow. He will not, however, maintain a hostile attitude towards the false pretensions of his age; he will content himself with not being overwhelmed by them. He will esteem himself fortunate if he can succeed in banishing from his mind all feelings of contradiction, and irritation, and impatience; in order to delight himself with the contemplation of some noble action of a heroic time, and to enable others, through his representation of it, to delight in it also.

I am far indeed from making any claim, for myself, that I possess this discipline; or for the following poems, that they breathe its spirit. But I say, that in the sincere endeavour to learn and practise, amid the bewildering confusion of our times, what is sound and true in poetical art, I seemed to myself to find the only sure guidance, the only solid footing, among the ancients. They, at any rate, knew what they wanted in art, and we do not. It is this uncertainty which is disheartening, and not hostile criticism. How often have I felt this when reading words of disparagement or of cavil: that it is the uncertainty as to what is really to be aimed at which makes our difficulty, not the dissatisfaction of the critic, who himself suffers from the same uncertainty! *Non me tua fervida terrent Dicta; ... Dii me terrent, et Jupiter hostis.*[21]

Two kinds of *dilettanti*, says Goethe, there are in poetry: he who neglects the indispensable mechanical part, and thinks he has done enough if he shows spirituality and feeling: and he who seeks to arrive at poetry merely by mechanism, in which he can acquire an artisan's readiness, and is without soul and matter. And he adds, that the first does most harm to art, and the last to himself.[22] If we must be *dilettanti*: if it is impossible for us, under the circumstances amidst which we live, to think clearly, to feel nobly, and to delineate firmly: if we cannot attain to the mastery of the great artists; – let us, at least, have so much respect for our art as to prefer it to ourselves. Let us not bewilder our successors; let us transmit to them the practice of poetry, with its boundaries and wholesome regulative laws, under which excellent works may again, perhaps, at some future time, be produced, not yet fallen into oblivion through our neglect, not yet condemned and cancelled by the influence of their eternal enemy, caprice.

From Preface to Second Edition of *Poems* (1854)

Printed *1854* with the 1853 Preface (p. 115 above) as a comment on the issues it provoked. With A.'s views about subjects 'from the past' cp. his conception of 'adequacy', 'On the Modern Element in Literature' (1857), headnote opposite.

... An objection has been warmly urged to the classing together, as subjects equally belonging to a past time. Oedipus and Macbeth.[1] And it is no doubt true that to Shakespeare, standing on the verge of the middle ages, the epoch of Macbeth was more familiar than that of Oedipus. But I was speaking of actions as they presented themselves to us moderns: and it will hardly be said that the European mind, in our day, has much more affinity with the times of Macbeth than with those of Oedipus. As moderns, it seems to me, we have no longer any direct affinity with the circumstances and feelings of either. As individuals, we are attracted towards this or that personage, we have a capacity for imagining him, irrespective of his times, solely according to a law or personal sympathy; and those subjects for which we feel this personal attraction most strongly, we may hope to treat successfully. Prometheus or Joan of Arc, Charlemagne or Agamemnon, – one of these is not really nearer to us now than another. Each can be made present only by an act of poetic imagination; but this man's imagination has an affinity for one of them, and that man's for another.

It has been said that I wish to limit the poet, in his choice of subjects, to the period of Greek and Roman antiquity[2] but it is not so. I only counsel him to choose for his subjects great actions, without regarding to what time they belong. Nor do I deny that the poetic faculty can and does manifest itself in treating the most trifling action, the most hopeless subject. But it is a pity that power should be wasted; and that the poet should be compelled to impart interest and force to his subject, instead of receiving them from it, and thereby doubling his impressiveness. There is, it has been excellently said, an immortal strength in the stories of great actions; the most gifted poet, then, may well be glad to supplement with it that mortal weakness, which, in presence of the vast spectacle of life and the world, he must for ever feel to be his individual portion.

Again, with respect to the study of the classical writers of antiquity; it has been said that we should emulate rather than imitate them. I make no objection; all I say is, let us study them. They can help to cure us of what is, it seems to me, the great vice of our intellect, manifesting itself in our incredible vagaries in literature, in art, in religion, in morals: namely, that it is *fantastic*, and wants *sanity*. Sanity, – that is the great virtue of the ancient literature; the want of that is the great defect of the modern, in spite of all its variety and power. It is impossible to read carefully the great ancients, without losing something of our caprice and eccentricity; and to emulate them we must at least read them.

From On the Modern Element in Literature

A.'s inaugural lecture as Professor of Poetry at Oxford 14 Nov. 1857, designed as the first in a course of lectures on 'The Modern Element in Literature'. Not published until Feb. 1869 (*Macmillan's Magazine*), with a brief statement about its 'sketchy and generalising mode of treatment' and the hope that it might all the same 'give some notion of the Hellenic spirit and its works'; omitted by A. from all collections of his essays. Celebrated for first expressing at length his views about 'adequacy' in literature.

... An intellectual deliverance is the peculiar demand of those ages which are called modern; and those nations are said to be imbued with the modern spirit most eminently in which the demand for such a deliverance has been made with most zeal, and satisfied with most completeness. Such a deliverance is emphatically, whether we will or not, the demand of the age in which we ourselves live. All intellectual pursuits our age judges according to their power of helping to satisfy this demand; of all studies it asks, above all, the question, how far they can contribute to this deliverance.

I propose, on this my first occasion of speaking here, to attempt such a general survey of ancient classical literature and history as may afford us the conviction – in presence of the doubts so often expressed of the profitableness, in the present day, of our study of this literature – that, even admitting to their fullest extent the legitimate demands of our age, the literature of ancient Greece is, even for modern times, a mighty agent of intellectual deliverance;

even for modern times, therefore, an object of indestructible interest.

But first let us ask ourselves why the demand for an intellectual deliverance arises in such an age as the present, and in what the deliverance itself consists? The demand arises, because our present age has around it a copious and complex present, and behind it a copious and complex past; it arises, because the present age exhibits to the individual man who contemplates it the spectacle of a vast multitude of facts awaiting and inviting his comprehension. The deliverance consists in man's comprehension of this present and past. It begins when our mind begins to enter into possession of the general ideas which are the law of this vast multitude of facts. It is perfect when we have acquired that harmonious acquiescence of mind which we feel in contemplating a grand spectacle that is intelligible to us; when we have lost that impatient irritation of mind which we feel in presence of an immense, moving, confused spectacle which, while it perpetually excites our curiosity, perpetually baffles our comprehension.... [1]

What facts, then, let us ask ourselves, what elements of the spectacle before us, will naturally be most interesting to a highly developed age like our own, to an age making the demand which we have described for an intellectual deliverance by means of the complete intelligence of its own situation? Evidently, the other ages similarly developed, and making the same demand. And what past literature will naturally be most interesting to such an age as our own? Evidently, the literatures which have most successfully solved for *their* ages the problem which occupies ours: the literatures which in their day and for their own nation have adequately comprehended, have adequately represented, the spectacle before them. A significant, a highly developed, a culminating epoch, on the one hand, – a comprehensive, a commensurate, an adequate literature, on the other, – these will naturally be the objects of deepest interest to our modern age. Such an epoch and such a literature are, in fact, *modern*, in the same sense in which our own age and literature are modern; they are founded upon a rich past and upon an instructive fulness of experience.

It may, however, happen that a great epoch is without a perfectly adequate literature; it may happen that a great age, a great nation, has attained a remarkable fulness of political and social development, without intellectually taking the complete measure of itself, without adequately representing that development in its literature. In this case, the *epoch*, the *nation* itself, will still be an object of the greatest interest to us, but the *literature* will be an object of less interest to us: the facts, the material spectacle, are there; but the contemporary view of the facts, the intellectual interpretation, are inferior and inadequate.

It may happen, on the other hand, that great authors, that a powerful literature, are found in an age and nation less great and powerful than themselves; it may happen that a literature, that a man of genius, may arise adequate to the representation of a greater, a more highly developed age than that in which they appear; it may happen that a literature completely interprets its epoch, and yet has something over; that it has a force, a richness, a geniality, a power of view which the materials at its disposition are insufficient adequately to employ. In such a case, the literature will be more interesting to us than the epoch. The interpreting power, the illuminating and revealing intellect, are there; but the spectacle on which they throw their light is not fully worthy of them. ...

Now the culminating age in the life of ancient Greece I call, beyond question, a great epoch; the life of Athens in the fifth century before our era I call one of the highly developed, one of the marking, one of the modern periods in the life of the whole human race. It has been said that the 'Athens of Pericles was a vigorous man, at the summit of his bodily strength and mental energy.' There was the utmost energy of life there, public and private; the most entire freedom, the most unprejudiced and intelligent observation of human affairs. Let us rapidly examine some of the characteristics which distinguish modern epochs; let us see how far the culminating century of ancient Greece exhibits them; let us compare it, in respect of them, with a much later, a celebrated century; let us compare it with the age of Elizabeth in our own country.

To begin with what is exterior. One of the most characteristic outward features of a *modern* age, of an age of advanced civilization, is the banishment of the ensigns of war and bloodshed from the intercourse of civil life. Crime still exists, and wars are still carried on; but within the limits of civil life a circle has been formed within which man can move securely, and develop the arts of peace uninterruptedly. The private man does not go forth to his daily occupation prepared to assail the life of his neighbour or to have to defend his own. With the disappearance of the constant means of offence the occasions of offence diminish; society at least acquires repose, confidence, and free activity. An important inward characteristic, again, is the growth of a tolerant spirit; that spirit which is the offspring of an enlarged knowledge; a spirit patient of the diversities of habits and opinions. Other characteristics are the multiplication of the conveniences of life, the formation of taste, the capacity for refined pursuits. And this leads us to the supreme characteristic of all: the intellectual maturity of man himself; the tendency to observe facts with a critical spirit; to search for their law, not to wander among them at random; to judge by the rule of reason, not by the impulse of prejudice or caprice.

Well, now, with respect to the presence of all these characteristics in the age of Pericles, we possess the explicit testimony of an immortal work, – of the history of Thucydides. 'The Athenians first,' he says – speaking of the gradual development of Grecian society up to the period when the Peloponnesian War commenced – 'the Athenians first left off the habit of wearing arms:'[2] that is, this mark of superior civilization had, in the age of Pericles, become general in Greece, had long been visible at Athens. In the time of Elizabeth, on the other hand, the wearing of arms was universal in England and throughout Europe. Again, the conveniences, the ornaments, the luxuries of life, had become common at Athens at the time of which we are speaking. But there had been an advance even beyond this; there had been an advance to that perfection, that propriety of taste which proscribes the excess of ornament, the extravagance of luxury. The Athenians had given up, Thucydides says, had given up, although not very long before, an extravagance of dress and an excess of personal ornament which, in the first flush of newly discovered luxury, had been adopted by some of the richer classes. The height of civilization in this respect seems to have been attained; there was general elegance and refinement of life, and there was simplicity. What was the case in this respect in the Elizabethan age? The scholar Casaubon,[3] who settled in England in the reign of James I, bears evidence to the want here, even at that time, of conveniences of life which were already to be met with on the continent of Europe. On the other hand, the taste for fantastic, for excessive personal adornment, to which the portraits of the time bear testimony, is admirably set forth in the work of a great novelist, who was also a very truthful antiquarian – in the *Kenilworth* of Sr Walter Scott. We all remember the description, in the thirteenth and fourteenth chapters of the second volume of *Kenilworth*, of the barbarous magnificence, the 'fierce vanities,' of the dress of the period.

Pericles praises the Athenians that they had discovered sources of recreation for the spirit to counterbalance the labours of the body: compare these, compare the pleasures which charmed the whole body of the Athenian people through the yearly round of their festivals with the popular shows and pastimes in *Kenilworth*. 'We have freedom,' says Pericles, 'for individual diversities of opinion and character; we do not take offence at the tastes and habits of our neighbour if they differ from our own.' Yes, in Greece, in the Athens of Pericles, there is toleration; but in England, in the England of the sixteenth century? – the Puritans are then in full growth. So that with regard to these characteristics of civilization of a modern spirit which we have hitherto enumerated, the superiority, it will be admitted, rests with the age of Pericles.

Let us pass to what we said was the supreme characteristic of a highly developed, a modern age – the manifestation of a critical spirit, the endeavour after a rational arrangement and appreciation of facts. Let us consider one or two of the passages in the masterly introduction which Thucydides, the contemporary of Pericles, has prefixed to his history.[4] What was his motive in choosing the Peloponnesian War for his subject? Because it was, in his opinion, the most important, the most instructive event which had, up to that time, happened in the history of mankind. What is his effort in the first twenty-three chapters of his history? To place in their correct point of view all the facts which had brought Grecian society to the point at which that dominant event found it; to strip these facts of their exaggeration, to examine them critically. The enterprises undertaken in the early times of Greece were on a much smaller scale than had been commonly supposed. The Greek chiefs were induced to combine in the expedition against Troy, not by their respect for an oath taken by them all when suitors to Helen, but by their respect for the preponderating influence of Agamemnon; the siege of Troy had been protracted not so much by the valour of the besieged as by the inadequate mode of warfare necessitated by the want of funds of the besiegers. No doubt Thucydides' criticism of the Trojan War is not perfect; but observe how in these and many other points he labours to correct popular errors, to assign their true character to facts, complaining, as he does so, of men's habit of *uncritical* reception of current stories. 'So little a matter of care to most men,' he says, 'is the search after truth, and so inclined are they to take up any story which is ready to their hand.' 'He himself,' he continues, 'has endeavoured to give a true picture, and believes that in the main he has done so. For some readers his history may want the charm of the uncritical, half-fabulous narratives of earlier writers; but for such as desire to gain a clear knowledge of the past, and thereby of the future also, which will surely, after the course of human things, represent again hereafter, if not the very image, yet the near resemblance of the past – if such shall judge my work to be profitable, I shall be well content.'

What language shall we properly call this? It is *modern* language; it is the language of a thoughtful philosophic man of our own days; it is the language of Burke or Niebuhr[5] assigning the true aim of history. And yet Thucydides is no mere literary man; no isolated thinker, speaking far over the heads of his hearers to a future age – no: he was a man of action, a man of the world, a man of his time. He represents, at its best indeed, but he represents, the general intelligence of his age and nation; of a nation the meanest citizens of which could follow with comprehension the profoundly thoughtful speeches of Pericles.

Let us now turn for a contrast to a historian of the Elizabethan age, also a man of great mark and ability, also a man of action, also a man of the world, Sir Walter Ralegh. Sir Walter Ralegh writes the *History of the World*, as Thucydides has written the *History of the Peloponnesian War*; let us hear his language; let us mark his point of view: let us see what problems occur to him for solution. 'Seeing,' he says, 'that we digress in all the ways of our lives – yea, seeing the life of man is nothing else but digression – I may be the better excused in writing their lives and actions.'[6] What are the preliminary facts which he discusses, as Thucydides discusses the Trojan War and the early naval power of Crete, and which are to lead up to his main inquiry? Open the table of contents of his first volume. You will find: 'Of the firmament, and of the waters above the firmament, and whether there be any crystalline Heaven, or any primum mobile.' You will then find: 'Of Fate, and that the stars have great influence, and that their operations may diversely be prevented or furthered.' Then you come to two entire chapters on the place of Paradise, and on the two chief trees in the garden of Paradise. And in what style, with what power of criticism, does Ralegh treat the subjects so selected? I turn to the 7th section of the third chapter of his first book, which treats 'Of their opinion which make Paradise as high as the moon, and of others which make it higher than the middle region of the air.' Thus he begins the discussion of this opinion: – 'Whereas Beda saith, and as the schoolmen affirm Paradise to be a place altogether removed from the knowledge of men ("locus a cognitione hominum remotissimus"), and Barcephas conceived that Paradise was far in the east, but mounted above the ocean and all the earth, and near the orb of the moon (which opinion, though the schoolmen charge Beda withal, yet Pererius lays it off from Beda and his master Rabanus); and whereas Rupertus in his geography of Paradise doth not much differ from the rest, but finds it seated next or nearest Heaven – ' So he states the error, and now for his own criticism of it. 'First, such a place cannot be commodious to live in, for being so near the moon it had been too near the sun and other heavenly bodies. Secondly, it must have been too joint a neighbour to the element of fire. Thirdly, the air in that region is so violently moved and carried about with such swiftness as nothing in that place can consist or have abiding. Fourthly,' – but what has been quoted is surely enough, and there is no use in continuing.

Which is the ancient here, and which is the modern? Which uses the language of an intelligent man of our own days? which a language wholly obsolete and unfamiliar to us? Which has the rational appreciation and control of his facts? which wanders among them helplessly and without a clue? Is it our own country-man, or is it the Greek? And the language of Ralegh affords a fair sample of the critical power, of the point of view, possessed by the majority of intelligent men of his day; as the language of Thucydides affords us a fair sample of the critical power of the majority of intelligent men in the age of Pericles.

Well, then, in the age of Pericles we have, in spite of its antiquity, a highly developed, a modern, a deeply interesting epoch. Next comes the question: Is this epoch adequately inter-preted by its highest literature? Now, the peculiar characteristic of the highest literature – the poetry – of the fifth century in Greece before the Christian era, is its adequacy; the peculiar characteristic of the poetry of Sophocles is its consummate, its unrivalled *adequacy*; that it represents the highly developed human nature of that age – human nature developed in a number of directions, politically, socially, religiously, morally developed – in its com-pletest and most harmonious development in all these directions;

while there is shed over this poetry the charm of that noble serenity which always accompanies true insight. If in the body of Athenians of that time there was, as we have said, the utmost energy of mature manhood, public and private; the most entire freedom, the most unprejudiced and intelligent observation of human affairs – in Sophocles there is the same energy, the same maturity, the same freedom, the same intelligent observation; but all these idealized and glorified by the grace and light shed over them from the noblest poetical feeling. And therefore I have ventured to say of Sophocles, that he 'saw life steadily, and saw it whole.'[7] Well may we understand how Pericles – how the great statesman whose aim was, it has been said, 'to realize in Athens the idea which he had conceived of human greatness,' and who partly succeeded in his aim – should have been drawn to the great poet whose works are the noblest reflection of his success.

I assert, therefore, though the detailed proof of the assertion must be reserved for other opportunities, that, if the fifth century in Greece before our era is a significant and modern epoch, the poetry of that epoch – the poetry of Pindar, Aeschylus, and Sophocles – is an adequate representation and interpretation of it.

The poetry of Aristophanes is an adequate representation of it also. True, this poetry regards humanity from the comic side; but there is a comic side from which to regard humanity as well as a tragic one; and the distinction of Aristophanes is to have regarded it from the true point of view on the comic side. He too, like Sophocles, regards the human nature of his time in its fullest development; the boldest creations of a riotous imagination are in Aristophanes, as has been justly said, based always upon the foundation of a serious thought: politics, education, social life, literature – all the great modes in which the human life of his day manifested itself – are the subjects of his thoughts, and of his penetrating comment. There is shed, therefore, over his poetry the charm, the vital freshness, which is felt when man and his relations are from any side adequately, and therefore genially, regarded....

Let us now pass to the Roman world. There is no necessity to accumulate proofs that the culminating period of Roman history is to be classed among the leading, the significant, the modern periods of the world....

Let us begin with a great poet, a great philosopher, Lucretius.[8] In the case of Thucydides I called attention to the fact that his habit of mind, his mode of dealing with questions, were modern;

that they were those of an enlightened, reflecting man among ourselves. Let me call attention to the exhibition in Lucretius of a modern *feeling* not less remarkable than the modern *thought* in Thucydides. The predominance of thought, of reflection, in modern epochs is not without its penalties; in the unsound, in the over-tasked, in the over-sensitive, it has produced the most painful, the most lamentable results; it has produced a state of feeling unknown to less enlightened but perhaps healthier epochs – the feeling of depression, the feeling of *ennui*. Depression and *ennui*; these are the characteristics stamped on how many of the representative works of modern times! they are also the characteristics stamped on the poem of Lucretius. One of the most powerful, the most solemn passages of the work of Lucretius, one of the most powerful, the most solemn passages in the literature of the whole world, is the well-known conclusion of the third book. With masterly touches he exhibits the lassitude, the incurable tedium which pursue men in their amusements; with indignant irony he upbraids them for the cowardice with which they cling to a life which for most is miserable; to a life which contains, for the most fortunate, nothing but the old dull round of the same unsatisfying objects for ever presented. 'A man rushes abroad,' he says, 'because he is sick of being at home; and suddenly comes home again because he finds himself no whit easier abroad. He posts as fast as his horses can take him to his country-seat: when he has got there he hesitates what to do; or he throws himself down moodily to sleep, and seeks forgetfulness in that; or he makes the best of his way back to town again with the same speed as he fled from it. Thus every one flies from himself.' What a picture of *ennui!* of the disease of the most modern societies, the most advanced civilizations! 'O man,' he exclaims again, 'the lights of the world, Scipio, Homer, Epicurus, are dead; wilt thou hesitate and fret at dying, whose life is well-nigh dead whilst thou art yet alive; who consumest in sleep the greater part of thy span, and when awake dronest and ceasest not to dream; and carries about a mind troubled with baseless fear, and canst not find what it is that aileth thee when thou staggerest like a drunken wretch in the press of thy cares, and welterest hither and thither in the unsteady wandering of thy spirit!' And again: 'I have nothing more than you have already seen', he makes Nature say to man, 'to invent for your amusement; *eadem sunt omnia semper* – all things continue the same for ever.'

Yes, Lucretius is modern; but is he adequate? And how can a man adequately interpret the activity of his age when he is not in sympathy with it? Think of the varied, the abundant, the wide spectacle of the Roman life of his day; think of its fulness of occupation, its energy of effort. From these Lucretius withdraws himself, and bids his disciples to withdraw themselves; he bids them to leave the business of the world, and to apply themselves '*naturam cognoscere rerum* – to learn the nature of things'; but there is no peace, no cheerfulness for him either in the world from which he comes, or in the solitude to which he goes. With stern effort, with gloomy despair, he seems to rivet his eyes on the elementary reality, the naked framework of the world, because the world in its fulness and movement is too exciting a spectacle for his discomposed brain. He seems to feel the spectacle of it at once terrifying and alluring; and to deliver himself from it he has to keep perpetually repeating his formula of disenchantment and annihilation. In reading him, you understand the tradition which represents him as having been driven mad by a poison adminis-tered as a love-charm by his mistress, and as having composed his great work in the intervals of his madness. Lucretius is, therefore, over-strained, gloom-weighted, morbid; and he who is morbid is no adequate interpreter of his age....

From On Translating Homer: Last Words

A.'s fourth lecture on the subject, delivered at Oxford 30 Nov. 1861 as an answer to Francis Newman's pamphlet, *Homeric Translation in Theory and Practice: A Reply to Matthew Arnold, Esq.* (8 June 1861); published as a book 1862. Newman's 'reply' was prompted by A.'s unfavourable analysis of his translations of Homer in the first three lectures delivered 3 Nov., 8 Dec. 1860, 26 Jan. 1861, and published as a book 1861. For contemporary translations of Homer and the continuing debate since F. Wolfe's *Prolegomena ad Homerum* (1795), which stressed the oral tradition of the Homeric poems, see *CPW* i. 339. A. chose the subject because of its topicality and 'because of complaints that I did not enough lecture on poetry'.

[*The Grand Style*]

... Nothing has raised more questioning among my critics than these words, – *noble, the grand style*. People complain that I do

not define these words sufficiently, that I do not tell them enough
about them. 'The grand style, – but what *is* the grand style?' – they
cry; some with an inclination to believe in it, but puzzled; others
mockingly and with incredulity. Alas! the grand style is the last
matter in the world for verbal definition to deal with adequately.
One may say of it as is said of faith: 'One must feel it in order to
know what it is.' But, as of faith, so too one may say of nobleness,
of the grand style: 'Woe to those who know it not![1] Yet this
expression, though indefinable, has a charm; one is the better for
considering it; *bonum est, nos hic esse*; nay, one loves to try to
explain it, though one knows that one must speak imperfectly.
For those, then, who ask the question, – What is the grand style?
– with sincerity, I will try to make some answer, inadequate as it
must be. For those who ask it mockingly I have no answer, except
to repeat to them, with compassionate sorrow, the Gospel words:
Moriemini in peccatis inpeccatis vestris, – Ye shall die in your
sins.[2]

But let me, at any rate, have the pleasure of again giving, before
I begin to try and define the grand style, a specimen of what it *is*.

> Standing on earth, not rapt above the pole,
> More safe I sing with mortal voice, unchanged
> To hoarse or mute, though fall'n on evil days,
> On evil days though fall'n, and evil tongues.... [3]

There is the grand style in perfection; and any one who has a sense
for it, will feel it a thousand times better from repeating those lines
than from hearing anything I can say about it.

Let us try, however, what *can* be said, controlling what we say
by examples. I think it will be found that the grand style arises in
poetry, *when a noble nature, poetically gifted, treats with simplic-
ity or with severity a serious subject.* I think this definition will be
found to cover all instances of the grand style in poetry which
present themselves. I think it will be found to exclude all poetry
which is not in the grand style. And I think it contains no terms
which are obscure, which themselves need defining. Even those
who do not understand what is meant by calling poetry noble,
will understand, I imagine, what is meant by speaking of a noble
nature in a man. But the noble or powerful nature – the
bedeutendes Individuum of Goethe – is not enough. For instance,
Mr Newman has zeal for learning, zeal for thinking, zeal for
liberty, and all these things are noble, they ennoble a man; but he

has not the poetical gift: there must be the poetical gift, the 'divine faculty,' also. And, besides all this, the subject must be a serious one (for it is only by a kind of licence that we can speak of the grand style in comedy); and it must be treated *with simplicity or severity.* Here is the great difficulty: the poets of the world have been many; there has been wanting neither abundance of poetical gift nor abundance of noble natures; but a poetical gift so happy, in a noble nature so circumstanced and trained, that the result is a continuous style, perfect in simplicity or perfect in severity, has been extremely rare. One poet has had the gifts of nature and faculty in unequalled fulness, without the circumstances and training which make this sustained perfection of style possible. Of other poets, some have caught this perfect strain now and then, in short pieces or single lines, but have not been able to maintain it through considerable works; others have composed all their productions in a style which, by comparison with the best, one must call secondary.

The best model of the grand style simple is Homer; perhaps the best model of the grand style severe is Milton. But Dante is remarkable for affording admirable examples of both styles; he has the grand style which arises from simplicity, and he has the grand style which arises from severity; and from him I will illustrate them both. In a former lecture[4] I pointed out what that severity of poetical style is, which comes from saying a thing with a kind of intense compression, or in an allusive, brief, almost haughty way, as if the poet's mind were charged with so many and such grave matters, that he would not deign to treat any one of them explicitly. Of this severity the last line of the following stanza of the *Purgatory* is a good example. Dante has been telling Forese that Virgil had guided him through Hell, and he goes on:

> Indi m' han tratto su gli suoi conforti,
> Salendo e rigirando la Montagna
> *Che drizza voi che il mondo fece torti.* *

'Thence hath his comforting aid led me up, climbing and circling the Mountain *which straightens you whom the world made crooked.*' These last words, 'la Montagna *che drizza voi che il mondo fece torti,*' – 'the Mountain *which straightens you whom the world made crooked,*' – for the Mountain of Purgatory, I call an excellent specimen of the grand style in severity, where the

Purgatory, xxiii. 124

poet's mind is too full charged to suffer him to speak more explicitly. But the very next stanza is a beautiful specimen of the grand style in simplicity, where a noble nature and a poetical gift unite to utter a thing with the most limpid plainness and clearness:

> Tanto dice di farmi sua compagna
> Ch' io sarò là dove fia Beatrice;
> Quivi convien che senza lui rimagna.*

'So long,' Dante continues, 'so long he [Virgil] saith he will bear me company, until I shall be there where Beatrice is; there it behoves that without him I remain.' But the noble simplicity of that in the Italian no words of mine can render.

Both these styles, the simple and the severe, are truly grand; the severe seems, perhaps, the grandest, so long as we attend most to the great personality, to the noble nature, in the poet its author; the simple seems the grandest when we attend most to the exquisite faculty, to the poetical gift. But the simple is no doubt to be preferred. It is the more *magical*: in the other there is something intellectual, something which gives scope for a play of thought which may exist where the poetical gift is either wanting or present in only inferior degree: the severe is much more imitable, and this a little spoils its charm. A kind of semblance of this style keeps Young going, one may say through all the nine parts of that most indifferent production, the Night Thoughts. But the grand style in simplicity is inimitable:

> αἰὼν ἀσφαλὴς
> οὐκ ἔγεντ' οὔτ' Αἰακίδᾳ παρὰ Πηλεῖ,
> οὔτε παρ' ἀντιθέῳ Κάδμῳ· λέγονται μὰν βροτῶν
> ὄλβον ὑπέρτατον οἱ σχεῖν, οἵ τε καὶ χρυσαμπύκων
> μελπομενᾶν ἐν ὄρει Μοισᾶν, καὶ ἐν ἑπταπύλοις
> ἄϊον Θήξαις. . . . †

There is a limpidness in that, a want of salient points to seize and transfer, which makes imitation impossible, except by a genius akin to the genius which produced it....

Purgatory, xxiii. 127

†'A secure time fell to the lot neither of Peleus the son of Aecus, nor of the god-like Cadmus ; howbeit these are said to have had, of all mortals, the supreme of happiness, who heard the golden-snooded Muses sing, one of them on the mountain (Pelion), the other in seven-gated Thebes.' [Pindar, *Pythian Odes*, iii. 86–91. cp. 'Empedocles on Etna', p. 36 above]

[*'Simplicité'* and *'Simplesse'*: *Tennyson and Wordsworth*].

... One sees how needful it is to direct incessantly the English translator's attention to the essential characteristics of Homer's poetry, when so accomplished a person as Mr Spedding,[5] recognising these characteristics as indeed Homer's, admitting them to be essential, is led by the ingrained habits and tendencies of English blank verse thus repeatedly to lose sight of them in translating even a few lines. One sees this yet more clearly, when Mr Spedding, taking me to task for saying that the blank verse used for rendering Homer 'must not be Mr Tennyson's blank verse,' declares that in most of Mr Tennyson's blank verse all Homer's essential characteristics, – 'rapidity of movement, *plainness of words and style, simplicity and directness of ideas*, and, above all, nobleness of manner, are as conspicuous as in Homer himself.' This shows, it seems to me, how hard it is for English readers of poetry, even the most accomplished, to feel deeply and permanently what Greek plainness of thought and Greek simplicity of expression really are: they admit the importance of these qualities in a general way, but they have no ever-present sense of them; and they easily attribute them to any poetry which has other excellent qualities, and which they very much admire. No doubt there are plainer things in Mr Tennyson's poetry than the three lines I quoted[6] in choosing them, as in choosing a specimen of ballad-poetry, I wished to bring out clearly, by a strong instance, the qualities of thought and style to which I was calling attention; but, when Mr Spedding talks of a plainness of thought *like Homer's*, of a plainness of speech *like Homer's*, and says that he finds these constantly in Mr Tennyson's poetry, I answer that these I do not find there at all. Mr Tennyson is a most distinguished and charming poet; but the very essential characteristic of his poetry is, it seems to me, an extreme subtlety and curious elaborateness of thought, an extreme subtlety and curious elaborateness of expression. In the best and most characteristic productions of his genius, these characteristics are most prominent. They are marked characteristics, as we have seen, of the Elizabethan poets; they are marked, though not the essential, characteristics of Shakespeare himself. Under the influences of the nineteenth century, under wholly new conditions of thought and culture, they manifest themselves in Mr Tennyson's poetry in a wholly new way. But they are still there. The essential bent of his poetry is towards such expressions as

> Now lies the Earth all Danaë to the stars ...

or

> O'er the sun's bright eye
> Drew the vast eyelid of an inky cloud ...

or

> When the cairn'd mountain was a shadow, sunn'd
> The world to peace again ...

or

> The fresh young captains flash'd their glittering teeth,
> The huge bush-bearded barons heaved and blew ...

or

> He bared the knotted column of his throat,
> The massive square of his heroic breast,
> The arms on which the standing muscle sloped
> As slopes a wild brook o'er a little stone,
> Running too vehemently to break upon it ...[7]

And this way of speaking is the least *plain*, the most *unHomeric*, which can possibly be conceived. Homer presents his thought to you just as it wells from the source of his mind: Mr Tennyson carefully distils his thought before he will part with it. Hence comes, in the expression of the thought, a heightened and elaborate air. In Homer's poetry it is all natural thoughts in natural words; in Mr Tennyson's poetry it is all distilled thoughts in distilled words. Exactly this heightening and elaboration may be observed in Mr Spedding's

> While the steeds mouth'd their corn aloof ...

(an expression which might have been Mr Tennyson's), on which I have already commented; and to one who is penetrated with a sense of the real simplicity of Homer, this subtle sophistication of the thought is, I think, very perceptible even in such lines as these,

> And drunk delight of battle with my peers
> Far on the ringing plains of windy Troy ...[8]

which I have seen quoted as perfectly Homeric. Perfect simplicity can be obtained only by a genius of which perfect simplicity is an essential characteristic.

So true is this, that when a genius essentially subtle, or a genius which, from whatever cause, is in its essence not truly and broadly

simple, determines to be perfectly plain, determines not to admit
a shade of subtlety or curiosity into its expression, it cannot even
then attain real simplicity; it can only attain a semblance of
simplicity.* French criticism, richer in its vocabulary than ours,
has invented a useful word to distinguish this semblance (often
very beautiful and valuable) from the real quality. The real quality
it calls *simplicité*, the semblance *simplesse*. The one is natural
simplicity, the other is artificial simplicity. What is called simplic-
ity in the productions of a genius essentially not simple, is in truth
simplesse. The two are distinguishable from one another the
moment they appear in company. For instance, let us take the
opening of the narrative in Wordsworth's 'Michael':

> Upon the forest-side in Grasmere Vale
> There dwelt a shepherd, Michael was his name;
> An old man, stout of heart, and strong of limb.
> His bodily frame had been from youth to age
> Of an unusual strength; his mind was keen,
> Intense, and frugal, apt for all affairs;
> And in his shepherd's calling he was prompt
> And watchful more than ordinary men.

Now let us take the opening of the narrative in Mr Tennyson's
'Dora':

> With Farmer Allan at the farm abode
> William and Dora. William was his son,
> And she his niece. He often look'd at them,
> And often thought, 'I'll make them man and wife.'

The simplicity of the first of these passages is *simplicité*; that of
the second, *simplesse*. Let us take the end of the same two poems; first,
of 'Michael':

> The cottage which was named the Evening Star
> Is gone – the ploughshare has been through the ground
> On which it stood; great changes have been wrought
> In all the neighbourhood: yet the oak is left
> That grew beside their door: and the remains
> Of the unfinish'd sheepfold may be seen
> Beside the boisterous brook of Green-head Ghyll.

---

*I speak of poetic genius as employing itself upon narrative or dramatic poetry, – poetry in
which the poet has to go out of himself and to create. In lyrical poetry, in the direct expression
of personal feeling, the most subtle genius may, under the momentary pressure of passion,
express itself simply. Even here, however, the native tendency will generally be discernible.

And now, of 'Dora':

> So those four abode
> Within one house together; and as years
> Went forward, Mary took another mate;
> But Dora lived unmarried till her death.

A heedless critic may call both of these passages simple if he will. Simple, in a certain sense, they both are; but between the simplicity of the two there is all the difference that there is between the simplicity of Homer and the simplicity of Moschus....[9]

[*Ballad style and the 'Lyrical Cry'*]

... Every one knows the 'Lucy Gray' and the 'Ruth' of Wordsworth. Both poems are excellent; but the subject-matter of the narrative of 'Ruth' is much more weighty and impressive to the poet's own feeling than that of the narrative of 'Lucy Gray', for which latter, in its unpretending simplicity, the ballad-form is quite adequate. Wordsworth, at the time he composed 'Ruth', – his great time, his *annus mirabilis*, about 1800, – strove to be simple; it was his mission to be simple; he loved the ballad-form, he clung to it, because it was simple. Even in 'Ruth' he tried, one may say, to use it; he would have used it if he could: but the gravity of his matter is too much for this somewhat slight form; he is obliged to give to his form more amplitude, more augustness, to shake out its folds.

> The wretched parents all that night
>   Went shouting far and wide;
> But there was neither sound nor sight
>   To serve them for a guide.

That is beautiful, no doubt, and the form is adequate to the subject-matter. But take this, on the other hand:

> I, too, have passed her on the hills,
> Setting her little water-mills
>   By spouts and fountains wild;
> Such small machinery as she turned,
> Ere she had wept, ere she had mourned,
>   A young and happy child.

Who does not perceive how the greater fulness and weight of his matter has here compelled the true and feeling poet to adopt a form of more *volume* than the simple ballad-form?

It is of narrative poetry that I am speaking; the question is

about the use of the ballad-form for *this*. I say that for this poetry
(when in the grand style, as Homer's is) the ballad-form is entirely
inadequate; and that Homer's translator must not adopt it, be-
cause it even leads him, by its own weakness, away from the grand
style rather than towards it. We must remember that the matter
of narrative poetry stands in a different relation to the vehicle
which conveys it, – is not so independent of this vehicle, so
absorbing and powerful in itself, – as the matter of purely emo-
tional poetry. When there comes in poetry what I may call the
lyrical cry, this transfigures everything, makes everything grand;
the simplest form may be here even an advantage, because the
flame of the emotion glows through and through it more easily.
To go again for an illustration to Wordsworth; – our great poet,
since Milton, by his performance, as Keats, I think, is our great
poet by his gift and promise; – in one of his stanzas to the Cuckoo,
we have:

> And I can listen to thee yet;
> Can lie upon the plain
> And listen, till I do beget
> That golden time again.

Here the lyrical cry, though taking the simple ballad form, is as
grand as the lyrical cry coming in poetry of an ampler form, as
grand as the

> An innocent life, yet far astray!

of 'Ruth'; as the

> There is a comfort in the strength of love

of 'Michael'. In this way, by the occurrence of this lyrical cry, the
ballad-poets themselves rise sometimes, though not so often as
one might perhaps have hoped, to the grand style.

> O lang, lang may their ladies sit,
> Wi' their fans into their hand,
> Or ere they see Sir Patrick Spence
> Come sailing to the land.
>
> O lang, lang may the ladies stand,
> Wi' their gold combs in their hair,
> Waiting for their ain dear lords,
> For they'll see them nae mair.[10]

But from this impressiveness of the ballad-form, when its subject-
matter fills it over and over again, – is, indeed, in itself, all in all,

– one must not infer its effectiveness when its subject-matter is not thus overpowering, in the great body of a narrative.

But, after all, Homer is not a better poet than the balladists, because he has taken in the hexameter a better instrument; he took this instrument because he was a *different* poet from them; so different, – not only so much better, but so essentially different, – that he is not to be classed with them at all. Poets receive their distinctive character, not from their subject, but from their application to that subject of the ideas (to quote the *Excursion*)

On Man, on Nature, and on human life,[11]

which they have acquired for themselves. In the ballad poets in general, as in men of a rude and early stage of the world, in whom their humanity is not yet variously and fully developed, the stock of these ideas is scanty, and the ideas themselves not very effective or profound. [For] them the narrative itself is the great matter, not the spirit and significance which underlies the narrative. Even in later times of richly developed life and thought, poets appear who have what may be called a *balladist's mind*; in whom a fresh and lively curiosity for the outward spectacle of the world is much more strong than their sense of the inward significance of that spectacle. When they apply ideas to their narrative of human events, you feel that they are, so to speak, travelling out of their own province: in the best of them you feel this perceptibly, but in those of a lower order you feel it very strongly. Even Sir Walter Scott's efforts of this kind, – even, for instance, the

Breathes there the man with soul so dead,

or the

O woman! in our hours of ease, –

even these leave, I think, as high poetry, much to be desired; far more than the same poet's descriptions of a hunt or a battle. But Lord Macaulay's

Then out spake brave Horatius,
   The captain of the gate:
'To all the men upon this earth
   Death cometh soon or late,'

(and here, since I have been reproached with undervaluing Lord Macaulay's *Lays of Ancient Rome*, let me frankly say, that, to my mind, a man's power to detect the ring of false metal in those Lays is a good measure of his fitness to give an opinion about poetical matters at all), – I say, Lord Macaulay's

> To all the men upon this earth
> Death cometh soon or late,

it is hard to read without a cry of pain. But with Homer it is very different. This 'noble barbarian,' this 'savage with the lively eye', – whose verse, Mr Newman thinks, would affect us, if we could hear the living Homer, 'like an elegant and simple melody from an African of the Gold Coast,' – is never more at home, never more nobly himself, than in applying profound ideas to his narrative. As a poet he belongs – narrative as is his poetry, and early as is his date – to an incomparably more developed spiritual and intellectual order than the balladists, or than Scott and Macaulay; he is here as much to be distinguished from them, and in the same way, as Milton is to be distinguished from them. He is, indeed, rather to be classed with Milton than with the balladists and Scott; for what he has in common with Milton – the noble and profound applications of ideas to life – is the most essential part of poetic greatness....

[*Homeric Simplicity: Arthur Hugh Clough*[12]]

It is for the future translator that one must work. The successful translator of Homer will have (or he cannot succeed) that true sense for his subject, and that disinterested love of it, which are, both of them, so rare in literature, and so precious; he will not be led off by any false scent; he will have an eye for the real matter, and, where he thinks he may find any indication of this, no hint will be too slight for him, no shade will be too fine, no imperfections will turn him aside, – he will go before his adviser's thought, and help it out with his own. This is the sort of student that a critic of Homer should always have in his thoughts; but students of this sort are indeed rare.

And how, then, can I help being reminded what a student of this sort we have just lost in Mr Clough[13] whose name I have already mentioned in these lectures? He, too, was busy with Homer, but it is not on that account that I now speak of him. Nor do I speak of him in order to call attention to his qualities and powers in general, admirable as these were. I mention him because, in so eminent a degree, he possessed these two invaluable literary qualities, – a true sense for his object of study, and a single-hearted care for it. He had both; but he had the second even more eminently than the first. He greatly developed the first through means of the second. In the study of art, poetry, or philosophy, he had the most undivided and disinterested love for his object in itself, the greatest aversion to mixing up with it anything accidental or personal. His interest was in literature itself; and it was this which gave so rare a stamp to his character, which kept him so free from all taint of littleness. In the saturnalia of ignoble personal passions, of which the struggle for literary success, in old and crowded communities, offers so sad a spectacle, he never mingled. He had not yet traduced his friends, nor flattered his enemies, nor disparaged what he admired, nor praised what he despised. Those who knew him well had the conviction that, even with time, these literary arts would never be his. His poem, of which I before spoke, has some admirable Homeric qualities; – out-of-doors freshness, life, naturalness, buoyant rapidity. Some of the expressions in that poem, – 'Dangerous Corrievreckan ... Where roads are unknown to Loch Nevish,'[14] – come back now to my ear with the true Homeric ring. But that in him of which I think oftenest is the Homeric simplicity of his literary life.

From Democracy

Introduction to *The Popular Education in France* (1861), A.'s report completed 1860 of his work March–Aug. 1859 in France, Switzerland and Holland as Foreign Commissioner to the Royal Commission in Education (established 1858 under the chairmanship of the Duke of Newcastle). Considered for inclusion in *Essays in Criticism* (1865) as 'one of the things I have taken most pains with' (*Buckler* 68) but finally printed separately 1879 with present title. R. Super notes, 'In many ways the Introduction is the keystone of his thinking about politics and education' (*CPW* ii. 330).

[State Action]

... I am convinced that if the worst mischiefs of democracy ever happen in England, it will be, not because a new condition of things has come upon us unforeseen, but because, though we all foresaw it, our efforts to deal with it went in the wrong direction. At the present time, almost every one believes in the growth of democracy, almost every one talks of it, almost every one laments it; but the last thing people can be brought to do is to make timely preparation for it. Many of those who, if they would, could do most to forward this work of preparation, are made slack and hesitating by the belief that, after all, in England, things may probably never go very far; that it will be possible to keep much more of the past than speculators say. Others, with a more robust faith, think that all democracy wants is vigorous putting-down; and that, with a good will and strong hand, it is perfectly possible to retain or restore the whole system of the Middle Ages.[1] Others, free from the prejudices of class and position which warp the judgment of these, and who would, I believe, be the first and greatest gainers by strengthening the hands of the State, are averse from doing so by reason of suspicions and fears, once perfectly well-grounded, but, in this age and in the present circumstances, well-grounded no longer.

I speak of the middle classes. I have already shown how it is the natural disposition of an aristocratical class to view with jealousy the development of a considerable State-Power. But this disposition has in England found extraordinary favour and support in regions not aristocratical, – from the middle classes; and, above all, from the kernel of these classes, the Protestant Dissenters. And for a very good reason. In times when passions ran high, even an aristocratical executive was easily stimulated into using, for the gratification of its friends and the abasement of its enemies, those administrative engines which, the moment it chose to stretch its hand forth, stood ready for its grasp. Matters of domestic concern, matters of religious profession and religious exercise, offered a peculiar field for an intervention gainful and agreeable to friends, injurious and irritating to enemies. Such an intervention was attempted and practised. Government lent its machinery and authority to the aristocratical and ecclesiastical party, which it regarded as its best support. The party which suffered comprised the flower and strength of that middle class of society, always very flourishing and robust in this country. That powerful class, from this specimen of the administrative activity of government, conceived a strong antipathy against all intervention of the State in certain spheres. An active, stringent administration in those spheres, meant at that time a High Church and Prelatic administration in them, an administration galling to the Puritan party and to the middle class; and this aggrieved class had naturally no proneness to draw nice philosophical distinctions between State-action in these spheres, as a thing for abstract consideration, and

State-action in them as they practically felt it and supposed themselves likely long to feel it, guided by their adversaries. In the minds of the English middle class, therefore, State-action in social and domestic concerns became inextricably associated with the idea of a Conventicle Act, a Five-Mile Act, an Act of Uniformity.[2] Their abhorrence of such a State-action as this they extended to State-action in general; and, having never known a beneficent and just State-power, they enlarged their hatred of a cruel and partial State-power, the only one they had ever known, into a maxim that no State-power was to be trusted, that the least action, in certain provinces, was rigorously to be denied to the State, whenever this denial was possible.

Thus that jealousy of an important, sedulous, energetic executive, natural to grandees unwilling to suffer their personal authority to be circumscribed, their individual grandeur to be eclipsed, by the authority and grandeur of the State, became reinforced in this country by a like sentiment among the middle classes, who had no such authority or grandeur to lose, but who, by a hasty reasoning, had theoretically condemned for ever an agency which they had practically found at times oppressive. *Leave us to ourselves!* magnates and middle classes alike cried to the State. Not only from those who were full and abounded went up this prayer, but also from those whose condition admitted of great amelioration. Not only did the whole repudiate the physician, but also those who were sick.[3]

For it is evident, that the action of a diligent, an impartial, and a national government, while it can do little to better the condition, already fortunate enough, of the highest and richest class of its people, can really do much, by institution and regulation, to better that of the middle and lower classes. The State can bestow certain broad collective benefits, which are indeed not much if compared with the advantages already possessed by individual grandeur, but which are rich and valuable if compared with the make-shifts of mediocrity and poverty. A good thing meant for the many cannot well be so exquisite as the good things of the few; but it can easily, if it comes from a donor of great resources and wide power, be incomparably better than what the many could, unaided, provide for themselves....[4]

The State, – but what is the State? cry many. Speculations on the idea of a State abound, but these do not satisfy them; of that which is to have practical effect and power they require a plain

account. The full force of the term, *the State*, as the full force
of any other important term, no one will master without going
a little deeply, without resolutely entering the world of ideas:
but it is possible to give in very plain language an account of it
sufficient for all practical purposes. The State is properly just
what Burke called it: *the nation in its collective and corporate
character.*[5] The State is the representative acting-power of the
nation; the action of the State is the representative action of the
nation. Nominally emanating from the Crown, as the ideal
unity in which the nation concentrates itself, this action, by the
constitution of our country, really emanates from the Ministers
of the Crown. It is common to hear the depreciators of State-
action run through a string of Ministers' names, and then say:
'Here is really your *State*; would you accept the action of these
men as your own representative action? in what respect is their
judgment on national affairs likely to be any better than that
of the rest of the world?' In the first place I answer: Even
supposing them to be originally no better or wiser than the rest
of the world, they have two great advantages from their posi-
tion: access to almost boundless means of information, and the
enlargement of mind which the habit of dealing with great
affairs tends to produce. Their position itself, therefore, if they are
men of only average honesty and capacity, tends to give them a
fitness for acting on behalf of the nation superior to that of other
men of equal honesty and capacity who are not in the same
position. This fitness may be yet further increased by treating
them as persons on whom, indeed, a very grave responsibility
has fallen, and from whom very much will be expected; –
nothing less than the representing, each of them in his own
department, under the control of Parliament, and aided by the
suggestions of public opinion, the collective energy and intelli-
gence of his nation. By treating them as men on whom all this
devolves to do, to their honour if they do it well, to their shame
if they do it ill, one probably augments their faculty of well-
doing; as it is excellently said: 'To treat men as if they were
better than they are, is the surest way to *make* them better than
they are.' ...

But in the second place I answer: If the executive government
is really in the hands of men no wiser than the bulk of mankind,
of men whose action an intelligent man would be unwilling to
accept as representative of his own action, whose fault is that? It

is the fault of the nation itself, which, not being in the hands of a despot or an oligarchy, being free to control the choice of those who are to sum up and concentrate its action, controls it in such a manner that it allows to be chosen agents so little in its confidence, or so mediocre, or so incompetent, that it thinks the best thing to be done with them is to reduce their action as near as possible to a nullity. Hesitating, blundering, unintelligent, inefficacious, the action of the State may be; but, such as it is, it is the collective action of the nation itself, and the nation is responsible for it. It is our own action which we suffer to be thus unsatisfactory. Nothing can free us from this responsibility. The conduct of our affairs is in our own power. To carry on into its executive proceedings the indecision, conflict, and discordance of its parliamentary debates, may be a natural defect of a free nation, but it is certainly a defect; it is a dangerous error to call it, as some do, a perfection. The want of concert, reason, and organisation in the State, is the want of concert, reason, and organisation in the collective nation....

I will not deny that to give a more prominent part to the State would be a considerable change in this country; that maxims once very sound, and habits once very salutary, may be appealed to against it. The sole question is, whether those maxims and habits are sound and salutary at this moment. A yet graver and more difficult change, – to reduce the all-effacing prominence of the State, to give a more prominent part to the individual, – is imperiously presenting itself to other countries. Both are the suggestions of one irresistible force, which is gradually making its way everywhere, removing old conditions and imposing new, altering long-fixed habits, undermining venerable institutions, even modifying national character: *the modern spirit*....

From Maurice de Guérin

Delivered 15 Nov. 1862 as a lecture at Oxford entitled 'A Modern French Poet'; pub. *Fraser's Magazine* Jan. 1863; repr. *Essays in Criticism* 1865 as the earliest of the pieces collected and A.'s first attempt at this kind of critique. Guérin (1810–39), who abandoned his religious calling to devote himself to nature and poetry, published nothing in his short lifetime, but *Maurice de Guérin: Reliquae* appeared 1861 with a preface by Sainte-Beuve, to whose critical approach, especially in his *Causeries du Lundi*, A. is deeply indebted. Guérin's best known works include the prose poem *La Centaure* (quoted by A.), pub. *La Revue des Deux Mondes* (May 1840), and his *Journal Intime* written 1832–35. A.'s essay includes a sensitive account of his life with frequent quotations from his work rendered in his own translation, but it is also notable for its passages (printed below) on the 'interpretative power of poetry' and 'natural magic'.

... The grand power of poetry is its interpretative power; by which I mean, not a power of drawing out in black and white an explanation of the mystery of the universe, but the power of so dealing with things as to awaken in us a wonderfully full, new, and intimate sense of them, and of our relations with them. When this sense is awakened in us, as to objects without us, we feel ourselves to be in contact with the essential nature of those objects, to be no longer bewildered and oppressed by them, but to have their secret, and to be in harmony with them; and this feeling calms and satisfies us as no other can.... The interpretations of science do not give us this intimate sense of objects as the interpretations of poetry give it; they appeal to a limited faculty, and not to the whole man. It is not Linnaeus, or Cavendish, or Cuvier who gives us the true sense of animals, or water, or plants, who seizes their secret for us, who makes us participate in their life; it is Shakespeare, with his

> daffodils
> That come before the swallow dares, and take
> The winds of March with beauty;

it is Wordsworth, with his

> voice .... heard
> In spring-time from the cuckoo-bird,
> Breaking the silence of the seas.
> Among the farthest Hebrides;

it is Keats, with his

> moving waters at their priest-like task
> Of pure ablution round earth's human shores;

it is Chateaubriand, with his, '*cîme indéterminée des forêts*'; it is
Senancour, with his mountain birch tree: '*Cette écorce blanche,
lisse et crevassée; cette tige agreste; ces branches qui s'inclinent
vers la terre; la mobilité des feuilles, et tout cet abandon, simplicité
de la nature, attitude des déserts.*'[1]

Eminent manifestations of this magical power of poetry are
very rare and very precious; the compositions of Guérin manifest
it, I think, in singular eminence. Not his poems, strictly so called,
– his verse, – so much as his prose; ... poetry is interpretative both
by having *natural magic*[2] in it, and by having *moral profundity*. In
both ways it illuminates man; it gives him a satisfying sense of reality;
it reconciles him with himself and the universe. Thus Aeschylus's
'δράσαντι παθεῖν' and his 'ἀ νήριθμον γέλασμα' are alike inter-
pretative. Shakespeare interprets both when he says,

> Full many a glorious morning have I seen
> Flatter the mountain-tops with sovereign eye;

and when he says,

> There's a divinity that shapes our ends,
> Rough-hew them how we will.[3]

These great poets unite in themselves the faculty of both kinds of
interpretation, the naturalistic and the moral. But it is observable
that in the poets who unite both kinds, the latter (the moral)
usually ends by making itself the master. In Shakespeare the two
kinds seem wonderfully to balance one another; but even in him
the balance leans; his expression tends to become too little
sensuous and simple, too much intellectualized. The same thing
may be yet more strongly affirmed of Lucretius[4] and of Words-
worth. In Shelley there is not a balance of the two gifts, nor even
a co-existence of them, but there is a passionate straining after
them both, and this is what makes Shelley, as a man, so interesting:
I will not now inquire how much Shelley achieves as a poet, but
whatever he achieves, he in general fails to achieve natural
magic in his expression; in Mr Palgrave's charming *Treasury* may
be seen a gallery of his failures.* But in Keats and Guérin, in whom
the faculty of naturalistic interpretation is overpoweringly pre-
dominant, the natural magic is perfect; when they speak of the
world they speak like Adam naming by divine inspiration the

---

* Compare, for example, his 'Lines Written in the Euganean Hills', with Keats's 'Ode to Autumn'
(*Golden Treasury*, pp. 256, 284). The latter piece *renders* Nature ; the former *tries to render* her.
I will not deny, however, that Shelley has natural magic in his rhythm ; what I deny is, that he has
it in his language. It always seems to me that the right sphere for Shelley's genius was the sphere
of music, not of poetry ; the medium of sounds he can master, but to master the more difficult
medium of words he has neither intellectual force enough nor sanity enough.

creatures; their expression corresponds with the thing's essential reality. Even between Keats and Guérin, however, there is a distinction to be drawn. Keats has, above all, a sense of what is pleasurable and open in the life of nature; for him she is the *Alma Parens*: his expression has, therefore, more than Guérin's, something genial, outward, and sensuous. Guérin has, above all, a sense of what there is adorable and secret in the life of Nature; for him she is the *Magna Parens*; his expression has, therefore, more than Keats's, something mystic, inward, and profound....[5]

From Heinrich Heine

Delivered as a lecture at Oxford 13 June 1863; pub. *Cornhill Magazine* Aug. 1863; repr. *Littell's Living Age* (Boston) Oct. 1863, *Revue Britannique* (in transl.), July 1864, *Essays in Criticism* (1865). 'My object is not so much to give a literary history of Heine's works as to mark his place in modern European letters, and the special tendency and significance of what he did' (A.'s letter of 14 May 1863, *L* i. 193). The extracts below illustrate the early origins of A.'s concern with 'Philistinism': his interest in Heine dates from at least 1852 (see headnote to 'The Neckan' (1853), A.'s ballad poem in Heine's manner, *Poems* 281).

... To ascertain the master-current in the literature of an epoch, and to distinguish this from all minor currents, is one of the critic's highest functions; in discharging it he shows how far he possesses the most indispensable quality of his office, – justness of spirit. The living writer who has done most to make England acquainted with German authors, a man of genius, but to whom precisely this one quality of justness of spirit is perhaps wanting, – I mean Mr Carlyle, – seems to me in the result of his labours on German literature to afford a proof how very necessary to the critic this quality is.[1] Mr Carlyle has spoken admirably of Goethe; but then Goethe stands before all men's eyes, the manifest centre of German literature; and from this central source many rivers flow. Which of these rivers is the main stream? which of the courses of spirit which we see active in Goethe is the course which will most influence the future, and attract and be continued by the most powerful of Goethe's successors? – that is the question. Mr Carlyle attaches, it seems to me, far too much importance to the romantic school of Germany, – Tieck, Novalis, Jean Paul Richter, – and gives to these writers, really gifted as two, at any rate, of them are, an undue prominence. These writers, and others with aims and a general tendency the same as theirs, are not the real inheritors and continuators of Goethe's power; the current of their activity is not the main current of German literature after Goethe. Far more in Heine's works flows this main current; Heine, far more than Tieck or Jean Paul Richter, is the continuator of that which, in Goethe's varied activity, is the most powerful and vital; on Heine, of all German authors who survived Goethe, incomparably the largest portion of Goethe's mantle fell....

Goethe's profound, imperturbable naturalism is absolutely fatal to all routine thinking; he puts the standard, once for all, inside every man instead of outside him; when he is told such a thing must be so, there is immense authority and custom in favour of its being so, it has been held to be so for a thousand years, he answers with Olympian politeness, 'But *is* it so? is it so to *me*?' Nothing could be more really subversive of the foundations on which the old European order rested; and it may be remarked that no persons are so radically detached from this order, no persons so thoroughly modern, as those who have felt Goethe's influence most deeply. If it is said that Goethe professes to have in this way deeply influenced but a few persons, and those persons poets, one may answer that he could have taken no better way to secure, in the end, the ear of the world; for poetry is simply the most beautiful, impressive, and widely effective mode of saying things, and hence its importance. Nevertheless the process of liberation, as Goethe worked it, though sure, is undoubtedly slow; he came, as Heine says, to be eighty years old in thus working it, and at the end of that time the old Middle-Age machine was still creaking on, the thirty German courts and their chamberlains subsisted in all their glory; Goethe himself was a minister, and the visible triumph of the modern spirit over prescription and routine seemed as far off as ever. It was the year 1830; the German sovereigns had passed the preceding fifteen years in breaking the promises of freedom they had made to their subjects when they wanted their help in the final struggle with Napoleon. Great events were happening in France; the revolution, defeated in 1815, had arisen from its defeat, and was wresting from its adversaries the power. Heinrich Heine, a young man of genius, born at Hamburg,[2] and with all the culture of Germany, but by race a Jew; with warm sympathies for France, whose revolution had given to his race the rights of citizenship, and whose rule had been, as is well known, popular in the Rhine provinces, where he passed his youth; with a passionate admiration for the great French Emperor, with a passionate contempt for the sovereigns who had overthrown him, for their agents, and for their policy, – Heinrich Heine was in 1830 in no humour for any such gradual process of liberation from the old order of things as that which Goethe had followed. His counsel was for open war.[3] With that terrible modern weapon, the pen, in his hand, he passed the remainder of his life in one fierce battle. What was that battle? the reader will ask. It was a life and death battle with Philistinism.[4]

Philistinism! – we have not the expression in English. Perhaps we have not the word because we have so much of the thing. At Soli,[5] I imagine, they did not talk of solecisms; and here, at the very headquarters of Goliath, nobody talks of Philistinism. The French have adopted the term *épicier* (grocer), to designate the sort of being whom the Germans designate by the term Philistine; but the French term, – besides that it casts a slur upon a respectable class, composed of living and susceptible members, while the original Philistines are dead and buried long ago, – is really, I think, in itself much less apt and expressive than the German term. Efforts have been made to obtain in English some term equivalent to *Philister* or *épicier*; Mr Carlyle has made several such efforts: 'respectability with its thousand gigs', he says[6] – well, the occupant of every one of these gigs is, Mr Carlyle means, a Philistine. However, the word *respectable* is far too valuable a word to be thus perverted from its proper meaning; if the English are ever to have a word for the things we are speaking of, – and so prodigious are the changes which the modern spirit is introducing, that even we English shall perhaps one day come to want such a word, – I think we had much better take the term *Philistine* itself.

Philistine must have originally meant, in the mind of those who invented the nickname, a strong, dogged, unenlightened opponent of the chosen people, of the children of the light.[7] The party of change, the would-be remodellers of the old traditional European order, the invokers of reason against custom, the representatives of the modern spirit in every sphere where it is applicable, regarded themselves, with the robust self-confidence natural to reformers as a chosen people, as children of the light. They regarded their adversaries as humdrum people, slaves to routine, enemies to light; stupid and oppressive, but at the same time very strong. This explains the love which Heine, that Paladin of the

FROM HEINRICH HEINE 159

modern spirit, has for France; it explains the preference which he gives to France over Germany: 'the French', he says, 'are the chosen people of the new religion, its first gospels and dogmas have been drawn up in their language; Paris is the new Jerusalem, and the Rhine is the Jordan which divides the consecrated land of freedom from the land of the Philistines'. He means that the French, as a people, have shown more accessibility to ideas than any other people; that prescription and routine have had less hold upon them than upon any other people; that they have shown most readiness to move and to alter at the bidding (real or supposed) of reason. This explains, too, the detestation which Heine had for the English: 'I might settle in England', he says, in his exile, 'if it were not that I should find there two things, coal-smoke and Englishmen; I cannot abide either.' What he hated in the English was the 'ächtbritische Beschränktheit', as he called it, – the *genuine British narrowness*.[8] In truth, the English, profoundly as they have modified the old Middle-Age order, great as is the liberty which they have secured for themselves, have in all their changes proceeded, to use a familiar expression, by the rule of thumb; what was intolerably inconvenient to them they have suppressed, and as they have suppressed it, not because it was irrational, but because it was practically inconvenient, they have seldom in suppressing it appealed to reason, but always, if possible, to some precedent, or form, or letter, which served as a convenient instrument for their purpose, and which saved them from the necessity of recurring to general principles. They have thus become, in a certain sense, of all people the most inaccessible to ideas and the most impatient of them; inaccessible to them, because of their want of familiarity with them; and impatient of them because they have got on so well without them, that they despise those who, not having got on as well as themselves, still make a fuss for what they themselves have done so well without. But there has certainly followed from hence, in this country, somewhat of a general depression of pure intelligence: Philistia has come to be thought by us the true Land of Promise, and it is anything but that; the born lover of ideas, the born hater of commonplace, must feel in this country that the sky over his head is of brass and iron.[9] The enthusiast for the idea, for reason, values reason, the idea, in and for themselves; he values them, irrespectively of the practical conveniences which their triumph may obtain for him; and the man who regards the possession of these practical conveniences as something sufficient in itself, something which compensates for the absence or surrender of the idea, of reason, is, in his eyes, a Philistine. This is why Heine so often and so mercilessly attacks the liberals; much as he hates conservatism he hates Philistinism even more, and whoever attacks conservatism itself ignobly, not as a child of light, not in the name of the idea, is a Philistine. Our Cobbett is thus for him, much as he disliked our clergy and aristocracy whom Cobbett attacked, a Philistine with six fingers on every hand and on every foot six toes, four-and-twenty in number: a Philistine, the staff of whose spear is like a weaver's beam. ...[10]

We in England, in our great burst of literature during the first thirty years of the present century, had no manifestation of the modern spirit, as this spirit manifests itself in Goethe's works or Heine's. And the reason is not far to seek. We had neither the German wealth of ideas, nor the French enthusiasm for applying ideas. There reigned in the mass of the nation that inveterate inaccessibility to ideas, that Philistinism, – to use the German nickname, – which reacts even on the individual genius that is exempt from it. In our greatest literary epoch, that of the Elizabethan age, English society at large was accessible to ideas, was permeated by them, was vivified by them, to a degree which has never been reached in England since. Hence the unique greatness in English literature of Shakespeare and his contemporaries; they were powerfully upheld by the intellectual life of their nation; they applied freely in literature the then modern ideas, – the ideas of the Renascence and the Reformation. A few years afterwards the great English middle class, the kernel of the nation, the class whose intelligent sympathy had upheld a Shakespeare, entered the prison of Puritanism, and had the key turned on its spirit there for two hundred years. *He enlargeth a nation*, says Job, *and straiteneth it again.*[11] In the literary movement of the beginning of the nineteenth century the signal attempt to apply freely the modern spirit was made in England by two members of the aristocratic class, Byron and Shelley. Aristocracies are, as such, naturally impenetrable by ideas; but their individual members have a high courage and a turn for breaking bounds; and a man of genius, who is the born child of the idea, happening to be born in the aristocratic ranks, chafes against the obstacles which prevent him from freely developing it. But Byron and Shelley did not succeed in their attempt freely to apply the modern spirit in

English literature; they could not succeed in it; the resistance to baffle them, the want of intelligent sympathy to guide and uphold them, were too great. Their literary creation, compared with the literary creation of Shakespeare and Spenser, compared with the literary creation of Goethe and Heine, is a failure. The best literary creation of that time in England proceeded from men who did not make the same bold attempts as Byron and Shelley. What, in fact was the career of the chief English men of letters, their contemporaries? The greatest of them, Wordsworth, retired (in Middle-Age phrase) into a monastery. I mean, he plunged himself in the inward life, he voluntarily cut himself off from the modern spirit. Coleridge took to opium. Scott became the historiographer royal of feudalism. Keats passionately gave himself up to a sensuous genius, to his faculty for interpreting nature; and he died of consumption at twenty-five. Wordsworth, Scott, and Keats have left admirable works; far more solid and complete works than those which Byron and Shelley have left. But their works have this defect, – they do not belong to that which is the main current of the literature of modern epochs, they do not apply modern ideas to life; they constitute, therefore, *minor currents*, and all other literary work of our day, however popular, which has the same defect, also constitutes but a minor current. Byron and Shelley will long be remembered, long after the inadequacy of their actual work is clearly recognized for their passionate, their Titanic effort to flow in the main stream of modern literature; their names will be greater than their writings; *stat magni nominis umbra*....[12]

From Spinoza and the Bible

Originally planned as an article for *The Times* in reply to criticisms of A.'s 'The Bishop and the Philosopher' (*Macmillan's Magazine*, Jan. 1863), contrasting Bishop Colenso's 'jejune and technical manner of dealing with Biblical controversy with that of Spinoza in his famous treatise on the Interpretations of Scripture' (A.'s letter of 19 Nov. 1862, L i. 75), but eventually published *Macmillan's Magazine* (Dec. 1863) as 'A Word More about Spinoza'; repr. *Essays in Criticism* (1865), with the present title and incorporating passages on the *Tractatus Theologico-Politicus* from the Jan. 1863 article. A.'s interest in Spinoza dates from at least 23 Oct. 1850 (see his letter of this date to Clough about his 'positive and vivifying atmosphere ... I have been studying [him] lately with profit', *CL* 117); for a probable longer acquaintance see K. Allott in *Victorian Studies*, March 1960, iii. 320 and for Spinoza's seminal influence on Victorian thinkers Basil Willey's *Nineteenth-century Studies* (1949) and *CPW* iii. 415–16. The extracts below, taken from the later part of the essay, define in Spinoza qualities of temperament and character (qualities 'in the grand style') which A. profoundly admired.

... Mr Maurice, seeking for the cause of Goethe's great admiration for Spinoza, thinks that he finds it in Spinoza's Hebrew genius. 'He spoke to God', says Mr Maurice, 'as an actual being, to those who had fancied him a name in a book. The child of the circumcision had a message for Lessing and Goethe which the pagan schools of philosophy could not bring.[1] This seems to me, I confess, fanciful. An intensity and impressiveness, which came to him from his Hebrew nature, Spinoza no doubt has; but the two things which are most remarkable about him, and by which, as I think, he chiefly impressed Goethe, seem to me not to come to him from his Hebrew nature at all, – I mean his denial of final causes, and his stoicism, a stoicism not passive, but active. For a mind like Goethe's, – a mind profoundly impartial and passionately aspiring after the science, not of men only, but of universal nature, – the popular philosophy which explains all things by reference to man, and regards universal nature as existing for the sake of man, and even of certain classes of men, was utterly repulsive. Unchecked, this philosophy would gladly maintain that the donkey exists in order that the invalid Christian may have donkey's milk before breakfast; and such views of nature as this were exactly what Goethe's whole soul abhorred. Creation, he thought, should be made of sterner stuff; he desired to rest the donkey's existence on larger grounds. More than any philosopher who has ever lived, Spinoza satisfied him here. The full exposition of the counter-doctrine to the popular doctrine of final causes is to be found in the Ethics; but this denial of final causes was so essential an element of all Spinoza's thinking that we shall, as has been said already, find it in the work with which we are here concerned, the *Tractatus Theologico-Politicus*, and, indeed, permeating that work and all his works....[2]

Spinoza's ideal is the intellectual life; the Christian's ideal is the religious life. Between the two conditions there is all the difference which there is between the being in love, and the following, with delighted comprehension, a reasoning of Plato. For Spinoza, undoubtedly, the crown of the intellectual life is a transport, as for the saint the crown of the religious life is a transport; but the two transports are not the same.

This is true; yet it is true, also, that by thus crowning the intellectual life with a sacred transport, by thus retaining in philosophy, amid the discontented murmurs of all the army of atheism, the name of God, Spinoza maintains a profound affinity with that which is truest in religion, and inspires an indestructible interest....

And Spinoza's life was not unworthy of this elevated strain. A philosopher who professed that knowledge was its own reward, a devotee who professed that the love of God was its own reward, this philosopher and this devotee believed in what he said. Spinoza led a life the most spotless, perhaps, to be found among the lives of philosophers; he lived simple, studious, even-tempered, kind; declining honours, declining riches, declining notoriety. He was poor, and his admirer Simon de Vries sent him two thousand florins; – he refused them. The same friend left him his fortune; – he returned it to the heir. He was asked to dedicate one of his works to the magnificent patron of letters in his century, Louis the Fourteenth; – he declined.[3] His great work, his Ethics, published after his death, he gave injunctions to his friends to publish anonymously, for fear he should give his name to a school. Truth, he thought, should bear no man's name.[4] And finally, – 'Unless', he said, 'I had known that my writings would in the end advance the cause of true religion, I would have suppressed them, – *tacuissem*.'[5] It was in this spirit that he lived; and this spirit gives to all he writes not exactly unction, – I have already said so, – but a kind of sacred solemnity. Not of the same order as the saints, he yet follows the same service: *Doubtless thou art our Father, though Abraham be ignorant of us, and Israel acknowledge us not.*[6]

Therefore he has been, in a certain sphere, edifying, and has inspired in many powerful minds an interest and an admiration such as no other philosopher has inspired since Plato. The lonely precursor of German philosophy, he still shines when the light of his successors is fading away; they had celebrity, Spinoza has fame. Not because his peculiar system of philosophy has had more adherents than theirs; on the contrary, it has had fewer. But schools of philosophy arise and fall; their bands of adherents inevitably dwindle; no master can long persuade a large body of disciples that they give to themselves just the same account of the world as he does; it is only the very young and the very enthusiastic who can think themselves sure that they possess the whole mind of Plato, or Spinoza, or Hegel, at all. The very mature and the very sober can even hardly believe that these philosophers possessed it themselves enough to put it all into their works, and to let us know entirely how the world seemed to them. What a remarkable philosopher really does for human thought, is to throw into circulation a certain number of new and striking ideas and expressions, and to stimulate with them the thought and imagination of his century or of after-times. So Spinoza has made his distinction between adequate and inadequate ideas a current notion for educated Europe. So Hegel seized a single pregnant sentence of Heracleitus, and cast it, with a thousand striking applications, into the world of modern thought. But to do this is only enough to make a philosopher noteworthy; it is not enough to make him great. To be great, he must have something in him which can influence character, which is edifying; he must, in short, have a noble and lofty character himself, a character, – to recur to that much-criticized expression of mine, – *in the grand style*.[7] This is what Spinoza had; and because he had it, he stands out from the multitude of philosophers, and has been able to inspire in powerful minds a feeling which the most remarkable philosophers, without this grandiose character, could not inspire.

From Joubert

Originally planned as an essay for early 1863 but eventually (on A.'s discontinuing his projected series of lectures on the Modern Element in Literature) delivered 28 Nov. 1863 as the final Oxford lecture for the year with title 'A French Coleridge'; repr. as 'Joubert; or a French Coleridge', *National Review* Jan. 1864, *Littell's Living Age* (Boston), 5 March 1864, *Essays in Criticism* 1865. Joseph Joubert (1754–1824), friend of Chateaubriand and Madame de Recamier, appointed by Napoleon 1809 to the governing body of Paris University, was renowned for his lucid reflections on life, literature and philosophy. A. draws on Pierre de Reynal's collection of his *Pensées, Maximes, Essais et Correspondance* (1842), a revision of Chateaubriand's 1838 edn. of *Recueil des Pensées* and was also affected by Sainte-Beuve on Joubert in *Causeries du lundi* (10 Dec. 1849) and *Chateaubriand et son groupe littéraire sous l'Empire* (1861). The *Spectator* found A.'s translations from Joubert had 'a spirit and meaning given to them in their English dress which makes them not merely equal, but in some respects superior impressions of the same thought ... by far the ablest [essay] on the subject we have seen' (30 Jan. 1864, xxxvii. 131). The extracts below include an instance of A.'s well known definition of literature as 'a criticism of life'.

... I have likened Joubert to Coleridge; and indeed the points of resemblance between the two men are numerous. Both of them great and celebrated talkers, Joubert attracting pilgrims to his upper chamber in the Rue St-Honoré, as Coleridge attracted pilgrims to Mr Gilman's at Highgate[1] both of them desultory and incomplete writers, – here they had an outward likeness with one another. Both of them passionately devoted to reading in a class of books, and to thinking on a class of subjects, out of the beaten line of the reading and thought of their day; both of them ardent students and critics of old literature, poetry, and the metaphysics of religion; both of them curious explorers of words, and of the latent significance hidden under the popular use of them; both of them, in a certain sense, conservative in religion and politics, by antipathy to the narrow and shallow foolishness of vulgar modern liberalism; – here they had their inward and real likeness. But that in which the essence of their likeness consisted is this, – that they both had from nature an ardent impulse for seeking the genuine truth on all matters they thought about, and a gift for finding it and recognizing it when it was found. To have the impulse for seeking this truth is much rarer than most people think; to have the gift for finding it is, I need not say, very rare indeed. By this they have a spiritual relationship of the closest kind with one another, and they become, each of them, a source of stimulus and progress for all of us.

Coleridge had less delicacy and penetration than Joubert, but more richness and power; his production, though far inferior to what his nature at first seemed to promise, was abundant and varied. Yet in all his production how much is there to dissatisfy us! How many reserves must be made in praising either his poetry, or his criticism, or his philosophy! How little either of his poetry, or of his criticism, or of his philosophy, can we expect permanently to stand! But that which will stand of Coleridge is this: the stimulus of his continual effort, – not a moral effort, for he had no morals, – but of his continual instinctive effort, crowned often with rich success, to get at and to lay bare the real truth of his matter in hand, whether that matter were literary, or philosophical, or political, or religious; and this in a country where at that moment such an effort was almost unknown; where the most powerful minds threw themselves upon poetry, which conveys truth, indeed, but conveys it indirectly; and where ordinary minds were so habituated to do without thinking altogether, to regard considerations of established routine and practical convenience as paramount, that any attempt to introduce within the domain of these the disturbing element of thought, they were prompt to resent as an outrage. Coleridge's great action lay in his supplying in England, for many years and under critical circumstances, by the spectacle of this effort of his, a stimulus to all minds, in the generation which grew up around him, capable of profiting by it. His action will still be felt as long as the need for it continues; when, with the cessation of the need, the action too has ceased, Coleridge's memory, in spite of the disesteem – nay, repugnance – which his character may and must inspire, will yet for ever remain invested with that interest and gratitude which invests the memory of founders....

There is, however, in France a sympathy with intellectual activity for its own sake, and for the sake of its inherent pleasurableness and beauty, keener than any which exists in England; and Joubert had more effect in Paris, – though his conversation was his only weapon, and Coleridge wielded besides his conversation his pen, – than Coleridge had or could have in London. I mean, a more immediate, appreciable effect; an effect not only upon the young and enthusiastic, to whom the future belongs, but upon formed and important personages to whom the present belongs, and who are actually moving society. He owed this partly to his real advantages over Coleridge. If he had, as I have already said, less power and richness than his English parallel, he had more tact and penetration. He was more *possible* than Coleridge; his doctrine was more intelligible than Coleridge's, more receivable. And yet with Joubert, the striving after a consummate and attractive clearness of expression came from no mere frivolous dislike of labour and inability for going deep, but was a part of his native love of truth and perfection. The delight of his life he found in truth, and in the satisfaction which the enjoying of truth gives to the spirit; and he thought the truth was never really and worthily said, so long as the least cloud, clumsiness, and repulsiveness hung about the expression of it.

Some of his best passages are those in which he upholds this doctrine. Even metaphysics he would not allow to remain difficult and abstract: so long as they spoke a professional jargon, the language of the schools, he maintained, – and who shall gainsay him? – that metaphysics were imperfect; or, at any rate, had not yet reached their ideal perfection.

> The true science of metaphysics [he says] consists not in rendering

> abstract that which is sensible, but in rendering sensible that which is abstract; apparent that which is hidden; imaginable, if so it may be, that which is only intelligible; and intelligible, finally, that which an ordinary attention fails to seize.[2]

and therefore:

> Distrust, in books on metaphysics, words which have not been able to get currency in the world, and are only calculated to form a special language....

I do not know whether the metaphysician will ever adopt Joubert's rules; but I am sure that the man of letters, whenever he has to speak of metaphysics, will do well to adopt them. He, at any rate, must remember:

> It is by means of familiar words that style takes hold of the reader and gets possession of him. It is by means of these that great thoughts get currency and pass for true metal, like gold and silver which have had a recognized stamp put upon them. They beget confidence in the man who, in order to make his thoughts more clearly perceived, uses them; for people feel that such an employment of the language of common human life betokens a man who knows that life and its concerns, and who keeps himself in contact with them. Besides, these words make a style frank and easy. They show that an author has long made the thought or the feeling expressed his mental food; that he has so assimilated them and familiarized them, that the most common expression suffice him in order to express ideas which have become everyday ideas to him by the length of time they have been in mind. And lastly, what one says in such words looks more true; for, of all the words in use, none are so clear as those which we call common words; and clearness is so eminently one of the characteristics of truth that often it even passes for truth itself.

These are not, in Joubert, mere counsels of rhetoric; they come from his accurate sense of perfection, from his having clearly seized the fine and just idea that beauty and light are properties of truth, and that truth is incompletely exhibited if it is exhibited without beauty and light....

Joubert was all his life a passionate lover of Plato; I hope other lovers of Plato will forgive me for saying that their adored object has never been more truly described than he is here:

> Plato shows us nothing, but he brings brightness with him; he puts light into our eyes, and fills us with a clearness by which all objects afterwards become illuminated. He teaches us nothing; but he

prepares us, fashions us, and makes us ready to know all. Somehow or other, the habit of reading him augments in us the capacity for discerning and entertaining whatever fine truths may afterwards present themselves. Like mountain air, it sharpens our organs, and gives us an appetite for wholesome food.

'Plato loses himself in the void' (he says again); 'but one sees the play of his wings, one hears their rustle.' And the conclusion is: 'It is good to breathe his air, but not to live upon him.' ...[3]

Joubert was not famous while he lived, and he will not be famous now that he is dead. But, before we pity him for this, let us be sure what we mean, in literature, by *famous*. There are the famous men of genius in literature, – the Homers, Dantes, Shakespeares: of them we need not speak; their praise is for ever and ever. Then there are the famous men of ability in literature: their praise is in their own generation. And what makes this difference? The work of the two orders of men is at the bottom the same, – *a criticism of life*. The end and aim of all literature, if one considers it attentively, is, in truth, nothing but that. But the criticism which the men of genius pass upon human life is permanently acceptable to mankind; the criticism which the men of ability pass upon human life is transitorily acceptable. Between Shakespeare's criticism of human life and Scribe's[4] the difference is there; – the one is permanently acceptable, the other transitorily. Whence then, I repeat, this difference. It is that the acceptableness of Shakespeare's criticism depends upon its inherent truth: the acceptableness of Scribe's upon its suiting itself, by its subject-matter, ideas, mode of treatment, to the taste of the generation that hears it. But the taste and ideas of one generation are not those of the next. This next generation in its turn arrives; – first its sharpshooters, its quick-witted, audacious light troops; then the elephantine main body. The imposing array of its predecessor it confidently assails, riddles it with bullets, passes over its body. It goes hard then with many once popular reputations, with many authorities once oracular. Only two kinds of authors are safe in the general havoc. The first kind are the great abounding fountains of truth, whose criticism of life is a source of illumination and joy to the whole human race for ever, – the Homers, the Shakespeares. These are the sacred personages, whom all civilized warfare respects. The second are those whom the out-skirmishers of the new generation, its forerunners, – quick-witted soldiers, as I have said, the select of the army, – recognize, though the bulk of their comrades behind might not, as of the same family and character with the sacred personages, exercising like them an immortal function, and like them inspiring a permanent interest. They snatch them up, and set them in a place of shelter, where the oncoming multitude may not overwhelm them. These are the Jouberts. They will never, like the Shakespeares, command the homage of the multitude; but they are safe; the multitude will not trample them down. Except these two kinds, no author is safe....

From Pagan and Religious Medieval Sentiment

Delivered as a lecture at Oxford 5 March 1864 as 'Pagan and Christian Religious Sentiment'; pub. with excisions *Cornhill Magazine* April 1864; repr. in the same form with the more appropriate present title *Essays in Criticism* (1865). A. wrote 17 March 1864 (*L* i. 229), 'a good deal about Protestantism is left out ... as it could not be stated fully enough quite to explain and secure itself' (for A. on dissent and education see his writings of this period on French education, especially 'A French Eton' (*CPW* ii. 262–325). The concluding passages of the essay, of which extracts are given below, follow on from A.'s comparison of Theocritus's fifteenth idyll with St. Francis's hymn to the sun and include one of his celebrated pronouncements on the art of criticism ('to get oneself out of the way and to let humanity decide' *CPW* iii. 227), his view of the 'religion of pleasure' ('to live by it one must never be sick or sorry', *CPW* iii. 227–8 and cp. *Empedocles on Etna* [1.i.20], p. 36 above) and his reference to 'imaginative reason' ('the element by which the modern spirit, if it would live right, has chiefly to live', quoted below).

... Now, the poetry of Theocritus's hymn is poetry treating the world according to the demand of the senses; the poetry of St Francis's hymn is poetry treating the world according to the demand of the heart and imagination. The first takes the world by its outward, sensible side; the second by its inward, symbolical side. The first admits as much of the world as is pleasure-giving; the second admits the whole world, rough and smooth, painful and pleasure-giving, all alike, but all transfigured by the power of a spiritual emotion, all brought under a law of supersensual love, having its seat in the soul. It can thus even say: 'Praised be my Lord for *our sister, the death of the body*.'

But these very words are, perhaps, an indication that we are touching upon an extreme. When we see Pompeii, we can put our finger upon the pagan sentiment in its extreme. And when we read of Monte Alverno and the *stigmata*[1] when we read of the repulsive, because self-caused, sufferings of the end of St Francis's life; when we find him even saying, 'I have sinned against my brother the ass', meaning by these words that he had been too hard upon his own body; when we find him assailed, even himself, by the doubt 'whether he who had destroyed himself by the severity of his penances could find mercy in eternity', we can put our finger on the medieval Christian sentiment in its extreme. Human nature is neither all senses and understanding, nor all heart and imagination. Pompeii was a sign that for humanity at large the measure of sensualism had been over-passed; St Francis's doubt was a sign that for humanity at large the measure of spiritualism had been over-passed. Humanity, in its violent rebound from one extreme, had swung from Pompeii to Monte Alverno; but it was sure not to stay there.

The Renascence is, in part, a return towards the pagan spirit, in the special sense in which I have been using the word pagan; a return towards the life of the senses and the understanding. The Reformation, on the other hand, is the very opposite to this; in Luther there is nothing Greek or pagan; vehemently as he attacked the adoration of St Francis, Luther had himself something of St Francis in him; he was a thousand times more akin to St Francis than to Theocritus or to Voltaire. The Reformation – I do not mean the inferior piece given under that name, by Henry the Eighth and a second-rate company, in this island, but the real Reformation, the German Reformation, Luther's Reformation – was a reaction of the moral and spiritual sense against the carnal and pagan sense; it was a religious revival like St Francis's, but this time against the Church of Rome, not within her; for the carnal and pagan sense had now, in the government of the Church of Rome herself, its prime representative. But the grand reaction against the rule of the heart and imagination, the strong return towards the rule of the senses and understanding, is in the eighteenth century. And this reaction has had no more brilliant champion than a man of the nineteenth, of whom I have already spoken; a man who could feel not only the pleasureableness but the poetry of the life of the senses (and the life of the senses has its deep poetry); a man who, in his very last poem, divided the whole world into 'Barbarians and Greeks', – Heinrich Heine. ...[2]

I have said a great deal of harm of paganism; and, taking

paganism to mean a state of things which it is commonly taken to mean, and which did really exist, no more harm than it well deserved. Yet I must not end without reminding the reader that, before this state of things appeared, there was an epoch in Greek life – in pagan life – of the highest possible beauty and value; an epoch which alone goes far towards making Greece the Greece we mean when we speak of Greece, – a country hardly less important to mankind than Judaea. The poetry of later paganism lived by the senses and understanding; the poetry of medieval Christianity lived by the heart and imagination. But the main element of the modern spirit's life is neither the senses and understanding, nor the heart and imagination; it is the imaginative reason. And there is a century in Greek life, – the century preceding the Peloponnesian war, from about the year 530 to the year 430 B.C., – in which poetry made, it seems to me, the noblest, the most successful effort she has ever made as the priestess of the imaginative reason, of the element by which the modern spirit, if it would live right, has chiefly to live. Of this effort, of which the four great names are Simonides, Pindar, Aeschylus, Sophocles, I must not now attempt more than the bare mention; but it is right, it is necessary, after all I have said, to indicate it. No doubt that effort was imperfect. Perhaps everything, take it at what point in its existence you will, carries within itself the fatal law of its ulterior development. Perhaps, even of the life of Pindar's time, Pompeii was the inevitable bourne. Perhaps the life of their beautiful Greece could not afford to its poets all that fullness of varied experience, all that power of emotion, which

> ... the heavy and the weary weight
> Of all this unintelligible world[3]

affords the poet of after-times. Perhaps in Sophocles the thinkingpower a little overbalances the religious sense, as in Dante the religious sense overbalances the thinking-power. The present has to make its own poetry, and not even Sophocles and his compeers, any more than Dante and Shakespeare, are enough for it. That I will not dispute; nor will I set up the Greek poets, from Pindar to Sophocles, as objects of blind worship. But no other poets so well show to the poetry of the present the way it must take; no other poets have lived so much by the imaginative reason; no other poets have made their work so well balanced; no other poets, who

have so well satisfied the thinking-power, have so well satisfied
the religious sense:

> Oh! that my lot may lead me in the path of holy innocence of word
> and deed, the path which august laws ordain, laws that in the highest
> empyrean had their birth, of which Heaven is the father alone, neither
> did the race of mortal men beget them, nor shall oblivion ever put
> them to sleep. The power of God is mighty in them, and groweth not
> old.[4]

Let St Francis – nay, or Luther either – beat that!

From The Literary Influence of Academies

Delivered as a lecture at Oxford 4 June 1864 entitled 'The Influence of Academies on
National Spirit and Literature'; pub. with modifications *Cornhill Magazine*, Aug.
1864; repr. *Littell's Living Age* (Boston) 17 Sept. 1864, *Revue Britannique* (shortened
version), May 1871. A.'s interest in the subject dates from his visit to France for the Royal
Commission 1859 (p. above) and there meeting prominent literary figures of the day,
notably Renan, whose *Essais de morale et de critique* (1859), much admired by A.,
includes 'L'Académie Française' (directed against the Academy's French critics). For a
summary of Renan's argument and Sainte-Beuve on the same subject, including his
reference to '*provincialisme*', A.'s theme in the extract below, see *CPW* iii. 463–65, 232–57.

[*The Provincial Spirit*]

... where there is no centre like an academy, if you have genius
and powerful ideas, you are apt not to have the best style going;
If you have precision of style and not genius, you are apt not to
have the best ideas going.

The provincial spirit, again, exaggerates the value of its ideas
for want of a high standard at hand by which to try them. Or
rather, for want of such a standard, it gives one idea too much
prominence at the expense of others; it orders its ideas amiss;
it is hurried away by fancies; it likes and dislikes too passionately,
too exclusively. Its admiration weeps hysterical tears, and its
disapprobation foams at the mouth. So we get the *eruptive* and
the *aggressive* manner in literature; the former prevails most in
our criticism, the latter in our newspapers. For, not having the
lucidity of a large and centrally placed intelligence, the provincial
spirit has not its graciousness; it does not persuade, it makes war;

it has not urbanity, the tone of the city, of the centre, the tone which always aims at a spiritual and intellectual effect, and not excluding the use of banter, never disjoins banter itself from politeness, from felicity. But the provincial tone is more violent, and seems to aim rather at an effect upon the blood and senses than upon the spirit and intellect; it loves hard-hitting rather than persuading. The newspaper, with its party spirit, its thorough-goingness, its resolute avoidance of shades and distinctions, its short, highly charged, heavy-shotted articles, its style so unlike that style *lenis minimèque pertinax*[1] – easy and not too violently insisting – which the ancients so much admired, is its true literature; the provincial spirit likes in the newspaper just what makes the newspaper such bad food for it, – just what made Goethe say, when he was pressed hard about the immorality of Byron's poems, that, after all, they were not so immoral as the newspapers.[2] The French talk of the *brutalité des journaux anglais*. What strikes them comes from the necessary inherent tendencies of newspaper-writing not being checked in England by any centre of intelligence and urbane spirit, but rather stimulated by coming in contact with a provincial spirit. Even a newspaper like the *Saturday Review*, that old friend of all of us, a newspaper expressly aiming at an immunity from the common newspaper-spirit, aiming at being a sort of organ of reason, – and, by thus aiming, it merits great gratitude and has done great good, – even the *Saturday Review*, replying to some foreign criticism on our precautions against invasion, falls into a strain of this kind:

> 'To do this [to take these precautions] seems to us eminently worthy of a great nation, and to talk of it as unworthy of a great nation, seems to us eminently worthy of a great fool'.

There is what the French mean when they talk of the *brutalité des journaux anglais*; there is a style certainly as far removed from urbanity as possible, – a style with what I call the note of provinciality. And the same note may not unfrequently be observed even in the ideas of this newspaper, full as it is of thought and cleverness: certain ideas allowed to become fixed ideas, to prevail too absolutely. I will not speak of the immediate present, but, to go a little while back, it had the critic who so disliked the Emperor of the French; it had the critic who so disliked the subject of my present remarks – academies; it had the critic who was so fond of the German element in our nation, and, indeed, everywhere; who ground his teeth if one said *Charlemagne*, instead of *Charles the Great*,[3] and, in short, saw all things in Teutonism, as Malebranche[4] saw all things in God. Certainly anyone may fairly find faults in the Emperor Napoleon or in academies, and merit in the German element; but it is a note of the provincial spirit not to hold ideas of this kind a little more easily, to be so devoured by them, to suffer them to become crotchets....

From The Function of Criticism at the Present Time

Planned as the introduction to A.'s first collection of essays, delivered as a lecture at Oxford 29 Oct. 1864, pub. the *National Review* 1864, repr. (with 'The Function ...' for 'The Functions ...') *Essays in Criticism*, First Series (1865). One of A.'s best known essays, celebrated for its emphasis on 'disinterestedness', a word whose frequent use today to mean 'indifference' would have confirmed A. in his worst fears for England 'losing immeasurably in all ways ... for want of what I must still call ideas ... This conviction haunts me, and at times even overwhelms me with depression' (letter of Nov. 1865, *L* i. 309–10). For the essay's critical reputation and its profound influence on other critics from Pater to T.S. Eliot and, in more recent years, F.W. Bateson, founder of the periodical *Essays in Critisism*, see *CPW* iii. 472–4.

Many objections have been made to a proposition which, in some remarks of mine on translating Homer, I ventured to put forth; a proposition about criticism, and its importance at the present day. I said: 'Of the literature of France and Germany, as of the intellect of Europe in general, the main effort, for now many years, has been a critical effort, the endeavour, in all branches of knowledge, theology, philosophy, history, art, science, to see the object as in itself it really is.' I added, that owing to the operation in English literature of certain causes, 'almost the last thing for which one would come to English literature is just that very thing which now Europe most desires, – criticism'; and that the power and value of English literature was thereby impaired.[1] More than one rejoinder declared that the importance I here assigned to criticism was excessive, and asserted the inherent superiority of the creative effort of the human spirit over its critical effort. And the other day, having been led by an excellent notice of

Wordsworth* published in the *North British Review*,[2] to turn
again to his biography, I found, in the words of this great man,
whom I, for one, must always listen to with the profoundest
respect, a sentence passed on the critic's business, which seems to
justify every possible disparagement of it. Wordsworth says in one
of his letters:

> The writers in these publications [the Reviews], while they
> prosecute their inglorious employment, can not be supposed to be in
> a state of mind very favourable for being affected by the finer
> influences of a thing so pure as genuine poetry.

And a trustworthy reporter of his conversation quotes a more
elaborate judgment to the same effect:

> Wordsworth holds the critical power very low, infinitely lower
> than the inventive; and he said today that if the quantity of time
> consumed in writing critiques on the works of others were given to
> original compositions, of whatever kind it might be, it would be
> much better employed; it would make a man find out sooner his own
> level, and it would do infinitely less mischief. A false or malicious
> criticism may do much injury to the minds of others, a stupid
> invention, either in prose or verse, is quite harmless.[3]

It is almost too much to expect of poor human nature, that a
man capable of producing some effect in one line of literature,
should, for the greater good of society, voluntarily doom himself
to impotence and obscurity in another. Still less is this to be
expected from men addicted to the composition of the 'false or
malicious criticism', of which Wordsworth speaks. However,
everybody would admit that a false or malicious criticism had
better never have been written. Everybody, too, would be willing
to admit, as a general proposition, that the critical faculty is lower
than the inventive. But is it true that criticism is really, in itself, a
baneful and injurious employment; is it true that all time given to
writing critiques on the works of others would be much better
employed if it were given to original composition, of whatever
kind this may be? Is it true that Johnson had better have gone on

---

*I cannot help thinking that a practice, common in England during the last century, and still
followed in France, of printing a notice of this kind, – a notice by a competent critic, – to serve
as an introduction to an eminent author's works, might be revived among us with advantage.
To introduce all succeeding editions of Wordsworth, Mr Sharp's notice (it is permitted, I hope,
to mention his name) might, it seems to me, excellently serve ; it is written from the point of
view of an admirer, nay, of a disciple, and that is right ; but then the disciple must be also, as
in this case he is, a critic, a man of letters, not, as too often happens, some relation or friend
with no qualification for his task except affection for his author.

producing more *Irenes* instead of writing his *Lives of the Poets*; nay, is it certain that Wordsworth himself was better employed in making his Ecclesiastical Sonnets than when he made his celebrated Preface, so full of criticism, and criticism of the works of others? Wordsworth was himself a great critic, and it is to be sincerely regretted that he has not left us more criticism; Goethe was one of the greatest of critics, and we may sincerely congratulate ourselves that he has left us so much criticism. Without wasting time over the exaggeration which Wordsworth's judgment on criticism clearly contains, or over an attempt to trace the causes, – not difficult I think to be traced, – which may have led Wordsworth to this exaggeration, a critic may with advantage seize an occasion for trying his own conscience, and for asking himself of what real service, at any given moment, the practice of criticism either is, or may be made, to his own mind and spirit, and to the minds and spirits of others.

The critical power is of lower rank than the creative. True; but in assenting to this proposition, one or two things are to be kept in mind. It is undeniable that the exercise of a creative power, that a free creative activity, is the highest function of man; it is proved to be so by man's finding in it his true happiness. But it is undeniable, also, that men may have the sense of exercising this free creative activity in other ways than in producing great works of literature or art; if it were not so, all but a very few men would be shut out from the true happiness of all men. They may have it in well-doing, they may have it in learning, they may have it even in criticizing. This is one thing to be kept in mind. Another is, that the exercise of the creative power in the production of great works of literature or art, however high this exercise of it may rank, is not at all epochs and under all conditions possible; and that therefore labour may be vainly spent in attempting it, which might with more fruit be used in preparing for it, in rendering it possible. This creative power works with elements, with materials; what if it has not those materials, those elements, ready for its use? In that case it must surely wait till they are ready. Now in literature, – I will limit myself to literature, for it is about literature that the question arises, – the elements with which the creative power works are ideas; the best ideas, on every matter which literature touches, current at the time. At any rate we may lay it down as certain that in modern literature no manifestation of the creative power not working with these can be very important or fruitful.

And I say *current* at the time, not merely accessible at the time; for creative literary genius does not principally show itself in discovering new ideas; that is rather the business of the philosopher: the grand work of literary genius is a work of synthesis and exposition, not of analysis and discovery; its gift lies in the faculty of being happily inspired by a certain intellectual and spiritual atmosphere, by a certain order of ideas, when it finds itself in them; of dealing divinely with these ideas, presenting them in the most effective and attractive combinations, – making beautiful works with them, in short. But it must have the atmosphere, it must find itself amidst the order of ideas, in order to work freely; and these it is not so easy to command. This is why great creative epochs in literature are so rare; this is why there is so much that is unsatisfactory in the productions of many men of real genius; because for the creation of a master-work of literature two powers must concur, the power of the man and the power of the moment, and the man is not enough without the moment; the creative power has, for its happy exercise, appointed elements, and those elements are not in its own control....

It has long seemed to me that the burst of creative activity in our literature, through the first quarter of this century, had about it, in fact, something premature; and that from this cause its productions are doomed, most of them, in spite of the sanguine hopes which accompanied and do still accompany them, to prove hardly more lasting than the productions of far less splendid epochs.[4] And this prematureness comes from its having proceeded without having its proper data, without sufficient materials to work with. In other words, the English poetry of the first quarter of this century, with plenty of energy, plenty of creative force, did not know enough. This makes Byron so empty of matter, Shelley so incoherent, Wordsworth even, profound as he is, yet so wanting in completeness and variety. Wordsworth cared little for books, and disparaged Goethe. I admire Wordsworth, as he is, so much that I cannot wish him different; and it is vain, no doubt, to imagine such a man different from what he is, to support that he could have been different. But surely the one thing wanting to make Wordsworth an even greater poet than he is, – his thought richer, and his influence of wider application, – was that he should have read more books, among them, no doubt, those of that Goethe whom he disparaged without reading him.

But to speak of books and reading may easily lead to a

misunderstanding here. It was not really books and reading that lacked to our poetry at this epoch; Shelley had plenty of reading, Coleridge had immense reading. Pindar and Sophocles – as we all say so glibly, and often with so little discernment of the real import of what we are saying – had not many books; Shakespeare was no deep reader. True; but in the Greece of Pindar and Sophocles, in the England of Shakespeare, the poet lived in a current of ideas in the highest degree animating and nourishing to the creative power; society was, in the fullest measure, permeated by fresh thought, intelligent and alive; and this state of things is the true basis for the creative power's exercise, – in this it finds its data, its materials, truly ready for its hand; all the books and reading in the world are only valuable as they are helps to this. Even when this does not actually exist, books and reading may enable a man to construct a kind of semblance of it in his own mind, a world of knowledge and intelligence in which he may live and work: this is by no means an equivalent, to the artist, for the nationally diffused life and thought of the epochs of Sophocles or Shakespeare, but, besides that it may be a means of preparation for such epochs, it does really constitute, if many share in it, a quickening and sustaining atmosphere of great value. Such an atmosphere the many-sided learning and the long and widely combined critical effort of Germany formed for Goethe, when he lived and worked. There was no national glow of life and thought there as in the Athens of Pericles, or the England of Elizabeth. That was the poet's weakness. But there was a sort of equivalent for it in the complete culture and unfettered thinking of a large body of Germans. That was his strength. In the England of the first quarter of this century, there was neither a national glow of life and thought, such as we had in the age of Elizabeth, nor yet a culture and a force of learning and criticism, such as were to be found in Germany. Therefore the creative power of poetry wanted, for success in the highest sense, materials and a basis; a thorough interpretation of the world was necessarily denied to it.

At first sight it seems strange that out of the immense air of the French Revolution and its age should not have come a crop of works of genius equal to that which came out of the stir of the great productive time of Greece, or out of that of the Renascence, with its powerful episode the Reformation. But the truth is that the stir of the French Revolution took a character which essentially distinguished it from such movements as these. These were, in the main, disinterestedly intellectual and spiritual movements; movements in which the human spirit looked for its satisfaction in itself and in the increased play of its own activity: the French Revolution took a political, practical character. The movement which went on in France under the old régime, from 1700 to 1789, was far more really akin than that of the Revolution itself to the movement of the Renascence; the France of Voltaire and Rousseau told far more powerfully upon the mind of Europe than the France of the Revolution. Goethe reproached this last expressly with having 'thrown quiet culture back'. Nay, and the true key to how much in our Byron, even in our Wordsworth, is this! – that they had their source in a great movement of feeling, not in a great movement of mind. The French Revolution, however, – that object of so much blind love and so much blind hatred, – found undoubtedly its motive-power in the intelligence of men and not in their practical sense; – this is what distinguishes it from the English Revolution of Charles the First's time; this is what makes it a more spiritual event than our Revolution, an event of much more powerful and world-wide interest, though practically less successful; – it appeals to an order of ideas which are universal, certain, permanent. 1789 asked of a thing, Is it rational? 1642 asked of a thing, Is it legal? or, when it went furthest, Is it according to conscience? This is the English fashion; a fashion to be treated, within its own sphere, with the highest respect; for its success, within its own sphere, has been prodigious. But what is law in one place, is not law in another; what is law here today, is not law even here tomorrow; and as for conscience, what is binding on one man's conscience is not binding on another's; the old woman who threw her stool at the head of the surpliced minister in St Giles's Church at Edinburgh obeyed an impulse to which millions of the human race may be permitted to remain strangers.[5] But the prescriptions of reason are absolute, unchanging, of universal validity; *to count by tens is the easiest way of counting* – that is a proposition of which every one, from here to the Antipodes, feels the force; at least, I should say so, if we did not live in a country where it is not impossible that any morning we may find a letter in *The Times* declaring that a decimal coinage is an absurdity.[6] That a whole nation should have been penetrated with an enthusiasm for pure reason, and with an ardent zeal for making its prescriptions triumph, is a very remarkable thing, when we consider how little of mind, or anything so worthy and quickening as mind, comes into the natives which alone, in general, impel great masses of men. In spite of the extravagant direction given to this enthusiasm, in spite of the crimes and follies in which it lost itself, the French Revolution derives from the force, truth, and universality of the ideas which it took for its law, and from the passion with which it could inspire a multitude for these ideas, a unique and still living power; it is – it will probably long remain – the greatest, the most animating event in history. And, as no sincere passion for the things of the mind, even though it turns out in many respects an unfortunate passion, is ever quite thrown away and quite barren of good, France has reaped from hers one fruit – the natural and legitimate fruit, though not precisely the grand fruit she expected: she is the country in Europe where *the people* is most alive.

But the mania for giving an immediate political and practical application to all these fine ideas of the reason was fatal. Here an Englishman is in his element: on this theme we can all go on for hours. And all we are in the habit of saying on it has undoubtedly a great deal of truth. Ideas cannot be too much prized in and for themselves, cannot be too much lived with; but to transport them abruptly into the world of politics and practice, violently to revolutionize this world to their bidding, – that is quite another thing. There is the world of ideas and there is the world of practice; the French are often for suppressing the one and the English the other; but neither is to be suppressed. A member of the House of Commons said to me the other day: 'That a thing is an anomaly, I consider to be no objection to it whatever.' I venture to think he was wrong; that a thing is an anomaly *is* an objection to it, but absolutely and in the sphere of ideas: it is not necessarily, under such and such circumstances, or at such and such a moment, an objection to it in the sphere of politics and practice. Joubert has said beautifully: 'C'est la force et la droit qui règlent toutes choses dans le monde; la force en attendant le droit.'[7] (Force and right are the governors of this world; force till right is ready.) *Force till right is ready*; and till right is ready, force, the existing order of things, is justified, is the legitimate ruler. But right is something moral, and implies inward recognition, free assent of the will; we are not ready for right, – *right*, so far as we are concerned, *is not ready*, – until we have attained this sense of seeing it and willing it. The way in which for us it may change and transform force, the existing order of things, and become, in its turn, the legitimate ruler of the world, should depend on the way in which, when our time comes, we see it and will it. Therefore for other people enamoured of their own newly discerned right, to attempt to impose it upon us as ours, and violently to substitute their right for our force, is an act of tyranny, and to be resisted. It sets at nought the second great half of our maxim, *force till right is ready*. This was the grand error of the French Revolution; and its movement of ideas, by quitting the intellectual sphere and rushing furiously into the political sphere, ran, indeed, a prodigious and memorable course, but produced no such intellectual fruit as the movement of ideas of the Renascence, and created, in opposition to itself, what I may call an *epoch of concentration*. The great force of that epoch of concentration was England; and the great voice of that epoch of concentration was Burke....

But Burke is so great because, almost alone in England, he brings thought to bear upon politics, he saturates politics with thought; it is his accident that his ideas were at the service of an epoch of concentration, not of an epoch of expansion; it is his characteristic that he so lived by ideas, and had such a source of them welling up within him, that he could float even an epoch of concentration and English Tory politics with them.[8] It does not hurt him that Dr Price and the Liberals were enraged with him; it does not even hurt him that George the Third and the Tories were enchanted with him. His greatness is that he lived in a world which neither English Liberalism nor English Toryism is apt to enter; – the world of ideas, not the world of catch-words and party habits. So far is it from being really true of him that he 'to party gave up what was meant for mankind',[9] that at the very end of his fierce struggle with the French Revolution, after all his invectives against its false pretensions, hollowness, and madness, with his sincere conviction of its mischievousness, he can close a memorandum on the best means of combating it, some of the last pages he ever wrote, – the *Thoughts on French Affairs*, in December 1791, – with these striking words:

> The evil is stated, in my opinion, as it exists. The remedy must be where power, wisdom, and information, I hope, are more united with good intentions than they can be with me. I have done with this subject, I believe, for ever. It has given me many anxious moments for the last two years. *If a great change is to be made in human affairs, the minds of men will be fitted to it; the general opinions and feelings will draw that way. Every fear, every hope will forward it; and then they*

who persist in opposing this mighty current in human affairs, will appear rather to resist the decrees of Providence itself, than the mere designs of men. They will not be resolute and firm, but perverse and obstinate.[10]

That return of Burke upon himself has always seemed to me one of the finest things in English literature, or indeed in any literature. This is what I call living by ideas; when one side of a question has long had your earnest support, when all your feelings are engaged, when you hear all round you no language but one, when your party talks this language like a steam-engine and can imagine no other, – still to be able to think, still to be irresistibly carried, if so it be, by the current of thought to the opposite side of the question, and, like Balaam, to be unable to speak anything *but what the Lord has put in your mouth.*[11] I know nothing more striking, and I must add that I know nothing more unEnglish....

But epochs of concentration cannot well endure for ever; epochs of expansion, in the due course of things, follow them. Such an epoch of expansion seems to be opening in this country. In the first place all danger of a hostile forcible pressure of foreign ideas upon our practice has long disappeared; like the traveler in the fable, therefore, we begin to wear our cloak a little more loosely.[12] Then, with a long peace, the ideas of Europe steal gradually and amicably in, and mingle, though in infinitesimally small quantities at a time, with our own notions. Then, too, in spite of all that is said about the absorbing and brutalizing influence of our passionate material progress, it seems to me indisputable that this progress is likely, though not certain, to lead in the end to an apparition of intellectual life; and that man, after he has made himself perfectly comfortable and has now to determine what to do with himself next, may begin to remember that he has a mind, and that the mind may be made the source of great pleasure. I grant it is mainly the privilege of faith, at present, to discern this end to our railways, our business, and our fortune-making; but we shall see if, here as elsewhere, faith is not in the end the true prophet. Our ease, our travelling, and our unbounded liberty to hold just as hard and securely as we please to the practice to which our notions have given birth, all tend to beget an inclination to deal a little more freely with these notions themselves, to canvass them a little, to penetrate a little into their real nature. Flutterings of curiosity, in the foreign sense of the word, appear amongst us, and it is in these that criticism must look to find its account. Criticism first; a time of true creative activity, perhaps, – which, as I have said, must inevitably be preceded amongst us by a time of criticism, – hereafter, when criticism has done its work.

It is of the last importance that English criticism should clearly discern what rule for its course, in order to avail itself of the field now opening to it, and to produce fruit for the future, it ought to take. The rule may be summed up in one word, – *disinterestedness*.[13] And how is criticism to show disinterestedness? By keeping aloof from practice; by resolutely following the law of its own nature, which is to be a free play of the mind on all subjects which it touches; by steadily refusing to lend itself to any of those ulterior, political, practical considerations about ideas which plenty of people will be sure to attach to them, which perhaps ought often to be attached to them, which in this country at any rate are certain to be attached to them quite sufficiently, but which criticism has really nothing to do with. Its business is, as I have said, simply to know the best that is known and thought in the world, and by in its turn making this known, to create a current of true and fresh ideas....

It is because criticism has so little kept in the pure intellectual sphere, has so little detached itself from practice, has been so directly polemical and controversial, that it has so ill accomplished, in this country, its best spiritual work; which is to keep man from a self-satisfaction which is retarding and vulgarizing, to lead him towards perfection, by making his mind dwell upon what is excellent in itself, and the absolute beauty and fitness of things. A polemical practical criticism makes men blind even to the ideal imperfection of their practice, makes them willingly assert its ideal perfection, in order the better to secure it against attack; and clearly this is narrowing and baneful for them. If they were reassured on the practical side, speculative considerations of ideal perfection they might be brought to entertain, and their spiritual horizon would thus gradually widen. Mr Adderley says to the Warwickshire farmers:

> Talk of the improvement of breed! Why, the race we ourselves represent, the men and women, the old Anglo-Saxon race, are the best breed in the whole world.... The absence of a too enervating climate, too unclouded skies, and a too luxurious nature, has produced so vigorous a race of people, and has rendered us so superior to all the world.[14]

Mr Roebuck says to the Sheffield cutlers:

> I look around me and ask what is the state of England? Is not property safe? Is not every man able to say what he likes? Can you not walk from one end of England to the other in perfect security? I ask you whether, the world over or in past history, there is anything like it? Nothing. I pray that our unrivalled happiness may last.[15]

Now obviously there is a peril for poor human nature in words and thoughts of such exuberant self-satisfaction, until we find ourselves safe in the streets of the Celestial City.

> Das wenige verschwindet leicht dem Blicke
> Der vorwärts sieht, wie viel noch übrig bleibt –[16]

says Goethe; the little that is done seems nothing when we look forward and see how much we have yet to do. Clearly this is a better line of reflection for weak humanity, so long as it remains on this earthly field of labour and trial.

But neither Mr Adderley nor Mr Roebuck is by nature inaccessible to considerations of this sort. They only lose sight of them owing to the controversial life we all lead, and the practical form which all speculation takes with us. They have in view opponents whose aim is not ideal, but practical; and in their zeal to uphold their own practice against these innovators, they go so far as even to attribute to this practice an ideal perfection. Somebody has been wanting to introduce a six-pound franchise, or to abolish church-rates, or to collect agricultural statistics by force, or to diminish local self-government. How natural, in reply to such proposals, very likely improper or ill-timed, to go a little beyond the mark and to say stoutly: 'Such a race of people as we stand, so superior to all the world ! The old Anglo-Saxon race, the best breed in the whole world! I pray that our unrivalled happiness may last! I ask you whether, the world over or in past history, there is anything like it?' And so long as criticism answers this dithyramb by insisting that the old Anglo-Saxon race would be still more superior to all others if it had no church-rates, or that our unrivalled happiness would last yet longer with a six-pound franchise, so long will the strain, 'The best breed in the whole world!' swell louder and louder, everything ideal and refining will be lost out of sight, and both the assailed and their critics will remain in a sphere, to say the truth, perfectly unvital, a sphere in which spiritual progression is impossible. But let criticism leave church-rates and the franchise alone, and in the most candid spirit, without a single lurking thought of practical innovation, confront with our dithyramb this paragraph on which I stumbled in a newspaper immediately after reading Mr Roebuck:

> A shocking child murder has just been committed at Nottingham. A girl named Wragg left the workhouse there on Saturday morning with her young illegitimate child. The child was soon afterwards found dead on Mapperly Hills, having been strangled. Wragg is in custody.[17]

Nothing but that; but, in juxtaposition with the absolute eulogies of Mr Adderley and Mr Roebuck, how eloquent, how suggestive are those few lines! 'Our old Anglo-Saxon breed, the best in the whole world!' – how much that is harsh and ill-favoured there is in this best! *Wragg*! If we are to talk of ideal perfection, of 'the best in the whole world', has anyone reflected what a touch of grossness in our race, what an original shortcoming in the more delicate spiritual perceptions, is shown by the natural growth amongst us of such hideous names, – Higginbottom, Stiggins, Bugg! In Ionia and Attica they were luckier in this respect than 'the best race in the world'; by the Ilissus there was no Wragg, poor thing! And 'our unrivalled happiness'; – what an element of grimness, bareness, and hideousness mixes with it and blurs it; the workhouse, the dismal Mapperly Hills, – how dismal those who have seen them will remember; – the gloom, the smoke, the cold, the strangled illegitimate child! 'I ask you whether, the world over or in past history, there is anything like it?' Perhaps not, one is inclined to answer; but at any rate, in that case, the world is very much to be pitied. And the final touch, – short, bleak, and inhuman: *Wragg is in custody*. The sex lost in the confusion of our unrivalled happiness; or (shall I say?) the superfluous Christian name lopped off by the straightforward vigour of our old Anglo-Saxon breed! There is profit for the spirit in such contrasts as this; criticism serves the cause of perfection by establishing them. By eluding sterile conflict, by refusing to remain in the sphere where alone narrow and relative conceptions have any worth and validity, criticism may diminish its momentary importance, but only in this way has it a chance of gaining admittance for those wider and more perfect conceptions to which all its duty is really owed. Mr Roebuck will have a poor opinion of an adversary who replies to his defiant songs of triumph only by murmuring under his breath, *Wragg is in custody*; but in no other way will these songs of triumph be induced gradually to moderate themselves, to get rid of what in them is excessive and offensive, and to fall into a softer and truer key.

It will be said that it is a very subtle and indirect action which I am thus prescribing for criticism, and that, by embracing in this manner the Indian virtue of detachment[18] and abandoning the sphere of practical life, it condemns itself to a slow and obscure work. Slow and obscure it may be, but it is the only proper work of criticism. The mass of mankind will never have any ardent zeal for seeing things as they are; very inadequate ideas will always satisfy them. On these inadequate ideas reposes, and must repose, the general practice of the world. That is as much as saying that whoever sets himself to see things as they are will find himself one of a very small circle; but it is only by this small circle resolutely doing its own work that adequate ideas will ever get current at all. The rush and roar of practical life will always have a dizzying and attracting effect upon the most collected spectator, and tend to draw him into its vortex; most of all will this be the case where that life is so powerful as it is in England. But it is only by remaining collected, and refusing to lend himself to the point of view of the practical man, that the critic can do the practical man any service; and it is only by the greatest sincerity in pursuing his own course, and by at last convincing even the practical man of his sincerity, that he can escape misunderstandings which perpetually threaten him....

Do what he will, however, the critic will still remain exposed to frequent misunderstandings, and nowhere so much as in this country. For here people are particularly indisposed even to comprehend that without this free disinterested treatment of things, truth and the highest culture are out of the question. So immersed are they in practical life, so accustomed to take all their notions from this life and its processes, that they are apt to think that truth and culture themselves can be reached by the processes of this life, and that it is an impertinent singularity to think of reaching them in any other. 'We are all *terrae filii*,'[19] cries their eloquent advocate; 'all Philistines together. Away with the notion of proceeding by any other course than the course dear to the Philistines; let us have a social movement, let us organize and combine a party to pursue truth and new thought, let us call it *the liberal party*, and let us all stick to each other, and back each other up. Let us have no nonsense about independent criticism, and

intellectual delicacy, and the few and the many. Don't let us trouble ourselves about foreign thought; we shall invent the whole thing for ourselves as we go along: if one of us speaks well, applaud him; if one of us speaks ill, applaud him too; we are all in the same movement, we are all liberals, we are all in pursuit of truth.' In this way the pursuit of truth becomes really a social, practical, pleasurable affair, almost requiring a chairman, a secretary, and advertisements; with the excitement of an occasional scandal, with a little resistance to give the happy sense of difficulty overcome; but, in general, plenty of bustle and very little thought. To act is so easy, as Goethe says; to think is so hard! It is true that the critic has many temptations to go with the stream, to make one of the party movement, one of these *terrae filii*; it seems ungracious to refuse to be a *terrae filius*, when so many excellent people are; but the critic's duty is to refuse, or, if resistance is vain, at least to cry with Obermann: *Périssons en résistant....*
[20]

From on the Study of Celtic Literature

Delivered as a series of lectures at Oxford, 6, 7 Dec. 1865 and 24 Feb., 26 March 1866; pub. *Cornhill Magazine*, March–July 1865; repr. *Eclectic Magazine* June–Oct. 1865 and as a book, with a preface and some alterations, 4 June 1867. A.'s interest in the Celtic temperament, first reflected in two Oxford lectures 1860–1 (notably 'The Claim of the Celtic Race, and the Claim of the Christian Religion, to Have Originated Chivalrous Sentiment', 8 June 1861), was fostered by his 1859 stay in France; his expeditions to Llandudno and the Highlands in summer 1864; and his reading of Renan, 'La Poésie des races celtiques', *Essais de morale et de critique* (see headnote p. 172 above). For the origin, reception and influence of this work, including the establishment of a Chair of Celtic at Jesus College Oxford 1877 see *CPW* iii. 490–8. With A. on 'natural magic' and Keats in the extracts below cp. Maurice de Guérin, pp. 154–6 above.

[*Natural Magic*]

... The Celt's quick feeling for what is noble and distinguished gave his poetry style; his indomitable personality gave it pride and passion; his sensibility and nervous exaltation gave it a better gift still, the gift of rendering with wonderful felicity the magical charm of nature. The forest solitude, the bubbling spring, the wild flowers, are everywhere in romance. They have a mysterious life and grace there; they are Nature's own children, and utter her secret in a way which makes them something quite different from the woods, waters, and plants of Greek and Latin poetry. Now of this delicate magic, Celtic romance is so pre-eminent a mistress, that it seems impossible to believe the power did not come into romance from the Celts.* Magic is just the word for it, – the magic of nature; not merely the beauty of nature, – that the Greeks and Latins had; not merely an honest smack of the soil, a faithful realism, – that the Germans had; but the intimate life of Nature, her weird power and her fairy charm. As the Saxon names of places, with the pleasant wholesome smack of the soil in them, – Weathersfield, Thaxted, Shalford, – are to the Celtic names of places, with their penetrating, lofty beauty, – Velindra, Tyntagel, Caernarvon, – so is the homely realism of German and Norse nature to the fairy-like loveliness of Celtic nature....

Magic is the word to insist upon, – a magically vivid and near interpretation of nature; since it is this which constitutes the special charm and power of the effect I am calling attention to, and it is for this that the Celt's sensibility gives him a peculiar aptitude. But the matter needs rather fine handling, and it is easy to make mistakes here in our criticism. In the first place, Europe tends constantly to become more and more one community, and we tend to become Europeans instead of merely Englishmen, Frenchmen, Germans, Italians; so whatever aptitude or felicity one people imparts into spiritual work, gets imitated by the others, and thus tends to become the common property of all. Therefore anything so beautiful and attractive as the natural magic I am speaking of, is sure, nowadays, if it appears in the production of the Celts, or of the English, or of the French, to appear in the productions of the Germans also, or in the productions of the Italians; but there will be a stamp of perfectness and inimitableness about it in the literatures where it is native, which it will not have in the literatures where it is not native. Novalis or Rückert, for instance, have their eye fixed on nature, and have undoubtedly a feeling for natural magic; a rough-and-ready critic easily credits them and the Germans with the Celtic fineness of tact, the Celtic nearness to Nature and her secret; but the question is whether the

---

*Rhyme, – the most striking characteristic of our modern poetry as distinguished from that of the ancients, and a main source, to our poetry, of its magic and charm, of what we call its *romantic element*, – rhyme itself, all the weight of evidence tends to show, comes into our poetry from the Celts.[1]

strokes in the German's picture of nature have ever the indefinable
delicacy, charm, and perfection of the Celt's touch in the pieces
I just now quoted, or of Shakespeare's touch in his daffodil,
Wordsworth's in his cuckoo, Keats's in his Autumn, Obermann's
in his mountain birch-tree or his Easter-daisy among the Swiss
farms.[2] To decide where the gift for natural magic originally lies,
whether it is properly Celtic or Germanic, we must decide this
question.

In the second place, there are many ways of handling nature,
and we are here only concerned with one of them; but a rough-
and-ready critic imagines that it is all the same so long as nature
is handled at all, and fails to draw the needful distinction between
modes of handling her. But these modes are many; I will mention
four of them now: there is the conventional way of handling
nature, there is the faithful way of handling nature, there is the
Greek way of handling nature, there is the magical way of
handling nature. In all these three last the eye is on the object, but
with a difference; in the faithful way of handling nature, the eye
is on the object, and that is all you can say; in the Greek, the eye
is on the object, but lightness and brightness are added; in the
magical, the eye is on the object, but charm and magic are added.
In the conventional way of handling nature, the eye is not on the
object; what that means we all know, we have only to think of
our eighteenth-century poetry: –

> 'As when the moon, refulgent lamp of night' –

to call up any number of instances. Latin poetry supplies plenty
of instances too; if we put this from Propertius's *Hylas*:

> ... 'manus heroum ....
> Mollia composita litora fronde tegit' –

side by side with the line of Theocritus by which it was suggested:

> 'λειμὼν γάρ σφιν ἔκειτο μέγας, στιβάδεσσιν ὄυειαρ'–

we get at the same moment a good specimen both of the conventional
and of the Greek way of handling nature. But from our own poetry we
may get specimens of the Greek way of handling nature, as well as of
the conventional: for instance, Keats's: –

> 'What little town, by river or seashore,
> Or mountain-built with quiet citadel,
> Is emptied of its folk, this pious morn?'

is Greek, as Greek as a thing from Homer or Theocritus,[3] it is composed with the eye on the object, a radiancy and light clearness being added. German poetry abounds in specimens of the faithful way of handling nature; an excellent example is to be found in the stanzas called *Zueignung*, prefixed to Goethe's poems; the morning walk, the mist, the dew, the sun, are as faithful as they can be, they are given with the eye on the object, but there the merit of the work, as a handling of nature, stops; neither Greek radiance nor Celtic magic is added, the power of these is not what gives the poem in question its merit, but a power of quite another kind, a power of moral and spiritual emotion. But the power of Greek radiance Goethe could give to his handling of nature, and nobly too, as any one who will read his *Wanderer*, – the poem in which a wanderer falls in with a peasant woman and her child by their hut, built out of the ruins of a temple near Cuma, – may see. Only the power of natural magic Goethe does not, I think, give; whereas Keats passes at will from the Greek power to that power which is, as I say, Celtic; from his:

> 'What little town, by river or seashore' –

to his:

> 'White hawthorn and the pastoral eglantine,
> Fast-fading violets cover'd up in leaves' –

or his:

> ... 'magic casements, opening on the foam
> Of perilous seas, in fairy lands forlorn' – [4]

in which the very same note is struck as in those extracts which I quoted from Celtic romance, and struck with authentic and unmistakable power.

Shakespeare, in handling nature, touches this Celtic note so exquisitely, that perhaps one is inclined to be always looking for the Celtic note in him, and not to recognize his Greek note when it comes. But if one attends well to the difference between the two notes, and bears in mind, to guide one, such things as Virgil's 'moss-grown springs and grass softer than sleep:'

> 'Muscos fontes et somno mollior herba' –

as his charming flower-gatherer, who:

> Pallentes violas et summa papavera carpens
> Narcissum et florem jungit bene olentis anethi' –

as his quinces and chestnuts:

> ... 'cana legam tenera lanugine mala
> Castaneasque nuces' ...[5]

then, I think, we shall be disposed to say that in Shakespeare's:

> 'I know a bank whereon the wild thyme blows,
> Where oxlips and the nodding violet grows,
> Quite over-canopied with luscious woodbine,
> With sweet musk-roses and with eglantine' –

it is mainly a Greek note which is struck. Then, again in his:

> .... . 'look how the floor of heaven
> Is thick inlaid with patines of bright gold!'

we are at the very point of transition from the Greek note to the Celtic; there is the Greek clearness and brightness, with the Celtic aërialness and magic coming in. Then we have the sheer, inimitable Celtic note in passages like this:

> 'Met we on hill, in dale, forest or mead,
> By paved fountain or by rushy brook,
> Or in the beached margent of the sea' –

or this, the last I will quote:

> 'The moon shines bright. In such a night as this,
> When the sweet wind did gently kiss the trees,
> And they did make no noise, in such a night
> Troilus, methinks, mounted the Trojan walls –
>
> .. . 'in such a night
> Did Thisbe fearfully o'ertrip the dew –
>
> .. . 'in such a night
> *Stood Dido, with a willow in her hand,*
> *Upon the wild sea-banks, and waved her love*
> *To come again to Carthage.*'[6]

And those last lines of all are so drenched and intoxicated with the fairy-dew of that natural magic which is our theme, that I cannot do better than end with them.

And now, with the pieces of evidence in our hand, let us go to those who say it is vain to look for Celtic elements in any Englishman, and let us ask them, first, if they seize what we mean by the power of natural magic in Celtic poetry; secondly, if

English poetry does not eminently exhibit this power; and, thirdly, where they suppose English poetry got it from? ...

From Friendship's Garland

The 'Arminius Letters' appeared *Pall Mall Gazette* 1866–7 (Letters i–vii) and 1869–70 (Letters ix–xii), repr. as *Friendship's Garland* Feb. 1871, with the related 'My Countrymen' and 'A Courteous Explanation' (*Pall Mall Gazette*, Feb., March 1866), the latter as a light-hearted reply to a French critic's rallying response to 'My Countryman'. They form a particularly vivacious part of A.'s running debate with the 'philistines' and are intimately connected with his polemical articles written 1867–9 and collected 1869 as *Culture and Anarchy* (p. 197 below).

(The acquaintance of the ever-to-be-lamented Arminius was made by the present Editor on the Continent in the year 1865. The early history of the noble family of Von-Thunder-ten-Tronckh, to which Arminius belonged, their establishment in Westphalia, the sack of their castle in the middle of the last century by the Bulgarians, the fate of their principal dependents (among whom was the famous optimist philosopher, Dr Pangloss), the adventures of Arminius's grandfather and his deportation to the Jesuits at Rome, are recorded in a well-known treatise of Voltaire.[1] Additional information is supplied in several of the following letters.

Arminius came to England in 1866, and the correspondence now given in a collected form to the public commenced in the summer of that year, at the outbreak of the war between Prussia and Austria.[2] Many will yet remember the thrill with which they originally received, through the unworthy ministry of the present Editor, the communication of the great doctrine of 'Geist.' What, then, must it have been to hear that doctrine in its first newness from the lips of Arminius himself! Yet it will, I hope, be admitted, that even in this position of exceptional privilege, the present Editor succeeded in preserving his coolness, his independent judgment, and his proper feelings as a Briton.) – ED.

LETTER 1
I INTRODUCE ARMINIUS AND 'GEIST' TO THE
BRITISH PUBLIC

Sir,   *Grub Street*,[3] 19 July 1866
A Prussian acquaintance of mine, one of the party of foreigners
who so offensively criticised my countrymen to me when I was
abroad last year, has been over here just now, and for the last
week or so he has been favouring me with his remarks on all he
hears us say about the present crisis in Germany. In confidence I
will own to you that he makes himself intensely disagreeable. He
has the harsh, arrogant, Prussian way of turning up his nose at
things and laying down the law about them; and though, as a lover
of intellect, I admire him, and, as a seeker of truth, I value his
frankness, yet, as an Englishman, and a member of what the *Daily
Telegraph* calls 'the Imperial race,' I feel so uncomfortable under
it, that I want, through your kindness, to call to my aid the great
British public, which never loses heart and has always a bold front
and a rough word ready for its assailants.

My Prussian friend got a little mortification at the beginning
of his visit, and as it is my belief this mortification set him wrong
from the first, I shall relate what it was. I took him with me down
to Reigate by the railroad, and in the carriage was one of our
representative industrial men (something in the bottle way), a
famous specimen of that great middle class whose energy and
self-reliance make England what it is, and who give the tone to
our Parliament and to our policy. News had just come of the first
bloodshed between the Austrians and Prussians now at war
together in Germany. 'So they've begun fighting,' cried my coun-
tryman; 'what fools they both are!' And he handed us *Punch*
with that masterly picture in it of 'Denmark avenged;'[4] that
scathing satire which represents the King of Denmark sitting with
his glass of grog and his cigar, to gloat over the terrible retribution
falling upon his great enemy Prussia for her misdeeds towards
him. My Prussian glared at the striking moral lesson thus brought
to his notice, but rage and contempt made him speechless. I
hastened, with a few sentences taken from Mr Gladstone's recent
advice to the Roumanians, to pay my homage to the great
principles of peaceful, industrial development which were invoked
by my countryman.[5] 'Yes; war,' I said, 'interrupts business, and brings
intolerable inconvenience with it; whereas people have only to

persist steadily in the manufacture of bottles, railways, banks, and finance companies, and all good things will come to them of their own accord.' Before I had finished we reached Reigate, and I got my still speechless Prussian quickly out of the train.

But never shall I forget the flood when speech came at last: 'The dolt! the dunderhead! His ignorance of the situation, his ignorance of Germany, his ignorance of what makes nations great, his ignorance of what makes life worth living, his ignorance of everything except bottles, – those infernal bottles!' I heard so much of all this that I am glad to forget it without going through it again with the British public. I only mention it to make the rudeness of expression in what follows less unaccountable.

The day before yesterday the *Daily News* published that powerful letter from Mr Goldwin Smith,[6] pronouncing in favour of the Prussian alliance. In great excitement I ran with it to my friend. 'At last I have got something,' I cried, 'which will please you; a declaration by one of our best writers, in one of our best newspapers, for a united Germany under Prussian headship. She and we are thereupon to combine to curb France. Wherever I go, I hear people admiring the letter and approving the idea.' A sardonic smile, such as Alexander von Humboldt[7] used to have when he contemplated the late King of Prussia's missionary deaconesses, came over my Berliner's harsh countenance. 'Good God!' said he, 'the miracles that needle-gun[8] is working! It is only a year ago you were threatening Prussia with France, and suggesting to that great and sagacious ruler, as you called him, the French Emperor, to take the Rhine Province from us; it is not six weeks since I saw him styled in this very newspaper, with the dignity usual in Englishmen at present, "the arbiter of Europe."[9] He has done nothing in the meantime to injure you; he has done his best to keep well with you. How charmed he will be with his friends! But the declaration you are all so pleased at, who is it by?' 'Mr Goldwin Smith,' I answered. 'I know him,' he said; 'a good writer, but a fanatic.' 'Oh, no, no,' said I; 'a man of genius and virtue.'

Without answering, my Berliner took the newspaper and read the letter. 'He should have served with Nelson,' he said, as he finished it; 'he hates a Frenchman as he does the devil. However, it is true that a preponderance in the world such as the French, thanks to your stupidity, were fast getting, is enough to make any human being, let alone a Frenchman, unbearable; and it is a good thing to have a great Germany in the world as well as a great

France. It would be a good thing to have a great England too, if you would let us. But pray what is to unite Germany and England against France? What is to be the ground of sympathy between actual England and actual Germany?' 'You are a strong Liberal,' said I, 'so I can easily answer you. You are drawn towards England because of her liberalism, and away from the French Emperor because of his despotism.' 'Liberalism and despotism!' cried the Prussian; 'let us get beyond these forms and words. What unites and separates people now is *Geist*.'[10]

I had not the slightest idea what he meant, and my looks told my bewilderment. 'I thought you had read Mr Grant Duff's chapters on Germany,' said he.[11] 'But Mr Grant Duff knows what he writes about, so I suppose you have not. Your great Lord Palmerston used to call Germany "that country of d—d professors;" and the English public, which supposes professors to be people who know something, and hates anybody who knows anything, has always kept its mind as clear of my unfortunate country as it could. But I advise you, for the sake of the events now passing, to read Mr Grant Duff's book. There you will find that in Berlin we oppose "Geist," – *intelligence*, as you or the French might say, – to "Ungeist." The victory of "Geist" over "Ungeist" we think the great matter in the world. The same idea is at the bottom of democracy; the victory of reason and intelligence over blind custom and prejudice. So we German Liberals who believe in "Geist" have a sympathy with France and its governors, so far as they are believers in democracy. We have no sympathy with English liberalism, whose centre is in the "Ungeist" of such people as your wiseacre in the Reigate train.'

'But then you play,' cried I, 'the game of the Tories; for listen to Mr Goldwin Smith: "The Tories in Europe, with the sure instinct of a party, recognise the great patron of reaction in the Emperor of the French." You and we are to unite, in order to defeat the Tories and the Emperor of the French.'[12]

The Prussian answered: 'Mr Goldwin Smith blinds himself with the passions, as the Emperor of the French himself would say, of another age. The Tories of Europe have no real love for the Emperor of the French; they may admire and envy his absolutism and strength, but they hate his fundamental principles: they can have no real sympathy with the Sovereign who says boldly that he detests the actual public law of Europe, and who tells the people that it is among the people he finds the true genius of France, and breathes freely.[13] Such a man works for "Geist" in his way* not, perhaps, through a *Daily Telegraph*, or monster meetings in Trafalgar Square, or a Coles's Truss Manufactory standing where it ought not,[14] a glorious monument of individualism and industrialism, to adorn the "finest site in Europe;" but by making the common people feel they are alive and have a human spirit in them. We North-Germans have worked for "Geist" in our way, by loving knowledge, by having the best-educated middle and lower class in the world. You see what this has just done for us. France has "Geist" in her democracy, and Prussia in her education. Where have you got it? – got it as a force, I mean, and not only in a few scattered individuals. Your common people is barbarous; in your middle class "Ungeist" is rampant; and as for your aristocracy, you know "Geist" is forbidden by nature to flourish in an aristocracy.

'So do not,' he continued, 'suffer yourself to be deceived by parallels drawn from times before "Geist." What has won this Austrian battle for Prussia is "Geist;" "Geist" has used the King, and Bismarck, and the Junkers, and "Ungeist in uniform," all for its own ends; and "Geist" will continue so to use them till it has triumphed.† It will ally itself with "Geist" where it finds it, because there it has a ground for mutual respect and understanding; and where there is no "Geist," it has none.

'And now,' this odious man went on, 'now, my dear friend, I shall soon be leaving you, so one word more. You have lately been writing about the Celts and the Germans, and in the course of your remarks on the Germans you have said, among many impertinences, one thing which is true. You have said that the strength of North Germany lay in this, that the idea of science governed every department of human activity there. You, my dear friend, live in a country where at present the idea of clap-trap governs every department of human activity. Great events are happening in the world, and Mr Goldwin Smith tells you that "England will be compelled to speak at last." It would be truly sad if, when she does speak, she should talk nonsense. To prevent

---

*The indulgence of Arminius for this execrable and unsuccessful tyrant was unworthy of a member of our great Teutonic family. Probably, after Sedan, he changed his opinion of him. – ED.

†I am unwilling to triumph over Arminius in his grave ; but I cannot help remarking that 'Ungeist in uniform,' as Mr Bottles[15] observes to me, has just given a pretty good account of the 'Geist' in French democracy ; and I have a shrewd suspicion it will give an equally good account of the 'Geist' of Arminius's educated and liberal friends in Prussia. Perhaps Arminius was taken away from the evil to come ! – ED.

such a disaster, I will give you this piece of advice, with which I take my leave: "*Get Geist*." '

Thank God, this d—d professor (to speak as Lord Palmerston) is now gone back to his own *Intelligenz-Staat*. I half hope there may next come a smashing defeat of the Prussians before Vienna, and make my ghostly friend laugh on the wrong side of his mouth.[16] Meanwhile, I shall take care that he hears whatever answers he gets. I know that they will be conclusive, and I hope that they will be speedy, and in this hope,

I am, Sir,

Your obedient servant,

Matthew Arnold

To: The EDITOR *of the* PALL MALL GAZETTE

From Culture and Anarchy

Published as articles for the *Cornhill Magazine* over a period of 13 months, June 1867–Aug. 1868: 'Culture and its Enemies', planned 1866 as an article for publication Feb. 1867 but delivered May 1867 as A.'s final lecture as Professor of Poetry at Oxford, pub. *Cornhill* July 1867; five subsequent articles, with title, 'Anarchy and Authority', pub. *Cornhill* Jan., Feb., June, July, Sept. 1868; repr. 1869 as *Culture and Anarchy* with slight revisions, preface and conclusion, and again 1875 with further revisions and new titles for the six sections: Sweetness and Light; Doing as One Likes; Barbarians, Philistines, Populace; Hebraism and Hellenism; Porro Unum est Necessarium ('The One Thing Needful'); Our Liberal Practitioners. The discussion is closely connected with A.'s sequence of thinking since 'My Countryman' (1866), which led to the 'Arminius letters' and *Friendship's Garland* (p. 193 above), and, as with the latter, owes its amused, reiterative and lively polemical manner to his continuous engagement in the running debate provoked during the period when his articles first appeared (see, e.g., the contributions by Henry Sidgwick and Frederic Harrison to 'Culture, a Dialogue', *Fortnightly Review*).

[*Sweetness and Light*]

... the Greek word εὐφυΐα, a finely tempered nature, gives exactly the notion of perfection as culture brings us to conceive it: a harmonious perfection, a perfection in which the characters of beauty and intelligence are both present, which unites 'the two noblest of things,' – as Swift, who of one of the two, at any rate, had himself all too little, most happily calls them in his *Battle of the Books*, – 'the two noblest of things, *sweetness and light*.'[1] The εὐφυής is the man who tends towards sweetness and light; the ἀφυής, on the other hand, is our Philistine. The immense spiritual significance of the Greeks is due to their having been inspired with this central and happy idea of the essential character of human perception; and Mr Bright's misconception of culture, as a smattering of Greek and Latin, comes itself, after all, from this wonderful significance of the Greeks having affected the very machinery of our education, and is in itself a kind of homage to it.

In thus making sweetness and light to be characters of perfection, culture is of like spirit with poetry, follows one law with poetry. Far more than on our freedom, our population, and our industrialism, many amongst us rely upon our religious organisations to save us. I have called religion a yet more important manifestation of human nature than poetry, because it has worked on a broader scale for perfection, and with greater masses of men. But the idea of beauty and of a human nature perfect on all its sides, which is the dominant idea of poetry, is a true and invaluable idea, though it has not yet had the success that the idea of conquering the obvious faults of our animality, and of a human nature perfect on the moral side, – has been enabled to have; and it is destined, adding to itself the religious idea of a devout energy, to transform and govern the other....

The impulse of the English race towards moral development and self-conquest has nowhere so powerfully manifested itself as in Puritanism. Nowhere has Puritanism found so adequate an expression as in the religious organisation of the Independents. The modern Independents have a newspaper, the *Non-conformist*, written with great sincerity and ability. The motto, the standard, the profession of faith which this organ of theirs carries aloft, is: 'The Dissidence of Dissent and the Protestation of the Protestant religion.'[2] There is sweetness and light, and an ideal of complete harmonious human perfection! One need not go to culture and poetry to find language to judge it. Religion, with its instinct for perfection, supplies language to judge it, language too, which is in our mouths every day. 'Finally, be of one mind, united in feeling,' says St Peter.[3] There is an ideal which judges the Puritan ideal: 'The Dissidence of Dissent and the Protestation of the Protestant religion!' And religious organisations like this are what people believe in, rest in, would give their lives for! Such, I say, is the wonderful virtue of even the beginnings of perfection, of having conquered even the plain faults of our animality, that the religious organisation which has helped us to do it can seem to us something precious, salutary, and to be propagated, even when it wears such a brand of imperfection on its forehead as this. And men have got such a habit of giving to the language of religion a special application, of making it a mere jargon, that for the condemnation which religion itself passes on the shortcomings of their religious organisations they have no ear; they are sure to cheat themselves and to explain this condemnation away. They can only be reached by the criticism which culture, like poetry, speaking a language not to be sophisticated, and resolutely testing these organisations by the ideal of a human perfection complete on all sides, applies to them.

But men of culture and poetry, it will be said, are again and again failing, and failing conspicuously, in the necessary first stage to a harmonious perfection, in the subduing of the great obvious faults of our animality, which it is the glory of these religious organisations to have helped us to subdue. True, they do often so fail. They have often been without the virtues as well as the faults of the Puritan; it has been one of their dangers that they so felt the Puritan's faults that they too much neglected the practice of his virtues. I will not, however, exculpate them at the Puritan's expense. They have often failed in morality, and morality is indispensable. And they have been punished for their failure, as the Puritan has been rewarded for his performance. They have been punished wherein they erred; but their ideal of beauty, of sweetness and light, and a human nature complete on all its sides, remains the true ideal of perfection still; just as the Puritan's ideal of perfection remains narrow and inadequate, although for what he did well he has been richly rewarded. Notwithstanding the mighty results of the Pilgrim Fathers' voyage, they and their standard of perfection are rightly judged when we figure to ourselves Shakespeare or Virgil, – souls in whom sweetness and light, and all that in human nature is most humane, were eminent, – accompanying them on their voyage, and think what intolerable company Shakespeare and Virgil would have found them! In the same way let us judge the religious organisations which we see all around us. Do not let us deny the good and the happiness which they have accomplished; but do not let us fail to see clearly that their idea of human perfection is narrow and inadequate, and that the Dissidence of Dissent and the Protestantism of the Protestant religion will never bring humanity to its true goal. As I said with regard to wealth: Let us look at the life of those who live in and for it, – so I say with regard to the religious organisations. Look at the life imaged in such a newspaper as the *Nonconformist*, – a life of jealousy of the Establishment, disputes, tea-meetings, openings of chapels, sermons; and then think of it as an ideal of human life completing itself on all sides, and aspiring with all its organs after sweetness, light, and perfection!

Another newspaper, representing, like the *Nonconformist*, one of the religious organisations of this country, was a short time ago giving an account of the crowd at Epsom on the Derby day, and of all the vice and hideousness which was to be seen in that crowd; and then the writer turned suddenly round upon Professor Huxley,[4] and asked him how he proposed to cure all this vice and hideousness without religion. I confess I felt disposed to ask the asker this question: and how do you propose to cure it with such a religion as yours? How is the ideal of a life so unlovely, so unattractive, so incomplete, so narrow, so far removed from a true and satisfying ideal of human perfection, as is the life of your religious organisation as you yourself reflect it, to conquer and transform all this vice and hideousness? ...

The pursuit of perfection, then, is the pursuit of sweetness and light. He who works for sweetness and light, works to make reason and the will of God prevail. He who works for machinery, he who works for hatred, works only for confusion. Culture looks beyond machinery, culture hates hatred; culture has one great passion, the passion for sweetness and light. It has one even yet greater! – the passion for making them *prevail*. It is not satisfied till we *all* come to a perfect man; it knows that the sweetness and light of the few must be imperfect until the raw and unkind masses of humanity are touched with sweetness and light. If I have not shrunk from saying that we must work for sweetness and light, so neither have I shrunk from saying that we must have a broad basis, must have sweetness and light for as many as possible. Again and again I have insisted how those are the happy moments of humanity, how those are the marching epochs of a people's life, how those are the flowering times for literature and art and all the creative power of genius, when there is a *national* glow of life and thought, when the whole of society is in the fullest measure permeated by thought, sensible to beauty, intelligent and alive. Only it must be *real* thought and *real* beauty; *real* sweetness and *real* light. Plenty of people will try to give the masses, as they call them, an intellectual food prepared and adapted in the way they think proper for the actual condition of the masses. The ordinary popular literature is an example of this way of working on the masses. Plenty of people will try to indoctrinate the masses with the set of ideas and judgments constituting the creed of their own profession or party. Our religious and political organisations give an example of this way of working on the masses. I condemn neither way; but culture works differently. It does not try to teach down to the level of inferior classes; it does not try to win them for this or that sect of its own, with ready-made judgments and watchwords. It seeks to do away with classes; to make the best that has been thought and known in the world current every-where; to make all men live in an atmosphere of sweetness and light; where they may use ideas, as it uses them itself, freely, – nourished, and not bound by them.

This is the *social idea*; and the men of culture are the true apostles of equality....

[*Barbarians, Philistines, Populace*]

... It is awkward and tiresome to be always saying the aristocratic class, the middle class, the working class. For the middle class, for that great body which, as we know, 'has done all the great things that have been done in all departments',[1] and which is to be conceived as moving between its two cardinal points of our commercial member of Parliament and our fanatical Protestant Dissenter, – for this class we have a designation which now has become pretty well known, and which we may as well still keep for them, the designation of Philistines. What this term means I have so often explained that I need not repeat it here.[2] For the aristocratic class, conceived mainly as a body moving between the two cardinal points of our chivalrous lord and our defiant bar-onet, we have as yet got no special designation. Almost all my attention has naturally been concentrated on my own class, the middle class, with whom I am in closest sympathy, and which has been, besides, the great power of our day, and has had its praises sung by all speakers and newspapers.

Still the aristocratic class is so important in itself, and the weighty functions which Mr Carlyle proposes at the present critical time to commit to it[3] must add so much to its importance, that it seems neglectful and a strong instance of that want of coherent philosophic method for which Mr Frederic Harrison blames me,[4] to leave the aristocratic class so much without notice and denomination. It may be thought that the characteristic which I have occasionally mentioned as proper to aristocracies, – their natural inaccessibility, as children of the established fact, to ideas, – points to our extending to this class also the designation of Philistines; the Philistine being, as is well known, the enemy of the children of light or servants of the idea. Nevertheless, there seems to be an inconvenience in thus giving one and the same designation to two very different classes; and besides, if we look into the thing closely, we shall find that the term Philistine conveys a sense which makes it more peculiarly appropriate to our middle class than to our aristocratic. For *Philistine* gives the notion of something particularly stiff-necked and perverse in the resistance to light and its children; and therein it specially suits our middle class, who not only do not pursue sweetness and light, but who even prefer to them that sort of machinery of business, chapels, tea-meetings, and addresses from Mr Murphy[5] which makes up the dismal and liberal life on which I have so often touched. But the aristocratic class has actually, as we have seen, in its well-known politeness, a kind of image or shadow of sweetness; and as for light, if it does not pursue light, it is not that it perversely cherishes some dismal and illiberal existence in preference to light, but it is lured off from following light by those mighty and eternal seducers of our race which weave for this class their most irresistible charms, – by worldly splendour, security, power and pleasure. These seducers are exterior goods, but in a way they are goods; and he who is hindered by them from caring for light and ideas, is not so much doing what is perverse as what is too natural.

Keeping this in view, I have in my own mind often indulged myself with the fancy of employing, in order to designate our aristocratic class, the name of *The Barbarians.*[6] The Barbarians, to whom we all owe so much, and who reinvigorated and renewed our worn-out Europe, had, as is well known, eminent merits; and in this country, where we are for the most part sprung from the Barbarians, we have never had the prejudice against them which prevails among the races of Latin origin. The Barbarians brought with them that staunch individualism, as the modern phrase is, and that passion for doing as one likes, for the assertion of personal liberty, which appears to Mr Bright the central idea of English life, and of which we have, at any rate, a very rich supply. The stronghold and natural seat of this passion was in the nobles of whom our aristocratic class are the inheritors; and this class, accordingly, have signally manifested it, and have done much by their example to recommend it to the body of the nation, who already, indeed, had it in their blood. The Barbarians, again, had the passion for field-sports; and they have handed it on to our aristocratic class, who of this passion too, as of the passion for asserting one's personal liberty, are the great natural stronghold. The care of the Barbarians for the body, and for all manly exercises; the vigour, good looks, and fine complexion which they acquired and perpetuated in their families by these means, – all this may be observed still in our aristocratic class. The chivalry of the Barbarians, with its characteristics of high spirit, choice of manners, and distinguished bearing, – what is this but the attractive commencement of the politeness of our aristocratic class? In some Barbarian noble, no doubt, one would have admired, if one could have been then alive to see it, the rudiments of our politest peer. Only, all this culture (to call it by that name) of the Barbarians was an exterior culture mainly. It consisted principally in outward gifts and graces, in looks, manners, accomplishments, prowess. The chief inward gifts which had part in it were the most exterior, so to speak, of inward gifts, those which come nearest to outward ones; they were courage, a high spirit, self-confidence. Far within, and unawakened, lay a whole range of powers of thought and feeling, to which these interesting productions of nature had, from the circumstances of their life, no access. Making allowances for the difference of the times, surely we can observe precisely the same thing now in our aristocratic class. In general its culture is exterior chiefly; all the exterior graces and accomplishments, and the more external of the inward virtues, seem to be principally its portion. It now, of course, cannot but be often in contact with those studies by which, from the world of thought and feeling, true culture teaches us to fetch sweetness and light; but its hold upon these very studies appears remarkably external, and unable to exert any deep power upon its spirit. Therefore the one insufficiency which we noted in the perfect mean of this class was an insufficiency of light. And owing to the same causes, does not a subtle criticism lead us to make, even on the good looks and politeness of our aristocratic class, and of even the most fascinating half of that class, the feminine half, the one qualifying remark, that in these charming gifts there should perhaps be, for ideal perfection, a shade more *soul*?[7]

I often, therefore, when I want to distinguish clearly the aristocratic class from the Philistines proper, or middle class, name the former, in my own mind, *the Barbarians*. And when I go through the country, and see this and that beautiful and imposing seat of theirs crowning the landscape, 'There,' I say to myself, 'is a great fortified post of the Barbarians.'

It is obvious that that part of the working class which, working diligently by the light of Mrs Gooch's Golden Rule,[8] looks forward to the happy day when it will sit on thrones with commercial members of Parliament and other middle-class potentates, to survey, as Mr Bright beautifully says, 'the cities it has built, the railroads it has made, the manufactures it has produced, the cargoes which freight the ships of the greatest mercantile navy the world has ever seen,'[9] – it is obvious, I say, that this part of the working class is, or is in a fair way to be, one in spirit with the industrial middle class. It is notorious that our middle-class Liberals have long looked forward to this consummation, when the working class shall join forces with them, aid them heartily to carry forward their great works, go in a body to their tea-meetings, and, in short, enable them to bring about their millennium. That part of the working class, therefore, which does really seem to lend itself to these great aims, may, with propriety, be numbered by us among the Philistines. That part of it, again, which so much occupies the attention of philanthropists at present, – the part which gives all its energies to organising itself, through trades' unions[10] and other means, so as to constitute, first, a great working-class power independent of the middle and aristocratic classes, and then, by dint of numbers, give the law to them and itself reign absolutely, – this lively and promising part must also, according to our definition, go with the Philistines; because it is its class and its class instinct which it seeks to affirm, its ordinary self not its best self, and it is a machinery, an industrial machinery, and power and pre-eminence and other external goods, which fill its thoughts, and not an inward perfection. It is wholly occupied, according to Plato's subtle expression, with the things of itself and not its real self, with the things of the State and not the real State. But that vast portion, lastly, of the working class which, raw and half-developed, has long lain half-hidden amidst its poverty and squalor, and is now issuing from its hiding-place to assert an Englishman's heaven-born privilege of doing as he likes, and is beginning to perplex us by marching where it likes, meeting where it likes, bawling what it likes, breaking what it likes,[11] – to this vast residuum we may with great propriety give the name of *Populace*.

Thus we have got three distinct terms, *Barbarians, Philistines, Populace*, to denote roughly the three great classes into which our society is divided; and though this humble attempt at a scientific nomenclature falls, no doubt, very far short in precision of what might be required from a writer equipped with a complete and coherent philosophy, yet, from a notoriously unsystematic and unpretending writer, it will, I trust, be accepted as sufficient.

But in using this new, and, I hope, convenient division of English society, two things are to be borne in mind. The first is, that since, under all our class divisions, there is a common basis of human nature, therefore, in every one of us, whether we be properly Barbarians, Philistines, or Populace, there exists, sometimes only in germ and potentially, sometimes more or less developed, the same tendencies and passions which have made our fellow-citizens of other classes what they are. This consideration is very important, because it has great influence in begetting that spirit of indulgence which is a necessary part of sweetness, and which, indeed, when our culture is complete, is, as I have said, inexhaustible. Thus, an English Barbarian who examines himself will, in general, find himself to be not so entirely a Barbarian but that he has in him, also, something of the Philistine, and even something of the Populace as well. And the same with Englishmen of the two other classes.

This is an experience which we may all verify every day. For instance, I myself (I again take myself as a sort of *corpus vile* to serve for illustration in a matter where serving for illustration may not by everyone be thought agreeable), I myself am properly a Philistine, – Mr Swinburne would add, the son of a Philistine.[12] And although, through circumstances which will perhaps one day be known if ever the affecting history of my conversation comes to be written, I have, for the most part, broken with the ideas and the tea-meetings of my own class, yet I have not, on that account, been brought much the nearer to the ideas and works of the Barbarians or of the Populace. Nevertheless, I never take a gun or a fishing-rod in my hands without feeling that I have in the ground of my nature the self-same seeds which, fostered by circumstances, do so much to make the Barbarian; and that, with the Barbarian's advantages, I might have rivalled him.[13] Place me in one of his great fortified posts, with these seeds of a love for field-sports sown in my nature, with all the means of developing them, with all pleasures at my command, with most whom I met deferring to me, everyone I met smiling on me, and with every appearance of permanence and security before me and behind me, – then I too might have grown, I feel, into a very passable child of the established fact, of commendable spirit and politeness, and, at the same time, a little inaccessible to ideas and light; not, of course, with either the eminent fine spirit of our type of aristocratic perfection, or the eminent turn for resistance of our type of aristocratic excess, but, according to the measure of the common run of mankind, something between the two. And as to the Populace, who, whether he be Barbarian or Philistine, can look at them without sympathy, when he remembers how often, – every time that we snatch up a vehement opinion in ignorance and passion, every time that we long to crush an adversary by sheer violence, every time that we are envious, every time that we are brutal, every time that we adore mere power of success, every time that we add our voice to swell a blind clamour against some unpopular personage, every time that we trample savagely on the fallen, – he has found in his own bosom the eternal spirit of the Populace, and that there needs only a little help from circumstances to make it triumph in him untameably.

The second thing to be borne in mind I have indicated several times already. It is this. All of us, so far as we are Barbarians, Philistines, or Populace, imagine happiness to consist in doing what one's ordinary self likes. What one's ordinary self likes differs according to the class to which one belongs, and has its severer and its lighter side; always, however, remaining machinery, and nothing more. The graver self of the Barbarian likes honours and consideration; his more relaxed self, field-sports and pleasure. The graver self of one kind of Philistine likes fanaticism, business, and moneymaking; his more relaxed self, comfort and tea-meetings. Of another kind of Philistine, the graver self likes rattening;[14] the relaxed self, deputations, or hearing Mr Odger speak. The sterner self of the Populace likes bawling, hustling, and smashing; the lighter self, beer. But in each class there are born a certain number of natures with a curiosity about their best self, with a bent for seeing things as they are, for disentangling themselves from machinery, for simply concerning themselves with reason and the will of God, and doing their best to make these prevail; – for the pursuit, in a word, of perfection. To certain manifestations of this love for perfection mankind have accustomed themselves to give the name of genius; implying, by this name, something original and heaven-bestowed in the passion. But the passion is to be found far beyond those manifestations of it to which the world usually gives the name of genius, and in which there is, for the most part, a *talent* of some kind or other, a special and striking faculty of execution, informed by the heaven-bestowed ardour, or genius. It is to be found in many manifestations besides these, and may best be called, as we have called it, the love and pursuit of perfection; culture being the true nurse of the pursuing love, and sweetness and light the true character of the pursued perfection. Natures with this bent emerge in all classes, – among the Barbarians, among the Philistines, among the Populace. And this bent always tends to take them out of their class, and to make their distinguishing characteristic not their Barbarianism or their Philistinism, but their *humanity*. They have, in general, a rough time of it in their lives; but they are sown more abundantly than one might think, they appear where and when one least expects it, they set up a fire which enfilades, so to speak, the class with which they are ranked; and, in general, by the extrication of their best self as the self to develop, and by the simplicity of the ends fixed by them as paramount, they hinder the unchecked predominance of that class-life which is the affirmation of our ordinary self, and seasonably disconcert mankind in their worship of machinery.

Therefore, when we speak of ourselves as divided into Barbarians, Philistines, and Populace, we must be understood always to imply that within each of these classes there are a certain number of *aliens*, if we may so call them, – persons who are mainly led, not by their class spirit, but by a general *humane* spirit, by the love of human perfection; and that this number is capable of being diminished or augmented. I mean, the number of those who will succeed in developing this happy instinct will be greater or smaller, in proportion both to the force of the original instinct within them, and to the hindrance or encouragement which it meets with from without. In almost all who have it, it is mixed with some infusion of the spirit of an ordinary self, some quantity of class-instinct, and even, as has been shown, of more than one class-instinct at the same time; so that, in general, the extrication of the best self, the predominance of the *humane* instinct, will very much depend upon its meeting, or not, with what is fitted to help and elicit it. At a moment, therefore, when it is agreed that we want a source of authority, and when it seems probable that the right source is our best self, it becomes of vast importance to see whether or not the things around us are, in general, such as to help and elicit our best self, and if they are not, to see why they are not, and the most promising way of mending them.... [15]

[Hebraism and Hellenism]

... The uppermost idea with Hellenism is to see things as they really are; the uppermost idea with Hebraism is conduct and obedience. Nothing can do away with this ineffaceable difference. The Greek quarrel with the body and its desires is, that they hinder right thinking; the Hebrew quarrel with them is, that they hinder right acting. 'He that keepeth the law, happy is he,' 'Blessed is the man that feareth the Eternal, that delighteth greatly in his commandments,'[1] – that is the Hebrew notion of felicity; and, pursued with passion and tenacity, this notion would not let the Hebrew rest till, as is well known, he had at last got out of the law a network of prescriptions to enwrap his whole life, to govern every moment of it, every impulse, every action. The Greek notion of felicity, on the other hand, is perfectly conveyed in these words of a great French moralist: 'C'est le bonheur des hommes,' – when? when they abhor that which is evil? – no; when they exercise themselves in the law of the Lord day and night? – no; when they die daily? – no; when they walk about the New Jerusalem with palms in their hands? – no; but when they think aright, when their thought hits: 'quand ils pensent juste.'[2] At the bottom of both the Greek and the Hebrew notion is the desire, native in man, for reason and the will of God, the feeling after the universal order, – in a word, the love of God. But, while Hebraism seizes upon certain plain, capital intimations of the universal order, and rivets itself, one may say, with unequalled grandeur of earnestness and intensity on the study and observance of them, the bent of Hellenism is to follow, with flexible activity, the whole play of the universal order, to be apprehensive of missing any part of it, of sacrificing one part to another, to slip away from resting in this or that intimation of it, however capital. An unclouded clearness of mind, an unimpeded play of thought, is what this bent drives at. The governing idea of Hellenism is *spontaneity of consciousness*; that of Hebraism, *strictness of conscience*....

Both Hellenism and Hebraism arise out of the wants of human nature, and address themselves to satisfying those wants. But their methods are so different, they lay stress on such different points, and call into being by their respective disciplines such different activities, that the face which human nature presents when it passes from the hands of one of them to those of the other, is no longer the same. To get rid of one's ignorance, to see things as they are, and by seeing them as they are to see them in their beauty, is the simple and attractive ideal which Hellenism holds out before human nature; and from the simplicity and charm of this ideal, Hellenism, and human life in the hands of Hellenism, is invested with a kind of aerial ease, clearness, and radiancy; they are full of what we call sweetness and light. Difficulties are kept out of view, and the beauty and rationalness of the ideal have all our thoughts. 'The best man is he who most tries to perfect himself, and the happiest man is he who most feels that he *is* perfecting himself,' – this account of the matter by Socrates, the true Socrates of the *Memorabilia*,[3] has something so simple, spontaneous, and unsophisticated about it, that it seems to fill us with clearness and hope when we hear it. But there is a saying which I have heard attributed to Mr Carlyle about Socrates, – a very happy saying, whether it is really Mr Carlyle's or not, – which excellently marks the essential point in which Hebraism differs from Hellenism. 'Socrates,' this saying goes, 'is terribly *at ease in Zion*.'[4] Hebraism, – and here is the source of its wonderful strength, – has always been severely preoccupied with an awful sense of the impossibility of being at ease in Zion; of the difficulties of that perfection of which Socrates talks so hopefully, and, as from this point of view one might almost say, so glibly. It is all very well to talk of getting rid of one's ignorance, of seeing things in their reality, seeing them in their beauty; but how is this to be done when there is something which thwarts and spoils all our efforts?

This something is *sin*; and the space which sin fills in Hebraism, as compared with Hellenism, is indeed prodigious. This obstacle to perfection fills the whole scene, and perfection appears remote and rising away from earth, in the background. Under the name of sin, the difficulties of knowing oneself and conquering oneself which impede man's passage to perfection, become, for Hebraism, a positive, active entity hostile to man, a mysterious power which I heard Dr Pusey the other day, in one of his impressive sermons, compare to a hideous hunchback seated on our shoulders, and which it is the main business of our lives to hate and oppose.[5] The discipline of the Old Testament may be summed up as a discipline teaching us to abhor and flee from sin; the discipline of the New Testament, as a discipline teaching us to die to it. As Hellenism speaks of thinking clearly, seeing things in their essence and beauty, as a grand and precious feat for man to achieve, so Hebraism speaks of becoming conscious of sin, of awakening to a sense of sin, as a feat of this kind. It is obvious to what wide divergence these differing tendencies, actively followed, must lead. As one passes and repasses from Hellenism to Hebraism, from Plato to St Paul, one feels inclined to rub one's eyes and ask oneself whether man is indeed a gentle and simple being, showing the traces of a noble and divine nature; or an unhappy chained captive, labouring with groanings that cannot be uttered to free himself from the body of this death....[6]

But the evolution of these forces, separately and in themselves, is not the whole evolution of humanity, – their single history is not the whole history of man; whereas their admirers are always apt to make it stand for the whole history. Hebraism and Hellenism are, neither of them, the *law* of human development, as their admirers are prone to make them; they are, each of them, *contributions* to human development, – august contributions, invaluable contributions; and each showing itself to us more august, more invaluable, more preponderant over the other, according to the moment in which we take them, and the relation in which we stand to them. The nations of our modern world, children of that immense and salutary movement which broke up the Pagan world, inevitably stand by Hellenism in a relation which dwarfs it, and to Hebraism in a relation which magnifies it. They are inevitably prone to take Hebraism as the law of human development, and not as simply a contribution to it, however precious. And yet the lesson must perforce be learned, that the human spirit is wider than the most priceless of the forces which bear it onward, and that to the whole development of man Hebraism itself is, like Hellenism, but a contribution....

... by alterations of Hebraism and Hellenism, of a man's intellectual and moral impulses, of the effort to see things as they really are, and the effort to win peace by self-conquest, the human spirit proceeds; and each of these two forces has its appointed hours of culmination and seasons of rule. As the great movement of Christianity was a triumph of Hebraism and man's moral impulses, so the great movement which goes by the name of the Renascence* was an uprising and reinstatement of man's intellectual impulses and of Hellenism. We in England, the devoted children of Protestantism, chiefly know the Renascence by its subordinate and secondary side of the Reformation. The Reformation has been often called a Hebraising revival, a return to the ardour and sincereness of primitive Christianity. No one, however, can study the development of Protestantism and of Protestant churches without feeling that into the Reformation too, – Hebraising child of the Renascence and offspring of its fervour, rather than its intelligence, as it undoubtedly was, – the subtle Hellenic leaven of the Renascence found its way, and that the exact respective parts, in the Reformation, of Hebraism and of Hellenism, are not easy to separate. But what we may with truth say is, that all which Protestantism was to itself clearly conscious of, all which it succeeded in clearly setting forth in words, had the characters of Hebraism rather than of Hellenism. The Reformation was strong, in that it was an earnest return to the Bible and to doing from the heart the will of God as there written. It was weak, in that it never consciously grasped or applied the central idea of the Renascence, – the Hellenic idea of pursuing, in all lines of activity, the law and science, to use Plato's words, of things as they really are.[7] ...

From God and the bible

First published as a series of articles in the *Contemporary Review* October 1874–September 1875 replying to objections raised against *Literature and Dogma* (1873), A.'s best-selling work (5th edition 1876; 9,500 copies sold in his lifetime; 21,000 copies sold by 1924); re-printed as a book with present title Nov. 1875. For A. one of his critics' principal 'objections' was his refusal 'to admit what they call a personal God'. In reaffirming his views on 'verifiability', especially concerning received ideas about the identity of God and the truth or otherwise of the Christian miracles, A. in effect restates the belief underlying *Literature and Dogma* that if people cannot do without religion neither can they any longer do with it as it is. The book did not win the success of its predecessor, but A. was generally pleased with it, finding 'some chapters ... to be the best prose I have succeeded in writing' (*L* ii. 268).

---

*I have ventured to give to the foreign word *Renaissance*, – destined to become of more common use amongst us as the movement which it denotes comes, as it will come, increasingly to interest us, – an English form.

[*The alliance of Imagination and Conduct* (Introduction)]

... *Literature and Dogma* had altogether for its object, and so too has the present work, – a work which clears, develops and defends the positions taken in *Literature and Dogma*, – to show the truth and necessity of Christianity, and also its charm for the heart, mind, and imagination of man, even though the preternatural, which is now its popular sanction, should have to be given up. To show this, is the end for which both books were written.

For the power of Christianity has been in the immense emotion which it has excited; in its engaging, for the government of man's conduct, the mighty forces of love, reverence, gratitude, hope, pity, and awe – all that host of allies which Wordsworth includes under the one name of *imagination*, when he says that in the uprooting of old thoughts and old rules we must still always ask:

> Survives *imagination*, to the change
> Superior? Help to virtue does she give?
> If not, O mortals, better cease to live![1]

Popular Christianity has enjoyed abundantly and with profit this help from the imagination to virtue and conduct. I have always thought, therefore, that merely to destroy the illusions of popular Christianity was indefensible. Time, besides, was sure to do it; but when it is done, the whole work of again cementing the alliance between the imagination and conduct remains to be effected. To those who effect nothing for the new alliance but only dissolve the old, we take once more our text from Wordsworth, and we say:

> Why with such earnest pains dost thou provoke
> The years to bring the inevitable yoke,
> Thus blindly with man's blessedness at strife?
> Full soon his soul will have its earthly freight; –[2]

soon enough will the illusions which charmed and aided man's inexperience be gone; what have you to give him in the place of them? ...

[*The Eternal, not ourselves, that makes for righteousness* (Chap. I)]

To people disposed to throw the Bible aside *Literature and Dogma* sought to restore the use of it by two considerations: one, that the Bible requires for its basis nothing but what they can verify; the other, that the language of the Bible is not scientific, but *literary*. That is, it is the language of poetry and emotion, approximate language thrown out, as it were, at certain great objects which the human mind augurs and feels after, and thrown out by men very liable, many of them, to delusion and error. This has been violently impugned ...

First and foremost has been impugned the definition which, proceeding on the rule to take nothing as a basis for the Bible but what can be verified, we gave of God. And of this we certainly cannot complain. For we have ourselves said, that without a clear understanding in what sense this important but ambiguous term *God* is used, all fruitful discussion in theology is impossible. And yet, in theological discussion, this clear understanding is hardly ever cared for, but people assume that the sense of the term is something perfectly well known. 'A personal First Cause, that thinks and loves, the moral and intelligent governor of the universe,' is the sense which theologians in general assume to be the meaning, properly drawn out and strictly worded, of the term God. We say that by this assumption a great deal which cannot possibly be verified is put into the word 'God'; and we propose, for the God of the Bible and of Christianity, a much less pretentious definition, but which has the advantage of containing nothing that cannot be verified. The God of the Bible and of Christianity is, we say: *The Eternal, not ourselves, that makes for righteousness.*

Almost with one voice our critics have expostulated with us for refusing to admit what they call a personal God. Nothing would be easier for us than, by availing ourselves of the ambiguity natural to the use of the term God, to give such a turn to our expressions as might satisfy some of our critics, or might enable our language to pass muster with the common religious world as permissible. But this would be clean contrary to our design. For we want to recommend the Bible and its religion by showing that they rest on something which can be verified. Now, in the Bible God is everything. Unless therefore we ascertain what it is which we mean by God, and that what we mean we can verify, we cannot recommend the Bible as we desire. So against all ambiguity in the use of this term we wage war ...

[*The Stream of Tendency* (Chap. II)]

... Many excellent people are crying out every day that all is lost in religion unless we can affirm that God is a person who thinks and loves. We say, that unless we can verify this, it is impossible to build religion successfully upon it; and it cannot be verified. Even if it could be shown that there is a low degree of probability for it, we say that it is a grave and fatal error to imagine that religion can be built on what has a low degree of probability. However, we do not think it can be said that there is even a low degree of probability for the assertion that God is a person who thinks and loves, properly and naturally though we may make him such in the language of feeling; the assertion deals with what is so utterly beyond us. But we maintain, that, starting from what may be verified about God, – that he is the Eternal which makes for righteousness, – and reading the Bible with this idea to govern us, we have here the elements for a religion more serious, potent, awe-inspiring, and profound, than any which the world has yet seen. True, it will not be just the same religion which prevails now; but who supposes that the religion now current can go on always, or ought to go on? Nay, and even of that much-decried idea of God as *the stream of tendency by which all things seek to fulfill the law of their being,*[1] it may be said with confidence that it has in it the elements of a religion new, indeed, but in the highest degree hopeful, solemn, and profound. But our present business is not with this. Our present business is with the religion of the Bible; to show a new aspect of this, wherein it shall appear true, winning, and commanding ...

[*Disengaging Christianity from Materialism* (Conclusion)]

... We should do Christians generally a great injustice, if we thought that the entire force of their Christianity lay in the fascination and subjugation of their spirits by the miracles which they suppose Jesus to have worked, or by the materialistic promises of heaven which they suppose him to have offered. Far more does the vital force of their Christianity lie in the boundless confidence, consolation, and attachment, which the whole being and discourse of Jesus inspire. Whatever Jesus, then, himself thought sufficient, Christians too may bring themselves to accept with good courage as enough for them. What Jesus himself dismissed as chimerical, Christians too may bring themselves to put aside without dismay.

The central aim of Jesus was to transform for every religious soul the popular Messias-ideal of his time, the Jewish people's ideal of happiness and salvation; to disengage religion, one may say, from the materialism of the Book of Daniel ... To the mind of Jesus, his own 'resurrection' after a short sojourn in the grave was the victory of his cause after his death and at the price of his death. His disciples materialized his resurrection, and their version of the matter falls day by day to ruin. But no ruin or contradiction befalls the version of Jesus himself. He *has* risen, his cause has conquered; the course of events continually attests his resurrection and victory. The manifest unsoundness of popular Christianity inclines at present many persons to throw doubts on the truth and permanence of Christianity in general. Creeds are discredited, religion is proclaimed to be in danger, the pious quake, the world laughs. Nevertheless, *the prince of this world is judged*,* the victory of Jesus is won and sure. Conscience and self-renouncement, the method and the secret of Jesus, are set up as a leaven in the world, nevermore to cease working until the world is leavened. That this is so, that the resurrection and re-emergent life of Jesus are in this sense undeniable, and that in this sense Jesus himself predicted them, may in time, surely, encourage Christians to lay hold on this sense as Jesus did.

So, too, with the hope of immortality. Our common materialistic notions about the resurrection of the body and the world to come are, no doubt, natural and attractive to ordinary human nature. But they are in direct conflict with the new and loftier conceptions of life and death which Jesus himself strove to establish His secret, *He that will lose his life shall save it*,* is of universal application. It judges not only the life to which men cling here, but just as much the life we love to promise to ourselves in the New Jerusalem. The immortality propounded by Jesus must be looked for elsewhere than in the materialistic aspirations of our popular religion. *He lived in the eternal order, and the eternal order never dies*; this, if we may try to formulate in one sentence the result of the sayings of Jesus about life and death, is the sense in which, according to him, we can rightly conceive of the righteous man as immortal, and aspire to immortality ourselves ...

* John xvi. 11.

From Wordsworth

Written between Feb. – July 1879 as the introduction to A.'s selection of Wordsworth's poems, first proposed by Macmillan Jan. 1877; pub. *Macmillan's Magazine* July 1879, repr. *Poems of Wordsworth* Sept. 1879. See A. on reviving the practice of writing 'a notice by a competent critic, to serve as the introduction to an eminent author's works', *The Function of Criticism* ..., p. 174 above; and for a summary of his conscious propagandist aim ('it is this great public which I want to buy Wordsworth's poems as they buy Milton's') *CPW* ix. 338–40. A. opens his essay by emphasizing the decline of Wordsworth's popularity since 1830–40 when (especially at Cambridge) he was 'established in possession of the minds of all who care for poetry'; its continued diminution with the waning of Coleridge's influence and the appearance of Tennyson's *Poems* (1842); and his belief in Wordsworth meriting the 'glory' bestowed when all 'civilized nations' recognize 'one ... as a master, or even as a seriously and eminently worthy workman, in one's own line of spiritual or intellectual activity'.

... Wordsworth has been in his grave for some thirty years, and certainly his lovers and admirers cannot flatter themselves that this great and steady light of glory as yet shines over him. He is not fully recognized at home; he is not recognized at all abroad. Yet I firmly believe that the poetical performance of Wordsworth is, after that of Shakespeare and Milton, of which all the world now recognizes the worth, undoubtedly the most considerable in our language from the Elizabethan age to the present time ...

The *Excursion* and the *Prelude*, his poems of greatest bulk, are by no means Wordsworth's best work. His best work is in his shorter pieces, and many indeed are there of these which are of first-rate excellence. But in his seven volumes the pieces of high merit are mingled with a mass of pieces very inferior to them; so inferior to them that it seems wonderful how the same poet should have produced both. Shakespeare frequently has lines and passages in a strain quite false, and which are entirely unworthy of him. But one can imagine his smiling if one could meet him in the Elysian Fields and tell him so; smiling and replying that he knew it perfectly well himself, and what did it matter? But with Wordsworth the case is different. Work altogether inferior, work quite uninspired, flat and dull, is produced by him with evident unconsciousness of its defects, and he presents it to us with the same faith and seriousness as his best work. Now a drama or an epic fill the mind, and one does not look beyond them; but in a collection of short pieces the impression made by one piece requires to be continued and sustained by the piece following. In reading Wordsworth the impression made by one of his fine pieces is too often dulled and spoiled by a very inferior piece coming after it ...

There is another thing. Wordsworth classified his poems not according to any commonly received plan of arrangement, but according to a scheme of mental physiology. He has poems of the fancy, poems of the imagination, poems of sentiment and reflection, and so on. His categories are ingenious but far-fetched, and the result of his employment of them is unsatisfactory. Poems are separated one from another which possess a kinship of subject or of treatment far more vital and deep than the supposed unity of mental origin, which was Wordsworth's reason for joining them with others.

The tact of the Greeks in matters of this kind was infallible. We may rely upon it that we shall not improve upon the classification adopted by the Greeks for kinds of poetry; that their categories of epic, dramatic, lyric, and so forth, have a natural propriety, and should be adhered to. It may sometimes seem doubtful to which of two categories a poem belongs; whether this or that poem is to be called, for instance, narrative or lyric, lyric or elegiac. But there is to be found in every good poem a strain, a predominant note, which determines the poem as belonging to one of these kinds rather than the other ; and here is the best proof of the value of the classification and of the advantage of adhering to it. Wordsworth's poems will never produce their due effect until they are freed from their present artificial arrangement, and grouped more naturally.[1]

Disengaged from the quantity of inferior work which now obscures them, the best poems of Wordsworth, I hear many people say, would indeed stand out in great beauty, but they would prove to be very few in number, scarcely more than half a dozen. I maintain, on the other hand, that what strikes me with admiration, what establishes in my opinion Wordsworth's superiority, is the great and ample body of powerful work which remains to him, even after all his inferior work has been cleared away. He gives us so much to rest upon, so much which communicates his spirit and engages ours! ...

To exhibit this body of Wordsworth's best work, to clear away obstructions from around it, and to let it speak for itself, is what every lover of Wordsworth should desire ...

Long ago, in speaking of Homer, I said that the noble and

profound application of ideas to life is the most essential part of poetic greatness.[2] I said that a great poet receives his distinctive character of superiority from his application, under the conditions immutably fixed by the laws of poetic beauty and poetic truth, from his application, I say, to his subject, whatever it may be, of the ideas

On Man, on nature, and on human life,[3]

which he has acquired for himself. The line quoted is Wordsworth's own; and his superiority arises from his powerful use, in his best pieces, his powerful application to his subject, of ideas 'on man, on nature, and on human life'.

Voltaire, with his signal acuteness, most truly remarked that 'no nation has treated in poetry moral ideas with more energy and depth than the English nation'. And he adds: 'There, it seems to me, is the great merit of the English poets.'[4] Voltaire does not mean, by 'treating in poetry moral ideas', the composing moral and didactic poems; – that brings us but a very little way in poetry. He means just the same thing as was meant when I spoke above 'of the noble and profound application of ideas to life'; and he means the application of these ideas under the conditions fixed for us by the laws of poetic beauty and poetic truth. If it is said that to call these ideas moral ideas is to introduce a strong and injurious limitation, I answer that it is to do nothing of the kind, because *moral* ideas are really so main a part of human life. The question, *how to live*, is itself a moral idea; and it is the question which most interests every man, and with which, in some way or other, he is perpetually occupied. A large sense is of course to be given to the term *moral*. Whatever bears upon the question, 'how to live', comes under it.

Nor love thy life, nor hate; but, what thou liv'st,
Live well; how long or short, permit to heaven.

In those fine lines Milton utters, as everyone at once perceives, a moral idea. Yes, but so too, when Keats consoles the forward-bending lover on the Grecian Urn, the lover arrested and presented in immortal relief by the sculptor's hand before he can kiss, with the line,

For ever wilt thou love and she be fair –

he utters a moral idea. When Shakespeare says that

> We are such stuff
> As dreams are made on, and our little life
> Is rounded with a sleep,[5]

he utters a moral idea... .

It is important, therefore, to hold fast to this: that poetry is at bottom a criticism of life; that the greatness of a poet lies in his powerful and beautiful application of ideas to life,[6] – to the question: How to live. Morals are often treated in a narrow and false fashion; they are bound up with systems of thought and belief which have had their day; they are fallen into the hands of pedants and professional dealers; they grow tiresome to some of us. We find attraction, at times, even in a poetry of revolt against them; in a poetry which might take for its motto Omar Khayyam's words: 'Let us make up in the tavern for the time which we have wasted in the mosque.'[7] Or we find attractions in a poetry indifferent to them; in a poetry where the contents may be what they will, but where the form is studied and exquisite. We delude ourselves in either case; and the best cure for our delusion is to let our minds rest upon that great and inexhaustible word *life*, until we learn to enter into its meaning. A poetry of revolt against moral ideas is a poetry of revolt against *life*; a poetry of indifference towards moral ideas is a poetry of indifference towards *life*... .

... I have named a number of celebrated poets above all of whom he [Wordsworth], in my opinion, deserves to be placed. He is to be placed above poets like Voltaire, Dryden, Pope, Lessing, Schiller, because these famous personages, with a thousand gifts and merits, never, or scarcely ever, attain the distinctive accent and utterance of the high and genuine poets –

> Quique pii vates et Phoebo digna locuti,[8]

at all. Burns, Keats, Heine, not to speak of others in our list, have this accent; – who can doubt it? And at the same time they have treasures of humour, felicity, passion, for which in Wordsworth we shall look in vain. Where, then, is Wordsworth's superiority? It is here; he deals with more of *life* than they do; he deals with *life*, as a whole, more powerfully.

No Wordsworthian will doubt this. Nay, the fervent Wordsworthian will add, as Mr Leslie Stephen does, that Wordsworth's poetry is precious because his philosophy is sound; that his 'ethical system is as distinctive and capable of systematical exposition as Bishop Butler's'; that his poetry is informed by ideas which 'fall spontaneously into a scientific system of thought'.[9] But we must be on our guard against the Wordsworthians, if we want to secure for Wordsworth his due rank as a poet. The Wordsworthians are apt to praise him for the wrong things, and to lay far too much stress upon what they call his philosophy. His poetry is the reality, his philosophy, – so far, at least, as it may put on the form and habit of 'a scientific system of thought', and the more that it puts them on, – is the illusion. Perhaps we shall one day learn to make this proposition general, and to say: Poetry is the reality, philosophy the illusion. But in Wordsworth's case, at any rate, we cannot do him justice until we dismiss his formal philosophy.

The *Excursion* abounds with philosophy, and therefore the *Excursion* is to the Wordsworthian what it never can be to the disinterested lover of poetry, – a satisfactory work. 'Duty exists,' says Wordsworth, in the *Excursion*; and then he proceeds thus –

> ... Immutably survive,
> For our support, the measures and the forms,
> Which an abstract Intelligence supplies,
> Whose kingdom is, where time and space are not.[10]

And the Wordsworthian is delighted, and thinks that here is a sweet union of philosophy and poetry. But the disinterested lover of poetry will feel that the lines carry us really not a step further than the proposition which they would interpret; that they are a tissue of elevated but abstract verbiage, alien to the very nature of poetry... .

Even the 'intimations' of the famous Ode, those cornerstones of the supposed philosophic system of Wordsworth, – the idea of the high instincts and affections coming out in childhood, testifying of a divine home recently left, and fading away as our life proceeds, – this idea, of undeniable beauty as a play of fancy, has itself not the character of poetic truth of the best kind; it has no real solidity. The instinct of delight in Nature and her beauty had no doubt extraordinary strength in Wordsworth himself as a child. But to say that universally this instinct is mighty in childhood, and tends to die away afterwards, is to say what is extremely doubtful. In many people, perhaps with the majority of educated persons, the love of nature is nearly imperceptible at ten years old but strong and operative at thirty. In general we may say of these high instincts of early childhood, the base of the alleged systematic philosophy of Wordsworth, what Thucydides says of the early achievements of the Greek race: 'It is impossible to speak with certainty of what is so remote; but from all that we can really investigate, I should say that they were no very great things.'[11]

Finally, the 'scientific system of thought' in Wordsworth gives us at last such poetry as this, which the devout Wordsworthian accepts –

> O for the coming of that glorious time
> When, prizing knowledge as her noblest wealth
> And best protection, this Imperial Realm,
> While she exacts allegiance, shall admit
> An obligation, on her part, to *teach*
> Them who are born to serve her and obey;
> Binding herself by statute to secure,
> For all the children whom her soil maintains,
> The rudiments of letters, and inform
> The mind with moral and religious truth.[12]

Wordsworth calls Voltaire dull,[13] and surely the production of these un-Voltairian lines must have been imposed on him as a judgment! One can hear them being quoted at a Social Science Congress; one can call up the whole scene.[14] A great room in one of our dismal provincial towns; dusty air and jaded afternoon daylight; benches full of men with bald heads and women in spectacles; an orator lifting up his face from a manuscript written within and without to declaim these lines of Wordsworth; and in the soul of any poor child of nature who may have wandered in thither, an unutterable sense of lamentation, and mourning, and woe!

'But turn we', as Wordsworth says, 'from these bold, bad men,'[15] the haunters of Social Science Congresses. And let us be on our guard, too, against the exhibitors and extollers of a 'scientific system of thought' in Wordsworth's poetry. The poetry will never be seen aright while they thus exhibit it. The cause of its greatness is simple, and may be told quite simply. Wordsworth's poetry is great because of the extraordinary power with which Wordsworth feels the joy offered to us in nature, the joy offered to us in the simple primary affections and duties; and because of the extraordinary power with which, in case after case, he shows us this joy, and renders it so as to make us share it.

The source of joy from which he thus draws is the truest and most unfailing source of joy accessible to man. It is also accessible universally. Wordsworth brings us word, therefore, according to his own strong and characteristic line, he brings us word

Of joy in widest commonalty spread.[16]

Here is an immense advantage for a poet. Wordsworth tells of what all seek, and tells of it at its truest and best source, and yet a source where all may go and draw for it.

Nevertheless, we are not to suppose that everything is precious which Wordsworth, standing even at this perennial and beautiful source, may give us. Wordsworthians are apt to talk as if it must be. They will speak with the same reverence of 'The Sailor's Mother', for example, as of 'Lucy Gray'. They do their master harm by such lack of discrimination. 'Lucy Gray' is a beautiful success; 'The Sailor's Mother' is a failure. To give right what he wishes to give, to interpret and render successfully, is not always within Wordsworth's own command. It is within no poet's command; here is the part of the Muse, the inspiration, the God, the 'not ourselves'.[17] In Wordsworth's case, the accident, for so it may almost be called, of inspiration, is of peculiar importance. No poet, perhaps, is so evidently filled with a new and sacred energy when the inspiration is upon him; no poet, when it fails him, is so left 'weak as is a breaking wave'.[18] I remember hearing him say that 'Goethe's poetry was not inevitable enough'.[19] The remark is striking and true; no line in Goethe, as Goethe said himself, but its maker knew well how it came there. Wordsworth is right, Goethe's poetry is not inevitable; not inevitable enough. But Wordsworth's poetry, when he is at his best, is inevitable, as inevitable as Nature herself. It might seem that Nature not only gave him the matter for his poem, but wrote his poem for him. He has no style. He was too conversant with Milton not to catch at times his master's manner, and he has fine Miltonic lines; but he has no assured poetic style of his own like Milton. When he seeks to have a style he falls into ponderosity and pomposity. In the *Excursion* we have his style, as an artistic product of his own creation; and although Jeffrey completely failed to recognize Wordsworth's real greatness, he was yet not wrong in saying of the *Excursion*, as a work of poetic style: 'This will never do.'[20] And yet magical as is that power, which Wordsworth has not, of assured and possessed poetic style, he has something which is an equivalent for it.

Everyone who has any sense for these things feels the subtle turn, the heightening, which is given to a poet's verse by his genius for style. We can feel it in the

> After life's fitful fever he sleeps well –

of Shakespeare; in the

> ... though fall'n on evil days,
> On evil days though fall'n, and evil tongues –

of Milton. It is the incomparable charm of Milton's power of poetic style which gives such worth to *Paradise Regained*, and makes a great poem of a work in which Milton's imagination does not soar high. Wordsworth has in constant possession, and at command, no style of this kind; but he had too poetic a nature, and had read the great poets too well, not to catch, as I have already remarked, something of it occasionally. We find it not only in his Miltonic lines; we find it in such a phrase as this, where the manner is his own, not Milton's –

> ... the fierce confederate storm
> Of sorrow barricadoed evermore
> Within the walls of cities;

although even here, perhaps, the power of style, which is undeniable, is more properly that of eloquent prose than the subtle heightening and change wrought by genuine poetic style. It is style, again, and the elevation given by style, which chiefly make the effectiveness of *Laodameia*. Still the right sort of verse to choose from Wordsworth, if we are to seize his true and most characteristic form of expression, is a line like this from *Michael* –

> And never lifted up a single stone.

There is nothing subtle in it, no heightening, no study of poetic style, strictly so called, at all; yet it is expression of the highest and most truly expressive kind.

Wordsworth owed much to Burns, and a style of perfect plainness, relying for effect solely on the weight and force of that which with entire fidelity it utters, Burns could show him:

> The poor inhabitant below
> Was quick to learn and wise to know,
> And keenly felt the friendly glow
> And softer flame;

> But thoughtless follies laid him low
> And stain'd his name.[21]

Everyone will be conscious of a likeness here to Wordsworth; and
if Wordsworth did great things with this nobly plain manner, we
must remember, what indeed he himself would always have been
forward to acknowledge, that Burns used it before him.

Still Wordsworth's use of it has something unique and un-
matchable. Nature herself seems, I say, to take the pen out of his
hand, and to write for him with her own bare, sheer, penetrating
power. This arises from two causes; from the profound sincereness
with which Wordsworth feels his subject, and also from the
profoundly sincere and natural character of his subject itself. He
can and will treat such a subject with nothing but the most plain,
first-hand, almost austere naturalness. His expression may often
be called bald, as, for instance, in the poem of *Resolution and
Independence*; but it is bald as the bare mountain tops are bald,
with a baldness which is full of grandeur.

Wherever we meet with the successful balance, in Wordsworth,
of profound truth of subject with profound truth of execution, he
is unique. His best poems are those which most perfectly exhibit
this balance. I have a warm admiration for 'Laodameia' and for
the great 'Ode';[22] but if I am to tell the very truth, I find
'Laodameia' not wholly free from something artificial, and the
great 'Ode' not wholly free from something declamatory. If I had
to pick out poems of a kind most perfectly to show Wordsworth's
unique power, I should rather choose poems such as 'Michael',
'The Fountain', 'The Highland Reaper'.[23] And poems with the
peculiar and unique beauty which distinguishes these, Words-
worth produced in considerable number; besides very many other
poems of which the worth, although not so rare as the worth of
these, is still exceedingly high ...

I have spoken lightly of Wordsworthians; and if we are to get
Wordsworth recognized by the public and by the world, we must
recommend him not in the spirit of a clique, but in the spirit of
disinterested lovers of poetry ... No Wordsworthian has a
tenderer affection for this pure and sage master than I, or is less
really offended by his defects. But Wordsworth is something more
than the pure and sage master of a small band of devoted followers,
and we ought not to rest satisfied until he is seen to be what he is.
He is one of the very chief glories of English Poetry; and by

nothing is England so glorious as by her poetry. Let us lay aside every weight which hinders our getting him recognized as this, and let our one study be to bring to pass, as widely as possible and as truly as possible, his own word concerning his poems: 'They will co-operate with the benign tendencies in human nature and society, and will, in their degree, be efficacious in making men wiser, better, and happier.'[24]

The Study of Poetry

Pub. May 1880 as the General Introduction to *The English Poets*, ed. T. Humphry Ward, husband of Arnold's niece (Mary Humphry Ward, novelist and critic), for which A. also edited selections from Gray and Byron. A.'s intention to reach and stimulate an audience not already closely familiar with reading poetry (cp. 'Wordsworth', p. 216 above) explains the shape and direction of his argument: especially his warning against judging by 'the historic and the personal estimate'; emphasis on poetry as 'a criticism of life' approaching classic status through 'high seriousness'; and, as a 'help for discovering what poetry belongs to the class of the truly excellent', advice 'to have always in one's mind lines and expressions of the great masters, and to apply them as a touchstone to other poetry'. For the essay's critical reputation and controversy over A.'s estimate of particular poets (notably Chaucer, Dryden and Pope) see *CPW* ix. 379–80, and for T.S. Eliot's praise ('... a classic in English criticism: so much is said in so little space with such economy and with such authority'), *The Use of Poetry and the Use of Criticism* (1933), 111.

'The future of poetry is immense, because in poetry, where it is worthy of its high destinies, our race, as time goes on, will find an ever surer and surer stay. There is not a creed which is not shaken, not an accredited dogma which is not shown to be questionable, not a received tradition which does not threaten to dissolve. Our religion has materialized itself in the fact, in the supposed fact; it has attached its emotion to the fact, and now the fact is failing it. But for poetry the idea is everything; the rest is a world of illusion, of divine illusion. Poetry attaches its emotion to the idea; the idea *is* the fact. The strongest part of our religion today is its unconscious poetry.'[1]

Let me be permitted to quote these words of my own, as uttering the thought which should, in my opinion, go with us and govern us in all our study of poetry. In the present work it is the course of one great contributory stream to the world-river of poetry that we are invited to follow. We are here invited to trace the stream of English poetry. But whether we set ourselves, as here, to follow only one of the several streams that make the mighty river of poetry, or whether we seek to know them all, our governing thought should be the same. We should conceive of poetry worthily, and more highly than it has been the custom to conceive of it. We should conceive of it as capable of higher uses, and called to higher destinies, than those which in general men have assigned to it hitherto. More and more mankind will discover that we have to turn to poetry to interpret life for us, to console us, to sustain us. Without poetry, our science will appear incomplete; and most of what now passes with us for religion and philosophy will be replaced by poetry. Science, I say, will appear incomplete without it. For finely and truly does Wordsworth call poetry 'the impassioned expression which is in the countenance of all science'[2] and what is a countenance without its expression? Again, Wordsworth finely and truly calls poetry 'the breath and finer spirit of all knowledge': our religion, parading evidences such as those on which the popular mind relies now; our philosophy, pluming itself on its reasonings about causation and finite and infinite being; what are they but the shadows and dreams and false shows of knowledge? The day will come when we shall wonder at ourselves for having trusted to them, for having taken them seriously; and the more we perceive their hollowness, the more we shall prize 'the breath and finer spirit of knowledge' offered to us by poetry.

But if we conceive thus highly of the destinies of poetry, we must also set our standard for poetry high, since poetry, to be capable of fulfilling such high destinies, must be poetry of a high order of excellence. We must accustom ourselves to a high standard and to a strict judgment. Sainte-Beuve relates that Napoleon one day said, when somebody was spoken of in his presence as a charlatan: 'Charlatan as much as you please; but where is there *not* charlatanism?' – 'Yes,' answers Sainte Beuve, 'in politics, in the art of governing mankind, that is perhaps true. But in the order of thought, in art, the glory, the eternal honour is that charlatanism shall find no entrance; herein lies the inviolableness of that noble portion of man's being.'[3] It is admirably said, and let us hold fast to it. In poetry, which is thought and art in one, it is the glory, the eternal honour, that charlatanism shall find no entrance; that this noble sphere be kept inviolate and inviolable. Charlatanism is for confusing or obliterating the distinctions between excellent and inferior, sound and unsound or only half-sound, true and untrue or only half-true. It is charlatanism, conscious or unconscious, whenever we confuse or obliterate these. And in poetry, more than anywhere else, it is unpermissible to confuse or obliterate them. For in poetry the distinction between excellent and inferior, sound and unsound or only half-sound, true and untrue or only half-true, is of paramount importance. It is of paramount importance because of the high destinies of poetry. In poetry, as a criticism of life under the conditions fixed for such a criticism by the laws of poetic truth and poetic beauty,[4] the spirit of our race will find, we have said, as time goes on and as other helps fail, its consolation and stay. But the consolation and stay will be of power in proportion to the power of the criticism of life. And the criticism of life will be of power in proportion as the poetry conveying it is excellent rather than inferior, sound rather than unsound or half-sound, true rather than untrue or half-true.

The best poetry is what we want; the best poetry will be found to have a power of forming, sustaining, and delighting us, as nothing else can. A clearer, deeper sense of the best in poetry, and of the strength and joy to be drawn from it, is the most precious benefit which we can gather from a poetical collection such as the present. And yet in the very nature and conduct of such a collection there is inevitably something which tends to obscure in us the consciousness of what our benefit should be, and to distract us from the pursuit of it. We should therefore steadily set it before our minds at the outset, and should compel ourselves to revert constantly to the thought of it as we proceed.

Yes; constantly, in reading poetry, a sense for the best, the really excellent, and of the strength and joy to be drawn from it, should be present in our minds and should govern our estimate of what we read. But this real estimate, the only true one, is liable to be superseded, if we are not watchful, by two other kinds of estimate, the historic estimate and the personal estimate, both of which are fallacious. A poet or a poem may count to us historically, they may count to us on grounds personal to ourselves, and they may count to us really. They may count to us historically. The course of development of a nation's language, thought, and poetry, is profoundly interesting; and by regarding a poet's work as a stage in this course of development we may easily bring ourselves to make it of more importance as poetry than in itself it really is,[5] we may come to use a language of quite exaggerated praise in criticizing it; in short, to overrate it. So arises in our poetic judgments the fallacy caused by the estimate which we may call historic. Then, again, a poet or a poem may count to us on grounds personal to ourselves. Our personal affinities, likings, and circumstances have great power to sway our estimates of this or that poet's work, and to make us attach more importance to it as poetry than in itself it really possesses, because to us it is, or has been, of high importance. Here also we overrate the object of our interest, and apply to it a language of praise which is quite exaggerated. And thus we get the source of a second fallacy in our poetic judgments – the fallacy caused by an estimate which we may call personal.

Both fallacies are natural. It is evident how naturally the study of the history and development of a poetry may incline a man to pause over reputations and works once conspicuous but now obscure, and to quarrel with a careless public for skipping, in obedience to mere tradition and habit, from one famous name or work in its natural poetry to another, ignorant of what it misses, and of the reason for keeping what it keeps, and of the whole process of growth in its poetry. The French have become diligent students of their own early poetry, which they long neglected; the study makes many of them dissatisfied with their so-called classical poetry, the court-tragedy of the seventeenth century, a poetry which Pellisson[6] long ago reproached with its want of the true poetic stamp, with its *politesse stérile et rampante*, but which nevertheless has reigned in France as absolutely as if it had been the perfection of classical poetry indeed. The dissatisfaction is natural; yet a lively and accomplished critic, M. Charles d'Héricault, the editor of Clément Marot, goes too far when he says that 'the cloud of glory playing round a classic is a mist as dangerous to the future of a literature as it is intolerable for the purposes of history'.[7] 'It hinders,' he goes on, 'it hinders us from seeing more than one single point, the culminating and exceptional point; the summary, fictitious and arbitrary, of a thought and of a work. It substitutes a halo for a physiognomy, it puts a statue where there was once a man, and, hiding from us all trace of the labour, the attempts, the weaknesses, the failures, it claims not study but veneration; it does not show us how the thing is done, it imposes upon us a model. Above all, for the historian this creation of classic personages is inadmissible; for it breaks historical relationships, it blinds criticism by conventional admiration, and renders the investigation of literary origins unacceptable. It gives us a human personage no longer, but a God seated immovable amidst His perfect work, like Jupiter on Olympus; and hardly will it be possible for the young student, to whom such work is exhibited at such a distance from him, to believe that it did not issue ready made from that divine head.'

All this is brilliantly and tellingly said, but we must plead for a distinction. Everything depends on the reality of a poet's classic character. If he is a dubious classic, let us sift him; if he is a false classic, let us explode him. But if he is a real classic, if his work belongs to the class of the very best (for this is the true and right meaning of the word *classic, classical*),[8] then the great thing for us is to feel and enjoy his work as deeply as ever we can, and to appreciate the wide difference between it and all work which has not the same high character. This is what is salutary, this is what is formative; this is the great benefit to be got from the study of poetry. Everything which interferes with it, which hinders it, is injurious. True, we must read our classic with open eyes, and not with eyes blinded with superstition; we must perceive when his work comes short, when it drops out of the class of the very best, and we must rate it, in such cases, at its proper value. But the use of this negative criticism is not in itself, it is entirely in its enabling us to have a clearer sense and a deeper enjoyment of what is truly excellent. To trace the labour, the attempts, the weaknesses, the failures of a genuine classic, to acquaint oneself with his time and his life and his historical relationships, is mere literary dilettantism unless it has that clear sense and deeper enjoyment for its end. It may be said that the more we know about a classic the better we shall enjoy him; and, if we lived as long as Methuselah and had all of us heads of perfect clearness and wills of perfect steadfastness, this might be true in fact as it is plausible in theory. But the case here is much the same as the case with the Greek and Latin studies of our schooldays. The elaborate philological groundwork which we require them to lay is in theory an admirable preparation for appreciating the Greek and Latin authors worthily. The more thoroughly we lay the groundwork, the better we shall be able, it may be said, to enjoy the authors. True, if time were not so short, and schoolboys' wits not so soon tired and their power of attention exhausted; only, as it is, the elaborate philological preparation goes on, but the authors are little known and less enjoyed. So with the investigator of 'historic origins' in poetry. He ought to enjoy the true classic all the better for his investigations; he often is distracted from the enjoyment of the best, and with the less good he overbusies himself, and is prone to overrate it in proportion to the trouble which it has cost him.

The idea of tracing historic origins and historical relationships cannot be absent from a compilation like the present. And naturally the poets to be exhibited in it will be assigned to those persons for exhibition who are known to prize them highly, rather than to those who have no special inclination towards them. Moreover, the very occupation with an author, and the business of exhibiting him, disposes us to affirm and amplify his importance. In the present work, therefore, we are sure of frequent temptation to adopt the historic estimate, or the personal estimate, and to forget the real estimate; which latter, nevertheless, we must employ if we are to make poetry yield us its full benefit. So high is that benefit, the benefit of clearly feeling and of deeply enjoying the really excellent, the truly classic in poetry, that we do well, I say, to set it fixedly before our minds as our object in studying poets and poetry, and to make the desire of attaining it the one principle to which, as the *Imitation* says, whatever we may read or come to know, we always return. *Cum multa legeris et cognoveris, ad unum semper oportet redire principium.*[9]

The historic estimate is likely in especial to affect our judgment and our language when we are dealing with ancient poets; the personal estimate when we are dealing with poets our contemporaries, or at any rate modern. The exaggerations due to the historic estimate are not in themselves, perhaps, of very much gravity. Their report hardly enters the general ear; probably they do not always impose even on the literary men who adopt them. But they lead to a dangerous abuse of language. So we hear Caedmon, amongst our own poets, compared to Milton.[10] I have already noticed the enthusiasm of one accomplished French critic for 'historic origins'. Another eminent French critic, M. Vitet, comments upon that famous document of the early poetry of his nation, the *Chanson de Roland*.[11] It is indeed a most interesting document. The *joculator* or *jongleur* Taillefer, who was with William the Conqueror's army at Hastings, marched before the Norman troops, so said the tradition, singing 'of Charlemagne and of Roland and of Oliver, and of the vassals who died at Roncevaux'; and it is suggested that in the *Chanson de Roland* by one Turoldus or Théroulde, a poem preserved in a manuscript of the twelfth century in the Bodleian Library at Oxford, we have certainly the matter, perhaps even some of the words, of the chant which Taillefer sang. The poem has vigour and freshness; it is not without pathos. But M. Vitet is not satisfied with seeing in it a document of some poetic value, and of very high historic and linguistic value; he sees in it a grand and beautiful work, a monument of epic genius. In its general design he finds the grandiose conception, in its details he finds the constant union of simplicity with greatness, which are the marks, he truly says, of the genuine epic, and distinguish it from the artificial epic of literary ages. One thinks of Homer, this is the sort of praise which is given to Homer, and justly given. Higher praise there cannot well be, and it is the praise due to epic poetry of the highest order only and to no other. Let us try, then, the *Chanson de Roland* at its best. Roland, mortally wounded, lays himself down under a pine-tree, with his face turned towards Spain and the enemy –

> De plusurs choses a remembrer li prist,
> De tantes teres cume li bers cunquist,
> De dulce France. des humes de sun lign,
> De Carlemagne sun seignor ki l'nurrit.*

That is primitive work, I repeat, with an undeniable poetic quality of its own. It deserves such praise, and such praise is sufficient for it. But now turn to Homer –

> Ὡς φάτο τοὺς δ' ἤδη κατέχευ φυσί ζοος αἶα
> ἐν Λακεδαίμονι αὖθι, φίλη. ἐν πατρί δι γαίῃ†

We are here in another world, another order of poetry altogether; here is rightly due such supreme praise as that which M. Vitet gives to the *Chanson de Roland*. If our words are to have any meaning, if our judgments are to have any solidity, we must not heap that supreme praise upon poetry of an order immeasurably inferior.

Indeed there can be no more useful help for discovering what poetry belongs to the class of the truly excellent, and can therefore do us most good, than to have always in one's mind lines and

*'Then began he to call many things to remembrance, – all the lands which his valour conquered, and pleasant France, and the men of his lineage, and Charlemagne his liege lord who nourished him.' – Chanson de Roland, iii. 939–42.

†'So said she ; they long since in Earth's soft arms were reposing,
There, in their own dear land, their fatherland, Lacedaemon.'
Iliad, iii. 243, 244 (translated by Dr Hawtrey)[12]

expressions of the great masters, and to apply them as a touch-stone to other poetry. Of course we are not to require this other poetry to resemble them; it may be very dissimilar. But if we have any tact we shall find them, when we have lodged them well in our minds, an infallible touchstone for detecting the presence or absence of high poetic quality, and also the degree of this quality, in all other poetry which we may place beside them. Short passages, even single lines, will serve our turn quite sufficiently. Take the two lines which I have just quoted from Homer, the poet's comment on Helen's mention of her brothers; – or take his

> Ἀ δελώ, τί σφῶϊ δόμευ Πηλήϊ ἀυακτι
> θνητῷ; ὑμεὶς δ᾽ ἐ στόν ἀγή ρω τ᾽ ἀθανά τω τε.
> ἦ ἵ να δυστή νοισι μετ᾽ ανδρά σιν ἄ λγε᾽ ἔ ητον; *

the address of Zeus to the horses of Peleus; – or take finally his

> Καὶ σέ , γέ ρον, τὸ πρὶν μὲν ἀ κού ομεν ὂ λβιον εἰ ναι †

the words of Achilles to Priam, a suppliant before him. Take that incomparable line and a half of Dante, Ugolino's tremendous words –

> Io. no piangeva; si dentro impietrai.
> Piangevan elli ...‡

take the lovely words of Beatrice to Virgil –

> Io son fatta da Dio, sua mercè, tale,
> Che la vostra miseria non mi tange,
> Nè fiamma d' esto incendio non m' assale ... §

take the simple, but perfect, single line –

> In la sua volontade è nostra pace.II

Take of Shakespeare a line or two of Henry the Fourth's expos-tulation with sleep –

> Wilt thou upon the high and giddy mast
> Seal up the ship-boy's eyes, and rock his brains
> In cradle of the rude imperious surge ...

---

*'An unhappy pair, why gave we you to King Peleus, to a mortal? but ye are without old age, and immortal. Was it that with men born in misery ye might have sorrow?' – Iliad xvii. 443–5.

† 'Nay, and thou too, old man, in former days wast, as we hear, happy.' – Iliad, xviv. 543.

‡ 'I wailed not, so of stone grew I within; – they wailed.' – Inferno, xxxiii 39, 40.

§ 'Of such sort hath God, thanked be his mercy made me that yiour misery toucheth me not neither doth the flame of this fire strike me.' – Infeno, ii. 91–3.

II 'In His will is our peace.' – Paradiso, iii. 85.

and take, as well, Hamlet's dying request to Horatio –

> If thou didst ever hold me in thy heart,
> Absent thee from felicity awhile,
> And in this harsh world draw thy breath in pain
> To tell my story ...

Take of Milton that Miltonic passage –

> Darken'd so, yet shone
> Above them all the archangel; but his face
> Deeps scars of thunder had intrench'd, and care
> Sat on his faded cheek ...

add two such lines as –

> And courage never to submit or yield
> And what is else not to be overcome ...

and finish with the exquisite close to the loss of Proserpine, the loss

> ... which cost Ceres all that pain
> To seek her through the world.[13]

These few lines, if we have tact and can use them, are enough even of themselves to keep clear and sound our judgments about poetry, to save us from fallacious estimates of it, to conduct us to a real estimate.

The specimens I have quoted differ widely from one another, but they have in common this: the possession of the very highest poetical quality. If we are thoroughly penetrated by their power, we shall find that we have acquired a sense enabling us, whatever poetry may be laid before us, to feel the degree in which a high poetical quality is present or wanting there. Critics give themselves great labour to draw out what in the abstract constitutes the characters of a high quality of poetry. It is much better simply to have recourse to concrete examples; – to take specimens of poetry of the high, the very highest quality, and to say: The characters of a high quality of poetry are what is expressed *there*. They are far better recognized by being felt in the verse of the master, than by being perused in the prose of the critic. Nevertheless if we are urgently pressed to give some critical account of them, we may safely, perhaps, venture on laying down, not indeed how and why the characters arise, but where and in what they arise. They are in the matter and substance of the poetry, and they are in its manner and style. Both of these, the substance and matter on the one hand, the style and manner on the other, have a mark, an accent, of high beauty, worth, and power. But if we are asked to define this mark and accent in the abstract, our answer must be: No, for we should thereby be darkening the question, not clearing it. The mark and accent are as given by the substance and matter of that poetry, by the style and manner of that poetry, and of all other poetry which is akin to it in quality.

Only one thing we may add as to the substance and matter of poetry, guiding ourselves by Aristotle's profound observation that the superiority of poetry over history consists in its possessing a higher truth and a higher seriousness (φιλοσοφώτερον καὶ σπουδαιότερον).[14] Let us add, therefore, to what we have said, this: that the substance and matter of the best poetry acquire their special character from possessing, in an eminent degree, truth and seriousness. We may add yet further, what is in itself evident, that to the style and manner of the best poetry their special character, their accent, is given by their diction, and, even yet more, by their movement. And though we distinguish between the two characters, the two accents, of superiority, yet they are nevertheless vitally connected one with the other. The superior character of truth and seriousness, in the matter and substance of the best poetry, is inseparable from the superiority of diction and movement marking its style and manner. The two superiorities are closely related, and are in steadfast proportion one to the other. So far as high poetic truth and seriousness are wanting to a poet's matter and substance, so far also, we may be sure, will a high poetic stamp of diction and movement be wanting to his style and manner. In proportion as this high stamp of diction and movement, again, is absent from a poet's style and manner, we shall find also, that high poetic truth and seriousness are absent from his substance and matter.[15]

So stated, these are but dry generalities; their whole force lies in their application. And I could wish every student of poetry to make the application of them for himself. Made by himself, the application would impress itself upon his mind far more deeply than if made by me. Neither will my limits allow me to make any full application of the generalities above propounded; but in the hope of bringing out, at any rate, some significance in them, and of establishing an important principle more firmly by their means, I will, in the space which remains to me, follow rapidly from the commencement the course of our English poetry with them in my view.

Once more I return to the early poetry of France, with which our own poetry, in its origins, is indissolubly connected. In the twelfth and thirteenth centuries, that seed-time of all modern langʻuage and literature, the poetry of France had a clear predominance in Europe. Of the two divisions of that poetry, its productions in the *langue d'oil* and its productions in the *langue d'oc*,[16] the poetry of the *langue d'oc*, of southern France, of the troubadours, is of importance because of its effect on Italian literature; – the first literature of modern Europe to strike the true and grand note, and to bring forth, as in Dante and Petrarch it brought forth, classics. But the predominance of French poetry in Europe, during the twelfth and thirteenth centuries, is due to its poetry of the *langue d'oil*, the poetry of northern France and of the tongue which is now the French language. In the twelfth century the bloom of this romance-poetry was earlier and stronger in England, at the court of our Anglo-Norman kings, than in France itself. But it was a bloom of French poetry; and as our native poetry formed itself, it formed itself out of this. The romance-poems which took possession of the heart and imagination of Europe in the twelfth and thirteenth centuries are French; 'they are', as Southey justly says, 'the pride of French literature, nor have we anything which can be placed in competition with them'. Themes were supplied from all quarters; but the romance-setting which was common to them all, and which gained the ear of Europe, was French. This constituted for the French poetry, literature, and language, at the height of the Middle Age, an unchallenged predominance. The Italian Brunetto Latini, the master of Dante, wrote his *Treasure* in French because, he says, 'la parleure en est plus délitable et plus commune a toutes gens'.[17] In the same century, the thirteenth, the French romance-writer, Christian of Troyes, formulates the claims, in chivalry and letters, of France, his native country, as follows:

> Or vous ert par ce livre apris,
> Que Gresse ot de chevalerie
> Le premier los et de clergie;
> Puis vint chevalerie à Rome,
> Et de la clergie la some,
> Qui ore est en France venue.
> Diex doinst qu'ele i soit retenue,
> Et que li lius li abelisse

Tant que de France n'isse
L'onor qui s'i est arestée![18]

(Now by this book you will learn that first Greece has the
renown for chivalry and letters; then chivalry and the primacy in
letters passed to Rome, and now it is come to France. God grant
it may be kept there; and that the place may please it so well, that
the honour which has come to make stay in France may never
depart thence!)

Yet it is now all gone, this French romance-poetry, of which
the weight of substance and the power of style are not unfairly
represented by this extract from Christian of Troyes. Only by
means of the historic estimate can we persuade ourselves now to
think that any of it is of poetical importance.

But in the fourteenth century there comes an Englishman
nourished on this poetry, taught his trade by this poetry, getting
words, rhyme, metre[19] from this poetry; for even of that stanza
which the Italians used, and which Chaucer derived immediately
from the Italians, the basis and suggestion was probably given in
France. Chaucer (I have already named him) fascinated his
contemporaries, but so too did Christian of Troyes and Wolfram
of Eschenbach.[20] Chaucer's power of fascination, however, is endur-
ing; his poetical importance does not need the assistance of the
historic estimate; it is real. He is a genuine source of joy and strength,
which is flowing still for us and will flow always. He will be read,
as time goes on, far more generally than he is read now. His language
is a cause of difficulty for us; but so also, and I think in quite as great
a degree, is the language of Burns. In Chaucer's case, as in that of
Burns, it is a difficulty to be unhesitatingly accepted and overcome.

If we ask ourselves wherein consists the immense superiority
of Chaucer's poetry over the romance-poetry – why it is that in
passing from this to Chaucer we suddenly feel ourselves to be in
another world, we shall find that his superiority is both in the
substance of his poetry and in the style of his poetry. His superiority
in substance is given by his large, free, simple, clear yet kindly view
of human life, – so unlike the total want, in the romance-poets, of
all intelligent command of it. Chaucer has not their helplessness;
he has gained the power to survey the world from a central, a truly
human point of view. We have only to call to mind the Prologue
to The Canterbury Tales. The right comment upon it is Dryden's:

'It is sufficient to say, according to the proverb, that *here is God's plenty*.' And again: 'He is a perpetual fountain of good sense.'[21] It is by a large, free, sound representation of things, that poetry, this high criticism of life, has truth of substance; and Chaucer's poetry has truth of substance.

Of his style and manner, if we think first of the romance-poetry and then of Chaucer's divine liquidness of diction, his divine fluidity of movement, it is difficult to speak temperately. They are irresistible, and justify all the rapture with which his successors speak of his 'gold dew-drops of speech'.[22] Johnson misses the point entirely when he finds fault with Dryden for ascribing to Chaucer the first refinement of our numbers, and says that Gower also can show smooth numbers and easy rhymes.[23] The refinement of our numbers means something far more than this. A nation may have versifiers with smooth numbers and easy rhymes, and yet may have no real poetry at all. Chaucer is the father of our splendid English poetry; he is our 'well of English undefiled',[24] because by the lovely charm of his diction, the lovely charm of his movement, he makes an epoch and founds a tradition. In Spenser, Shakespeare, Milton, Keats, we can follow the tradition of the liquid diction, the fluid movement, of Chaucer; at one time it is his liquid diction of which in these poets we feel the virtue, and at another time it is his fluid movement. And the virtue is irresistible.

Bounded as is my space, I must yet find room for an example of Chaucer's virtue, as I have given examples to show the virtue of the great classics. I feel disposed to say that a single line is enough to show the charm of Chaucer's verse; that merely one line like this –

O martyr souded* in virginitee![25]

has a virtue of manner and movement such as we shall not find in all the verse of romance-poetry; – but this is saying nothing. The virtue is such as we shall not find, perhaps, in all English poetry, outside the poets whom I have named as the special inheritors of Chaucer's tradition. A single line, however, is too little if we have not the strain of Chaucer's verse well in our memory; let us take a stanza. It is from *The Prioress's Tale*, the story of the Christian child murdered in a Jewry –

My throte is cut unto my nekke-bone
Saidè this child, and as my way of kinde

*the French *soudé* ; soldered, fixed fast.

> I should have deyd, yea, longè time agone;
> But Jesu Christ, as ye in bookès finde,
> Will that his glory last and be in minde,
> And for the worship of his mother dere
> Yet may I sing O *Alma* loud and clere.[26]

Wordsworth has modernized this Tale,[27] and to feel how delicate and evanescent is the charm of verse, we have only to read Wordsworth's first three lines of this stanza after Chaucer's –

> My throat is cut unto the bone, I trow,
> Said this young child, and by the law of kind
> I should have died, yea, many hours ago.

The charm is departed. It is often said that the power of liquidness and fluidity in Chaucer's verse was dependent upon a free, a licentious, dealing with language, such as is now impossible; upon a liberty, such as Burns too enjoyed, of making words like *neck*, *bird*, into a dissyllable by adding to them, and words like *cause*, *rhyme*, into a dissyllable by sounding the e mute. It is true that Chaucer's fluidity is conjoined with this liberty, and is admirably served by it; but we ought not to say that it was dependent upon it. It was dependent upon his talent. Other poets with a like liberty do not attain to the fluidity of Chaucer; Burns himself does not attain to it. Poets, again, who have a talent akin to Chaucer's, such as Shakespeare or Keats, have known how to attain to his fluidity without the like liberty.

   And yet Chaucer is not one of the great classics. His poetry transcends and effaces, easily and without effort, all the romance-poetry of Catholic Christendom; it transcends and effaces all the English poetry contemporary with it; it transcends and effaces all the English poetry subsequent to it down to the age of Elizabeth. Of such avail is poetic truth of substance, in its natural and necessary union with poetic truth of style. And yet, I say, Chaucer is not one of the great classics. He has not their accent. What is wanting to him is suggested by the mere mention of the name of the first great classic of Christendom, the immortal poet who died eighty years before Chaucer, – Dante.[28] The accent of such verse as

> In la sua volontade è nostra pace ...

is altogether beyond Chaucer's reach; we praise him, but we feel that this accent is out of the question for him. It may be said that it was necessarily out of the reach of any poet in the England of that stage of growth. Possibly; but we are to adopt a real, not a historic, estimate of poetry. However we may account for its absence, something is wanting, then, to the poetry of Chaucer, which poetry must have before it can be placed in the glorious class of the best. And there is no doubt what that something is. It is the σπουδαιότης, the high and excellent seriousness, which Aristotle assigns as one of the grand virtues of poetry. The substance of Chaucer's poetry, his views of things and his criticism of life, has largeness, freedom, shrewdness, benignity; but it has not this high seriousness. Homer's criticism of life has it, Dante's has it, Shakespeare's has it. It is this chiefly which gives to our spirits what they can rest upon; and with the increasing demands of our modern ages upon poetry, this virtue of giving us what we can rest upon will be more and more highly esteemed. A voice from the slums of Paris, fifty or sixty years after Chaucer, the voice of poor Villon out of his life of riot and crime, has at its happy moments (as, for instance, in the last stanza of *La Belle Heaulmière**) more of this important poetic virtue of seriousness than all the productions of Chaucer. But its apparition in Villon, and in men like Villon, is fitful; the greatness of the great poets, the power of their criticism of life, is that their virtue is sustained.

To our praise, therefore, of Chaucer as a poet there must be this limitation; he lacks the high seriousness of the great classics, and therewith an important part of their virtue. Still, the main fact for us to bear in mind about Chaucer is his sterling value according to that real estimate which we firmly adopt for all poets. He has poetic truth of substance, though he has not high poetic seriousness, and corresponding to his truth of substance he has an exquisite virtue of style and manner. With him is born our real poetry.

*The name *Heaulmière* is said to be derived from a head-dress (helm) worn as a mark by courtesans. In Villon's ballad, a poor old creature of this class laments her days of youth and beauty. The last stanza of the ballad runs thus –

> 'Ainsi le bon temps regretons
> Entre nous, pauvres vieilles sottes.
> Assises bas, à croppetons,
> Tout en ung tas comme pelottes
> A petit feu de chenevottes
> Tost allumées, tost estainctes.
> Et jadis fusmes si mignottes !
> Ainsi en prend à maintz et maintes.'[29]

('Thus amongst ourselves we regret the good time, poor silly old things, low-seated on our heels, all in a heap like so many balls, by a little fire of hemp-stalks, soon lighted, soon spent. And once we were such darlings ! So fares it with many and many a one.')

For my present purpose I need not dwell on our Elizabethan poetry, or on the continuation and close of this poetry in Milton. We all of us profess to be agreed in the estimate of this poetry; we all of us recognize it as great poetry, our greatest, and Shakespeare and Milton as our poetical classics. The real estimate, here, has universal currency. With the next age of our poetry divergency and difficulty begin. An historic estimate of that poetry has established itself; and the question is, whether it will be found to coincide with the real estimate.

The age of Dryden, together with our whole eighteenth century which followed it, sincerely believed itself to have produced poetical classics of its own, and even to have made advance, in poetry, beyond all its predecessors. Dryden regards as not seriously disputable the opinion 'that the sweetness of English verse was never understood or practised by our fathers'.[30] Cowley could see nothing at all in Chaucer's poetry. Dryden heartily admired, and, as we have seen, praised its matter admirably; but of its exquisite manner and movement all he can find to say is that 'there is the rude sweetness of a Scotch tune in it, which is natural and pleasing, though not perfect.'[31] Addison, wishing to praise Chaucer's numbers, compares them with Dryden's own. And all through the eighteenth century, and down even into our own times, the stereotyped phrase of approbation for good verse found in our early poetry has been that it even approached the verse of Dryden, Addison, Pope, and Johnson.

Are Dryden and Pope poetical classics? Is the historic estimate, which represents them as such, and which has been so long established that it cannot easily give way, the real estimate? Wordsworth and Coleridge, as is well known, denied it; but the authority of Wordsworth and Coleridge does not weigh much with the young generation, and there are many signs to show that the eighteenth century and its judgments are coming into favour again. Are the favourite poets of the eighteenth century classics?

It is impossible within my present limits to discuss the question fully. And what man of letters would not shrink from seeming to dispose dictatorially of the claims of two men who are, at any rate, such masters in letters as Dryden and Pope; two men of such admirable talent, both of them, and one of them, Dryden, a man, on all sides, of such energetic and genial power? And yet, if we are to gain the full benefit from poetry, we must have the real estimate of it. I cast about for some mode of arriving, in the present case, at such an estimate without offence; and perhaps the best way is to begin, as it is easy to begin, with cordial praise.

When we find Chapman, the Elizabethan translator of Homer, expressing himself in his preface thus: 'Though truth in her very nakedness sits in so deep a pit, that from Gades to Aurora and Ganges few eyes can sound her, I hope yet those few here will so discover and confirm that, the date being out of her darkness in this morning of our poet, he shall now gird his temples with the sun', – we pronounce that such a prose is intolerable. When we find Milton writing: 'And long it was not after, when I was confirmed in this opinion, that he, who would not be frustrate of his hope to write well hereafter in laudable things, ought himself to be a true poem ', – we pronounce that such a prose has its own grandeur, but that it is obsolete and inconvenient. But when we find Dryden telling us: 'What Virgil wrote in the vigour of his age, in plenty and at ease, I have undertaken to translate in my declining years; struggling with wants, oppressed with sickness, curbed in my genius, liable to be misconstrued in all I write', – then we exclaim that here at last we have the true English prose, a prose such as we would all gladly use if we only knew how.[32] Yet Dryden was Milton's contemporary.

But after the Restoration the time had come when our nation felt the imperious need of a fit prose. So, too, the time had likewise come when our nation felt the imperious need of freeing itself from the absorbing preoccupation which religion in the Puritan age had exercised. It was impossible that this freedom should be brought about without some negative excess, without some neglect and impairment of the religious life of the soul; and the spiritual history of the eighteenth century shows us that the freedom was not achieved without them. Still, the freedom was achieved; the preoccupation, an undoubtedly baneful and retarding one if it had continued, was got rid of. And as with religion amongst us at that period, so it was also with letters. A fit prose was a necessity; but it was impossible that a fit prose should establish itself amongst us without some touch of frost to the imaginative life of the soul. The needful qualities for a fit prose are regularity, uniformity, precision, balance. The men of letters, whose destiny it may be to bring their nation to the attainment of a fit prose, must of necessity, whether they work in prose or in verse, give a predominating and almost exclusive attention to the qualities of regularity, uniformity, precision, balance. But an almost exclusive attention to these qualities involved some repression and silencing of poetry.

We are to regard Dryden as the puissant and glorious founder, Pope as the splendid high priest, of our age of prose and reason, of our excellent and indispensable eighteenth century. For the purposes of their mission and destiny their poetry, like their prose, is admirable. Do you ask me whether Dryden's verse, take it almost where you will, is not good?

> A milk-white Hind, immortal and unchanged,
> Fed on the lawns and in the forest ranged.

I answer: Admirable for the purposes of the inaugurator of an age of prose and reason. Do you ask me whether Pope's verse, take it almost where you will, is not good?

> To Hounslow Heath I point, and Banstead Down;
> Thence comes your mutton, and these chicks my own.[33]

I answer: Admirable for the purposes of the high priest of an age of prose and reason. But do you ask me whether such verse proceeds from men with an adequate poetic criticism of life, from men whose criticism of life has a high seriousness, or even, without that high seriousness, has poetic largeness, freedom, insight, benignity? Do you ask me whether the application of ideas to life in the verse of these men, often a powerful application, no doubt, is a powerful *poetic* application? Do you ask me whether the poetry of these men has either the matter or the inseparable manner of such an adequate poetic criticism; whether it has the accent of

> Absent thee from felicity awhile ...

or of

> And what is else not to be overcome ...

or of

> O martyr souded in virginitee!

I answer: It has not and cannot have them; it is the poetry of the builders of an age of prose and reason. Though they may write in verse, though they may in a certain sense be masters of the art of versification, Dryden and Pope are not classics of our poetry, they are classics of our prose.

Gray is our poetical classic of that literature and age; the position of Gray is singular, and demands a word of notice here. He has not the volume or the power of poets who, coming in times more favourable, have attained to an independent criticism of life. But he lived with the great poets, he lived, above all, with the Greeks, through perpetually studying and enjoying them; and he caught their poetic point of view for regarding life, caught their poetic manner. The point of view and the manner are not self-sprung in him, he caught them of others; and he had not the free and abundant use of them. But whereas Addison and Pope never had the use of them, Gray had the use of them at times. He is the scantiest and frailest of classics in our poetry, but he is a classic.

And now, after Gray, we are met, as we draw towards the end of the eighteenth century, we are met by the great name of Burns. We enter now on times where the personal estimate of poets begins to be rife, and where the real estimate of them is not reached without difficulty. But in spite of the disturbing pressures of personal partiality, let us try to reach a real estimate of the poetry of Burns.

By his English poetry Burns in general belongs to the eighteenth century, and has little importance for us.

> Mark ruffian Violence, distain'd with crimes,
> Rousing elate in these degenerate times;
> View unsuspecting Innocence a prey,
> As guileful Fraud points out the erring way;
> While subtle Litigation's pliant tongue
> The life-blood equal sucks of Right and Wrong![34]

Evidently this is not the real Burns, or his name and fame would have disappeared long ago. Nor is Clarinda's love-poet, Sylvander, the real Burns either. But he tells us himself: 'These English songs gravel me to death. I have not the command of the language that I have of my native tongue. In fact, I think that my ideas are more barren in English than in Scotch. I have been at 'Duncan Gray' to dress it in English, but all I can do is desperately stupid.'[35] We English turn naturally, in Burns, to the poems in our own language, because we can read them easily; but in those real poems we have not the real Burns.

The real Burns is of course in his Scotch poems. Let us boldly say that of much of this poetry, a poetry dealing perpetually with Scotch drink, Scotch religion, and Scotch manners, a Scotchman's estimate is apt to be personal.[36] A Scotchman is used to this world

of Scotch drink, Scotch religion, and Scotch manners; he has a
tenderness for it; he meets its poet half way. In this tender mood
he reads pieces like the 'Holy Fair' or 'Halloween'. But this world
of Scotch drink, Scotch religion, and Scotch manners is against a
poet, not for him, when it is not a partial countryman who reads
him; for in itself it is not a beautiful world, and no one can deny
that it is of advantage to a poet to deal with a beautiful world.
Burns's world of Scotch drink, Scotch religion, and Scotch man-
ners, is often a harsh, a sordid, a repulsive world; even the world
of his 'Cotter's Saturday Night' is not a beautiful world. No doubt
a poet's criticism of life may have such truth and power that it
triumphs over its world and delights us. Burns may triumph over
his world, often he does triumph over his world, but let us observe
how and where. Burns is the first case we have had where the bias
of the personal estimate tends to mislead; let us look at him closely
– he can bear it.

Many of his admirers will tell us that we have Burns, convivial,
genuine, delightful, here –

> Leeze me on drink! It gies us mair
> Than either school or college;
> It kindles wit, it waukens lair,
> It pangs us fou o' knowledge.
> Be't whisky gill or penny wheep
> Or ony stronger potion,
> It never fails, on drinking deep,
> To kittle up our notion
>   By night or day.[37]

There is a great deal of that sort of thing in Burns, and it is
unsatisfactory, not because it is bacchanalian poetry, but be-
cause it has not that accent of sincerity which bacchanalian
poetry, to do it justice, very often has. There is something in it of
bravado, something which makes us feel that we have not the man
speaking to us with his real voice; something, therefore, poetically
unsound.

With still more confidence will his admirers tell us that we have
the genuine Burns, the great poet, when his strain asserts the
independence, equality, dignity, of men, as in the famous song
'For a' that and a' that' –

> A prince can mak' a belted knight,
>   A marquis, duke, and a' that;
> But an honest man's aboon his might,

> Guid faith he mauna fa' that!
> For a' that, and a' that,
>   Their dignities, and a' that,
> The pith o' sense, and pride o' worth,
>   Are higher rank than a' that.

Here they find his grand, genuine touches; and still more, when this puissant genius, who so often set morality at defiance, falls moralizing –

> The sacred lowe o' weel-placed love
>   Luxuriantly indulge it;
> But never tempt th' illicit rove,
>   Tho' naething should divulge it.
> I waive the quantum o' the sin,
>   The hazard o' concealing,
> But och! it hardens a' within,
>   And petrifies the feeling.

Or in a higher strain –

> Who made the heart, 'tis He alone
>   Decidedly can try us;
> He knows each chord, its various tone;
>   Each spring, its various bias.
> Then at the balance let's be mute,
>   We never can adjust it;
> What's *done* we partly may compute,
>   But know not what's resisted.

Or in a better strain yet, a strain, his admirers will say, unsurpass-able –

> To make a happy fire-side clime
>   To weans and wife,
> That's the true pathos and sublime
>   Of human life.

There is criticism of life for you, the admirers of Burns will say to us; there is the application of ideas to life! There is, undoubtedly. The doctrine of the last-quoted lines coincides almost exactly with what was the aim and end, Xenophon tells us, of all the teaching of Socrates. And the application is a powerful one; made by a man of vigorous understanding, and (need I say?) a master of language.

But for supreme poetical success more is required than the powerful application of ideas to life; it must be an application under the conditions fixed by the laws of poetic truth and poetic beauty. Those laws fix as an essential condition, in the poet's treatment of such matters as are here in question, high seriousness; – the high seriousness which comes from absolute sincerity. The accent of high seriousness, born of absolute sincerity, is what gives to such verse as

> In la sua volontade è nostra pace ...

to such criticism of life as Dante's, its power. Is this accent felt in the passages which I have been quoting from Burns? Surely not; surely, if our sense is quick, we must perceive that we have not in those passages a voice from the very inmost soul of the genuine Burns; he is not speaking to us from these depths, he is more or less preaching. And the compensation for admiring such passages less, from missing the perfect poetic accent in them, will be that we shall admire more the poetry where that accent is found.

No; Burns, like Chaucer, comes short of the high seriousness of the great classics, and the virtue of matter and manner which goes with that high seriousness is wanting to his work. At moments he touches it in a profound and passionate melancholy, as in those four immortal lines taken by Byron as a motto for *The Bride of Abydos*, but which have in them a depth of poetic quality such as resides in no verse of Byron's own –

> Had we never loved sae kindly,
> Had we never loved sae blindly,
> Never met, or never parted,
> We had ne'er been broken-hearted.

But a whole poem of that quality Burns cannot make; the rest, in the 'Farewell of Nancy', is verbiage.

We arrive best at the real estimate of Burns, I think, by conceiving his work as having truth of matter and truth of manner, but not the accent or the poetic virtue of the highest masters. His genuine criticism of life, when the sheer poet in him speaks, is ironic; it is not –

> Thou Power Supreme, whose mighty scheme
> These woes of mine fulfil,
> Here firm I rest, they must be best
> Because they are Thy will!

It is far rather: 'Whistle owre the lave o't!' Yet we may say of him as of Chaucer, that of life and the world, as they come before him, his view is large, free, shrewd, benignant, – truly poetic, therefore; and his manner of rendering what he sees is to match. But we must note, at the same time, his great difference from Chaucer. The freedom of Chaucer is heightened, in Burns, by a fiery, reckless energy; the benignity of Chaucer deepens, in Burns, into an overwhelming sense of the pathos of things; – of the pathos of human nature, the pathos, also of non-human nature. Instead of the fluidity of Chaucer's manner, the manner of Burns has spring, bounding swiftness. Burns is by far the greater force, though he has perhaps less charm. The world of Chaucer is fairer, richer, more significant than that of Burns; but when the largeness and freedom of Burns get full sweep, as in 'Tam o'Shanter', or still more in that puissant and splendid production, 'The Jolly Beggars', his world may be what it will, his poetic genius triumphs over it. In the world of 'The Jolly Beggars' there is more than hideousness and squalor, there is bestiality; yet the piece is a superb poetic success. It has a breadth, truth, and power which make the famous scene in Auerbach's Cellar, of Goethe's 'Faust', seem artificial and tame beside it, and which are matched only by Shakespeare and Aristophanes.

Here, where his largeness and freedom serve him so admirably, and also in those poems and songs where to shrewdness he adds infinite archness and wit, and to benignity infinite pathos, where his manner is flawless, and a perfect poetic whole is the result, – in things like the address to the mouse whose home he had ruined, in things like 'Duncan Gray', 'Tam Glen', 'Whistle and I'll come to you my Lad', 'Auld Lang Syne' (this list might be made much longer) – here we have the genuine Burns of whom the real estimate must be high indeed. Not a classic, nor with the excellent σπουδαιότης of the great classics, nor with a verse rising to a criticism of life and a virtue like theirs; but a poet with thorough truth of substance and an answering truth of style, giving us a poetry sound to the core. We all of us have a leaning towards the pathetic, and may be inclined perhaps to prize Burns most for his touches of piercing, sometimes almost intolerable, pathos; for verse like –

> We twa hae paidl't i' the burn
>   From mornin' sun till dine;
> But seas between us braid hae roar'd
>   Sin auld lang syne ...

where he is as lovely as he is sound. But perhaps it is by the perfection of soundness of his lighter and archer masterpieces that he is poetically most wholesome for us. For the votary misled by a personal estimate of Shelley, as so many of us have been, are, and will be, – of that beautiful spirit building his many-coloured haze of words and images

> Pinnacled dim in the intense inane –

no contact can be wholesomer than the contact with Burns at his archest and soundest. Side by side with the

> On the brink of the night and the morning
>   My coursers are wont to respire,
> But the Earth has just whispered a warning
>   That their flight must be swifter than fire ... [38]

of *Prometheus Unbound*, how salutary, how very salutary, to place this from *Tam Glen* –

> My minnie does constantly deave me
>   And bids me beware o' young men;
> They flatter, she says, to deceive me;
>   But wha can think sae o' Tam Glen?[39]

But we enter on burning ground as we approach the poetry of times so near to us – poetry like that of Byron, Shelley, and Wordsworth – of which the estimates are so often not only personal, but personal with passion. For my purpose, it is enough to have taken the single case of Burns, the first poet we come to of whose work the estimate formed is evidently apt to be personal, and to have suggested how we may proceed, using the poetry of the great classics as a sort of touchstone, to correct this estimate, as we had previously corrected by the same means the historic estimate where we met with it. A collection like the present, with its succession of celebrated names and celebrated poems, offers a good opportunity to us for resolutely endeavouring to make our estimates of poetry real. I have sought to point out a method which will help us in making them so, and to exhibit it in use so far as to put any one who likes in a way of applying it for himself.

At any rate the end to which the method and the estimate are designed to lead, and from leading to which, if they do lead to it, they get their whole value, – the benefit of being able clearly to feel and deeply to enjoy the best, the truly classic, in poetry, – is an end, let me say it once more at parting, of supreme importance.

We are often told that an era is opening in which we are to see multitudes of a common sort of readers, and masses of a common sort of literature; that such readers do not want and could not relish anything better than such literature, and that to provide it is becoming a vast and profitable industry. Even if good literature entirely lost currency with the world, it would still be abundantly worth while to continue to enjoy it by oneself. But it never will lose currency with the world, in spite of momentary appearances; it never will lose supremacy. Currency and supremacy are insured to it, not indeed by the world's deliberate and conscious choice, but by something far deeper, – by the instinct of self-preservation in humanity.

NOTES

For abbreviated references to editions of Arnold see Bibliography.

Shakespeare (p. 3)

1–2. ' ... to solve the universe as you try to do is as irritating as Tennyson dawdling with its painted shell ... I keep saying, "Shakespeare, Shakespeare, you are as obscure as life is" ' (A. to Clough, Dec. 1847, *CL* 63).

3. *Out-topping knowledge*: Exceeding our own power of understanding; *loftiest hill*: cp., e.g., Goethe and Emerson who image Shakespeare among poets as, respectively, Mont Blanc and Chimborazo (*Conversations*, 2 Jan. 1824; 'The Poet', *Essays* 1844).

5. cp. Cowper's 'Light Shining out of Darkness', l. 3, 'He plants his footsteps in the sea ...'

In Harmony with Nature: To A Preacher (p. 3)

12. cp. Epictetus, *Discourses* i. ch. 6 *Long* (1877) 21, ' ... it is dreadful for man to begin and end where irrational minds do ... he ought to begin where they begin, and to end where nature ends in us; and nature ends in contemplation and understanding'.

In Utrumque Paratus (p. 4)

1. *One all pure*: Plotinus, *Ennead* 1. vi. 7: ' ... that solitary duelling Existence, the Apart, the Unmingled, the Pure, that from Which all things depend ... The Source of Life and of Intellection and Being' (*The Ethical Treatises*, tr. S. Mackenna (1917) 86).

3. *procession*: In the theological sense of emanation.

11–14. Plotinus urges 'purity of being' for 'the manna of our flight' towards the ultimate Good (loc. cit. 87–9). A. also knew Emerson, 'The Oversoul', Essays (1841), 'The soul gives itself alone, original and pure, to the Lonely, Original and Pure' (*Works*, Riverside edn. ii. 277).

15–21. Similar imagery for intellectual exploration in Coleridge's *Biographia Literaria* (1817) ch. xii, ed. J. Shawcross i. 165– 6; read by A. 1846.

31, 36. The 'brother-world' dreams because it lacks man's consciousness;

man is the 'Chief dreamer' because of his illusion that he is 'a monarch'
and the world exists for his sake. cp. 'No, we are strangers here',
Empedocles on Etna, ii. 177–81, p. 53 above.

The Sick King in Bokhara (p. 5)
5– 8.   Details from *Burnes* i. 270.
　12.   *Ferdousi*: Persian epic poet (c. 950–1020), author of the
Sháhnámeh, containing the story of Sohrab and Rustum.
16 –17.   Details about the Registàn of Bokhara ('a spacious area – near
the palace') in *Burnes* i. 272–3.
22–3.   Probably suggested by the Balkh fever which afflicted Burnes and
his fellow travellers (op. cit. i. 258–9), but the sickness of the king,
vizier and mullah in the arid land also suggests spiritual malaise.
Images of fever and sickness are frequent in A. when describing the
'waste land' of modern life (e.g. 'The Scholar-Gipsy' 164 (and *n.*)
203–5, pp. 112, 113–14 above).
　31.   *Moollah*: Mullah. A Mohammedan title for one learned in theol-
ogy and sacred laws (OED).
　49.   *way*: path *1849–77*.
58 – 64.   Bokhara's scanty water supply and the sufferings of a long
summer drought recorded in *Burnes* i. 301–2.
116.   *Hinder*: Forbid *1849–55*.
161.   *Russian*: northern *1849*.
166 – 8.   An early example of A.'s liking for exotic and resonant oriental
names (notable later in 'Sohrab and Rustum' pp. 106–7 above).
167.   *Shiah dogs*: The Shiahs, an Islamic sect, are despised by the Vizier,
who is a Sunni.
173.   *kaffirs*: ' … the Siahposh kaffirs, or Black-vested Infidels … This
race is entirely confined to the mountains, and persecuted by all the
surrounding races' (*Burnes* ii. 221).
195– 6.   ' … sherbet of cherries, cooled by ice … grape jelly or syrup …
mixed up with chopped ice … It is a refreshing sight to see the huge
masses of it, with the thermometer at 90° … piled into heaps like snow'
(op. cit. 259, 277–8).
207–8.   Obscure, but the meaning is: And that his will be not satisfied,
from all time the law is fixed.
224.   See ll. 166–8n. above.

Resignation: To Fausta (p. 12)
Sub-title.   Perhaps 'a female Faust' who 'desires poignant experience to
relieve the dulness of her life' (*Trilling* 99); but see K. A., 'equally with
the Latin meaning … in mind, it may hint a gentle rebuke – in spite of
her sense of frustration Jane is "fortunate" ' (*Poems* 84; see Introduc-
tion, p. xix above).
　1.   cp. Byron, 'The Giaour' l. 1113, 'I knew but to obtain or die … '

21. *Past straits*: 'Past difficulties and also narrow gorges already passed through' (K. A., unpub. *n.*).

40 –1. 'Those who have long been familiar with the English Lake-Country will find no difficulty in recalling, from the description in the text, the roadside inn of Wythburn on the descent from Dunmail Rise towards Keswick; its sedentary landlord of twenty years ago, and the passage over the Wythburn Fells to Watendlath' (A.'s note *1869*). The Arnold family's 1833 expedition on foot and by carriage via Keswick to Cockermouth and the coast is reconstructed *Poems* 86.

70 –1. cp. Scott; *Marmion* (1808) Canto III, ll. 11–12 (of Marmion's all-day journey north), 'On wings of jet, from his repose/In the deep heath, the black-cock rose … '

85. *Wide-glimmering sea*: Probably the Irish Sea (see above).

86–107. cp. Clough, 'Blank Misgivings … ' ix. 1–21 beginning 'Once more the wonted road I tread … '

98–101. cp. *Marmion*, intr. to Canto IV, ll. 33–6, beginning 'The same November gale once more/Whirls the dry leaves on Yarrow shore … '

116–19. Recollecting the 'torpid life' in Wordsworth's 'Gipsies', ll. 1–2, 5–8.

144 – 69. Resembles Goethe's account of the poet in *Wilhelm Meister* ii. ch. 2, read by A. c. 1845 in Carlyle's translation (1824).

161. *Uncravingly*: With the 'Indian' detachment which A. fastened on when first reading the *Bhagavad-Gita* 1845–6. See 'The Function of Criticism … ', p. 201 above.

164. 'That is a fine saying of Plato: That he who is discoursing about men should look also at earthly things as if he viewed them from some higher place … ' (*The Thoughts of the Emperor M. Aurelius Antoninus* vii., 48 tr. G. Long (1875 ed. 138: see also ix. 30, quoted by A., 'Marcus Aurelius' *E in C* I (*CPW* iii. 154) and Lucretius, *De Rerum Natura* ii. 7–10).

170 – 85. Similarly idyllic settings in 'The Scholar-Gipsy', 'Thyrsis' pp. 108, 120 above.

181–3. cp. Milton's ploughman whistling in the dawn countryside, 'l'Allegro' ll. 63–4.

190–2. Nature's calm resigned acceptance of eternal change contrasts with Wordsworth's conception in 'Tintern Abbey' (see headn.).

198. 'He sees things as they are … in their stern simplicity. The sight is a severe and mind-tasking one' (from A.'s analysis of Empedocles, *Yale MS*).

201–2. Fausta is attracted by action, excitement, change. A's 'scanning' of her thoughts in ll. 203–14 is part of his own 'dialogue of the mind with itself' (see 1853 preface, p. 129 above).

209–10. Recalled in 'Memorial Verses' ll. 45–7, p. 87 above.

211–12. Added *1881*.

214. ' … a slight gift of poetical expression … is overlaid and crusted in a profound thinker … "Not deep the poet sees but wide":– think of

this as you gaze from the Cumner Hill towards Cirencester and Cheltenham' (A. to Clough Feb. 1849, *CL* 99): cp. A. on Empedocles, *Yale MS*, 'the service of reason is freezing to feeling ... '

237. *life's uncheered ways*: cp. Lucretius, *De Rerum Natura* ii. 15-16 and A. on Lucretius, pp. 151-2 above.

253. 'The image is the Tree of Life. Those who can distinguish the variety of life without experience are like "leaves by suns not yet uncurled" ' (*Poems* 94).

257- 60. 'At every moment men are being born and men are dying' (Ibid.).

268. Striations in Lake District boulders made by the movement of ancient glaciers.

270. A. was familiar with the similar feelings in *Obermann* (Lettre iv. 128, '... je ne veux plus en jouir [i.e. 'ma vie'], mais seulement la tolérer ... ').

277. cp. 'The Buried Life' l. 43 (p. 98 above) and 'Tristram and Iseult' iii. 135, 'diseased unrest' (p. 83 above).

278. 'Necessity, which thwarts our Romantic expectations' (*Poems* 95). cp. 'To Marguerite – Continued' (p. 28 above) which again salutes necessity but is more explicitly sympathetic towards the longings which are here both 'intemperate' (l. 271 above) and also victims of the 'infection'.

The Forsaken Merman (p. 19)

96. *spindle drops*: shuttle falls *1849-77*. Clough pointed out the error (*CL* 107).

112-19. Following Byron's *Manfred* I. i. 76-87 (see 'Empedocles on Etna', II. i. 2*n*. below), beginning 'In the blue depths of the waters,/Where the wave hath no strife/Where the Wind is a stranger;/And the Sea-snake hath life,/Where the Mermaid is decking/Her green hair with shells ... '

To a Friend (p. 23)

1. *these bad days*: 1848, the 'year of revolutions'. cp. Carlyle, *Past and Present* (1843), ' ... French Revolutions, Chartisms ... that make the heart sick in these bad days' (*Traill*, 36).

2. *the old man*: Homer.

3. *The Wide Prospect*: A. notes *1849*, 'E'υρωπη' (the wide prospect) adding in later edns. that the Greeks probably used the term because of the view of the European coast as seen from Asia Minor.

4. Smyrna, at the foot of Mt. Timolus, was one of seven cities claimed as Homer's birthplace.

5-8. The Stoic philosopher Epictetus: expelled with other philosophers from Rome by Domitian AD 89; resided at Nicopolis, where Arrian recorded his teachings. A. commented on this densely informative stanza, 'There's for you, but the style is not hard tho' rather taking' (*CL* 90).

9–14. Sophocles: born Colonus 498 BC, died 406 BC; *Oedipus at Colonus* was his last play. For A. on his 'unrivalled *adequacy*' see 'On the Modern Element in Literature' (p. 150 above) and with 'even-balanced soul' (1.9) cp. *Lucretius*, i.41, ' ... in this time of our country's troubles neither can I do my part with untroubled mind' (Loeb transl.).

Quiet Work (p. 24)

1. *One lesson*: Two lessons *1849*. See Wordsworth on Nature's teaching in 'Hartleap Well' ll. 177–8, 'One lesson, Shepherd, let us two divide/Taught both by what she shows, and what she conceals ... '.

5–13. Coleridge in *Biographia Literaria* quotes Plotinus on Nature's adjuration to man, '... it behoves thee ... to understand in silence, even as I am silent and work without words ... ' (ed. Shawcross i. 66; see 'In Utrumque Paratus' 15–21 *n.*, above).

6. *lasting fruit*: one short hour *1849*; still advance *1853–7*.

9–12. In keeping with many early 19th-century allusions to the steadiness and calm of nature's 'ministers', particularly the stars, e.g., Goethe's lines, transl. by Carlyle, 'Like as a star/That maketh not haste/That taketh not rest/But each one fulfilling/His God-given best ... ' (*Traill* xxvii. 432); Wordsworth's 'Gipsies' ll. 23–4; Keats's 'Nature's patient sleepless eremite' in his 'Bright star!' sonnet (first pub. 1848; see Introduction p. xxii above).

12. *glorious tasks*: glorious course *1849* (confirms the identity of the 'sleepless ministers' (l. 11) with the stars).

Meeting (p. 24)

3 – 4. 'See, among "Early Poems", the poem called "A Memory Picture" ' (A.'s *n.* 1877).

6. Her pallor is mentioned in 'A Memory Picture' l. 30 (*Poems* 109), 'A Farewell' l. 10, p. 29 above.

11. cp. 'To Marguerite – Continued' l. 22, p. 29 above.

15. 'Do not let us forsake one another: we have the common quality, now rare, of being unambitious ... Some must be contented not to be at the top' (A. to Clough, March 1848, *CL* 76).

Isolation. To Marguerite (p. 25)

1. *apart*: For a year; see 'Meeting', p. 26 above.

10. *may oft be*: is often *1857–69*; may well be *1877*.

11. As the moon sways the tides. cp. l. 16 'remote and sphere'd course', and the moon-goddess's love for Endymion, ll. 19–20.

13–30. Out of keeping with A.'s marriage to Frances Lucy Wightman June 1851 (see 'Dover Beach' p. 88 above) and, with other sentiments

in the poem, helping to explain its exclusion from *1852*.
16. See the similar image in 'A Farewell', ll. 73–6 (p. 31 above).

To Marguerite – Continued (p. 26)
Title. 'To Marguerite, in Returning a Volume of the Letters of Ortis'
1852; 'To Marguerite' *1853*;'Isolation' *1857*; present title *1869*.
Foscolo's *Ultime Lettere di Jocopo Ortis* (1802) probably read by A.
in the French transl. by A. Dumas (1839; repr. 1847). (Ortis is
romantically melancholy and unhappy in love.)
1–4. cp. Thackeray's *Pendennis* (1848–50), ch. xvi, 'How lonely we are
in the world ... you and I are but a pair of infinite isolations, with
some fellow-islands a little more or less near to us'. The 'sea of life' is
frequent in A., e.g. 'Human Life' l. 27, 'A Summer Night' ll. 52–3
(*Poems* 140, p. 95 above).
2. 'Making communication confused and uncertain' (*Poems* 124).
6. *endless*: Unending. cp. 'Isolation. To Marguerite' ll. 40–1, p. 28
above. K. A. notes the ambivalency of 'enclasping' (l. 5) which sug-
gests both protectiveness and imprisonment and, 'in conjunction with
"shoreless" (l. 3), may imply that the individual also knows that he
belongs to a General Life, which seems ..., boundless (i.e. without
apparent beginning or end).'
7–12. Suggesting a mood of romantic enchantment as in human love.
13. cp. 'The Buried Life' ll. 12–15, p. 97 above.
15–16. With the idea of a total unity from which men are separated cp.
'Empedocles on Etna' II. i. 372, p. 75 above.
22–4. With 'A God, a God', cp. Horace's *Epodes* xiv. 6, 'deus, deus,
nam me vetat ... ', and with estranging, his *Odes* I. iii. 21–3
'necquicquam dues abscidit/prudens Oceano dissociabili/terras ... ' K.
Tillotson (loc. cit.) notes A.'s probable familiarity with the oral transl.
of 'oceano dissociabili' by A. Tait (taught at Rugby and Balliol, later
Archbishop of Canterbury) as 'with the estranging sea'.

A Farewell (p. 27)
10. *poured flushing*: came flooding *1852*; came flushing *1854–7*.
23–5. Clough has, *Amours de Voyage* ii. 293–5,
... the woman, they tell you,
Ever prefers the audacious, the wilful, the vehement hero;
She has no heart for the timid, the sensitive soul ...
56. *affinities*: Affinity: a spiritual attraction believed to exist between
persons; also the subject of the affinity 1868 (OED).
73–6. Image perhaps suggested by Clough, 'Our orbits ... early in
August might ... cross, and we two serene undeviating souls salute
each other once again for a moment amid the infinite space' (letter to
A. 23 June 1849, *CL* 108).
81–2. *boon*: Benign, gracious, as in 'Thyrsis' l. 175 (p. 124 above).

Stanzas in Memory of the Author of 'Obermann', November, 1849 (p. 30)

3. *Rack* est un mot de la vieille langue anglaise pour signifier les *bords, la frange* d'une nuage qui passe. Shakespeare s'en sert dans *La Tempête'* (A. to Saint-Beuve, 8 March 1855, *Bonnerot* 525.)

12. The last time was Sept. 1848.

18. *cast*: Turning the ship's head away from the wind to ease its passage.

27–8. 'Les glaciers *prêtent, donnent quelque chose* de l'âme de leurs nuages aux livres d'Obermann' (A. to Sainte-Beuve, March 1855, op. cit. 526).

28. *white*: mute *1852*.

44. cp. Luke 23:34. Perhaps implying 'the poet who tells "deep secrets" is crucified by the world's neglect' (*Poems* 131).

49–50. 'Written November, 1849', A.'s *n. 1852–1869*. Wordsworth died 1850.

51–2. Goethe died 1832. Linked with Wordsworth again 'Memorial Verses', pp. 86–7 above.

53–4. 'Wordsworth ... plunged himself in the inward life, he voluntarily cut himself off from the modern spirit' ('Heinrich Heine', *CPW* iii. 121). See Introduction, p. xxviii–ix above.

66. *a tremendous*: Europe's stormiest *1855*:'... the fiery storm of the French Revolution', A.'s *1869 n.* on Senancour (headn.).

72. *leisure to grow wise*: The phrase occurs in S. Johnson's 'Life of Pope', *Lives of the Poets*, ed. G. Birkbeck Hill iii. 239 (1903).

79–80. cp. 'Resignation' l. 214, p. 18 above.

85–8. *Obermann* (3me Fragment) i. 148:'Le vent apporte ou recule ces sons alpestres; et quand il les perd, tout paraît froid, immobile et mort'.

93–6. On the 'divided self' see the 1853 Preface, 'Empedocles on Etna' II. i. 220 –30, 'On the Modern Element in Literature', pp. 129, 70–1, 151, above.

97. *The glow*, he cries: The glow of thought *1852*. Probably altered because of the contradiction in l. 107.

101–4. cp. 'Resignation' ll. 144–69 (pp. 16–17 above) and on renouncing the world in order to understand it 'Obermann Once More' ll. 75–6 ('Ah me! we anchorites read things best,/Clearest their course discern!')

109–12. 'Besides the inwardness ... sincerity ... renouncement, there was the poetic emotion and deep feeling for nature', A.'s essay on Obermann (headn.)

114. *Jaman*: Above Vevey on the Lake of Geneva (Obermann's château is situated near Vevey).

121. *Lake Leman*: The Lake of Geneva.

125–6. *Obermann* (Lettre xlviii) ii. 19–20, 'Et moi aussi, j'ai des moments d'oubli ... Je m'arrête étonné ... je cherche ... dans le bruit des pins quelques-un des accents de la langue éternelle'.

132. 'the poetic half of the divided self, but A. is also probably thinking of Marguerite' (*Poems* 135).

133– 4. cp. 'Meeting' l. 13, p. 26 above.

143. 'Except a man be born again, he cannot see the kingdom of God', John 3:3, 7 (quoted by A. 23 Sept. 1849, *CL* 109–10).

156. Epistle of James 1:27.

161– 4. Sainte-Beuve informed A. Sept. 1854 of Senancour's death and burial, attended by only two mourners, at Sèvres near Paris, and of his chosen epitaph, 'Eternité deviens mon asyle' (quoted 'Obermann Once More' ll. 268–72, *Poems* 530).

171– 4. cp. Gray's 'Elegy in a Country Church-yard' ll. 97–116.

183– 4. 'It is his own "unstrung will" and "broken heart" as much as Obermann's that A. is dismissing ... The lines are A.'s farewell to youth, insouciance and Marguerite – and also, in the long run, to the writing of poetry' (*Poems* 138).

Self-dependence (p. 35)

Title. See *Poems* 142, 'Perhaps suggested by Emerson's "Self-Reliance", (*Essays*, 1st series 1841). A. would have endorsed Emerson's comment, "Discontent is the want of self-reliance: it is infirmity of will" (*Works*, Riverside ed. ii. 77).'

1–2. cp. 'The disease of the present age is divorce from self' (A.'s *Yale MS*). See 'Obermann' ll. 93–6 *n*. above.

5–8. See Introduction, p. xxii above.

16 –28. cp. 'Quiet Work', p. 25 above.

17. 'Le silence éternel de ces espaces infinis m'effraie' (Pascal's *Pensées, Oeuvre* ... 1941 edn. 848. A. may first have read Pascal c. 1848.

21. In 'Resignation', however, nature seems 'to bear rather than rejoice' (l. 270, p. 20 above).

22. cp. 'Empedocles on Etna' II. i. 425.

23. *self-poised*: alone *1852–7*.

24. cp. A. to Clough 12 Feb. 1853, '... you ... could never finally ... "resolve to be thyself" – but were ... doubting whether you ought not to adopt this or that mode of being ... because it might possibly be nearer the truth than your own' (*CL* 130).

25–8. See Basil Willey, ' ... the two fixed marks of Stoic doctrine; the Stars and Duty – the starry heavens above and the moral law within' (op. cit.[headn.] 66).

29–32. Variations on the Sophoclean adjuration, 'know thyself' known to A. in Goethe (' ... man ... knows not whence he comes, nor where he goes;he knows little of the world, and least of himself. I know not myself, and God forbid I should', *Conversations* 10 April 1892), and Carlyle, *Sartor Resartus*, 'the folly of that impossible Precept; till it be transl. into this partially possible one, *know* what thou canst work at' (*Traill* i. 132).

Empedocles on Etna: A Dramatic Poem (p. 36)

Scene. The three scenes on Etna are in the forest early morning (I. i), on the unshaded upper slopes at noon (I. ii), on the barren summit at evening (II. i): the journey is 'from youth to middle age, from elasticity of spirit to world weariness, from a proper balance of man's mental powers to his "enslavement" by thought' (*Poems* 149).

I. i. 20. *sick or sorry*: cp. 'Pagan and Medieval Religious Sentiment', headn. p. 184 above.

I. i. 23– 43. Based on Karsten's *Philosophorum Graecorum Veterum ... Operum Reliquae* (1838), Introduction, ii. 34–5.

I. i. 52. *Viewless*: Invisible. So used in Shakespeare, Milton, Keats; here echoing the Spirit, *Comus* ll. 91–2, ' ... I hear the tread/Of hatefull steps, I must be viewless now ... '

I. i. 59– 63 (and 108–11, 115, 116, 117, 118, 138–9). Based on notes from *Karsten* ii.

I. i. 85–98. Perhaps suggested by the Abbot's following behind Manfred and trying to save him, *Manfred* III. i. 160–71.

I. i. 147– 8. *Georgias*: Empedocles's most famous pupil (*Karsten* ii. 56).

I. i. 151–3. A. found 'a root of failure, powerlessness, and ennui ... in the constitution of Senancour's own nature' ('Obermann', 1869, *CPW* v. 300) and saw Byron's heroes,'... breaking on some rock of revolt and misery in the depths of their own nature; Manfred, self-consumed, fighting blindly and passionately with I know not what ... ' ('On the Study of Celtic Literature', 1867, *CPW* iii. 372–3.)

I. ii. 4–5. cp. the setting in 'Obermann', p. 32 above.

I. ii. 14–16. See ll. 427–60 *n.* below.

I. ii. 19–21 (and 30–1). See *Karsten* ii. 25, 88.

I. ii. 31. *confound*: confuse *1852–69*.

I. ii. 36 –76. Repr. *1855* as 'the Harp-Player on Etna. 1. The Last Glen'.

I. ii. 51. *muffle*: '... the vegetation of the south [of Italy] ... is all above ... in the branches and leaves of the trees ... not muffling and cooling the ground itself in the way I love' (A. 5 July 1865, *L* i. 286). cp. 'The Scholar-Gipsy' l. 69, p. 109 above.

I. ii. 56 –76. Chiron teaches Achilles traditional love (accounts in Statius's *Achillead* ii, Pindar's *Nemean Odes* iii); deliberately contrasted with Empedocles' philosophical instruction of Pausanias below.

I. ii. 77– 426. 'Empedocles' attempt to free Pausanias from superstitious fears is so far Lucretian, but this long philosophical chant ... is primarily stoical in its insistence on recognising and accepting the limits of human freedom' (*Poems* 159). The stanza has two hexameters broken to form a quatrain rhyming abab and an unbroken hexameter rhyming with the corresponding hexameter in the following stanza.

I. ii. 77. *out-spread world*: howling void *1852*.

I. ii. 81.   *Obermann* (Lettre xli) i. 165:'... jouet lamentable d'une destinée rien n'explique, l'homme abandonnera sa vie aux hasards et des choses et des temps'.

I. ii. 82– 6.   Following Empedocles, *Karsten* ii. 88, 90.

I. ii. 101.   i.e. tries to believe in at least a limited freedom, a view less 'degrading' than the implication of I. ii. 93 – 6 above.

I. ii. 102.   Epicurean comment. The evils of life are due to fear. Belief in God is due to fear. Fear leads to superstition.

I. ii. 108.   *Pantheia*: See I. i. 19 ff.

I. ii. 111.   *son of Anchitus*: ' ... son of wise Anchitus', Empedocles, *Karsten* ii. 92. See l. 216.

I. ii. 122–6.   Ironically alluding to his supposed miracles (I. i. 108–111, 117–18).

I. ii. 127– 8.   See 1853 Preface, p. 129 above.

I. ii. 129–30.   For the difficulty involved see 'The Buried Life' ll. 55– 6, p. 98 above. Similar adjurations to 'look within' in M. Aurelius, vii. 59 (*Long* 140); Carlyle's *Past and Present* (1843), *Traill* x. 26; Lucretius *De Rerum Natura* iii. 273–5.

I. ii. 136.   M. Aurelius: ' ... think steadily as a Roman and a man to do what thou hast in hand', ' ... let men see, let them know, a real man, who lives according to nature', *Long* ii. 27, x. 15.

I. ii. 147– 61.   Stoical. See A.'s note (*Yale MS*),'Epicureanism is Stoical, and there is no theory of life but is.'

I. ii. 160 –1.   'Foolish soul! What Act of Legislature was there that *thou* shouldst be Happy' (Carlyle, *Sartor Resartus, Traill* i. 153. But see ll. 172–6 for a defence of man's desire for happiness and ll. 387– 426 epitomizing the harmony with nature through which he can satisfy it.

I. ii. 175 – 6.   Lucretius in *De Rerum Natura*, v. 156– 65, declares it is 'the act of a fool' to believe that the gods made the universe for the sake of man.

I. ii. 177– 86.   A.'s ideas here and in his prose summary (*Yale MS*, quoted *Poems* 164) are in tune with Spinoza's *Ethics*, '... human power is extremely limited ... infinitely surpassed by the power of external causes ... Nevertheless we shall bear with an equal mind all that happens to us ... remembering that we are a part of universal nature and that we follow her order' (*Ethics* Pt. iv. appendix, *Works* tr. R. H. M. Elves (1891)

I. ii. 242–3; and cp. Stoic teaching, e.g. Epictetus, '... the law of life, that we must act conformably to nature'. (*Discourses* i. ch. 26, *Long* 77). But see also 'In Harmony with Nature' p. 1 above.

I. ii. 177–81.   cp. 'In Utrumque Paratus' ll. 36– 42, p. 3 above.

I. ii. 187–96.   Added *1867*.

I. ii. 197–201.   'The Spirit of the world enounces the problems which this or that generation of Men is to work: men do not fix for themselves' (A.'s note, *Yale MS*.).

I. ii. 203, 205. *hold dear ... clear*: maintain ... plain *1852*.

I. ii. 217–20. 'Nature how long ... kept this inn, the Earth ... no swagger of any new comer can impose upon her' (A.'s note, *Yale MS.*).

I. ii. 221. *course ... take*: ways ... learn *1852*.

I. ii. 222–3. Similarly *Obermann* (Lettre xii) i. 160, 'Nul individu ne saurait arrêter le cours universel ... rien n'est plus vain que la plainte des maux attachés nécessairement à notre nature.'

I. ii. 237. Echoing the General Confession, *Book of Common Prayer*.

I. ii. 241. 'We learn late the truth of *Cause and Effect*, that this or that operation will bring forth this or that result, and not another ... that there is no pity – no compromise' (A.'s note, *Yale MS.*).

I. ii. 247–8, 254 –5. cp. Lucretius, *De Rerum Natura* ii. 1103–4 on the thunderbolt 'which often passes the guilty by and slays the innocent and undeserving'.

I. ii. 256. '... good and evil fortunes fall to the lot of pious and impious alike' (Spinoza, *Ethics* Pt. I. appendix, *Works*, ed. cit. ii. 76).

I. ii. 261. *foundering*: founder'd *1852–69*.

I. ii. 272– 6. Perhaps suggested by Epictetus, *Discourses* iii. ch. 19,'... while we were still children, the nurse, if we ever stumbled through want of care ... did not chide us, but would beat the stone' (*Long* 241).

I. ii. 287–301. 'A God identical with the world and with the sum of being and force therein contained: not exterior to it ... determines it à son gré' and 'We learn not to *abuse* or *storm* at the Gods or Fate ... as there is nothing wilfully operating against us ... the power we would curse is the same with ourselves' (A.'s notes, *Yale MS.*). Similarly *Bhagavad-Gita* x. 20, 'I am the soul which dwells in the heart of all things ...' and, in Stoic philosophy, Empedocles, *Karsten* ii. 13 ('... but he is only sacred and ineffable mind speeding through the whole world with rapid thought ...'), Epictetus, *Discourses*; ed. cit. 46; Marcus Aurelius, Bk. vii. chap. 9.

I. ii. 288. *one stuff*: cp. Emerson, 'Nature', *Essays* (1844),' ... nature, with all her craft ... from the beginning to the end of the universe ... has but one stuff ... Compound it how she will ... it is but one stuff' (*Works*, Riverside ed. iii. 174).

I. ii. 291– 6. A. sees the 'one stuff' under the two aspects of power and a material intractable to that by which it is informed and from which it is inseparable. This is not compatible with Stoicism or Spinoza's thought, but cp. *Obermann* (Lettre lxxxv), 'la nature parait empêchée dans sa marche, et comme embarrassée et incertaine ...'

I. ii. 341. *mete the immeasurable All*: span the illimitable All *1852*.

I. ii. 347(and 382). *Fools*: Empedocles shows his impatience and arrogance in the Fragments (*Karsten*) by this expression.

I. ii. 356. ' A pertinent allusion. The gazer's delight depends on his "youthful blood" and is in this sense narcissistic' (*Poems* 170).

I. ii. 362– 6. Characteristic personal feeling: 'How life rushes away, and youth. One has dawdled and scrupled and fiddle-faddled – and it is all over' (*CL* 120).

I. ii. 368.   cp. A.'s 'The Second Best' ll. 1– 4 (beginning 'Moderate tasks and moderate leisure …') and Carlyle's precept in *Sartor Resartus* (1838), '… the Fraction of Life can be increased in value not so much by increasing your Numerator as by lessening your Denominator' (*Traill* i. 152–3).

I. ii. 397– 411.   In a draft version originally part of A.'s projected 'Lucretius' (*Commentary* 294).

I. ii. 401.   cp. *Manfred* I. i. 19–20, 'I have had my foes,/And none have baffled, many fallen before me … '

I. ii. 409–16.   Similar feelings expressed in *Obermann* (Lettre xviii) i. 74–5.

I. ii. 414.   Recalls Horace, *Epodes* ii. 41–2.

I. ii. 422–3.   cp. 'A Summer Night' ll. 91–2, p. 96 above.

I. ii. 427–60.   Printed separately as 'Cadmus and Harmonia' *1853–57*. A.'s use of the lyrical passages of Callicles, poet of 'natural magic', are in keeping with his views on the chorus in Greek tragedy which bring 'relief and relaxation' and 'combine … harmonise … deepen the feelings … excited … by the sight of what was passing upon the stage' (Preface to *Merope* (1858), *CPW* i. 61).

I. ii. 435– 42.   Story related in Ovid, *Metamorphoses* iv. 563–603. Cadmus founded Thebes and was given Harmonia as his wife by Zeus. His flight from Thebes parallels Empedocles's flight from the world.

I. ii. 440.   *Sphinx*: The Theban Sphinx.

I. ii. 445–7.   Echoing Sophocles, *Trachiniae* ll. 112 ff. (probably also affecting 'Dover Beach' ll. 15–18, p. 89 above),'… as the tireless South or Northern blast/Billow on billow rolls o'er ocean wide,/So on to son of Cadmus follows fast/Sea upon sea of trouble … ' (Loeb transl.)

I. ii. 445– 6.   Story related in Apollodorus, *Biblioteca* iii. 4.

I. ii. 450– 1.   Related in Pindar, *Pythian Odes* iii. 86–96.

I. ii. 457– 60.   Ovid, op. cit., iv. 600–3, where such forgetfulness is seen as sad rather than happy.

I. ii. 471.   Follows references to reincarnation in Empedocles's Fragments.

I. i. 2.   Empedocles at the summit of Etna, the 'blackened, melancholy waste', resembles Byron's hero contemplating suicide on the Jungfrau (*Manfred* I. ii); with his despondency cp. *Manfred* I. ii. 25–7.

II. i. 21–2.   Fuller reasons in ll. 235–75 below. On aridity and withering of hope cp. 'Memorial Verses' ll. 54–7, 'Tristram and Iseult' iii. 119–26, pp. 87, 82–3 above. See Introduction p. xxv above.

II. i. 23.   See further ll. 198–234.

II. i. 25– 6.   cp. Epictetus, *Discourses* iii. ch. 13, ed. cit., 230, 'Go whither? To nothing terrible, but to … your friends and kinsmen, to the elements: what was in you of fire goes to fire; of earth, to earth; of air, to air; of water to water ... ' Empedocles refers to the elements as 'the four roots of all things' (*Karsten* ii. 96: copied by A. in the original Greek, *Yale MS.*).

II. i. 27. *helpers*: servants 1852-8.

II. i. 29-32. A. expresses his own despondency about 'these damned times' in various letters to Clough, notably 23 Sept. 1849, 7 June 1852 (*CL* 123).

II. i. 37-88. Printed separately *1855* as 'The Harp-Player on Etna. ii. Typho', 'Fashioned to suggest the symmetry of a Greek tragic chorus' *(Poems* 178; on the metre see P. F. Baum, *Ten Studies in the Poetry of Matthew Arnold*(1958) 125). See I.ii. 427- 60*n*. above. The subject follows Pindar, *Pythian Odes* i. 1-28; on the myth's meaning see ll. 89-107 above.

II. ii. 54. A.'s note *1855* records the legend of Typho's last battle with Zeus;he was betrayed by the Destinies and his blood soaked Mount Haemus (hence its name).

II. i. 55. *still weep*: still see *1852, 1867*; still flee *1869*. For the effect of the revised readings on A.'s original rhyme scheme see *Poems* 179.

II. i. 57. Thy last defeat in this Sicilian sea? *1852- 69*.

II. i. 60. *rest*: sleep *1852- 69*.

II. i. 62. *thunder pressed*: thunder deep *1852- 69*.

II. i. 67-83. Follows *Pythian Odes* i. 5-12 and Gray's reworking of Pindar's eagle, 'The Progress of Poesy' ll. 20 - 4.

II. i. 90 -1. cp. 'The Scholar-Gipsy' l. 205, p. 114 above. For 'heart' *1852* has hand.

II. i. 92- 4. The increasing weakness of the individual in relation to the mass is a common theme at the time. See A.'s letter 7 June 1872 (*CL* 122); Carlyle, 'Sign of the Times' (1829: *Traill* xxvii. 61); J. S. Mill, 'Civilization' (1836: Mill's *Essays* ..., ed. J. B. Schneewind (1956) 157).

II. i 109-10. Renounces his symbols of necromancy. Clearly recollecting Prospero's renunciation in *The Tempest* V. i. 50 -1, 54 -7.

II. i. 121-90. Printed separately *1855* as 'The Harp-Player on Etna, III, Marsyas'. Story known to A. from Apollodorus (*Biblioteca* i. 4. (2)), Ovid (*Metamorphoses* vi. 383-95): ' ... but neither account mentions Pan's jealousy or the presence of the Muses. The song ... is about the price of being a poet – Empedocles, like Marsyas, is Apollo's victim and finds the final price too high' (*Poems* 181).

II. i. 128 (and 131). Pan, inventor of the shepherd's flute, is jealous of Apollo's skill with the lyre. The setting is traditionally Phrygia, where flutes were used in the cult of Cybele.

II. i. 136. *Maeander*: Phrygian river, flowing for part of its course on the southern slopes of Mt. Messogis.

II. i. 148. The fir was sacred to Pan.

II. i. 165-8. Follows Ovid (in Apollodorus Olympus is the father of Marsyas and does not appear at the contest).

II. i. 191–7. See II. i. 109–10n. above.

II. i. 204 –5. Apollo slew Python, the dragon guarding Delphi.

II. i. 210. Contrasts with the more serene, Goethean, attitude to the poet's being set apart in 'Resignation'. 144– 69, pp. 16–17 above.

II. i. 213. 'La fuite de l'eau est comme la fuite de nos années ... ' *Obermann* (Lettre xc) ii. 230.

II. i. 228–9. The 'divided self' once more. See 'Obermann' 93– 6, p. 35 above.

II. i. 233– 4. *only death ... poise*: But see ll. 345–72.

II. i. 235–7. 'Empedocles is an older Callicles. Neither has realised ... that the capacity for joy entails the capacity for suffering' (*Poems* 185, citing in support Wordsworth, 'Resolution and Independence' ll. 48–9).

II. i. 235. *Parmenides*: Said to have taught Empedocles: ll. 238–9 follows one of his Fragments (A.'s note in *1867*). See also ll. 293 – 4.

II. i. 241. *outward things*: See Coleridge's 'Dejection' ll. 45–6, 'I may not hope from outward forms to win/The passion and the life, whose fountains are within ... '

II. i. 249. '... *congestion of the brain* is what we suffer from – I always feel it and say it – and cry for air like my own Empedocles' (A. to Clough 12 Feb. 1853, *CL* 130).

II. i. 261–75. See 1853 Preface; p. 129 above ('I intended to delineate ... influence of the Sophists to prevail').

II. i. 276–300. Printed separately as 'The Philosopher and the Stars' *1855*.

II. i. 293–4. 'Necessity took and bound [the sky] so as to set a limit to the courses of the stars' (Parmenides, *Karsten* i. Fr. ii. 44).

II. i. 295. 'In a space so empty that it would echo like a bare room' (*Poems* 187).

II. i. 301–2. cp. 'A Summer Night' ll. 78–9, 'Self-dependence' ll. 21–3 (pp. 96, 39 above. An acceptance of hylozoism by Empedocles; the cosmos is alive.

II. i. 313. From Stromboli, one of the volcanic Lipari islands near Sicily.

II. i. 315. cp. 'Sohrab and Rustum' ll. [889–91] 15–17, p. 107 above.

II. i. 331– 6. See ll. 25–6 n. above.

II. i. 344. *nimble*: active *1852*.

II. i. 354. 'The All is the noumen behind phenomenal appearances. Kant and the unknowability of the thing-in-itself (*Ding-an-sich*) are in the background here, but cp. Carlyle' (*Poems* 189: cites *Sartor Resartus*, e.g. 'Space is but a mode of our human sense ... likewise Time ...', *Traill* i. 43).

II. i. 360 –3. Close to Empedocles on the force and power of the elements, *Karsten* ii. 86.

II. i. 360. *unallied*: A.'s single use of the epithet may be owed to Byron, in 'Prometheus' (1816) l. 52, on man's 'sad unallied existence ... '

II. i. 365. *meadow of calamity*: cp. Empedocles, 'meadow of Ate' (*Karsten* ii. 88).

II. i. 366. *uncongenial place*: cp. Empedocles, 'joyless place' (*Karsten* ii. 86).

II. i. 368. See l. 471*n*. above.

II. i. 371–2. Renewing the difficult search for the buried self. See I.ii. 29–30 above and 'The Buried Life', p. 96 above.

II. i. 404–16. A.'s note in *Yale MS*. emphasises the exaltation in Empedocles's leap to death: 'Before he becomes the victim of depression and overtension of mind, to the utter deadness to joy, grandeur, spirit, and animated life, he desires to die; to be reunited with the universe, before by exaggerating his human side he has become utterly estranged from it.'

II. i. 407–8. See II. i. 215–17 above.

II. i. 417–68. Repr. *1855* as 'the Harp-player on Etna. IV. Apollo'; 'Apollo Musagetes', *Selected Poems* (1878). Mostly adapted from the first part of Hesiod's *Theogony*.

II. i. 417–20. See *Poems* 192 for the parallel with the Fourth Spirit's song, *Manfred* I. i. 88–9 (beginning 'Where the slumbering earthquake/Lies pillowed on fire … ').

II. i. 427. *Thisbe*: A town in Boetia between Mt. Helicon and the Gulf of Corinth;famous for its wild pigeons (ll. 431–2 above).

II. i. 441–44. Echoes Aeschylus, *Prometheus Bound* ll. 114 –15, 'What music, what fragrance invisible comes to enfold me –/From God is it wafted, or man, or some being between … ' (G. Murray's transl.).

II. i. 457–6, 61–8. Following *Theogony* ll. 36 –9, 11–21.

From Tristram and Iseult: III Iseult of Brittany (p. 68)

1–2. A year had flown, and in the chapel old
      Lay Tristram and queen Iseult dead and cold. *1852*.

3 – 4. Added *1853* after A. read in Dunlop (ed. cit. 87) that the lovers were buried in Cornwall.

7. La Villemarqué (headn.) describes the Val-des-Fées, scene of his 'Visite au Tombeau de Merlin,' as 'un immense amphithéâtre'.

13 –15. cp. Wordsworth, *Excursion* iii. 50, '… a semicirque of turf-clad ground … '

52. cp. 'Balder Dead' (*1855*) i.80, 'Where in and out the screaming seafowl fly … ' (affected by Percy's transl. of Mallet's *Northern Antiquities* (1770; 2nd edn. 1819) ii. 72: see 'Stanzas from the Grande Chartreuse' l. 83*n*., below.

112–50. Omitted *1853*, *1854*, perhaps as too lengthy a digression; *Poems* 220 –1 which rightly emphasises that ll. 112– 42 are autobiographical, adding 'This would not have been obvious to the poem's first readers …' The 'narrator' here is apparently the Breton bard who records events in Parts I and II.

119–22. cp. 'Empedocles on Etna' II. i. 21–2, 'Memorial Verses' l. 56, 'The Scholar Gipsy' ll. 142–5, pp. 64, 87, 112 above.

122. *bloom*: See 'The Youth of Nature' l. 54 and *n.*, p. 91 above.

133–5. A 'Stoic sermon on restlessness' with traditional examples. (So described by W. D. Anderson, *Matthew A. and the Classical Tradition* (1965) 138).

136. See Tristram's fever and also his love-fever, Part I (headn.).

142. *Are furious with themselves*: Can never end their tasks *1852*; Are fretful of themselves *1857, 1859*.

143–5. See Caesar on Alexander in Suetonius, *De Vita Caesarum* i. 7; also *Paradise Regained* iii. 31–5, 39–42.

149. *the Soudan's realm*: The empire of Darius.

179 (and see l. 200). Suggests that A. is recalling 'Marguerite'.

193. *last year's fern*: Corrected to 'the green fern' *1858–77* ('for the sake of botanical accuracy', *Poems* 223).

198. *weird*: light *1852–7*.

202. *light sea*: green sea *1852–77*.

203. *plays*: lay *1852–77*.

224. 'And always Merlyn, lay aboute the lady to have her mayden hode, and she was ever passynge wery of him ...', *The Byrth, Lyf, and Actes of Kyng Arthur ...* ', ed. R. Southey i. 91 (1817).

Memorial Verses: April 1850 (p. 74)

1–2. Goethe died 1832 (see 'Obermann' ll. 51–2, p. 34 above), Byron 1824 at Missolonghi in Greece.

6–14. For A. on Byron see 'Stanzas from the Grande Chartreuse' ll. 133–8; 'Haworth Churchyard' ll. 48–51, pp. 104, 118 above; 'Byron', *E in C* II (quotes Goethe on B.'s weakness, 'The moment he reflects he is a child', *CPW* ix. 227); and, on his exemplifying 'the Titanism of the Celt' (ll. 13–14), 'On the Study of Celtic Literature', *CPW* iii. 370.

14. *which served*: suffic'd *MS*; which flow'd *Fraser 1850*.

19–24. The 'sickness' of modern life: cp. 1853 Preface and 'The Scholar-Gipsy' l. 203, pp. 129, 113 above; similar references familiar to A. in Carlyle's 'Characteristics' (1831) and Goethe, *Conversations*, 2 April 1829.

29–33. Echoing Virgil's *Georgics* ii. 470 –2 (beginning 'Fortunate is he who can know the causes of things ... ').

43. *this iron time*: Carlyle has '... an iron ignoble circle of Necessity embraces all things' (*Characteristics, Traill* xxviii, 30); cp. 'this iron coast', 'Tristram and Iseult' III l. 81, p. 81 above.

46. Our spirits in a brazen round, *MS, Fraser 1850*; followed by lines cancelled *1852*,

He tore us from the prison-cell
Of festering thoughts and personal fears

Where we had long been doom'd to dwell ...
cp. 'A Summer Night' l. 37, p. 95 above.

49–57. See 'Wordsworth', pp. 231–2 above, and for a source of weakness omitted here 'Obermann' ll. 53– 4, p. 34 above.

56. cp. 'Empedocles on Etna' II. i. 21–2, p. 64 above. For 'dried up' *MS, Fraser 1850* have 'deep-crushed'.

57. cp.'The Youth of Nature' ll. 53–5, p. 91 above.

63. *healing power*: 'The reference recalls ll. 17–22. Goethe diagnoses but Wordsworth heals' (*Poems* 229).

72–3. The Rotha flows beside Grasmere churchyard.

Dover Beach (p. 76)

1–14. A's characteristic feeling for sea and moonlight, here informed by memories of *Obermann* (Lettre iv) i. 22, transl. in his 1869 essay, 'Nature is unspeakably grand, when, plunged in a long reverie, one hears the washing of waves upon a solitary strand, in the calm of a night still enkindled and luminous with the setting moon' (*CPW* v. 302).

4. *Gleams*: shines *MS*.

6. *sweet*: sweet
hushed *MS*.

8. *Where the sea*: Where the ebb *1867–1877*. Restored from *MS* probably to avoid confusing the ebbing of the tide (l. 2) with that of successive waves, A.'s meaning here.

10. *draw*: suck *MS, 1867*.

11. *high*: barr'd *MS*.
steep

12. *Begin, and cease*: Cease and begin *MS*.

13. *tremulous cadence slow*: regular cadence slow *MS*. cp. the Miltonic inversion at 1.27 below, 'vast edges drear'.

14–20. The beat of the waves on the shore reminds the hearer of the erosions of time and change. No passage in Sophocles directly expresses this thought, but A. sees him as responding thus to the sound of the waves of the Aegean, possibly because he is recollecting *Trachiniae* l.112ff. (quoted 'Empedocles on Etna' I. ii. 445–7 *n*., above).

20. See 'Stanzas from the Grande Chartreuse' ll. 80 –2, p. 102 above.

21–5. cp. 'Obermann Once More' ll. 189–90,
But slow that tide of common thought,
Which bathed our life, retired ...

23. *girdle*: garment *MS*. On the obscurity of this 'one, dubiously "poetical" line' see *Poems* 242 and G. H. Ford's gloss, 'at high tide the sea envelopes the land closely. Its forces are "gathered" up (to use Wordsworth's term for it) like the "folds" of bright clothing ("girdle") which have been compressed ("furled"). At ebb tide, as the sea

retreats, it is unfurled and spread out' (*Norton Anthology of English Literature* (rev. edn. 1968) ii. 1039.

24–8. 'Probably the most musically expressive passage in all A.'s poetry and a valid poetic equivalent for his feelings of loss, exposure and dismay' (*Poems* 242).

24. *I*: I
   We *MS*.

33–4. Delight in the beauty of nature should not deceive us into forgetting the indifference of the universe towards man.

35. The image of a battle by night, with friend and foe confused in the darkness, stems from Thucydides on the Battle of Epipolie (413 BC), *History of the Peloponnesian War* vii. ch. 44 (ed. Dr. A. 1830 –5), and was familiar at the time among A. and others with similar training; cp. Clough's *The Bothie of Toper-na-Fuosich* (1848) ix. 51– 4 and Newman's sermon (probably A.'s source) 6 Jan. 1869, 'Controversy, at least in this age, does not lie between the hosts of heaven, Michael and his angels on the one side, and the powers of evil on the other; but it is a sort of night battle, where each fights for himself, and friend and foe stand together' (*University Sermons* (1843) 193).

The Youth of Nature (p. 78)

1–2. Deliberately echoes Wordsworth's echo in 'Remembrance of Collins' ll. 17–18, 21–2, of Collins's 'Ode on the Death of Mr Thomson' ll. 15–16. (Wordsworth: 'Now let us, as we float along, for *him* suspend the dashing oar ... /How calm! how still! the only sound/The dripping of the oar suspended!' Collins: 'And oft suspend the dashing Oar/To bid his gentle spirit rest!')

6. Almost certainly June 1850 (A. did not visit the Lakes summer 1851, the time of his marriage). cp. l. 9 suggesting his still recent memory of Wordsworth's death.

15–17. The rock known as 'The Pillar' and the town of Egremont (near Ennerdale Lake) appear in Wordsworth's 'The Brothers' (1800).

18. *The Evening Star*: The cottage in Wordsworth's 'Michael' (1800).

22– 4. See Wordsworth's 'Ruth' (1800).

28 –35. Wordsworth survived all the Romantic poets and in late years abandoned his ardent youthful libertarianism for high Toryism.

34. *Theban seer*: Tiresias: see ll. 41–5 below.

36. Near Thebes.

53 –5. See 'Memorial Verses' ll. 45–50, p. 87 above, and cp. Carlyle on 'The Hero as Man of Letters' (*Traill* v. 145).

54. *bloom*: A favourite word with A., suggesting both freshness and transience. See l. 111. 'The Scholar-Gipsy' l. 28, 'Thyrsis' l. 52, 'Growing Old' l. 7, pp. 108, 121, 127.

92–8. cp. Shelley, 'A Defence of Poetry','... the mind in creation is as a fading coal ... the most glorious poetry that has ever been communicated to the world is probably a feeble shadow of the original conception of the poet' (*Peacock's Four Ages of Poetry* ed. H. F. B. Brett-Smith 53– 4 (1921).

102. cp. 'The Buried Life', l. 73, p. 98 below. Nature's answer to ll. 59–74 stresses that its own Beauty does reside in the world (ll. 80 –1), that perception of it varies with individuals and is never fully grasped (ll. 81–90), that the perception nevertheless increases with our knowledge of our deepest self (ll. 99–102).

115–16. Shelley's 'Adonais' l. 40 has 'the One remains, the many change and pass ... '

A Summer Night (p. 81)

1. *moon-blanched*: Also in 'Dover Beach' l. 8, 'The Scholar-Gipsy' l. 9, pp. 88, 108 above.

24. *vainly throbbing heart*: agitated heart *1852*.

27–33. The 'divided self' once more. cp. 'Obermann' ll. 93–6, 'Empedocles on Etna' II. i. 220 –34 pp. 35, 70 –1 above. See Introduction, pp. xv–xvi, xxiii, xxiv–xxv above.

37–8. See the prison image in 'Memorial Verses' ll. 45– 6, p. 87 above; perhaps here remembering Wordsworth's 'Immortality Ode' ll. 67–8, 'Shades of the prison-house begin to close/Upon the growing Boy ... '

51–73. 'The tone betrays some involuntary admiration for the Romantic poet-outlaw who prefers "self-selected good" even if it entails destruction, to obedience to any law human or divine' (*Poems* 269; followed by the suggestion of a possibly unconscious echo of Shelley's 'Adonais' ll. 488–92 beginning ' ... my spirit's bark is driven/Far from the shore, far from the trembling throng ...').

74–5. '... but for God's sake, let us neither be fanatics nor yet chalf[*sic*] blown by the wind' (A. to Clough 23 Sept. 1849, *CL* 111).

76–82. So in *Obermann*, 'Profondeurs de l'espace, serait-ce en vain qu'il nous est donné de vous apercevoir? La majesté de la nuit repète d'âge en âge: malheur à toute âme qui se complaint dans la servitude' (Lettre xc. ii. 231). On A.'s feeling for the 'stars in their calm' see 'Quiet work' ll. 9–12 *n.*, above.

78–9. cp. 'Empedocles on Etna' II. i. 301–2, p. 73 above.

The Buried Life (p. 84)

9–11. Perhaps remembering Keats's 'Ode on Melancholy' ll. 19–20, 'Imprison her soft hand, and let her rave,/And feed deep, deep upon her powerless eyes ... '

12. 'A. is less pessimistic than in "Isolation. To Marguerite" ll. 37–42[p. 28 above] about ... understanding between lovers ... as the poem develops his ... interest shifts to the possibility of self-knowledge at rare moments of happiness in love' (*Poems* 270). See headn.

13. cp. l. 28, 'unchained' and l. 84, 'a bolt is shot back'.

29. In 'To Marguerite – Continued' l. 22, p. 29 above, the sense of inexorable law is unmitigated by feelings of release: see preceding *n*.

40 – 4 (and 38– 40, 55– 6). See on 'the buried self ' 'Empedocles on Etna' I. ii. 129–30, p. 51 above. The image of the self as a stream, with surface eddies as the everyday self and the real self as the current below, co-exists confusingly with A.'s other favourite image of the river of life (e.g. 'In Utrumque Paratus' ll. 11–14, p. 3 above).

45–6. Wordsworth has in 'Tintern Abbey' ll. 25– 6, 'But oft in lonely rooms, and 'mid the din/Of towns and cities … '

47. Echoing *Paradise Lost* iii. 662–3, 'Unspeakable desire to see and know/All these his wondrous works, But chiefly Man …'

55. Preceding poem, 27–33 *n*.

57–60. See Introduction, p. xxix above.

58. *spirit and power*: talent and power *1852–5*.

67. *we will no more be*: i.e. we wish no more to be.

73. See 'The Youth of Nature' l. 102*n*., above.

79–80. Reiterates the 'sick hurry', fever and noise of the modern world: cp. 'Tristram and Iseult', iii. 119–26, 'A Summer Night', ll. 37–50 (pp. 82–3, 95 above).

97–8. cp. ll. 54 –55 above and *n*. to ll. 40 – 4 above.

Stanzas from the Grande Chartreuse (p. 87)

2. *crocus*: The autumn crocus.

10. The source of the Guiers Mort is near the Grande Chartreuse.

12. *boiling*: black-worn *MS*.

27. The infirmary outside the main gate.

30. St Bruno founded the first Carthusian settlement 1084.

42. They circulate the Pax, not the Host.

47–8. In fact they are buried in their habits on a bare wooden plank.

56 – 60. Refers to the making of the celebrated liquor.

67. 'Carlyle, Goethe, Senancour and Spinoza are certainly among those indicated' (*Poems* 288). Probably also Epictetus and Lucretius.

68. *purged … trimmed*: prun'd … quench'd *Fraser 1855*.

69. *high, white*: pale cold *Fraser 1855*.

81–3. A.'s Greek 'laments over two dead faiths as A. regrets that the Protestant and Catholic forms of Christian orthodoxy are alike incredible' (*Poems* 288).

83. Probably from Mallet's *Northern Antiquities* (1847 English ed.), read by A. for 'Balder Dead' (*1855*) Dec. 1853 and taken with him on his honeymoon.

85– 6. A familiar idea at the time to A. and his associates. cp. Carlyle's 'Characteristics' (1831), *Traill* xxviii. 29–30, J. S. Mill's 'The Spirit of the Age' (1831) *Essays on Literature and Society*, ed. J. B. Schneewind (1965)30, and Tom Arnold to Clough 16 April 1847, '… an evil time

... we cannot accept the present, and we shall not live to see the future ... nothing is left but sadness and isolation' (*AHC* i. 180).

85. *between two worlds*: Byron has *Don Juan* Canto xv. st. 99, 'Between two worlds life hovers like a star ... '

87. Matthew 8:20.

93. Invest me, steep me, fold me round ... *Fraser 1855*

99. *sciolist*: A superficial pretender to knowledge; conceited smatterer (OED).

108. *fret*: pang *Fraser 1855*.

113–14. Stoically so.

115. 'The reference is clumsy: it suggests that "the best" are sulking as Achilles sulked apart in his tent after the death of Patroclus' (*Poems* 290).

116. From Shelley's 'Adonais' ll. 430 –1, ' ... the kings of thought/Who waged contention with their time's decay ... '

122. cp. the 'sea of life ' in 'To Marguerite – Continued'. l. 1, 'A Summer Night' l. 53, pp. 28, 95 above.

133 – 42. Carlyle's 'Characteristics': 'Behold a Byron, in melodious tones, "cursing the day" ... Hear a Shelley filling the earth with inarticulate wail; like the infinite inarticulate grief of forsaken infants' (*Traill* xxviii. 31).

140. 'The right sphere for Shelley's genius was the sphere of music, not of poetry' ('Maurice de Guérin', headn. p. 168 above), *E in C* I, *CPW* iii. 34.

145– 6. See headn. to 'Obermann', p. 32 above.

151– 6. *Ye ... your*: They ... their *Fraser 1855*.

157. Carlyle (op. cit.): ' ... our feeling that we stand in the bodeful Night [but] ... our assurance that the Morning also will not fail' (*Traill* xxxviii. 37).

169. 'The shadow of Romantic melancholy' (*Poems* 292).

181– 6. Parallels the lively 'medieval' hunting scenes in 'Tristram and Iseult' ii. 153– 6, 186–9.

201. *hope over*: light above *Fraser 1855*.

210. *desert*: forest *1855*. Reflects A.'s determined effort by 1867 to leave those 'who grieve' ('at least one foot in the camp of the sciolists', *Poems* 294).

From **Sohrab and Rustum** (coda) (p. 92)

1 [878]. cp. Shelley, 'Alastor' ll. 272– 4, 'At length upon the lone Chorasmian shore/He paused, a wide and melancholy waste/Of putrid marshes ... '

16–17 [890–1]. cp. 'Empedocles on Etna' II. i. 315, p. 73 above.

The Scholar-Gipsy (p. 93)

1. See 'Thyrsis' l. 35, p. 120 above.

5. *herbage*: grasses *1853-81*.

9. *moon-blanched*: See 'A Summer Night' l. 1 *n*. above.

10. *begin*: renew *1853-87, 1877-81*. The quest is both the scholar-gipsy's and also A.'s for what he represents: simplicity, integrity, imaginative truth (cp. *Poems* 334).

11-23. Diffused Keatsian echoes: cp., e.g., 'To Autumn' ll. 12-15, 'On a half-reap'd furrow sound asleep,/Drowsed with a fume of poppies ... '

25. *pink*: blue *1853-81*.

35. cp. Johnson's 'The Vanity of Human Wishes' l. 73, 'Unnumber'd suppliants crowd Preferment's gate ... '

45-7. cp. A.'s summary from Glanvil *1853*, 'they [the gipsies joined by the young Oxford scholar] had a traditional kind of learning among them, and could do wonders by the power of the imagination, their fancy binding that of others'.

50. *heaven sent*: happy *1853*.

54. *seen by rare glimpses*: ' ... suggested by Gray's "Elegy ... " ll. 98-112 ... describing how the country-folk see the poet in different places at different times of the day' (*Poems* 335).

57. With the Cumnor Hurst setting cp. 'Thyrsis' ll. 216-17, p. 126 above.

61ff. See *Poems* 336, 'The Scholar-gipsy is seen only by the young and happy, the simple, and the innocent. Many epithets applied to the scenes in which he appears — e.g. lone, quiet, shy, retired — apply equally well to him ... another way of saying that he is for A. "un moyen d'animer le paysage" (*Bonnerot* 472).'

69. *green-muffled*: See 'Empedocles on Etna' I. ii. 51, p. 49 above.

76. *punt's rope chops*: slow punt swings *1853-7*.

88. cp. Keats's 'Ode to a Nightingale' ll. 49-50, 'The coming musk-rose, full of dewy wine,/The murmurous haunt of flies on summer eves ... '

94. cp. Keats's 'Sir Calidore' l. 14 (of swallows over water), 'The freaks and darting of the black-winged swallows ... '

107. *eying*: watching *1853-7*; haunting *1869*.

120. Resembles Carlyle's 'Characteristics', *Critical and Miscellaneous Essays* (1839), 'The lightning-spark of thought ... heaven-kindled, in a solitary mind ... ' (*Traill* xxviii. 11). The conception here and in A. has behind it the descent of the Holy Ghost on the Apostles.

131. cp. K.'s return to the everyday world in 'Ode to a Nightingale' l. 79, 'was it a vision or a waking dream? ... ' A. now 'moves from pastoral description to criticism of modern life' (*Poems* 338).

136-40. cp. Gray's 'Elegy' ll. 13-15.

141(and 155). Echoing 'Ode to a Nightingale' ll. 61-2, 'Thou wast not born for death, immortal Bird!/No hungry generations tread thee down ... '

147. *teen*: Archaic: grief; woe.

149. *Genius*: The tutelary spirit, both judge and protector, accompanying each of us through life.

152 (and 167). On the restlessness of modern life, from which the Scholar-Gipsy is freed, cp. 'A Summer Night' ll. 27, 31–3, p. 94 above.

161–70. 'Romantic *contemptus mundi*' *(Poems* 339, citing Shelley's 'contagion of the world's slow stain', 'Adonais' l. 356, Keats's view of the world, 'The weariness, the fever, and the fret ... ', in 'Ode to a Nightingale' ll. 23– 4).

164. *sick fatigue*: Images suggesting modern life as 'a strange disease' (l. 203) continue in ll. 204, 221–2. A. quotes the line in his letter to Clough 27 July 1853, commenting, 'You will laugh if I tell you I am deplorably ennuyé. I seem to myself to have lost all ressort' (*CL* 138).

182–90. The 'one' is generally taken to be either Goethe or Tennyson;(for the evidence on either side see *Poems* 341); the tone and temper of the lines, together with Tennyson's recent election to the Poet Laureateship and the publication of his 'In Memoriam', suggest the latter to the present editor.

190. cp. Tennyson, 'In Memoriam' v. 7–8, 'The sad mechanic exercise,/Like dull narcotics, numbing pain ... '

201–2. Less a picture of the 17th century than an expression of A.'s sad 'modern' sense of lost youthful happiness.

203. cp. 'Memorial Verses' ll. 19–22, p. 86 above.

204. See l. 164*n*. above.

205. cp. 'Empedocles on Etna' II. i. 90 –1, 248–9, pp. 66, 71 above.

207–9. Virgil's *Aeneid* vi. 469–73.

211–12. cp. 'A Summer Night' ll. 68–9, p. 95 above.

217. *pales*: A set of pales, a fence. 1834 (OED).

221. See l. 164 *n*. above.

230. cp. 'Ode to a Nightingale' l. 26, 'Where youth grows pale, and spectre thin, and dies ...' and see 'Empedocles on Etna' I. ii. 362– 6 p. 75 above.

232. 'The Tyrian trader's flight before the clamorous spirited Greeks is exactly analogous to the scholar-gipsy's flight before the drink and clatter of the smock-frocked boors ... the bathers or ... the Oxford riders blithe. Both flights express a desire for calm, a desire for aloofness', E. K. Brown, *Revue Anglo-Américaine* xxi. 224 –5 (1934– 5). A. is recollecting the graphic account of the retiring Carthaginian traders in Herodotus iv. 196. See G. F. Ford's note that William Beloe, a translator of Herodotus, commented 1844, 'They transact their exchange, without seeing each other, or without the least instance of dishonesty on either side' (*Norton Anthology of English Literature* (1968) ii. 1038 *n*.); see also Isaiah 23:8, 'Tyre ... whose traffickers are the honourable of the earth.'

Requiescat (p. 100)

13. *cabined*: Echoing *Macbeth* VI. iv. 24, 'But now I am cabin'd, cribb'd, confin'd, bound in ... '

From **Haworth Churchyard: April 1855** (p. 101)

1 [l.47]. Preceded in *Fraser 1855* by 30 lines, cancelled *1877*, reflecting in part the general feeling raised by the political crisis of Feb. 1855 over the conduct of the Crimean War.

13 [l.59]. *poach*: 'Cut up and turn into mire' (*Poems* 393).

19 [l.65]. Followed in *Fraser 1855* by 16 lines alluding to Patrick Brontë ('the childless father') and his curate A. B. Nicholls ('another grief I see/Younger ...'), who married Charlotte 29 June 1854.

27 [1.73]. Followed in *Fraser 1855* by the 19 lines printed separately as 'Early Death and Fame' *1867* and subsequent editions.

33 –5 [ll.79–81]. Emily died at Haworth 19 Dec. 1848; Anne at Scarborough 28 May 1849.

42– 43 [ll.88–9]. Erroneous. A. did not visit the grave. Anne is buried at Scarborough; Charlotte, Emily and Branwell are buried in a vault in the church.

44 –50 [ll.90 – 6]. Anne (ll.44– 6); Emily (ll.46–50).

50 [l.96]. On A. and Byron see 'Memorial Verses' ll. 6–14 *n*., above.

53 – 4 [ll.99–100]. Follows Charlotte on 'No coward soul is mine ...', first printed in her 1850 ed. of *Wuthering Heights and Agnes Grey*, but the poem is dated 2 Jan. 1846, three years before Emily's death: 'too bold' to A. perhaps because of ll.90 –100, which see 'the thousand creeds/That move men's hearts' as 'unutterably vain'.

55– 65 [ll.101–11]. Branwell's story became better known through Mrs Gaskell's *Life of Charlotte Brontë* (1857).

59[1.105]. *eloquent – the child*: beautiful; the cause *Fraser 1855*.

66 –78 [ll.112–24]. Inspired by the closing paragraph of *Wuthering Heights* (1848).

79–92 [ll.125–38]. Added *1877*.

88. cp. Lockwood's comment at the close of *Wuthering Heights*, 'I ... wondered how anyone could ever imagine unquiet slumbers for the sleepers in that quiet earth.'

90. cp. Charlotte Brontë's 1850 Preface to *Wuthering Heights*, '... hewn in a wild workshop ... The statuary found a granite block on a solitary moor ... With time and labour [it] took human shape; and there it stands colossal, dark, and frowning, half statue, half rock ...'

Thyrsis: A Monody, to commemorate the author's friend Arthur Hugh Clough, who died at Florence 1861 (p. 104)

1–10. Returns to the Keatsian stanza of 'The Scholar-Gipsy' (headn. p. 107 above).

2– 4. See 'The Scholar-Gipsy Country', *Commentary* 355– 6. Sybella

Carr, who kept the Cross Keys inn in South Hinksey, died 1860. The 'haunted mansion' was in North Hinksey.

14. Photographs of the 'signal-elm' appear in Henry W. Taunt, *Oxford in Camera* (n.d.), containing a note on the elm by A. C. Bradley and a chapter 'Rambles with Matthew Arnold'.

18. A. was in Oxford 28 Nov. 1863: see 'Joubert', headn. p. 179 above.

19. 'Beautiful city! so venerable, so lovely, so unravaged by the fierce intellectual life of our century ... Adorable dreamer, whose heart has been so romantic' (Preface to *E in C1*, CPW iii. 290).

26–30. 'The "single elm-tree bright/Against the west" is the central symbol of "Thyrsis" as the scholar-gipsy is of the earlier elegy. The search for the tree ... is a repetition of the scholar-gipsy's quest' (*Poems* 499).

34. cp. 'The Scholar-Gipsy' l. 104, p. 110 above.

42–50. Clough resigned his fellowship at Oriel College because he objected to the 'fetters of Subscription to the thirty-nine articles' (*AHC* i. 221): ll.45–6 misleadingly suggest concern with social injustice as a cause.

57. The cuckoo migrates August, not June.

60. See 'The Youth of Nature' l. 54, p. 91 above.

61–70. Keatsian in feeling and texture.

62. *high Midsummer pomps*: cp. Browning, 'Pippa Passes' (1841) ll. 154 –8,' ... all glaring pomps/That triumph at the heels of June the god ...'

71–77. Individual reworking of 'Lament for Bion' ll. 99–104, 115–26.

71. *flown*: gone *Macmillan* 1866.

78. cp. A. to Clough on 'a deficiency of the *beautiful* in your poems' (*CL 66*).

80. Corydon defeats Thyrsis in their singing competition (Virgil's *Eclogues* vii: see too Theocritus, *Idylls* iv).

84. Said to have died by poison: 'Lament for Bion' ll. 109–12.

86. *relax*: unbend *Macmillan* 1866.

88–90. See Ovid's *Metamorphoses* v. 391–2, 395 (widely influential in English poetry, notably *Paradise Lost* iv. 268–71) and, on Orpheus, 'Lament for Bion' ll. 123–4, *Georgics* iv. 404–503.

105–115. Echoes by conflation of Milton's *Comus* ll. 311–13 ('I know each lane and every alley green ...') and of *A Midsummer Night's Dream* ll II. i., 249–50 ('I know a bank whereon the wild thyme blows ...')

106–125. cp. 'The Scholar-Gipsy', ll. 82–3 (p. 110 above); l. 94 *n.* above.

133 and 161. Echoing Collins, 'Ode to Evening', ll. 39–40, 'Thy dewy fingers draw/The gradual dusky veil ...'

137. *pausefully*: 'A neologism combining the two senses of "purpose-

fully" and "so as to induce a pause" ' (*Poems* 504).

141-5. cp. the ascent in 'In Utrumque Paratus' ll. 15-21, p. 3 above.

144. *the throne of Truth*: Johnson has in 'The Vanity of Human Wishes', ll. 141-2, 'Proceed, illustrious youth/And virtue guard thee to the throne of Truth.'

153-5; 156. cp. 'The Scholar-Gipsy' ll. 72-3; 221, 231, pp. 110, 114 above.

166. Truth is there to be found, even if with difficulty.

167. Clough was buried in Florence.

169. cp. 'Lament for Bion' l. 104.

175. See 'A Farewell' l. 81-2 *n.*, above.

177. *Great Mother*: Demeter, mother of Proserpine.

181-90. A.'s note in *1869* records of the shepherd Daphnis (i) he followed Piplea to Phrygia and killed King Lityerses in a reaping contest, the 'Lityerses song' becoming traditional in Greek popular poetry (ii) his father Mercury raised him to heaven when a jealous nymph struck him blind, and made a fountain spring in the place where he ascended.

201. cp. A. on Joubert as a man 'of extraordinary ardour in the search for truth' who 'seized the fine and just idea that beauty and light are properties of truth' ('Joubert' E in CI (1865), *CPW* iii. 193, 196). See also p. 182 above, ' ... his accurate sense of perfection, ... beauty and light.'

203-5. cp. 'On Translating Homer' (*CPW* i. 215-16; on Clough's integrity).

224. See 'Ode to a Nightingale', quoted 'The Scholar-Gipsy' l.88*n.*, above.

231. Repeating l. 31.

226. Clough published no new poems in England after 1849.

Growing Old (p. 110)

Title. Probably glancing ironically at Browning, 'Grow old along with me!/The best is yet to be,/The last of life, for which the first was made ...'

16-18. Replies to Wordsworth on age as 'a final EMINENCE', 'A place of power,/A throne that may be likened unto his,/Who in some placid day of summer, looks/Down from a mountain-top ...'(*Excursion* ix. 52, 55-8).

23-5. cp. 'A Summer Night' ll. 37-40, p. 95 above.

35. cp. *As You Like It* II. vii. 163-5 'Last scene of all/That ends this strange eventful history/Is second childishness and mere oblivion ...'

Preface to First Edition of Poems (1853) (p. 115)

1. 'Empedocles on Etna', repr. 1867. See p. 40 above.

2. *Poetics* 4: 1-5.

3. *Theogony* 55.

4. cp. Horace, *Ars Poetica* 333– 4.

5. Preface to *Die Braut von Messina, Sämmtliche Werke* (1862) v. 344.

6. cp. *Poetics* 11: 6.

7. cp. *Poetics* 6: 9–10.

8. In the *Iliad*; Aeschylus's *Prometheus Bound* and *Agamemnon*; Virgil's *Aeneid* iv.

9. By Goethe (1797); Byron (1812–18); Lamartine (1836); Wordsworth (1814).

10. See *On Translating Homer. Last Words*, pp. 152– 6 above.

11. cp. *Poetics* 17: 1–2.

12. In J. M. Ludlow's 'Theories of Poetry and a New Poet', *North British Review* (Aug. 1853).

13. See *Conversations* 3 Jan. 1830. On A.'s feeling for Goethe see 'Stanzas in Memory of ... "Obermann" ' 51–2 *n.* above; 'Memorial Verses' ll. 15–33, 61 (pp. 86–7); 'Stanzas from the Grande Chartreuse,' 67 *n.* above; Introduction, *n.* 47, p. xliv above; 'Heinrich Heine' and 'Spinoza' (pp. 170, 176 above).

14. Goethe's 'Uber den sogenannten Dilettantismus' (1799), *Werke* (Stuttgart 1833) xliv. 271–2.

15. See *CPW*, i. 221 for the view that this may summarize Alfred Crampon's review of Gautier and others, *Revue des Deux Mondes* (1 Nov. 1852), n.s. xvi. 382–97.

16. ' ... the difference between a mature and youthful age of the world compels the poetry of the former to use great plainness of speech as compared with that of the latter ... Keats and Shelley were on a false track when they set themselves to reproduce the exuberance of expression, the charm, the richness of images, and the felicity of the Elizabethan poets ... modern poetry can only subsist by its *contents*: by becoming a complete Magister vitae as the poetry of the ancients did: by including as theirs did, religion with poetry ... the language, style and general proceedings of a poetry which has such an immense task to perform, must be very plain direct and severe: and it must not lose itself in parts and episodes and ornamental work, but must press forward to the whole' (A. to Clough, 28 Oct. 1852, *CL* 124). For Keats's reworking of Boccaccio see *The Poems of John Keats*, ed. M. Allott (1970, rev. 1972) 326 ff.

17. H. Hallam, *Introduction to the Literature of Europe* ... (1843 ed.) iii. 91–2.

18. F. Guizot, *Shakespeare et son temps* (1852) 114.

19. 'It's hard to be good'.

20. B. G. Niebuhr (1776–1831), whose *History of Rome* (1827–8) was transl. into English 1828. On A.'s feeling for Goethe see *n.* 13 above.

21. Virgil's *Aeneid*, 'It is not your fiery words that daunt me ... it is

the gods and the enmity of Jupiter' (xii. 894 –5).
22. Goethe, 'Über den sogenannten Dilettantismus', *Werke* (1833) xliv. 291.

From Preface to Second Edition of Poems (1854) (p. 128)

1. See the review of *Poems* (1853), *Spectator* (3 Dec. 1853), no. 1327, 5.
2. For instance in reviews of A.'s *Poems* (1853) by J. A. Froude, *Westminster Review* (Jan. 1854), lxi. 84 and J. D . Coleridge, *Christian Remembrancer* (April 1854), xxvii. 318–20.

From On the Modern Element in Literature (p. 129)

1. ' … such modern poets as Browning and Keats … will not … understand that they must begin with an idea of the world in order not be prevailed over by the world's multitudinous' (A. to Clough, late 1848–9, *CL* 97).
2. Thucydides I. vi.
3. Isaac Casaubon (1559–1614), French Huguenot scholar and theologian, lived in London 1610 –14; Mark Pattison reviewed his Diary, *Quarterly Review* (Oct. 1853), xciii. 264.
4. References in this paragraph are chiefly to Thucydides II. xxxvii, xxxviii; I. i, ix–xi, xx, xxii.
5. See 'Preface to First Edition of Poems' *n*. 22 above, and on Burke, 'The Function of Criticism at the Present Time', p. 196 above.
6. Preface to his *History of the World* (1614).
7. See 'To a Friend', p. 24 above.
8. See headn. to 'Empedocles on Etna' (p. 40 above) for A.'s unwritten tragedy on Lucretius. The paragraph largely summarizes Lucretius's *De Rerum Natura* iii. 944–1072.
9. cp. 1853 Preface (p. 129 above) and A.'s characterization of Empedocles, 'Resignation' 198 *n*. above.

From On Translating Homer: Last Words (p. 138)

1. Matthew 17: 4; Mark 9: 5.
2. John 8: 4.
3. *Paradise Lost* vii. 23– 6.
4. Lecture III, *CPW* i. 145– 47.
5. In 'Arnold on Translating Homer', *Fraser's Magazine* (June 1861).
6. 'Ulysses', ii. 19–21,
   Yet all experience is an arch, wherethrough
   Gleams that untravelled world, whose margin fades
   For ever and for ever, when I move;
   see CPW i. 147
7. *The Princess* vii. 182; *Idylls of the King*, 'Merlin and Vivian' ll. 633 – 4, 638–9; *The Princess* v. 20 –1; *Idylls of the King*, 'Marriage of

Geraint' ll. 74 – 8.

8. Tennyson's *Ulysses* 16–17.

9. Syracusan pastoral poet, fl. c. 150 BC; author of 'Lament for Bion', which affected Milton's 'Lycidas', Shelley's 'Adonais' and 'A's 'Thyrsis' (headn. p. 119 above).

10. 'Sir Patrick Spens' ll. 33 – 40 (Percy's version).

11. This and the following three quotations from the opening of 'The Recluse' ('On Man, on Nature, and on human life ...'); *Lay of the Last Minstrel* vi. 1; *Marmion* VI. xxx. 1; *Lays of Ancient Rome*, 'Horatius', st.27).

12. Clough died 1861 (see 'Thyrsis', p. 119 above), having worked intermittently at translating Homer into English hexameters since 1849, frequently discussing problems with A.

13. In Lecture III A. describes Clough's *The Bothie of Tober-na-Vuolich* (1848) as, 'more than any English poem I can call to mind, like the *Iliad*: in the rapidity of its movement and the plainness and directness of its style'; he also found the thought too 'curious and subtle', to be Homeric and the hexameters 'too rough and irregular', notwithstanding Clough's avoidance of the common English fault of being 'much too dactylic' and hence 'lumbering' in this metre, instead of learning 'to use spondees freely' *CPW* i. 150–1.

14. *The Bothie of Tober-na-Vuolich* (1848) ix. 79, iv. 12. cp Lecture III, 'the diction is often grotesque, and that is not Homeric.... Still ... this poem ... being a serio-comic poem, had a right to be grotesque, and it is grotesque *truly*, not, like Mr Newman's version of the *Iliad*, *falsely*' (loc. cit.).

From **Democracy** (p. 149)

1. e.g. Carlyle in *Past and Present* (1843); Ruskin in *The Stones of Venice* (1853).

2. Measures against Nonconformists taken by the first Restoration Parliament (1661–65).

3. Philippians 4:2; Matthew 9:12.

4. In subsequent paragraphs A. elects to 'dwell for a moment' on the practical matter of advocating State intervention in public education, commending the French lyceums founded by the State 'for the vast middle class of Frenchmen' which 'may not be so good as Eton or Harrow; but ... are a great deal better than a *Classical and Commercial Academy*' – A.'s phrase for the numerous English middle-class private schools established to compete with public and grammar schools. See further Introduction pp. xxxi–xxxii above.

5. But cp. Super, 'Although Burke uses both the words *collective* and *corporate* in describing the State, he nowhere uses the exact phrase that Arnold credits him with' (*CPW* ii. 377).

From **Maurice de Guérin** (p. 154)

1. Quotations from *Winter's Tale* IV. iv. 118–20; 'The Solitary Reaper' ll. 13–16; *Atala* 'Les Chasseurs' (also admired by Sainte-Beuve); *Obermann*, Lettre xi.

2. cp. 'On the Study of Celtic Literature', p. 202 above.

3. Quotations from *Choephoroi* I. 313 ('Let the doer be done by'), *Prometheus Bound*, l. 90 ('multitudinous laughter' [of the waves of the sea]); Sonnet 38; *Hamlet* V. ii. 10 –11.

4. cp. 'On the Modern Element …' pp. 151–2 above.

5. For A. on Keats elsewhere see 1853 Preface, 'On the Study of Celtic Literature' (pp. 203–5 above) and 'Keats', *Essays in Criticism* (1865; *CPW* ix. 205–16).

From **Heinrich Heine** (p. 156)

1. Carlyle's essays on Goethe, Jean Paul and Tieck's edn. of Novalis appeared with other of his German studies in *Critical and Miscellaneous Essays* (1838; repr. 1839, 1840, 1847, 1857). For A. and Goethe see 'Obermann' 51–2 *n*. above.

2. He spent his youth there but was born Düsseldorf (13 Dec. 1797), where under French government, 1795–1813, Jews had equal political rights with Germans (later withdrawn by the Prussians).

3. Quoting *Paradise Lost* ii. 51.

4. cp. *Culture and Anarchy*, p. 216 above.

5. Ancient Greek town in Asia Minor known for its bad Greek: hence 'solecism'.

6. 'Count Cagliostro', *Critical and Miscellaneous Essays* III (*Traill* 249–318).

7. Echoing Luke 16:8; John 12:36; Ephesians 5:8; 1 Thessalonians 5:5.

8. Quotations from *Reisebilder* iv, 'Englische Fragmente' chap. xi, close of 'Die Befreiung'; *Romanzero*, Book II, 'Jetzt Wohin?' st. 4; 'Englische Fragmente,' chap. x, 'Wellington.'

9. See Hebrews 11:9; Leviticus 26:19.

10. 1 Chronicles 20:5– 6.

11. Job 12:23.

12. Lucan *Pharsalia* I: 135.

From **Spinoza and the Bible** (p. 161)

1. 'Spinoza and Professor Arnold', *Spectator* (3 Jan. 1863), xxxvi. 1474.

2. Translated from the Latin with introduction and notes by Robert Willis, 1862; for A.'s review see *CPW* iii. 56– 64.

3. Recorded in John Colerus, *Life of Benedict de Spinoza* (1706) and C. H. Bruder's edn. of Spinoza, *Opera Quae Supersunt Omnia* (1843), l. ix.

4. See Spinoza's *Ethics* in his *Opera Quae Supersunt Omnia* ed. cit. 51 and C. H. Bruder's edn. of Spinoza's *Opera Quae Supersunt Omnia* l. ix.
5. *Tractatus*, ed. cit. xii. 4.
6. Isaiah 63:16
7. See 'On Translating Homer: Last Words', p. 152 above.

From Joubert (p. 164)

1. Where Coleridge lived from April 1816 until his death in 1834.
2. This and ensuing quotations from *Pensées* ii. 154; 293; 308; 343– 4.
3. cp. A. on Shelley, 'beautiful and ineffectual angel, beating in the void his luminous wings in vain' ('Byron', 1881, *CPW* iv 237).
4. Eugène Scribe (1791–1861), hugely successful French popular dramatist, author of some 300 plays.

From Pagan and Religious Medieval Sentiment (p. 169)

1. A. had recently read about St Francis receiving the *stigmata* in C. Berthoud, 'Françoise d'Assise', *Revue Germanique*, 1 July, 1 Sept. 1863 (xxvi. 224–52; xxvii. 69–101).
2. See p. 170 above.
3. Wordsworth, 'Tintern Abbey' ll. 39– 40.
4. Sophocles, *Oedipus Tyrannos* ll. 863–71.

From The Literary Influence of Academies (p. 172)

1. Cicero *De Officiis* I. xxxvii. 134.
2. In 'Byron's Don Juan', *Über kunst und Alterthum* (1821) iii. 82; *Werke* (1902), XLI. i. 249.
3. e.g. in 'Savoy', *Saturday Review* 11 Feb. 1860, ix. 175.
4. Nicolas Malebranche (1638–1715), French theologian, scientist and philosopher; replaced Cartesian dualism with belief in the correspondence between spirit and matter.

From The Function of Criticism at the Present Time (p. 174)

1. Conclusion of *On Translating Homer*, Lecture II (*CPW* i. 140). See headn. 189 above.
2. J. C. Shairp's 'Wordsworth: the Man and the Poet' loc. cit. xli (Aug. 1864) 1–54. A. followed his example in *Wordsworth*, headn. pp. 231–2 above.
3. Letter to Bernard Barton, 12 Jan. 1816; Lady Richardson's notes, Nov. 1843 (*CPW* iii. 474).
4. cp. Sainte-Beuve's comments on the Romantic movement, concluding, ' ... c'est pour cela que nous ne sommes pas en 1800 à l'aurore d'un grand siècle, mais seulement au début de la plus brillante des périodes de déclin' (*Chateaubriand et son groupe littéraire* (1889 edn.) i. 200).

5. Jenny Geddes on 23 July 1637: to protest against the introduction of the new service.

6. Decimal coinage and the metric system established in France 1700 –1803; English Decimal Association formed 1854; bill for decimalization in England withdrawn after second reading 1863.

7. *Pensées* (ed. P. de Raynal, 1877 edn.) ii. 178.

8. cp. A.'s enthusiasm for Burke in his letter to his sister Jan. 1864, ending 'I advise … you indeed to read something of Burke's every year' (*L* i. 215).

9. Goldsmith, 'Retaliation' l. 32.

10. *Works* (1852) iv. 591.

11. Numbers 22:38.

12. Aesop's fable of the wind and the sun.

13. On A.'s indebtedness for this conception to Sainte-Beuve see *CPW* iii. 477– 8; also A.'s citing in his Note-Books (1864) Renan on the duty of a university teacher to instruct 'sans aucune vue d'application immédiate, sans autre but que la culture désintéressée de l'esprit' ('L'Instruction supérieure en France', *Revue des Deux Mondes*, seconde période, li. 81, 1 May 1864).

14. Sir Charles Adderley, Conservative MP for North Staffordshire; address at Leamington 16 Sept. 1863.

15. John Arthur Roebuck (1801–79), MP for Sheffield; address at Sheffield 18 Aug. 1864.

16. *Iphigenie auf Tauris*, I. ii. 91–2.

17. She was found guilty of manslaughter and sentenced to 20 years' penal servitude.

18. Evidence of A.'s interest in the *Bhagavad-Gita*; see 'Resignation' 161 *n*. above.

19. Persius vi. 59: ' "We are all alike terrae filii" [creatures of low birth] is one of the closing sentences of a sprightly article entitled "the Few and the Many" [*London Review*, 31 Jan. 1863] attacking Arnold's doctrine (in "The Bishop and the Philosopher") that "the highly instructed few, and the not scantily instructed many, will ever be the organ to the human race of knowledge and truth" ' (*CPW* iii. 479).

20. Lettre xc. (see p. 32 above).

From On the Study of Celtic Literature (p. 187)

1. Super cites Edwin Guest on the Latinist probably getting his rhyme 'from the Celtic races; … the earliest poems of the Irish have final rhime, and we know that the Welsh used it, at least as early as the sixth century' (*A History of English Rhymes* (1850) I 120).

2. *Winter's Tale* IV. iv. 118–20; 'The Solitary Reaper' ll. 13–16; 'Ode to Autumn'; Senancour, *Obermann*, Lettres xi, xci.

3. Quotations from Pope's *Iliad* viii. 687; Elegies I. xx. 21–2; *Idylls* xiii. 34; *Ode on a Grecian Urn*, st. 4.

4. 'Ode to a Nightingale' sts. v, vii.

5. *Eclogues* vii. 45; ii. 47– 48, 51–52.

6. *Midsummer Night's Dream* II. i. 249–52; *Merchant of Venice* V. i. 58–9; *MND* II. i. 83–5; *MV* V. i. 1–4, 6–7, 9–12.

From **Friendship's Garland** (p. 193)

1. *Candide* (1759). Dr Pangloss believed all was for the best in the best of all possible worlds.

2. Lasted 7 weeks (15 June – 22 July 1866).

3. Traditionally the resort of hack-writers.

4. By Charles Keene, *Punch* 7 July 1866.

5. Reflecting the belief of the 'Manchester School' in free trade as the answer to war.

6. A.'s friend, whose 'The Part of England in the European Crisis' (*Daily News* 17 July 1866) prompted this initial Arminius letter. He and A. frequently argued against each other in print.

7. German statesman (1769–1859). His contemptuous description of the courtiers once surrounding the Prussian King Frederick William IV was used by M. E. Grant Duff, 'the brood of "court theologians, missionary deaconesses", and the like …' (*Studies in European Politics* 246–7 (1866)).

8. Breech-loading rifle used by the Prussians, much in the news at the time because of its rapidity and efficiency.

9. Reported in *Daily News* 14 June 1866 (p. 4, col. 6).

10. A favourite word used by A. since at least 1853 (see p. 129 above) to mean spirit, intelligence, light, reason. He called his beloved dachshund by this name (see his memorial poem, 'Geist's Grave', *Poems* 547–9).

11. *Studies in European politics*, chapters 3–5. Grant Duff felt some anxiety for Prussian liberalism because of the seductiveness of Bismarckian military success.

12. *Daily News* 17 July (p. 5, col. 1).

13. Reported in *The Times*, 8 May (p. 12, col. 2).

14. On the corner of Trafalgar Square: see *Culture and Anarchy*, chap. 2, 'Show him our symbolical Truss Manufactory on the finest site in Europe [so described by Sir Robert Peel] and tell him that British industrialism and individualism can bring a man to that …' (*CPW* v. 121).

15. Mr Bottles and his family: A.'s invention, used as a target in his polemics against the Philistines. For 'Ungeist in Uniform' see Grant Duff's *European Politics* 250 –1.

16. In fact the Austrians capitulated the day after this letter appeared.

From **Culture and Anarchy** (p. 197)
Sweetness and Light

1. In the quarrel in Swift's *The Battle of the Books* between the Spider, standing for the moderns, and the Bee, standing for the ancients, Aesop sides with the Bee: 'The difference is, that, instead of dirt and poison, we have rather chosen to fill our lives with honey and wax, thus furnishing mankind with the two noblest of things, sweetness and light'.

2. *The Nonconformist*, Congregationalist paper ed. Edward Miall (1809–81) founded 1841; motto from Burke's speech 'On Conciliation with the Colonies'.

3. 1 Peter 3:8.

4. T. H. Huxley (1825–95), vigorous controversialist, ardent supporter of Darwin and coiner of the term 'agnostic' to describe his own philosophic position. Notable at this time among his numerous writings are *Man's Place in Nature* (1863), *The Physical Basis of Life* (1868).

Philistines, Barbarians, Populace

1. Quoted from *Daily News*, 7 Dec. p. 4; further quoted 'My Countrymen' (*CPW* v. 5).

2. See, for example 'Heinrich Heine', pp. 172– 4 above.

3. In 'Shooting Niagara: and After?' *Macmillan's Magazine* (Aug. 1867) xvi.

4. See headn., p. 212 above. Harrison (1831–1923), Positivist and Professor of Law to the Inns of Court 1877– 89, published widely, including, in A.'s lifetime, *The Making of History* (1862, enlarged 1892), *The Choice of Books* (1886), *Oliver Cromwell* (1888) and later, *Victorian Literature* (1895), *Ruskin* (1902), *The Positive Evolution of Religion* (1912).

5. William Murphy provoked riots when he inaugurated anti-Catholic lectures at Birmingham 16 June 1867 but still insisted on his right of free speech. Quoted by A. in 'Doing as One Likes' ('I will carry out my lectures if they walk over my body as a dead corse; and I say to the Mayor of Birmingham that he is my servant when I am in Birmingham, and as my servant he must do his duty and protect me') with ironical comment, 'Touching and beautiful words, which find a sympathetic chord in every British bosom' (*CPW* v. 120).

6. Used in preface to *Essays in Criticism* (1865), quoting Byron's *Childe Harold's Pilgrimage* IV. cxli. 5, ' *There* were his young barbarians all at play ...'

7. Glances at Carlyle's view of the aristocratic female as 'the prettiest and gracefullest kind of woman you will find in any country', 'Shooting Niagara ...' loc cit.

8. Sir Daniel Gooch (chairman of the board of directors of the Great Western Railway, 1865– 89) informed workmen that his mother had told him each morning, 'Ever remember, my dear Dan, that you should

look forward to being some day manager of that concern'. A. comments in 'Doing as One Likes', 'That beautiful sentence ... which I treasure as Mrs Gooch's Golden Rule or the Divine injunction, "Be ye perfect", done into British' (*CPW* v. 122).

9.　Speech reported *Morning Star* and *The Times* 9 Oct. 1866; noted by A. in his diary 12 Oct.

10.　Royal commission on trades unions established 12 Feb. 1867.

11.　For a summary of contemporary disturbances, especially demonstrations immediately after the defeat of the Reform Bill 1866, the protracted Hyde Park Riots some weeks later and the Fenian troubles see J. Dover Wilson intr. to *Culture and Anarchy* (1961) xxii–xxx.

12.　'From the son of his father and the pupil of his teacher [i.e. Wordsworth] none would have looked for such an efficient assault and battery of the Philistine outworks ... A profane alien in my hearing once defined him as "David the son of Goliath" ' ('Mr Arnold's New Poems', *Fortnightly Review* Oct. 1867).

13.　A. was an enthusiast for shooting and fishing. 'The shooting here is superb ... I shall go on blazing away, and then abandon for ever the vain attempt to mingle in the sport of the Barbarians' (17 Sept. 1873, *L* ii. 107).

14.　'1843. The act of ... abstracting tools, destroying machinery etc., as a means of enforcing compliance with the rules of a trade union ...' (OED).

15.　The argument continues in a direction parallel with A.'s thinking on the subject of Academies and their role in preserving 'excellence' (p. 187 above).

Hebraism and Hellenism

1.　Proverbs 29:18; Psalms 112:1.

2.　Frederick the Great, quoted by Sainte-Beuve, *Causeries du lundi*, noted by A. 20 Jan. 1867.

3.　Xenophon, *Memorabilia* IV. viii.

4.　Carlyle in a letter to J. L. Davies, 27 April 1852. See K. Tillotson, *N & Q* (March 1955) cc. 126.

5.　Edward Pusey (1800 – 82), regius professor of Hebrew at Oxford; with Keble and Newman a founder of the Oxford Movement 1833 and remaining throughout a pillar of high Anglicanism.

6.　Romans 8:26; 7:24.

7.　cp. *Republic* vii. 532.

From God and the Bible: A Sequel to Literature and Dogma (p. 211)
Preface

1.　Sonnet beginning 'The pibroch's note, discountenanced or mute ...', ll. 12–14.

2.　'Ode on the Intimations of Immortality', ll. 124–7 ('man's blessedness' for 'thy blessedness'; 'his soul' for 'thy soul').

Chapter II The God of Metaphysics

1. 'God is simply the stream of tendency by which all things fulfil the law of their being' (*Literature and Dogma*, *CPW* vi. 189; also used in *St Paul and Protestantism*, *CPW* vi. 10). cp. Wordsworth, *Excursion* ix. 82,' ... power to commune with the invisible world,/And hear the mighty stream of tendency/Uttering, for elevation of our thought,/A clear sonorous voice, inaudible/To the vast multitude ...'

Conclusion

1. Psalms 37:39; Proverbs 11:19.

From **Wordsworth** (p. 216)

1. For A.'s selection and classification of the poems see *CPW* ix. 318–20 and for his own taxonomic problems Introduction.

2. 'On Translating Homer' (*CPW* i. 116–17). cp. 'The Study of Poetry', pp. 234–5, 242–3, 255 above.

3. 'Prospectus' of *The Excursion* (1814), l. 1, originally from 'The Recluse'. Quoted in 'On Translating Homer,' p. 161 above.

4. 'Des beaux arts en Europe du temps de Louis XIV', *Siècle de Louis XIV*, chap. xxxiv.

5. Quotations from *Paradise Lost* xi. 553 –54; 'Ode on a Grecian Urn' st. 2; *Tempest* IV. i. 156–58.

6. cp. 'Joubert' and 'The Study of Poetry', pp. 183, 242–3 above.

7. Paraphrasing J. B. Nicholas, *Les Quartrains de Khèyam* (1867) st. 38; longer than FitzGerald's *Rubáiyat of Omar Khayyàm* (1859), read by A. March-April 1876.

8. Virgil, *Aeneid* vi. 662.

9. 'Hours in a Library. No. xiii. Wordsworth's Ethics', *Cornhill Magazine* xxxiv. 209–10. (Aug. 1876).

10. iv. 73– 6.

11. I. i. 2.

12. *Excursion* ix. 219–302.

13. See *Excursion* ii. 484; B. Haydon, *Autobiography and Journals*, ed. M. Elwin 317 (1950).

14. The National Association for the Promotion of Social Science, founded 1856, held congresses in various English cities 1857– 84; dissolved for want of money 1886; satirized as the Pantopragmatic Society in Peacock's *Gryll Grange* (1861).

15. 'To the Lady Fleming' l. 81.

16. 'Prospectus' of *The Excursion* (see *n.* 3. above) l. 18.

17. See A. on 'that power, not ourselves, in which we move and have our being' in *St Paul and Protestantism* (1869–70; *CPW* vi. 58 and *n.*).

18. 'A Poet's Epitaph' l. 58.

19. cp. C. Wordsworth, *Memoirs of William Wordsworth* (1851) ii. 438, 478–9.

20. Jeffrey's opening remark in his review of *The Excursion*, *Edinburgh Review* (Nov. 1814) XXIV. i.

21. Quotations from *Macbeth* III. ii. 23; *Paradise Lost* VII. 25– 6; 'Prospectus', loc. cit., ll. 78– 80; 'Michael' l. 466; Burns's 'A Bard's Epitaph' ll. 19–24.

22. 'On the Intimations of Immortality' (1807).

23. Correctly 'The Solitary Reaper'.

24. Letter to Lady Beaumont 21 May 1807.

The Study of Poetry (p. 225)

1. From final paragraph of A.'s 'Introduction on Poetry' for *The Hundred Greatest Men*, collection of portraits in 8 vols., ed. W. Wood 1879–80.

2. Preface to *Lyrical Ballads* (2nd edn. 1800).

3. Follows A.'s notebook entries from *Les Cahiers de Sainte-Beuve* 51 (1876).

4. cp. 'Joubert' and 'Wordsworth', pp. 182, 233 above.

5. With this (and below, 'to make us ... really possesses') cp. 'The Function of Criticism ...' on 'disinterestedness', p. 198 (and 13 *n*.)

6. Paul Pelisson (1624–93).

7. Clément Marot (1496–1544): A. is referring to his *Oeuvres*, ed. d'Hericault (1867) p. iii.

8. cp. Sainte-Beuve, 'Qu'est-ce qu'un classique?', *Causeries* 21 Oct. 1850.

9. Thomas à Kempis (1380–1471), *De imitatione Christi* III. xliii. 11–12.

10. e.g. Stopford Brooke's comparison of a passage in Caedmon's versification of *Genesis* (c. 670 AD) with the 'proud and angry cry of [Milton's] Satan against God', *English Literature* 12 (1879).

11. Louis Vitet, 'La Chanson de Roland', *Revue des Deux Mondes*, 1 June 1852, n.s. xiv. 851, 860; repr. *Essais historiques et littéraires* 73– 4 (1862).

12. A. uses this and the two following passages from Homer as touchstones for good translation in *On Translating Homer* (CPW ix. 382–3).

13. Quotations from *2 Henry IV* III. i. 18–20; *Hamlet* V. ii. 357– 60; *Paradise Lost* i. 599– 602, 108–9; iv. 271–2.

14. *Poetics* 9:3.

15. cp. 'the grand style' in *On Translating Homer: Last Words*, p. 153 above.

16. 'Oc' and 'oil' (ultimately 'oui') signify 'yes' in the two dialects.

17. In *Li livres dou trésor* (c. 1265), Book I, Part I, chap. 1 (conclusion): Dante movingly salutes Brunetto as his teacher in *Inferno* xv.

18. *Cligés* (c. 1170), ll. 30 –9.

19. 'Rime royal', the seven-line stanza (ababbcc) used in *Troilus and Criseyde* and 'The Prioress's Tale'.

20. Bavarian poet whose *Parzeval* was written early 13th century.
21. Preface to *Fables, Ancient and Modern* (1699).
22. John Lydgate, *The Life of our Lady* (c. 1410) ii. 1633.
23. In 'The History of the English Language', prefacing his Dictionary (1755).
24. Spenser's *Faerie Queene* IV. ii. 287.
25. 'The Prioress's Tale', l. 92 ('in' for 'to').
26. Ibid., ll. 162–68.
27. 1801; published 1820.
28. Died 1321.
29. From 'Les regrets de la belle Heaulmière', *Le Testament* (1461) sts. xlvii – lvi, ll. 453 –532.
30. *Essay of Dramatick Poesie* (1668).
31. Preface to *Fables*.
32. Quotations from Chapman, *The Iliads of Homer* (1865 edn.) i. 23 (quoted in A.'s *On Translating Homer* i (1860); Milton's 'Smectymnuus' pamphlet (1642), *Works* (1931 edn.) III. i. 303; opening of 'Postscript to the Reader' in Dryden's transl. of the *Aenid* (1697). Note the period of time separating the two latter passages.
33. *The Hind and the Panther* 1–2 (1687); *Imitation of the Second Satire of the Second Book of Horace* 143 – 4 (1734).
34. 'On the Death of the Late Lord President Dundas', ll. 25–30.
35. Slightly misquotes letter of 19 Oct. 1794, *Letters*, ed. J. D. Ferguson (1931) ii. 268.
36. cp. A.'s letter of Nov. 1879, 'I have been reading Chaucer a great deal, the early French poets a great deal, and Burns a great deal. Burns is a beast with splendid gleams, and the medium in which he lived, Scotch peasants, Scotch Presbyterianism, and Scotch drink, is repulsive. Chaucer on the other hand pleases me more and more, and his medium is infinitely superior'.
37. For this and the following eight quotations from Burns see 'The Holy Fair' ll. 163–71; 'For a' that and a' that', st. 4; 'Epistle to a Young Friend' ll. 41–8; 'Address to the Unco Guid, or the Rigidly Righteous' 57– 64; Epistle to Dr Thomas Blacklock', ll. 51– 4; 'Ae fond kiss, and then we sever …', ll. 13–16; 'Winter, A Dirge', ll. 17–20; 'Auld Lang Syne', ll. 17–20; 'Tam Glen' ll. 13–16.
38. *Prometheus Unbound* III. iv. 204; II. v. 1– 4.
39. *minnie … deave:* mother … deafen.

SUGGESTIONS FOR FURTHER READING

Abbreviations

1849	*The Strayed Reveller, and Other Poems* (1849)
1852	*Empedocles on Etna, and Other Poems* (1852)
1853	*Poems* A new edition (1853)
1854	*Poems* Second edition (1854)
1855	*Poems* Second series (1855)
1857	*Poems* Third edition (1857)
1867	*New Poems* (1867)
1868	*New Poems* Second edition (1868)
1869	*Poems* (1869). First collected edition (2 vols.)
Poems	*The Poems of Matthew Arnold*, ed. Kenneth Allott (1965)
E in C I	*Essays in Criticism* (1865)
E in C II	*Essays in Criticism*. Second series (1888)
CPW	*The Complete Prose Works of Matthew Arnold* (11 vols.), ed. R. H. Super (1960–1977)
L	*Letters of Matthew Arnold, 1848–1888* (2 vols.) ed. G. W. E. Russell (1895)
CL	*The Letters of Matthew Arnold to Arthur Hugh Clough* ed. H. F. Lowry (1932)
Allott	*Matthew Arnold: Writers and their Background*, ed. Kenneth Allott (1975)
AHC	*Correspondence of Arthur Hugh Clough*, ed. F. L. Mulhauser (Oxford 1957)
Bonnerot	*Matthew Arnold – Poète: Essai de biographie psychologique*, by L. Bonnerot (Paris 1947)
Buckler	William E. Buckler, *Matthew Arnold's Books: Towards a Publishing Diary* (Geneva 1958)
Commentary	*The Poetry of Matthew Arnold: A Commentary*, by C. B. Tinker and H. F. Lowry (1940)
Conversations	J. P. Eckermann's *Conversations with Goethe*, tr. John Oxenford (London 1850)
Obermann	*Obermann*, by E. P. de Senancour (2 vols.), ed. G. Michaut (Paris 1912–13)

PMLA	Publications of the Modern Language Association of America
Traill	*The Works of Thomas Carlyle* (30 vols.), ed. H. D. Traill (1896–9)
Trilling	*Matthew Arnold*, by L. Trilling (New York 1939)
Vict. Poetry	*Victorian Poetry: A Critical Journal of Victorian Literature* (West Virginia University, Morgantown, W.Va.)
Vict. Stud.	*Victorian Studies: A Quarterly Journal of the Humanities, Arts, and Sciences* (Indiana University, Bloomington, Indiana)
Yale MS	A collection of notes, poetic drafts, etc., kept by Matthew Arnold and now lodged at Yale.

Bibliographies and Concordance

There is a wealth of published material on Arnold. The fullest records include R. H. Super's list of primary and secondary items in the *New Cambridge Bibliography of English Literature* III (1969) and the chapters on Arnold in *Victorian Prose: A Guide to Research*, ed. D. J. DeLaura (New York 1973), and *Victorian Poetry: A Guide to Research*, ed. F. E. Faverty (Camb., Mass. 1956, rev. 1968). Useful bibliographical information is also found in *CPW* and *Poems; Allott* (containing a bibliography compiled by D. J. DeLaura); T. G. Ehrsam's and R. H. Deily's *Bibliographies of Twelve Victorian Authors* (New York 1936, rpt. 1968); *Matthew Arnold: The Poetry*, The Critical Heritage, ed. Carl Dawson (1973) and William E. Buckler, *Matthew Arnold's Books: Towards A Publishing Diary* (Geneva, 1958).

Bibliographical Studies

The first full-length biography of Matthew Arnold to appear was published in 1981 by Park Honan and entitled *Matthew Arnold. A Life*. This drew widely on the available materials, including various unpublished letters, but any new attempt at a full biographical study will need to await the publication of Cecil Lang's definitive edition of Arnold's letters, due to appear within the next two years. Several earlier studies which include valuable information are *Passages in a Wandering Life* (1900) by his brother Thomas Arnold, which is informative about his early life; the reminiscences of his famous niece, Mrs Humphry Ward, in her *A Writer's Recollections* (1918); A. G. Butler's *The Three Friends: A Story of Rugby in the Forties* (1900), which describes Arnold in his 'dandy' days; and *Matthew Arnold* (1904) by George W. E. Russell, who also edited *Letters* and is restricted in both books by the family's desire for reticence. Some of Arnold's unpublished letters appeared in various literary periodicals during the 1980's (see e.g. *Arnoldian*, 1985/86, 13:2; *MP*, 1987, 159–69; *N&Q*, 1988, Sept.; VN, Autumn 1988).

An important recent addition to Arnold studies is *The Yale Manuscript*, edited and with commentary by S. O. A. Ullman (Univ. of Mich. Press, 1989). A collection of documents written by Matthew Arnold between 1843 and 1856/7, including notes and drafts for poems, hitherto only available in manuscript at the Beinecke Rare Book and MS Library of Yale University.

General Studies

The range of Arnold's interests is so wide, and his work so central to our understanding of his age, that with the growth of nineteenth-century scholarship general studies of his writings have proliferated during the past two decades. The essays in *Allott* discuss among other topics Arnold and Literary Criticism, Arnold's Social and Political Thought, Arnold and Religion, Arnold and the Classics; 'in addition' as one of the contributors points out, 'Arnold and Celtic Literature, Arnold and education, Arnold and France, Arnold and race, Arnold and the Romantics, Arnold and the social classes, Arnold and the United States have all been the subject of extended and enlightened investigation' (Fraser Neiman, *Allott* 2). Some of these appear in the following – necessarily very selective – lists.

Allott, Kenneth, (ed.), *Matthew Arnold: Writers and their Background* (1975); *Matthew Arnold's reading-lists in three early diaries (Vict. Stud.* ll, 1959); *Matthew Arnold: Writers and their Work* (1955, repr. in British Writers and their Work 1963).

Allott, Miriam, (ed.), *Matthew Arnold. A Centennial Review*. Essays and Studies for the English Association (1988).

Anderson, Warren D., *Matthew Arnold and the Classical Tradition* (Ann Arbor 1965): *Arnold and the Classics (Allott* 1975).

apRoberts, Ruth, *Matthew Arnold and God* (Univ. Cal. Press, Berkeley, 1983).

Bush, Douglas, *Matthew Arnold* (1971).

Collini, Stefan, *Matthew Arnold* (OUP 1988).

DeLaura, David J., *Matthew Arnold and the nightmare of history (Vict. Poetry*, Stratford upon Avon Studies 15, ed. M. Bradbury and D. Palmer 1972); ed., *Matthew Arnold: A Collection of Critical Essays*. Twentieth Century Views (Englewood Cliffs, N.J. 1973); *Arnold and Literary Criticism: I Ideas (Allott* 1975).

Gottfried, Leon A., *Matthew Arnold and the Romantics* (Lincoln, Nebraska 1963).

Lowry, H. F., *Matthew Arnold and the Modern Spirit* (Princeton 1941).

Clough, Arthur H., *The Poems and Prose Remains*, 2 vols. (London 1869). Vol. l contains a review (1853) of Arnold's early poetry.

Simpson, James, *Matthew Arnold and Goethe*, MHRA texts and Dissertations, vol. 11 (1979).

Stone, Donald, 'Arnold, Nietzsche, and the Revaluation of values' *Nineteenth Century Literature* 43, pp. 289–318.

Super, R. H., *The Time-Spirit of Matthew Arnold* (Ann Arbor 1970); *Arnold and Literary Criticism: II Practice* (*Allott* 1975).

Tillotson, Geoffrey and Kathleen, *Mid-Victorian Studies* (1965).

Trilling, Lionel, *Matthew Arnold* (New York 1939, repr. 1955).

Willey, Basil, *Nineteenth Century Studies* (1949).

Studies of the Poetry

Allott, Kenneth, (ed.), *The Poems of Matthew Arnold* (London: Longmans 1965). Contains a detailed commentary on the poems. *Matthew Arnold. Poems* (London: Dent. 1965). Contains an Introductory essay. *A Background for 'Empedocles on Etna'* (*Essays and Studies by Members of the English Association* n.s. XXl, 1968).

Allott, Kenneth and Miriam, *Arnold the Poet: II Narrative and Dramatic Poems* (*Allott* 1975).

Baum, P. F., *Ten Studies in the Poetry of Matthew Arnold* (Durham 1958).

Bonnerot, Louis, *Matthew Arnold – Poète: Essai de biographie psychologique* (Paris 1947).

Buckler, William E., *On the Poetry of Matthew Arnold. Essays in Critical Reconstruction* (New York and London, 1982).

Culler, A. Dwight, *Imaginitive Reason: The Poetry of Matthew Arnold* (New Haven and London 1966.)

Madden, William, *Arnold the Poet: I Lyric and Elegaic Poems* (*Allott* 1975).

Pearson, Gabriel, *The Importance of Arnold's 'Merope'* (*The Major Victorian Poets*, ed. Isobel Armstrong, 1969).

Roper, Alan, *Arnold's Poetic Landscapes* (Baltimore 1969).

Studies of the Prose

Brown, E. K. *Matthew Arnold: A Study in Conflict* (Chicago 1948); *Studies in the Text of Matthew Arnold's Prose Works* (Paris 1935).

Carroll, Joseph, *The Cultural Theory of Matthew Arnold* (Berkeley, London, 1982).

Connell, W. F., *The Educational Thought and Influence of Matthew Arnold* (1950).

DeLaura, David J., *Arnold and Carlyle* (PMLA LXXIX, 1964); *Hebrew and Hellene in Victorian England: Newman, Arnold, and Pater* (Austin 1969); *The 'Wordsworth' of Pater and Arnold: (Studies in English*

Literature VI, 1966); *Arnold and Literary Criticism: Critical Ideas* (Allott 1975).

Keating, Peter, *Arnold's Social and Political Thought* (Allott 1975).

Madden, William A., *The divided tradition of English criticism* (PMLA LXXIII, 1958).

Schneider, Mary W., *Poetry in the Age of Democracy, The Literary Criticism of Matthew Arnold* (Univ. of Ka. Press, 1989).

Super, Robert H., *Arnold and Literary Criticism: Critical Practice* (Allott 1975).

Tillotson, Geoffrey, *Criticism and the Nineteenth Century* (1951); *Matthew Arnold's prose: theory and practice, The Art of Victorian Prose*, ed. G. Levine and W. Madden (New York 1968).

ACKNOWLEDGEMENTS

My chief debts are to R. H. Super's work on Arnold's prose and Kenneth Allott's work on the poems. I have had the opportunity to discuss Arnold informally with both these editors; with my late husband over several years and, more recently, with Professor Super who has generously come to my aid in the completing of various Arnold projects left unfinished by my husband at his death in 1973. It is a pleasure to record that I have benefited at every turn from the work of many other Arnoldians, especially the contributors to *Matthew Arnold* (1975), edited by Kenneth Allott for the series Writers and their Background. These include, besides Professor Super, Professor Fraser Neiman, Professor David DeLaura, Professor James Bertram, Dr Peter Keating, Professor Basil Willey, Professor Warren Anderson and Dr James Simpson. From many of these, and also from Professor S. O. A. Ullman and Dr Park Honan, whose names I would like to add here, I have had the advantage of receiving personal encouragement and advice.

Finally I must record my warm thanks to Mrs Joan Welford, who patiently and impeccably typed the work for me, putting up with my many second thoughts, deciphering my handwriting and keeping me up to the mark in meeting deadlines. I am also very grateful to Sara Helm for helping to bring the Select Bibliography up to date for the present edition.